The Place of the Audience

Cultural Geographies of Film Consumption

Mark Jancovich and Lucy Faire
with Sarah Stubbings

The College of St. Mark & St. John
LIBRARY

 Publishing

First published in 2003 by the
BRITISH FILM INSTITUTE
21 Stephen Street, London W1T 1LN

The British Film Institute promotes greater understanding of,
and access to, film and moving image culture in the UK.

Set by Fakenham Photosetting Limited, Norfolk
Printed in the UK by St Edmundsbury Press, Suffolk

British Library Cataloguing-in-Publication Data
A catalogue record for this book is available from the British Library

ISBN 0–85170–942–7 (pbk)
ISBN 0–85170–943–5 (hbk)

Contents

Acknowledgments

All books are collective efforts but it is particularly true of this volume. We would therefore like to thank the huge number of people and institutions who contributed to this book. The staff at the Local Studies Library and the Nottinghamshire Archive were always more than generous with their time, knowledge and connections, as were the staff of the University of Nottingham East Midlands Collection, the National Fairground Archive and the *Nottingham Evening Post*. We are also grateful to BBC Radio Nottingham, the *Nottingham Evening Post*, the Community Service Volunteers, the Broadway Media Centre, local libraries and the hosts of other institutions and individuals that helped with the project by passing on questionnaires and/or word of mouth.

We are also in debt to those who spared the time to fill in questionnaires or be interviewed. Their generosity was outstanding and their memories, ideas and enthusiasm continue to surprise and challenge us.

Without a major research grant from the Arts and Humanities Research Board, this book would have remained just an idea, and it was only with their funding that researchers were appointed to carry out the huge amounts of archival and audience research that lies behind the current volume. Indeed, even this research would have stayed mouldering away in boxes without a research fellowship from the Levelhulme Trust, which provided the time for Mark Jancovich to process the materials and write up the results in the form of this book.

The original ideas behind the project were tested in an MA module that Mark Jancovich taught in 1997, and he would like to thank all the students who attended the class, particularly Ian Brookes, Gavin Hibbert, James Lyons and Sarah Stubbings.

Perhaps most significantly, the project would have been impossible without the work of Kate Egan and Rhianydd Murray who stepped into the breach at short notice to distribute questionnaires, conduct interviews and organise focus groups. Their work was truly outstanding. Without their commitment and dedication, this book could never have happened.

The following people all read sections of the manuscript and gave valuable and incisive feedback: Douglas Gomery, Lee Grieveson, James Hay, Tim O'Sullivan, Roberta Pearson and Douglas Tallack. If we have not been able to resolve every issue that they raised, we were either constrained by the length of the current book or by our own intellectual abilities. We thank them profusely.

The following have also earned our gratitude for their encouragement and support over the years: Charles Acland, Thomas Austin, Martin Barker, Ian F. A. Bell, Mark Betz, Charlotte Brunsdon, Alan Burton, Joan C. Hawkins, Steve Cohan, Mike Cormack, Sue Currell, Robert Fish, Christine Geraghty, Paul Grainge, Sara Gwenllian-Jones, Ina Rae

Hark, Sarah Heaton, Dave Hesmondhalgh, Kevin Hetherington, Matt Mills, Michael Hoar, Jenn Holt, Leon Hunt, Peter Hutchings, Henry Jenkins, Janna Jones, Davis Joyce, Barbara Klinger, Peter Krämer, Peter Ling, Anna McCarthy, John McMurria, Tara McPherson, Sharon Monteith, Dave Morley, Rachel Moseley, Steve Neale, Martin Parker, James Patterson, Dana Polan, Eithne Quinn, Laraine Porter, Luca Prono, Jacinda Read, Eric Schaefer, Karen Schneider, Jeff Sconce, Gianluca Sergi, Bev Skeggs, Janet Staiger, Julian Stringer, Vanessa Toulmin, Andrew Tudor, William Uricchio, Haidee Wasson, Andy Willis and many, many others.

The School of American and Canadian Studies at the University of Nottingham also deserves thanks for the support that it has provided not only for the project, but also for the Institute of Film Studies more generally.

Lucy Faire would also like to thank Mr A. Sheldon, a local cinema enthusiast who photocopied various articles about Nottingham cinemas for her, and provided photos and photocopies, many from his own personal cinema memorabilia. He is a pertinent reminder that so much historical research is dependent on the personal passions of individuals, who put huge amounts of effort into preserving pasts that academics only come to appreciate at some future date, if at all.

On a more personal note, Lucy would like to thank Thomas Faire (who lent her books on cinema history) and Phil Hubbard, who contributed ideas and support to the writing of this book, even when she was supposed to be working for him as a research associate on another project. She would also like to give especial thanks to Chris Williams.

Sarah would also like to thank the Arts and Humanities Research Board for funding her PhD, which informs so much of Part Three, and Ian Brookes, who has offered her support and feedback throughout. She would also like to thank Sarah Dossor, who has offered advice on architecture, and her mother: it was her belief in Sarah's potential as a researcher that remains Sarah's central motivation in pursuing her studies.

Finally, Mark would like to thank Joanne Hollows, as ever, for her love, encouragement and ideas. She remains a source of inspiration, whose intellectual influence can be found on every page of this volume.

Note to the General Reader

The introduction to the book is largely written for an academic readership and may be of little interest to certain readers. Those primarily interested in the history of cinemagoing and other types of film consumption may wish to skip this section and move straight on to the historical material that begins at the start of Part Two.

PART ONE

Introduction

1

From Spectatorship to Film Consumption

In *Shared Pleasures: A History of Movie Exhibition in America*, Douglas Gomery demonstrates that film studies needs to be seen as more than the analysis of film texts, or even the study of their industrial production and of their interpretation by audiences. Cinemagoing (and more recently the activities of consuming films via television, video, cable and satellite) is about far more than the watching of a film. For example, as Gomery argues, while Balaban and Katz became the most successful and imitated exhibitors of the 1910s and 1920s, 'one of the variables that did *not* count in [their] rise to power and control was the movies themselves. Indeed the company grew and prospered despite having little access to Hollywood's top films.' Their success was due to a concentration on other aspects of the cinemagoing experience through which they 'differentiated [their] corporate product through five important factors – location, the theatre building, service, stage shows and air conditioning'.[1]

However, Gomery's account is an 'internal' or business history of exhibition practices and, in the process, the meaning of film consumption to actual cinemagoers is either absent from the account or seen as an unproblematic effect of industries' strategies.[2] Indeed, it has been a recurring complaint both within and against film studies that it has largely ignored audiences.[3] In response, many film scholars have challenged text-centred interpretation in favour of the study of film reception, but most of this work still concentrates on the interpretation of texts by audiences. The following study is an attempt to move beyond the analysis of how audiences interpret texts and to open up ways of studying film consumption as an activity.

From Interpretation to Consumption

As David Morley puts it, 'it is necessary to consider the *context of viewing* as much as the *object of viewing*':

> There is more to cinema going than seeing films. There is going out at night and the sense
> of relaxation combined with a sense of fun and excitement. The very name 'picture palace',
> by which cinemas were known for a long time, captures an important part of that
> experience ... Rather than selling individual films, cinema is best understood as having sold
> a habit, a certain type of socialized experience ... Any analysis of the film subject which
> does not take on board these issues of the context within which film is consumed is, to my
> mind, insufficient. Unfortunately a great deal of film theory has operated without reference

to these issues, given the effect of the literary tradition in prioritizing the status of the text abstracted from the viewing context.[4]

As the above quote makes clear, this absence has often been blamed on the fact that film studies developed within the arts and particularly out of literary studies. Film studies has therefore often been contrasted with television and media studies which largely emerged out of the social sciences and in which the study of the viewing context is far more common.[5]

However, there is an additional reason for this absence within film studies. The study of television, unlike that of film, seems to have a more easily identifiable social context – the domestic living room – the cultural politics of which was therefore more immediately open to analysis.[6] Television studies has therefore been able to concentrate not only on the different ways in which audiences decode television programmes, but also on the meanings of television viewing as an activity.[7] As David Morley has noted, the television can be on whether people are watching it or not, and can have a range of uses and meanings.[8] For example, it can be used as a babysitter; as a focus for familial interaction; as

Going to the cinema has always been about more than going to see films. The Capitol, Alfreton Road, illustration from the *Nottingham Journal*, 17 October 1936

a way of switching off after work; of scheduling or pacing one's day; and as an excuse for parents to pack the kids off to bed and have some time together or a 'cuddle on the sofa'. The focus on the domestic living room has therefore enabled television studies to analyse the cultural politics of television consumption and the domestic power relations that are involved with it.

However, television studies did not just develop differently from film studies, but as a criticism of its key trends. For example, Morley's early work was an overt rejection of the models of spectatorship associated with '*Screen* theory'. For Morley, viewers of a text are always already social subjects whose ideological construction will determine whether they accept or reject a text's ideological position, or negotiate a position in relation to that text. At this stage, then, Morley was concerned with the reasons that different social groups interpreted texts differently.[9]

However, in the course of this research, Morley began to see that other issues also affected interpretation, which he termed 'relevance' and 'comprehension'. These terms are similar to Bourdieu's 'disposition' and 'competence', and they suggest that an audience's response to a text is dependent on their engagement with it and their ability to make sense of it. In other words, a particular viewer might simply not care enough about a programme to even get to the level of acceptance or rejection, while another may have sufficient investment in its genre, for example, that he/she enjoys it regardless of whether he/she accepts or rejects its ideological position. Similarly, if one lacks a knowledge of contemporary art, a particular painting or sculpture may be simply incomprehensible, while if one has never seen a martial arts film before, one may not know what to make of such a film. As a result, while Morley demonstrated that different audiences consumed texts in different ways, he also stressed that these differences were not due to individual idiosyncrasies but that they were differentially distributed in relation to class, gender and other forms of cultural identity. They were both produced by social inequalities but also acted to legitimate and reproduce them.

Morley's research on audiences also began to throw up another issue. It became clear that interpretation was also affected by the context of viewing. Initially, Morley had held focus groups but he became interested in how the more 'ordinary' context of the home affected the ways in which audiences interpreted programmes, a shift that led him to appreciate that there was more to the activity of television viewing than the interpretation of programmes. In the process, he became aware that, as a piece of domestic technology, the television had meanings regardless of whether it was ever even watched. In a similar way, Charlotte Brunsdon has shown that, in the late 1980s and early 1990s, the ownership of satellite dishes became associated with subordinate social classes and certain neighbourhoods sought to distinguish themselves by banning these devices.[10] In this way, ownership of a satellite dish (or the lack of such ownership) came to say something about a person or household and, as Shaun Moores has shown, the decision to buy the technology was often less about the programmes to which it gave access, than the meanings of the technology itself.[11]

Television therefore needs to be seen in relation to other forms of domestic technology. Not only was it the case that, in the early days, there was often intense gender

conflict over the decision to buy a television (often seen as a predominantly male preference) or a washing machine (often seen as a predominantly female preference),[12] but
the meanings of domestic technologies are also related in other ways. For example, as
Ellen Seiter found: 'If the television is commonly considered the bad screen for children
because it causes passivity, the computer is the good screen because it is construed as
active and intellectual.'[13]

The analysis of television has therefore moved beyond a concern with the interpretation of programmes to a concern with consumption more generally.[14] In other words,
the consumption of television is not just about the watching of programmes but also
about the consumption of the technologies through which those programmes are
accessed.

From Spectatorship to Ethnography in Film Studies

This concern with consumption is largely absent from film studies, but audiences have
been of key importance to the discipline, and it could be argued that most studies of
film make claims about the effects that films have upon their audiences. For example,
concerns about the audience are central both to psychoanalytic work on spectatorship[15]
and to work in cognitive psychology that examines viewing as a problem-solving
process.[16] However, these kinds of work elide any concern with actual audiences and are
therefore representative of the positions that Morley and others have challenged. In
other words, they are not concerned with socially situated viewers but with an abstract
and hypothetical construct – the audience – which is presumed to have a single and unitary response to a text.

More recently, however, there has been a growing interest in reception, and it can be
divided into three main areas. The first concerns the audience as a market, while the second concerns the inter-textual contexts within which the reception of films takes place,
and is therefore concerned with the ways in which films are framed for audiences. The
third and final area is the ethnography of film audiences, or work that examines audiences' own accounts of their relationship to film.

The first area is represented by Bruce Austin's survey of the material produced by the
film industry and other agencies in their attempts to understand, organise and control
audiences.[17] The analysis of these kinds of material has largely concentrated on two main
issues: audience preferences[18] and audience demographics.[19] However, the most interesting work in this field is that of Richard Maltby, who uses these materials to analyse
how the industry's 'generic typology of its audience' provided 'a means through which
Hollywood could negotiate the generic organisation of its products'.[20] According to
Maltby, during the 1930s, the industry believed that there was a significant difference
between the tastes of the urban audiences and those of small-town audiences and this
belief caused it to question seriously its production, distribution and exhibition strategies.[21] However, while Maltby accepts that the industry's account 'may not have been
an accurate description of actual movie audiences', Peter Krämer has not only demonstrated that film industries have often been very wrong in their assumptions about
audiences, but has also tried to account for their taken-for-granted assumptions about

the relative importance of male and female audiences.[22] Ien Ang has also examined the reasons industries are routinely unsuccessful in their attempts to make sense of, and hence regulate, their audiences.[23]

The second major area has come to be known as reception studies, and Janet Staiger is the figure most directly associated with it. For Staiger, the meaning of a film does not reside within the text, where it waits to be discovered by the reader, but rather meanings need to be understood as the product of specific historical conditions. In other words, readers make meanings from texts on the basis of the specific assumptions and knowledges that they bring to their encounter with them. In order to study these events historically, Staiger turns to 'reviews, news articles, letters to papers, advertisements, illustrations, and publicity which circulated in the major mass media'.[24] These subsidiary texts are then analysed as the indicators of reception, and are used to identify the intertextual systems that constitute these events.

This work can end up in two related problems. First, it can suggest that there was only one way in which a text was understood within that period. Second, as Barbara Klinger has pointed out, it tends to ignore the ways in which the meanings of texts change over time. As a result, reception studies can sometimes amount to little more than a historically concrete version of reader-response criticism in which the task of the critic is to unearth the 'appropriate' competences necessary for the interpretation of film.[25] In this situation, the job of the critic is simply to discover how audiences were 'expected' to fill in gaps within the text and to identify the knowledge that audiences were 'required' to bring to their encounter with texts – a position which, as Jeffrey Sconce points out, divides the filmgoing public into '"skilled" and "unskilled" audiences'.[26]

Barbara Klinger's study of Douglas Sirk avoids many of these problems, and she examines the different ways in which his films were understood within different cultural contexts. In the process, she not only analyses how their meanings have changed over time, but also how they have been consumed differently within different contexts during the same period. For example, when these films are screened as part of a season of television matinees, they are usually presented very differently from when they are screened at film festivals or at art-house cinemas. In the first context, they are often explicitly presented as romantic melodramas while in the second they are usually presented as a critique of romantic melodrama.

Klinger is quite clear that her work is not a study of actual audiences, but only an account of the conditions within which audiences encountered films – an account that can only suggest how these films *might* have been understood. However, as Martin Barker has argued, while most forms of analysis can only deduce the reception of films, the strength of ethnographic research is that it can test these deductions.[27] For example, in her study of female viewers of the 1940s and 1950s, Jackie Stacey found that women used images of female stars as a cultural resource in 'the typical work of femininity: the production of oneself as both subject and object in accordance with cultural ideals of femininity'.[28] However, unlike many textual approaches to these dynamics, she also found that female stars were also used as a resource to resist and negotiate dominant definitions of femininity. In the United Kingdom, she notes, 'American feminine ideals are clearly remembered as transgressing restrictive British femininity and thus employed as strategies of resistance.'[29] Not only were women invited to choose between different notions of feminine beauty, but 'the production of a feminine self in relation to Americanness signified "autonomy", "individuality", and "resistance"'.[30]

Similarly, in Barker and Brooks' study of the audiences for *Judge Dredd*, they found that while most textual analyses tend to focus on the narrative pleasures of films, their respondents were usually routinely uninterested in talking about the film in narrative terms. Rather than focus on narrative, Barker and Brooks therefore identified six key languages though which *Judge Dredd* was discussed, each of which involved a distinct 'way of expressing a relation to the film or to the act of going to the cinema which seems to have wide and organising implications'.[31]

However, both these studies still remain focused on the relationship between audiences and texts, rather than the activities of film consumption itself, and much the same is also true of the initial findings in Annette Kuhn's study of memories of cinemagoing in the 1930s.[32] The study's concern was to investigate 'the ways in which films and cinema-going figured in the daily lives of people throughout the nation in the 1930s, and of situating cinema-going and fan behaviour in this period within their broader social and cultural contexts'.[33] Unfortunately, the material that has been published out of this research largely concerns people's tastes, preferences and investments in the films that they watched.[34]

Ethnographies of Film Consumption

However, there is more to cinemagoing than simply the watching of films. As Nicholas Hiley has pointed out, audiences in the 1920s and 1930s did not 'treat the cinema simply as a place to see films, but as somewhere to spend time and even to sleep'.[35] For other audiences, it simply 'offered a refuge from the cold outside'[36] while many 'young couples visited their local cinemas to escape the prying eyes of their parents'.[37] Furthermore, as Barker's own research suggests, film consumption is a social activity.[38] According to Sue Harper and Vincent Porter, 'in 1947, barely a quarter of those waiting to see *The Two Mrs Carrolls* (1947) were on their own', and most of those who were alone were housewives for whom 'the cinema was probably their only chance to get out of the house and enjoy solitude'.[39]

However, despite this observation, Harper and Porter do not devote much time to cinema as a social activity. They divide the cinemagoing public into three main groups: the indiscriminate moviegoer, the habitual moviegoer and the occasional moviegoer. Furthermore, they also point out, only '63% of the audience for Fox's *Sentimental Journey* (1946) had specifically chosen that film. An eighth had gone out of habit, and almost a quarter had gone for other reasons – because other cinemas were full, they had been taken by a friend, or the cinema was near a bus stop.'[40] They even stress that the 'proportion of indiscriminate cinema goers would have been higher for a less popular film'.[41] It is not even clear what people meant when they said they had chosen the film. For example, they may have chosen to go to the pictures first and then decided which film to see. Their cinemagoing might primarily have been habitual. However, Harper and Porter spend little time on the indiscriminate moviegoer, and devote only a couple of hundred words to the case of the regular cinemagoers, and they do so because, in both these cases, 'audience tastes' are largely irrelevant and it is precisely the social activities of cinemagoing – its meanings above and beyond the watching of films – that are central.

It is for this reason that Kevin J. Corbett's work is so interesting and promising. Corbett counters the claims that new technologies will mean the replacement of cinemagoing with home viewing on the grounds that these claims do not take account of the different meanings of 'going to the cinema' and 'staying in with a movie'. As a result, Corbett looks at 'how movie audiences historically have used the act of movie-watching in their everyday lives, how symbolically important the act was within their lives, or how it has contributed to forming, maintaining, and transforming their interpersonal relationships'.[42] To this end, he examines the role of film consumption within the relationships of married and dating couples, and finds that their film consumption was not motivated by the desire to see a particular film but was used to create opportunities for interaction. For example, he notes that many couples 'use movie-watching as a symbolic way to celebrate special events like Christmas and birthdays'.[43] As a result, while film consumption was sometimes valued because 'it was so convenient',[44] couples also valued its ability to distinguish an event:

Cinemagoing has always been a social event. The ABC (formerly the Carlton), Chapel Bar, City Centre

all the couples recognised the importance of what many of them referred to as 'making a night of' watching movies together and of the act to their relationship. Watching movies became a way of celebrating or – recalling Gerry Philipsen's definition of ritual – 'paying homage to' their relationship.[45]

Effort can make an event special, and distinguish the time together from other more mundane forms of interaction.

To the extent that film preferences were a factor, things were not as straightforward as one might expect. In his study of family audiences, Morley pointed out that there is often a significant discrepancy between people's stated preferences and the shows that they actually watch, and he claims that this is due to the fact that people tend to watch television in a social setting where the programmes watched are chosen through negotiation, rather than the decision of one individual.[46] In much the same way, Corbett found that people 'sometimes have to compromise so that they can spend time with their partner watching a movie',[47] although he also found that the event can even be given a special meaning if one member is willing to watch something that he/she would not normally watch. Such an act can also be a way of sharing in one another's interests, or learning about the other person. It can even be used to construct a relatively independent event that is outside common experience: a specific type of film can acquire a special meaning as part of the relationship precisely because it is something that one would not watch in other circumstances.

However, Corbett's account remains rather free of conflict, and these processes can often be much more tense than he acknowledges. It is therefore worth comparing his ethnographic study with that of Janna Jones, whose work on audiences at the Tampa Theatre in Florida never loses sight of the cultural politics involved in film consumption. Her account demonstrates that struggles for cultural distinction did not just affect the ways in which these audiences read specific films, but also the meaning of cinemagoing. For example, through their consumption of this cinema, the Tampa Theatre's audiences rejected other sites of film consumption, particularly the multiplex, which was associated with the obvious and easy pleasures of popular culture.[48] However, it is worth noting that when Corbett reconstructs histories of cinemagoing, he does not turn to audience research but rather to work on exhibition. The study of exhibition is a small but developing area and although, as we saw in relation to Gomery, it is not primarily or even necessarily interested in audiences, it is one of the few areas of film studies that acknowledges that there has always been more to film consumption than the watching of films.

Exhibition and Audiences

The two leading advocates of this area are Robert Allen and Douglas Gomery, who have been demonstrating its importance for about twenty years,[49] although it is only in recent years that this type of research has acquired momentum.[50] For Allen, exhibition is important for a number of different reasons. First, it is a neglected aspect of the film industry, which is too often equated with film production rather than distribution or exhibition. Second, the 'location and the physical sites of exhibition' are essential to an understanding of the meanings of cinema. This raises questions about the meanings of cinemagoing, but Allen also argues that film studies has been too concerned with spectacular but unrepresentative phenomena. Writing of the coming of sound, for example, Allen and Gomery stress that the experience of New York cannot be seen as representative of the whole country, but that the sound film came to New York first precisely because it was unrepresentative. As a result, they also provide a fascinating alternative account of the coming of sound by concentrating on the case of Milwaukee.[51] Similarly, Allen argues:

> [the] concentration on early moviegoing as an urban phenomenon has obscured the fact that during the first decade of the movies' commercial growth, 71% of the population of the United States lived in rural areas or small towns. The first audiences for the movies in these areas were not to be found in vaudeville theatres (the towns were too small to support them) or storefront movie theatres (which, if they came at all, came later), but in tents, amusement parks, the local opera house, YMCA hall, public library basement – wherever itinerant showmen could set up their projectors.[52]

The issue of exhibition is therefore related to another of Allen's concerns: 'performance'. According to Allen, 'we tend to talk of films being "screened" as though the only thing going on in a movie theatre were light being bounced off a reflective surface':

> in the 1920s in America, for example, many viewers were not particularly interested in what feature film was playing. They were attracted to the theatre by the theatre itself, with its sometimes bizarre architectural and design allusions to exotic cultures, its capacious public spaces, its air conditioning in the summer, and its auditorium, which may have been decorated to resemble the exterior of a Moorish palace at night – complete with heavenly dome and twinkling stars. Regardless of what feature the theatre chain had secured from the distributor that week, there was sure to be a newsreel, a comedy short, a programme of music by pit orchestra or on the mighty wurlitzer, and in many theatres elaborate stage shows.[53]

Indeed, as Douglas Gomery has observed, the slogan for Paramount's theatre chain was: 'You don't need to know what's playing at the Publix House. It's bound to be the best show in town.'[54]

As we have seen, the definitive history of exhibition is Douglas Gomery's *Shared Pleasures* and it covers mainstream cinemas from their origins to the present, alternative operations such as ethnic and art cinemas, technological transformations such as sound, colour and widescreen and, finally, non-cinematic forms of exhibition such as the showing of films on television, the emergence of cable television's movie channels and the emergence of home video. In the process, it provides a wealth of material on the potential meanings of film consumption to audiences. However, while Gomery covers the history of cinema from its origins to the present and does so from a national perspective, Gregory Waller has developed the more localised research that Allen and Gomery have called for elsewhere.[55] His study examines cinema in relation to other forms of commercial entertainment in Lexington between the years 1896 and 1930. In the process, he challenges the thesis that there was a 'standardization of recreation' during the period in which provincialism was eroded by a homogenised American culture, and argues that we can 'acknowledge the importance of local and regional variation and negotiation of mass culture without falling prey to problems that often beset local history: naïve boosterism or the yearning for a supposedly more autonomous provinciality'.[56]

As he demonstrates, while there was a pressure to standardise experiences across cinemas, there was an equally strong pressure for cinemas to distinguish their product in order to compete with one another. Thus, while the industry became centralised after World War I, Waller argues that 'moviegoing in this period looks far less homogeneous' if one looks beyond the feature film and takes into account 'the whole "show," the multipart bill, the "balanced program"'.[57] In other words, films were shown at a number of different sites within Lexington, each of which contextualised them differently. The choice between cinemas was therefore the choice between different types of experience, which meant that audiences' responses were never quite as 'unpredictable' as critics such as Miriam Hansen have implied.[58] As Waller puts, it, 'to a great extent context reined in unpredictability',[59] as different modes of exhibition, performance and reception came to be associated with different locations. In this way, audiences built up identifications and disidentifications with places of exhibition, and different cinemas not only had meanings that exceeded their function as places to show films, but even transformed the meaning of the films shown within them.

This work on exhibition is also part of a more general turn to social and cultural history within film studies, and Allen's study of nickelodeon audiences has created a more general interest in the audiences for early cinema and attempts to regulate them.[60] This research is best represented by Uricchio and Pearson's *Reframing Culture* and Grieveson's *Policing Cinema*.[61] In the first, the authors take the case of the Vitagraph Quality Films, and ask how we are to begin to understand their meanings for audiences in the late 1900s and early 1910s, when they were made. In this way, they represent a form of historical reception studies, but one that not only examines the inter-texts for these films but also places them within broader social struggles over the cinema audience – struggles that were part of larger conflicts over class and ethnicity in the period. From a slightly different perspective, Grieveson looks at roughly the same period to examine the ways in which audiences were understood in the period, and the ways in which these understandings were the product of progressivist attempts to regulate and control not only cinema audiences but social life more generally.

However, while these studies are exemplary, there are problems with certain tendencies within other social and cultural histories. For example, there is preoccupation with early cinema audiences to the virtual exclusion of any later period, and this is linked to a second problem. This period is often seen as a distinct and unique moment within cinema history, which represents a moment when 'options [were] still open':[62] a period of diversity and experimentation which came to an end some time between 1905 and 1915, when classical Hollywood cinema is established. The period is seen as one of contestation and possibility, before audiences were finally regulated and contained.[63]

This position, however, relies on a profoundly ahistorical view of history, in which nothing much seems to change in the nature of either the film industry or its audiences from the period around 1910 until the emergence of the 'new' Hollywood in the late 1960s and early 1970s. Furthermore, even a cursory examination of film history since the 1910s would find repeated claims that films and their audiences were still in need of both discipline and regulation.

Notes

1. Gomery, 1992, p. 43.
2. We have chosen the term 'film consumption' for a number of reasons. First, we are not simply concerned with cinemagoing, but also with the activities associated with other forms of distribution and exhibition: terrestrial television broadcasts, video rental and retail, satellite and cable, the internet, etc. Second, we want to distinguish these activities from the act of viewing itself: film consumption is about far more than simply the viewing of films.
3. Similar criticisms can be directed at other disciplines. Architectural histories of the cinema, for example, have tended to focus on the construction of these places of exhibition rather than their consumption by audiences. (See Gray, 1996; Atwell, 1980; Sharp, 1969; and Valentine, 1994.) This tendency is also evident in many of the local studies of the cinema: Williams, 1993; Clarke, 1991; Roddis, 1993; Charles Anderson, 1983. Alternatively, the experience of going to the cinema remains marginal in studies of everyday life and leisure: Davies, 1992; Langhamer, 2000; Roberts, 1984; and Roberts, 1995.
4. Morley, 1992, pp. 157–8.
5. See Jancovich, 1992, pp. 134–47; Morley, 1986; and Moores, 1993.
6. Though as we demonstrate in Chapter 12, television is not just watched in the living room, or even one's own living room.
7. The diversity of audience research and theory can be seen in the following brief selection: Abercrombie and Longhurst, 1998; Dickinson, Harindranath and Linné, 1998; Hay, Grossberg and Wartella, 1996; McQuail, 1997; Nightingale, 1996; Tulloch, 2000.
8. Morley, 1986.
9. Morley and Brunsdon, 1978; and Morley, 1980b.
10. Brunsdon, 1997.
11. Moores, 2000. For other material on the consumption of media technologies see, for example, Gauntlett and Hill, 1999; Gray, 1992; Petrie and Willis, 1995; Silverstone, 1994; and Silverstone and Hirsch, 1992.
12. Bowden and Offer, 1994, pp. 725–48. See Chapter 10: 'From Cinemagoing to Television Viewing: The Developing Meanings of a New Medium'.
13. Seiter, 1999, p. 42.
14. For work on consumption see: Lee, 2000; Lury, 1996; Miller, 1987; Miller, Jackson, Thrift, Holbrook and Rowlands, 1998; Miller, 1995; Slater, 1997; and, for a concrete study that applies and develops many of the key debates in the field of consumption studies, see Warde, 1997.

15. See, for example, Heath, 1981; Mulvey, 1985; and Mayne, 1993.

16. See, for example, Bordwell, 1985; Branigan, 1992; Carrol, 1988; and Smith, 1995.

17. Austin, 1989.

18. See, for example, Harper and Porter, 1999, pp. 66–82.

19. See, for example, Docherty, Morrison and Tracey, 1987; Corrigan, 1983; Hiley, 1998, pp. 96–103; and Hiley, 1999, pp. 39–53.

20. Maltby, 1999a, p. 4.

21. Maltby, 1999b.

22. Krämer, 1999.

23. Ang, 1991.

24. Staiger, 2000, p. 163. See also Staiger, 1992.

25. It can also end up as little more than a revision of '*Screen* theory'. In other words, much of this work identifies the period of early cinema with a specific mode of spectatorship that is then opposed to that of classical Hollywood cinema. For example, both Hansen and Gunning, despite the value of their work, see early cinema as a free space before narrative began to organise and regulate spectatorship, a position that tends to homogenise periods. Rather than acknowledging that different audiences had different competences and dispositions which meant that they consumed films in different ways, these writers try to identify the modes of address associated with the different epochs and hence suggest that audiences within each epoch were subject to the modes of spectatorship which these periods designate. See Gunning, 1990, pp. 56–62; and Hansen, 1991.

26. Sconce, 1995, p. 392.

27. Barker, 1998, pp. 131–47.

28. Stacey, 1994, p. 168.

29. Ibid., p. 204.

30. Ibid., p. 238.

31. Barker and Brooks, 1998, p. 145.

32. Annette Kuhn, *Cinema Culture in 1930s Britain: Ethnohistory of a Popular Cultural Practice*, ESRC project R000 23 5385.

33. Kuhn, 1999a, p. 531.

34. Kuhn, 1994; Kuhn, 1996; Kuhn, 1999a, pp. 531–43; Kuhn, 1999b, pp. 100–20; Kuhn, 1999c, pp. 135–46; and Kuhn, 2000.

35. Hiley, 1999, p. 39.

36. Hiley, 1998, p. 100.

37. Ibid., p. 101.

38. Barker and Brooks, 1998.

39. Harper and Porter, 1999, p. 68.

40. Ibid.

41. Ibid.

42. Corbett, 1998–1999, p. 34. See also Corbett, 2001, pp. 17–34.

43. Corbett, 1998–1999, p. 41

44. Ibid., p. 39.

45. Ibid., p. 41.

46. Morley, 1986.
47. Corbett, 1998–1999, p. 43.
48. Jones, 2001, pp. 122–133.
49. Allen and Gomery, 1985.
50. The field has even just acquired its first substantial textbooks: Hark, 2001; and Waller, 2001.
51. Allen and Gomery, 1985.
52. Allen, 1990, p. 351.
53. Ibid., p. 353.
54. Gomery, 1992, p. 58.
55. Allen and Gomery, 1985.
56. Waller, 1995, p. xvii.
57. Ibid., p. 218.
58. Hansen, 1991.
59. Waller, 1995, p. 37.
60. Allen, 1979, pp. 2–15; Allen, 1996, pp. 75–103; Singer, 1995, pp. 5–35; Singer, 1996, pp. 104–28; and Higashi, 1996, pp. 72–4.
61. Uricchio and Pearson, 1993; and Grieveson, forthcoming.
62. Kitses, 1969, p. 12.
63. Gunning, 1990; and Hansen, 1991.

2

Contexts of Film Consumption

Space, Place and the City

The relative absence of work on the activity of film consumption within film studies when compared with television studies is due to the fact that the social context of television viewing seemed more immediately apparent. Film consumption seemed to lack a clearly defined cultural context, such as the domestic living room, but this does not mean that there was *no* social context in relation to which it could be understood. On the contrary, the following study will demonstrate that the changing cultural politics of the city can offer a context that is as equally compelling and productive as the domestic living room. However, this is not to claim that film consumption is exclusively, or even predominantly, an urban experience. We simply chose the context of the city because it helped to focus and limit our study to a local area: Nottingham. Certainly, other cultural geographies of film consumption can be mapped, and it was necessary for our own study to address continually the ways in which Nottingham's own sense of place has been constructed in relation to local, national and even international arenas.

In this way, the project draws upon recent work in cultural geography which has emphasised the need to see spatial organisation as central to the organisation of social life. As Massey puts it, 'it seems important to me to establish the inherent dynamism of the spatial, at least in the sense that the spatial is not simply opposed to the temporal as its absence, as a lack'.[1] History does not just take place in space but social life is organised spatially, and spatial relations are therefore 'both open to, and a necessary element in, politics in the broadest sense of the word'.[2]

The spatial organisation of social relations therefore means that one must be careful about how one envisions place. Instead of autonomous and authentic sites of meaning, every place is defined through its relation to other places. This does not mean that there is anything 'inevitably reactionary about place-based identities, as long as they are founded on an "extroverted" definition, in which place is seen as constituted by the flows of people, objects and symbols passing through it'.[3] As a result, Massey calls for 'a global sense of place', which 'challenges any possibility of claims to internal histories or to timeless identities'.[4] The identities of places are therefore both mobile and multiple. On the one hand, if places are defined by their interactions with other places, they can neither be static nor have 'boundaries in the sense of divisions which frame simple enclosures'.[5] On the other, places cannot be seen to have single, unitary identities. They are inevitably composed of internal conflicts and contradictions, and hence there are competing meanings and definitions of any place as different social groups struggle over it. In other words, any place will be experienced differently by different social groups and will inevitably change over time.

The history of cities therefore needs to be understood in terms of their role in organising social relations, and it is:

> typically charted *from* the rise and fall of ancient cities (such as Athens and Rome), *through* the rise of mediaeval cities (such as Antwerp and Naples), onto the spectacular growth of cities during the industrial revolution and the age of empire (such as London and Paris), and finally *to* the sprawling 'post-modern' cities of today (normally exemplified by Los Angeles).[6]

The problems of such an account are numerous. For example, it not only privileges certain dominant, and hence unrepresentative, cities, but also fails to take account of the social relations that both 'stretch *beyond* the city' and exist '*within* the city'.[7] While many social critics have taken Los Angeles to be the exemplar of the 'post-modern' city,[8] there are numerous reasons why most cities will never become anything like Los Angeles. The form and character of Los Angeles is tied to a specific history and a specific place within the global relations of economic, political and cultural power.

None the less, the so-called post-modern world is supposed to have changed both the meaning and function of cities. Most centrally, it is claimed, culture has become more and more important to cities[9] as they are converted from places of production to places of consumption[10] and as they are forced to compete for finance capital in an increasingly competitive global economy.[11] On the one hand, these changes are related to processes of deindustrialisation, in which many city economies are increasingly dependent on cultural consumption, rather than industrial productions. On the other, these changes are also related to what has become known as 'time–space compression' in which communications allow goods and capital to move around the globe at accelerated rates,[12] and encourage cities to develop their images in order to attract capital investment.[13]

Communities, Culture and Spatial Relations

Media and communications are therefore intimately connected to the cultural geography of modern life. After all, their central function is to connect places to one another. Raymond Williams has therefore linked communications to the development of 'mobile privatisation' in which the distinction between the public and the private becomes permeable.[14] Rather than distinct and opposed realms, communications offer the possibility of travelling out of the home (such as in the car) while staying safely enclosed in private space, or of staying home (as with the home computer) while remaining connected to the outside world.

These processes can therefore often be seen as ways of controlling the world, of having access to the public world beyond while remaining safely enclosed within a privatised inner space. However, it can also offer exactly the opposite possibility, in which it becomes difficult to police the boundaries of the private. It is this concern, for example, which often motivates complaints over television content, but it can also manifest itself

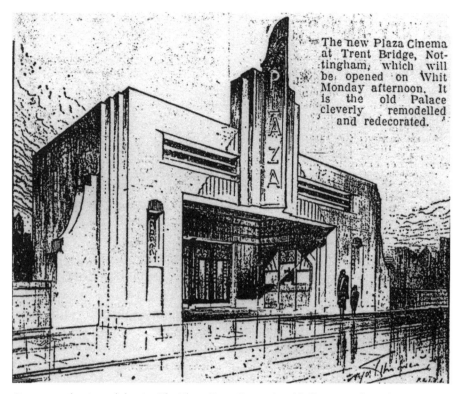

The new Plaza Cinema at Trent Bridge, Nottingham, which will be, opened on Whit Monday afternoon. It is the old Palace cleverly remodelled and redecorated.

Cinema, modernity and the city. The Plaza, Front Street, Arnold, illustration from the *Evening News*, 13 May 1932

in other ways. Harassment, both sexual and racial, often uses communication as a way invading the home, such as through the use of threatening phone calls or materials shoved through letterboxes.

However, if communications mediate the boundaries between the public and the private, they are also related to cultural geographies in other ways. They not only provide images of elsewhere[15] but also, as Benedict Anderson and others have pointed out, they provide the rituals for a sense of imagined community.[16] Senses of national unity are often constructed specifically through the ritualised schedules of the media as much as through the representation of large public events such as royal occasions, the opening of parliament, and so forth.[17] However, as has also been pointed out, while many media organisations were largely national in their identities, a series of processes has worked to break down the national or enable the production of new transnational identities. Certain media have enabled the development of new localisms, while there has been a development of niche media, such as science-fiction channels on cable, which increasingly address audiences that are not nationally or even spatially specific but exist across national lines. Indeed, the European Union has tried to foster a sense of European, rather than simply national, identity through its media policy.[18] Communications are therefore not only central to the ways in which social life is both organised and imagined in spatial terms, but the 'link between culture and place, it is argued, is being ruptured'.[19] In other words, it is argued that people's identities and affiliations are no longer (if indeed they ever were)[20] primarily place-based and, as Shaun Moores puts it: 'Where we are no longer determines who we are – or who we are "with" – to the same degree as it used to because electronically mediated communication has the potential to transform situation, interaction and identification.'[21]

However, as Massey has stressed, we need to be careful about these claims, and while these processes can be seen as producing an increasingly mobile and homogeneous global culture, they also produce the exact opposite tendencies. Not only are cities forced to rely on their identities as localities to differentiate themselves in the global finance markets,[22] but the very processes that create greater mobility for some inevitably create immobility for others. For example, as Massey points out, as a car culture makes some increasingly mobile, public transport systems are run down and so make others increasingly immobile.[23]

Thus, while there is a tendency to focus on the 'world cities' that dominate global economic, political and economic relations,[24] it is therefore important to remember that few of the world's population live in these places and that, even if they do, they do not necessarily share in the experiences of wealth, power and influence that are associated with these places. Of course, much of the current writing on the cultural geographies of cities is deeply concerned about the inequalities that these relations engender, but there is also considerable need for caution here, too. Much recent work has shown considerable concern about the new urban environments that these relations produce, and particularly the development of new spaces of leisure and consumption that have excluded large sections of the urban population.[25]

During the 1970s, many cities went into crisis and public spaces came to be seen as dangerous and threatening spaces. As a result, a series of new spaces emerged that are seen as replacing public space with private and commercial space.[26] However, while these processes may have economically divided cities into pleasure and leisure for some and poverty and unemployment for others, public space was never simply a place of plurality and diversity. Public space was always founded on the repression and exclusion of others, and both access to and freedom of movement within it has always been unequal. Thus, while criticisms of the new city spaces often imply that they are the product of an irrational fear of interaction with other social groups, or an overt form of political violence, it is not the most powerful and dominant groups who experience public spaces as dangerous and threatening. For example, historically, women have felt highly vulnerable in public space,[27] which is largely defined as masculine space, and it is usually the lower middle class who are singled out for their fear of otherness. The bourgeoisie achieved 'respectability' through the distinction between the public and private spheres but, once it had attained political hegemony, it had less need to prove its respectability.[28] In contrast, the lower middle class remains in an indeterminate position in which it tries to distinguish itself from the proletariat and aspires to be bourgeoisie. However, it lacks the capital to realise this ambition and has only its respectability on which to trade.[29] As a result, the petit-bourgeois has an investment in respectability that is not only unnecessary to the bourgeoisie, but which the bourgeois must also repudiate in order to distinguish itself from these cultural interlopers, a repudiation that is even more vehement from those who rely on their cultural capital to distinguish themselves.

In other words, it is those who are most insecure in their power and authority that fear public spaces, while those who champion such spaces are often those with sufficient power and authority that they are not threatened by them. As a result, many attacks on the new privatised places of the contemporary landscape reproduce familiar claims about the aesthetic poverty and homogeneity of lower-middle-class culture, and so work to assert the superiority of the cultural bourgeoisie over subordinate groups, rather than to champion the oppressed and excluded.

Film Consumption and the Case of Nottingham

As a result, while our research examined the meanings of film consumption as an activity, it focused on the ways in which these meanings were related to the meanings of sites of exhibition and distribution: city-centre cinemas; local cinemas; out-of-town multiplexes; inner-city multiplexes; terrestrial television; video rental and retail; and both satellite and cable. However, the research not only examined the different meanings of watching a film on broadcast television, renting a video or going to the pictures, but also the different meanings of these activities for different sections of society. As Morley pointed out, different members of the family usually have very different experiences of the domestic sphere. For men, it is largely defined as a place of leisure, while, for women, even those who are in full-time work outside the home, it is largely seen as a place of work.[30] As a result, the factors affecting the choice between the act of staying in with the television or a video, on the one hand, and the act of going out to the cinema, on the other, can have different gendered meanings. For example, for a male, who perceives the home as a place of leisure, staying in may be seen as a form of relaxation. Alternatively, for a woman, who is constantly aware of the domestic chores that need doing, going out may be seen as a way of escaping the demands of the domestic sphere and of breaking routine. However, the meanings of these activities can also be affected by the gendered meanings of places outside the home, which might contradict these other meanings in various ways. Just as getting out can represent an escape from domestic routine, the public space outside the home can also be perceived as potentially threatening by many women, so that the home can be seen as a place of comfort and safety.

The decision to focus on Nottingham was largely pragmatic: the grant for research funding was submitted by Mark Jancovich, who was already living and working within the city.[31] However, the decision to make the project a local study was quite deliberate. A local study enabled the project not only to achieve a necessary focus, but also to avoid an abstract conception of place and space. It is not that we view the local as the concrete and micro as opposed to global abstraction and the macro. As we have seen, different places have different narratives precisely because they occupy different positions within spatially organised social relations. The sound film came to New York first because it was a key metropolitan centre and, as a result, the experience of New York was not representative of other places – places that were not metropolitan centres. Similarly, Nottingham is not a microcosm of more abstract processes, nor a unique place defined by internal processes. Thus, we sought to examine the ways in which Nottingham's situation locally, nationally and internationally shaped its development.

For example, while the first reference to the town was in AD 868, Nottingham's significance was established in AD 920, when it became 'a key centre of royal administration'.[32] The city continued as a regional centre throughout the Middle Ages but it was dramatically transformed by the industrial revolution. During the first half of the 18th century, 'a revolution in consumer spending' was taking place, and the garden town became fashionable among the middle classes of the period. However, between 1750 and 1831, the population grew from about 11,000 to 50,000 as the textile trades expanded.

As we have seen, it is claimed that culture has become central to the economies of contemporary cities as consumption and leisure become increasingly important and cities are forced to trade on their images to attract tourism and finance capital. However, unlike many British cities in the 19th century, Nottingham had one crucial absence – heavy industry – and, as a result, its position has long been dependent on its role as a regional centre and as a place of leisure and consumption. This situation also had gendered implications. Heavy industry was associated with masculinity during the 19th century, and Nottingham's image was therefore strongly feminised. The Corporation of Nottingham, for example, had 'assiduously cultivated' its image as the 'Queen of the Midlands',[33] and this feminised image was used to signify the gentility and refinement of the city, rather than imply any masculine city to which it was subordinated.

Even its textiles industries contributed to this image. They were not only centred on a luxury consumer item, lace, but they also meant that the city had a large female workforce. As Beckett and Brand note, not only was it the case that 'about two-fifths of the Nottingham workforce was female', but many of these female workers were single as many employers refused to hire married women.[34] These women helped to bolster the city's image as a place of leisure and consumption through their consumer spending but they often came to figure as objects of consumption themselves. For example, it has long been claimed that Nottingham has more than its fair share of attractive women, many of whom, it is implied, are freer with their affections than women from other cities.

Nor did this situation change much during the 20th century, when the city's economy came to be dominated by 'three giants which came in to being at the end of the nineteenth century: Boots in pharmaceuticals, Raleigh in cycle manufacture, and Players in cigarette manufacture'.[35] However, as Beckett and Brand point out, although textiles firms are smaller and less visible than companies like Boots, Raleigh and Players, 'Nottingham was, and still is, a textile city', despite the rapid decline of the lace industry after World War I.

The war had little impact on the city, although many locals were killed during the conflict, but in its aftermath there was a change in the city's textile industries. If the lace industry contracted during the period, the hosiery industry expanded, and helped ensure Nottingham's relative prosperity during the inter-war period. Even during the Depression, the city was not as hard-hit as other areas of the country and still had a reputation as a lively centre of leisure and affluence. None the less, unemployment was still a problem with as many as 10.8 per cent of the insured population out of work during the 1930s, and even those in work during this period often suffered from low wages or short-time working.

During World War II, Nottingham was also relatively fortunate. Many cities suffered severe damage from German bombers. For example, much of Coventry was devastated by air raids, and required major rebuilding in the post-war period. However, Nottingham was largely unscathed, probably due to its lack of heavy industry, which meant that it was not an important strategic target. However, the city was not unaffected by the war, and it proved a popular centre of leisure and entertainment for soldiers on leave. Their presence even justified the relaxation of local prohibitions against the Sunday opening of cinemas and other places of leisure and entertainment. However, while there were a series of anxieties over the presence of foreign servicemen in Britain at the time,[36] there is little evidence that this was a particular problem in Nottingham.

None the less, the lack of damage did not stop the council from embarking on a major reconstruction of the city in the post-war period. The council undertook a series of building programmes that expanded the city beyond its pre-war boundaries. Slum clearance was also a feature of the period, as was the redevelopment of areas that had once been slums. The expansion of the city also required a major development of the city's transport systems. Car ownership in particular underwent a dramatic increase throughout the period and, by 1991, 50 per cent of households in the city had at least one car, a situation that has created inevitable traffic problems.

While the city grew in size, its population also began to change. From the 1950s onwards, Nottingham, like many other cities in the Midlands, became the home of migrants from the New Commonwealth, particularly those of Indian and Afro-Caribbean descent, many of whom were attracted by promises of work. However, many of the new residents did not receive a positive reception and 'race riots' erupted in Nottingham in both 1958 and the early 1980s. None the less, their presence has been an important addition to the city that has both transformed its character and enriched its culture.

The post-war period also saw a change in the fortunes of the city's key industries. The lace industry had already gone into decline after World War I, but hosiery continued to do well. Even in the mid-1980s, employment in textiles was not much lower than it had been during the mid-1920s. However, the industry has been subject to a growing concentration of ownership in which the small companies that composed the industry have gone through successive mergers and become increasingly dependent on sales through chain stores. The textile industry has also witnessed increasing competition from overseas, and particularly the economies of the Pacific rim.

Raleigh also experienced a similar history. After World War II, the company expanded and reached an output of 1 million cycles by 1951. However, with increases in car ownership and other forms of transport, and with increased competition from overseas, Raleigh went into decline as an employer. It still continued to produce in high numbers and, as late as 1994, it produced 750,000 cycles. However, it did so on the basis of a much smaller workforce. Immediately after World War I, Raleigh had the largest cycle factory in the world, but by the 21st century, much of its site had been converted into a campus for the University of Nottingham.

While both these industries were victim to competition from overseas, they were also subject to changing fashions, a pressure that hit Players particularly hard. While the company thrived up to the 1960s, revelations about the health risks of smoking had a severe impact on the company. Once a major industry and sponsor of cultural events, Players's importance to the city has been significantly diminished and is unlikely to see any reversal of its fortunes in the foreseeable future.

However, although the significance of these industries has waned over the course of the 20th century, new developments have only consolidated the importance of leisure and consumption to the city. While traditional industries have declined, the service sector has flourished and, as S. D. Chapman has noted, 'perhaps the greatest increase in the service sector is at the city's two universities, where student numbers have doubled between 1985 and 1995'. Not only do these students bring 'benefits to the town by augmentation of consumer expenditure', but many are drawn to Nottingham as much by the reputation of its club scene as by the reputation of its degree courses.[37] Furthermore, many students have chosen to stay on in Nottingham after graduation due to its cultural life and, given the profile of Nottingham Trent University's art and design courses, many of these work in fashion and design. The lace-market area of the city has therefore witnessed a significant regeneration that was based initially on fashion and clothing. Indeed, as is often pointed out, the 'most outstanding success story is Paul Smith, the menswear

The post-modern city as a place of spectacle and consumption? The Cornerhouse, Forman Street, City Centre

designer, who opened his first boutique in Byard Lane in 1970, and by 1996 was one of the country's 500 richest people'.[38]

However, while the Corporation has promoted Nottingham as a city of affluence and consumption, it has also been renowned for its slums and poverty.[39] Even today while the Corporation presents the city as a regional and even national centre of culture, leisure and consumption, Nottingham also has a national reputation for its social problems, particularly prostitution, homelessness and drugs.[40]

Like other cities, Nottingham is therefore diverse, heterogeneous and contradictory but it was not chosen as an object of study for any unique or special feature. However, while we do not want to imply that it is somehow typical or representative either, the advantage of using Nottingham as an object of study is precisely that it is a fairly 'ordinary' city, not a metropolitan centre such as London, New York or Los Angeles.

Indeed, Nottingham's location in the East Midlands places it on the divide between the North and South of England, a divide that has cultural as well as geographical significance.[41] While the North has often been associated with heavy industry and suffered greatly from deindustrialisation in the late 20th century, Nottingham's lack of heavy industry and its association with leisure, consumption and the service sector enabled it to escape the worst effects of deindustrialisation. In many ways, then, its economy and culture seem to display features both of the North and the South. Indeed, while the South operates as the national centre of commerce, consumption and administration, Nottingham claims to be 'the commercial, retailing and administrative centre of the East Midlands'.[42] Its relation to other towns and cities in the region is therefore one of a regional centre. While other cities in the region, such as Leicester and Derby, have their own centres of consumption and leisure, Nottingham's centre is a major draw and it represents a place of affluence and distinction. Its centre seems more up-market and it has heavily promoted itself as a regional centre for the arts through institutions such as the Playhouse theatre, the Royal Centre (which combines the Theatre Royal and Concert Hall), the Broadway Media Centre (the East Midlands' leading regional film theatre) and more recently the National Ice Stadium.

Archives and Ethnography

Our research approached its topic from a series of different angles. First, it examined different periods in the history of Nottingham in order to analyse the ways in which the meanings of places within the city have changed and so affected the activities of consumption associated with them. Second, it investigated the ways in which different places have different meanings for different sections of the population.

The project also employed two inter-related types of research. First, it concentrated on the analysis of local history archives in order to study the public debates over sites of film consumption. Second, it undertook an ethnographic study to access people's perceptions, experiences and memories of film consumption. The analysis of local archives mainly centred on reports in local newspapers, although it also consulted a number of other sources, such as papers from meetings of the council and the Watch Committee, who regulated Nottingham cinemas in the first half of the 20th century. These sources do not give us direct access to audiences' experience of the places of film consumption, but they do provide access to the public debates over them. As a result, while the presumed readerships of these papers influenced their selection of topics and the ways in which topics were discussed, these agendas can be useful to the film historian: they can reveal the different ways in which different social groups viewed these places.

Only one local daily newspaper still survives in Nottingham, the *Nottingham Evening Post*,[43] but during the first half of the 20th century, there were many more. In the 1930s, for example, there were four local daily newspapers. The *Nottingham Daily Guardian* was modelled on *The Times* and aimed at the Nottingham elite. It contained financial news, coverage of the local council, and reports on sports such as fox-hunting. The *Nottingham Evening Post*, on the other hand, was the most visually entertaining, and contained sensational news items, jokes and a women's page. It also presented itself as the most modern and youthful. In contrast, the *Nottingham Evening News* directed itself at respectable middle-class home-owners, and cultivated a reputation for community involvement. It not only put on events such as an ideal home exhibition but also organised holidays abroad. Finally, the *Nottingham Journal* had a largely male, working-class readership and was distinguished by its coverage of racing and football.[44]

The provincialism of the local press is often read as synonymous with its triviality, and it is often associated with stories of lost cats and parish tea parties. However, local newspapers are a rich and undervalued resource in film studies, whose importance is demonstrated by their readerships. For example, for much of the 20th century, 'the number of local papers sold exceeded that of nationals'[45] and, even as late as the 1990s, 'the *Birmingham Evening Mail* and the *Manchester Evening News* [had] circulations around a quarter of a million – in the same order of magnitude as that of *The Independent* or the *Guardian*, and more than that of the *Financial Times*'.[46] The importance of these figures is also borne out by the advertising revenues that the local press earns: 'In 1987 the regional press attracted £1,280 million in advertising, which represents 36 per cent of total press advertising and 22 per cent of the national advertising revenues total for all media.'[47]

However, the importance of the press is not simply based on their sales, but also their ability to produce and organise the public. During much of the 20th century, they not only 'remained the prime source of information for the reading public – especially for working-class readers',[48] but they were therefore 'highly influential in defining news for their readers and likely to be the single most important source of news, especially political news, within their area'.[49] Indeed, while Franklin and Murphy have claimed that the 'localism of the British local press is ersatz [and that] it is the product of an international corporate capitalism',[50] they also acknowledge that not only are they 'a highly significant component in local media networks',[51] but that they are even central to the production of community. The local press are not only committed to the promotion of 'local patriotism',[52] but the communities that they claim to represent have always been constructions, entities that did not pre-exist the papers that claim to represent them.[53] In other words, the local press are central to the production of local 'imagined communities' as much as the national press are central to the production of the 'imagined community' of the nation.

However, although they are often dismissed for their provincialism, the local press differ from the national press in one significant way. As Franklin and Murphy put it, 'the local press is significant because it may provide a relatively open and pluralistic forum for public discussion and debate at a time when large sections of the British national press are increasingly speaking with a monotonously homogeneous voice'.[54] Their reliance on local sources of information for regular news stories – 'local and regional government, voluntary organisations, the courts, the police and business'[55] – can create a tendency to conformity, for fear of alienating these potential sources. However, 'nonconforming opinions do get published' and 'the interplay of local politics [can often] disrupt the normal tendency to blandness'.[56]

As for the ethnographic study, we used as many different approaches as possible in order to solicit as many different respondents and types of response. We involved the local media which ran items that encouraged people to write to us about their experiences. A questionnaire was distributed to cinemas, local libraries, school, retirement homes and other agencies, while copies were also distributed to a range of institutions such as trade unions and voluntary organisations. This questionnaire was not designed to elicit quantifiable data, but contained some basic, open-ended questions that sought to identify the key terms through which people talked about film consumption. The questionnaire also asked people if they were willing to be interviewed in more depth, and a number of informal follow-up interviews were held. In addition, a series of focus groups was organised. Some of these groups were simply congregations of people united by a common agenda, such as a local history group or Women's Institute group, but others were targeted for specific reasons. For example, to ensure a large number of young respondents, meetings were held at playgroups and schools, and to ensure that certain ethnic minorities were represented, we interviewed a range of different organisations and groups. However, we were concerned that our questions should not define people as the representatives of specific identities determined by us, and it should be noted that while one disabled group made the issue of access central to their discussion of film consumption, certain ethnic groups never once made conscious reference to their ethnic identities as being in any way relevant.

Another reason that we used as many methods as possible and contacted a wide range of groups and organisations was to counteract one particular problem of the project. Most of the people who contacted us or returned our questionnaires had, almost inevitably, a fairly major investment in the cinema. Some groups, like the elderly, were much more prone to respond with only a minor investment in the cinema: they tended to have more time on their hands, and those with limited mobility clearly enjoyed the social contact. However, we did not want the project to be skewed by these factors and, as a result, interviewers went into the city centre for several days where they stopped shoppers and members of the general public to ask them questions. This produced a wealth of information and contacts, but it also reinforced our awareness of the problem. Many people believed that their views would simply not be important to us unless they had a major investment in the cinema, while others had such a lack of investment that they would not devote their spare time to talking to us.

Ethnography and Interpretation

We therefore tried to avoid the preoccupations with aberrant audiences and readings present in much cultural studies. Early cultural studies, for example, tended to divide the public rather too neatly into two distinct groups – the conformist and the resistant – and it was always implied that the former were a known entity and that all activity, interest and creativity was to be found in the usually subcultural groups who composed the latter position.[57] More recently, this tradition has produced an over-concentration on fan cultures within academic work on media audiences,[58] and there are two main reasons for this. First, it is fairly easy for researchers to gain access to fans: fans tend to congregate together, produce materials such as fanzines and webpages, and are usually willing to talk about their activities. Second, the study of fans has helped many academics to escape a central problem of audience research: the accusation that this research is inherently intrusive and comparable to the colonial gaze at racialised others that first produced the discipline of social anthropology and the practice of ethnography. By studying fandom, academics could claim that their own identities as fans meant that their research did not involve speaking *for* others.

However, as Ellen Seiter argues, researchers need to avoid 'the delusion of alliance', in which they try to escape the power relations involved in encounters with their respondents by claiming a shared identification with them. As Seiter points out, this tactic implies that researchers can only study those who are like themselves, and she rightly responds: 'Surely, researchers must be willing to engage subjects whose experiences are different as well as the same as our own, and to interrogate and even pursue situations in which some discomfort exists.'[59]

The 'delusions of alliance' can also have other dangers. For example, Valerie Walkerdine is highly critical of the 'colonial gaze' within audience research and, as a result, her own study of one family's viewing of *Rocky II* tries to avoid a clear distinction between the researcher and her object of research. Instead, her analysis involves a autobiographical self-investigation that acknowledges her own involvement within the dynamics that she is studying. This definitely produces considerable insights, but her sense of involvement not only creates a sense of empathy and investment, but it also produces its own form of imposition. The family that she studies is continually read in terms of herself and her own relationship to her father and, as a result, her respondents do not have lives of their own but become mere props for her own self-exploration.[60]

Similarly, Barker and Brooks have claimed that in a 'desire for political positions', ethnographic researchers usually interpret audiences in terms of their incorporation within, or resistance to, a dominant culture, and so impose their own agendas upon their respondents. In the process, Barker and Brooks also imply that most studies do not 'trust' their respondents – that they do not take what their respondents say at face value – but feel the need to explain (or explain away) their comments. Unfortunately, in order to draw any conclusions from their own study, Barker and Brooks are also forced to interpret what their respondents tell them: to identify patterns and tendencies that underpin what is said and draw conclusions from what it might mean. Their conclusion even sounds like the models of resistance from which they distance themselves:

the popularity of Action films is connected in precise ways with their historical 'moment'. In Britain and, in related ways, in many industrialised countries, the 1980–90s saw a down-turn in working class activity, and a rise in various kinds of right-wing populism. But a class does not disappear just because it members lack confidence for a time. Instead, their group-awareness goes underground, and comes out in strange forms. Action films, we suggest, are one of those.[61]

Not only does this imply that the popularity of 'Action films' is simply a distorted form of a 'real' political resistance, but also that Barker and Brooks are able to access this true meaning in a way that is not open to their respondents.[62]

Our point is that interpretation is not only necessary, but also inevitable. Even if it were possible to simply describe a phenomenon without making assumptions about its meaning and significance, it is not clear what the value of such an activity would be. Indeed, others criticise ethnography for not being intrusive enough. Jane Feuer, for example, has argued that ethnographic research cannot escape interpretation and that it provides no more access to the audience than textual analysis: the ethnographer has simply replaced the film text with the audience text.[63] Furthermore, she claims that ethnography only deals with conscious articulations of experience, while psychoanalysis demonstrates that the conscious mind is always the production of unconscious repression, and that one needs to be wary of what the audience say. However, as Andrew Tudor has demonstrated, psychoanalysis is not only unfalsifiable, but has an inherent tendency towards 'esoteric readings'. Its concern with the unconscious not only means that any argument made against it can be dismissed as evidence of repression but also that it is predisposed to offer accounts that contradict people's conscious experiences.[64] However, the psychoanalytic argument also pulls the rug from under itself. By its own logic, if any conscious articulation of experience must of necessity be the product of repression, psychoanalysis must also be the product of repression. Furthermore, while Feuer confirms the need for interpretation within ethnographic research, she does not prove that there is anything *more* problematic about interpreting audience responses than interpreting film texts.

Obviously audience work cannot fall 'back on a realist treatment of language, analysing transcription of speech as a pure and direct expression of the mind of the sub-ject'.[65] Researchers must strive to understand the contexts within which they interact with those that they study, and the ways in which these contexts will shape 'what gets said and how it is said'.[66] Indeed, rather than pursuing the impossible fantasy of a con-text that exists outside of power relations, researchers must constantly remind themselves, in their research planning, their research practice and in the interpretation of their findings, that the ways in which 'what gets said and how it is said' are influenced and affected by power relations. One noteworthy instance of such reflection can be found in Ellen Seiter's account of one particularly awkward interview, in which she not only demonstrates the difficulties of audience research, but used the encounter to reflect on the dynamics of the interviewing process and the cultural power of her position as an academic.[67]

As a result, in our meetings with the public, we were careful to put our cards on the table. We began each meeting with a very clear outline of the basic ideas behind the research. This did not predetermine what people would later go on to discuss but, on the contrary, it prevented them from trying to guess our agenda and provided them with a position from which to comment on, and even criticise, our agendas. As a result, many older respondents asserted that they used to go to the cinema to see particular films, and that the place of consumption was irrelevant to them. However, having stated this, they would often contradict this point again and again throughout the course of the meeting – a situation that not only demonstrates the danger of taking people's claims at face value but also requires explanation. Why is it that people claimed that when they went to the pictures, their primary motivation was the desire to see a particular film, when their later comments clearly contradicted this claim? In other words, researchers need to look for contradictions in what people say about their experiences: it is these very contradictions that both demonstrate the need for interpretation and provide the materials for such interpretation.

However, although we were interested in the activities of film consumption, the scope of the project did not allow us to actually accompany audiences while they consumed films, and the absence of such research means that our interviews need to be seen as memories of cinemagoing. Of course, some memories were older than others, but all share one problem: memory is not simply a record of the past, but a reconstruction of that past, a text whose meanings require interpretation. As Lynn Spigel has put it, memory 'aims to discover a past that makes the present more tolerable'.[68] Again this point reminds us of the textual nature of audience accounts, and of the need for interpretation, but this is not to imply that memory is simply a problem. As Stacey points out, to take 'account of the narrative formations of audiences' memories is not to rob them of their specificity, or treat them as fictional narratives like the films they were watching'.[69] Memories are memories *of* something, and the ways in which things are remembered have much to tell us. For example, the importance that many elderly women attach to their memories of going to the cinema as young women can tell us both about the function of cinemagoing within youth, and the ways in which these women relate that experience to their own current situation and circumstances. For many, the construction of this 'golden age' is a product of their dissatisfaction with the present.

Focus and Findings

Finally, although it is grounded in both the archival and the 'ethnographic' research, the following book will foreground the former. This is for two reasons. First, for much of the book, few respondents were old enough to provide much commentary on the periods covered. For example, there are few people old enough to remember the bioscopes that came to Nottingham's Goose Fair in the late 1890s, and there are not many more who remember the reorganisation of the city centre in the late 1920s and 1930s. These accounts are therefore forced to rely predominantly on written records, although actual audience accounts have been included where possible. Second, the sheer volume of material has convinced us that the project should form the basis of at least two books.

The current book will provide an initial history of cinemagoing in Nottingham, and its changing meanings over time, and while this will include extensive reference to the ethnographic research, the detailed examination of this material will be left until later volumes. This means that there will be few extended quotations from people, a practice that is often used to let people speak for themselves in their own words. Instead, we have concentrated on identifying broader patterns, although we have been concerned to ground these patterns through reference to specific examples.

In the process, the following book is divided into four further parts. Part Two concerns the emplacement of cinema within Nottingham from the late 19th century to the 1910s, and it therefore covers the emergence of the fairground bioscopes which associated film consumption with meanings of the fairground as a place of popular amusement. It then moves on to examine the emergence of the purpose-built cinemas following the passing of the Cinematographic Act in 1909. As will be demonstrated, in Nottingham, this Act was not just used as a way of regulating the health and safety of cinema buildings, nor even as a way of regulating the types of materials that were shown in them. It was also used to regulate the modes of film consumption available and their spatial location within the city. In other words, different places within the city were clearly associated with different modes of cultural consumption. As a result, certain venues were either denied a licence or encouraged not to apply for one in an attempt to regulate the modes of consumption appropriate to film. However, struggles also occurred over the placing of cinemas within certain areas. In this way, we can see the ways in which cinemas were associated with certain social groups and classes and their construction was spatially regulated.

Part Three moves on to the 1920s and 1930s, and it is concerned with the conditions that produced not only a boom in cinema building within the period, but also the creation of the large super cinemas. In Nottingham, it will be argued, this process was largely associated with the reorganisation of the city and its image, and this occurred in two different ways. First, there was a large slum clearance programme in the city centre which resulted in the removal of the old, popular market from the Old Market Square, the construction of a monumental council building, and the conversion of the Old Market Square into a place of high-income consumption. In the process, the focus of film consumption was shifted away from the 1920s' cinemas that had congregated around Upper Parliament Street and to the Ritz, a new cinema that was built within the Old Market Square on land made available by slum clearance. The second process was a massive programme of suburban building, which the council undertook in order to house those displaced by slum clearance. Although suburbanisation is often associated with the decline in cinema attendance in the period after World War II, in Nottingham it was largely responsible for what has become known as the 'age of the dream palace'. As we will demonstrate, most suburban estates had few if any local amenities, and even the public house, the traditional place of working-class leisure, was absent due to the intervention of the temperance movement. In this context, the vast majority of the cinemas built within Nottingham during the late 1920s and 1930s were built within these suburbs and, as the only local amenity and place of congregation, they became central to the life of these suburbs, and one of the predominant forms of leisure during the period.

Part Four then moves on to the post-war period, which saw a dramatic decline in cinema attendance and the closure of numerous cinemas. As we have already seen, this process is often related to either suburbanisation or television, but in this section we provide a different account. Rather than presenting a picture of increasing retreat into suburban privatisation, we demonstrate that the period was distinguished by a change in people's understanding of the 'local'. Home ownership and new systems of transport meant that many people were spending more leisure time at home *and* travelling further for their leisure. As a result, the definition of what constituted one's local environment was changing and it was not the city-centre cinemas that were hit hardest after World War II but the suburban cinemas themselves. This section also demonstrates the ways in which the introduction of television did not simply threaten cinemagoing, but rather enabled new and different modes of film consumption and so changed the meanings of cinemas and cinemagoing.

Finally, in Part Five, we extend this argument to look at a whole range of different types of film consumption that have emerged since the late 1970s: the video; the multiplex; the Broadway Media Centre, which developed out of transformations in the art cinema; the 'new media', from satellite and cable to the internet; and finally, the Cornerhouse, a new city-centre leisure complex featuring a multi-screen cinema that is the product of changing cultural policy concerning urban development within British cities.

In the process, we suggest the following: that the meanings of different modes of film consumption are tied to their location within the cultural geography of the city; that the emergence of each new mode of film consumption does not necessarily render older modes redundant but rather that it involves a redefinition of their meanings; that there is not a process of privatisation in which people retreat from public life and become increasingly isolated from one another, but rather a process in which people's perceptions of space change: while more leisure becomes centred in the home, people also travel further and further for their leisure; that these processes are mediated by a whole series of different factors such as class, gender, race and age, and that this means that different modes of film consumption, and the places associated within them, have different meanings for different sections of society.

Notes

1. Massey, 1994, p. 4.
2. Ibid.
3. Morley, 2000, p. 234.
4. Massey, 1994, p. 5.
5. Ibid., p. 155.
6. Pile, 1999, p. vii. See also Pile, Brook and Mooney, 1999. Indeed, 'city studies' has become a burgeoning interdisciplinary area across the disciplines as demonstrated, for example, by the following selection: David B. Clarke, 1997; Fainstein and Campbell, 1996; LeGates and Stout, 1996; Miles, Hall and Borden, 2000; Savage and Warde, 1993; Short, 1996; Taylor, Evans and Fraser, 1996; Westwood and Williams, 1997.
7. Pile, 1999, p. vii.

8. Davis, 1990; Davis, 2002, p. 151; Dear, 2000; Harvey, 1989a; Jameson, 1984, pp. 53–92; Jameson, 1991; Soja, 1989.

9. Zukin, 1995.

10. Hannigan, 1998; Harvey, 1989a and Zukin, 1995.

11. Ibid.; and Morley and Robins, 1995.

12. Harvey, 1989a.

13. Zukin, 1995; and Morley and Robins, 1995.

14. Williams, 1974; and Moores, 2000.

15. Williams, 1974; and Morley, 1992.

16. Benedict Anderson, 1983.

17. Ibid.; and Morley, 1992.

18. Morley and Robins, 1995.

19. Massey, 1994, p. 160

20. Appaduri, 1988, p. 39.

21. Moores, 2000, p. 109.

22. Zukin, 1995; and Morley and Robins, 1995.

23. Massey, 1994.

24. Hall, 1984; Sassen, 1991; and Sassen, 1994.

25. Hannigan, 1998.

26. Davis, 2002.

27. Massey, 1994.

28. Morley, 2000, p. 23.

29. Bourdieu, 1984, p. 333.

30. Morley, 1986.

31. The research was funded by a Major Research Award from the Arts and Humanities Research Board that was conducted between 1 February 1999 and 31 January 2000, and was entitled: *Film Consumption and the City: A Historical Case Study in the City of Nottingham, 1900–Present.*

32. Beckett and Brand, 1997, p. 8.

33. Ibid., p. 79. See also Griffin, 1997.

34. Beckett and Brand, 1997, p. 81.

35. Ibid.

36. See, for example, Webster, 1988.

37. Chapman 1997, p. 504.

38. Beckett and Brand, 1997, p. 82

39. Most famously, it was the site of one of the classic studies of poverty: Coates and Silburn, 1970.

40. See Griffin, 1997; and Beckett and Brand, 1997.

41. See Shields, 1991.

42. Quoted in Beckett and Brand, 1997, p. 84.

43. It is joined by two additional free weekly newspapers: the *Topper* and the *Recorder*.

44. See Stubbings, unpublished PhD.

45. Franklin and Murphy, 1992, p. 55. See also Franklin and Murphy, 1998.

46. Franklin and Murphy, 1992, p. 67.

47. Ibid., p. 7.

48. Ibid., p. 55

49. Ibid., p. 6.

50. Ibid., p. 31.

51. Ibid., p. 2.

52. Ibid.

53. Ibid., p. 56.

54. Ibid., p. 9.

55. Ibid., p. 63.

56. Ibid., p. 75.

57. See, for example, Hall and Jefferson, 1976; and Hebdige, 1979.

58. Jenkins, 1992; and Lewis, 1992.

59. Seiter, 1999, p. 37.

60. Walkerdine, 1986, pp. 167–99.

61. Barker and Brooks, 1998, p. 291.

62. Ang makes a similar criticism of Radway's *Reading the Romance* (1987) , which she argues works to reaffirm the authority of the academic over that of the respondents. Ang, 1996, p. 99.

63. Feuer, 1986. Also quoted in Morley, 1990, p. 24.

64. Tudor, 1989, p. 3. See also Tudor, 1997, pp. 443–63.

65. Seiter, 1999, p. 29.

66. Ibid., p. 30.

67. Seiter, 1990, pp. 61–84.

68. Spigel, 1995, p. 21.

69. Stacey, 1994, p.76.

PART TWO

The Construction of the Cinema: Fairgrounds, Theatres and Spatial Regulation

Introduction: Class, Gender and Public Space in Early Film Consumption

The early film period is often seen as one of fluidity and experimentation in which the possibilities of film technologies were explored and contested. The invention of a technology for the projection of moving images can in no way be seen as equivalent to the invention of 'cinema' as a social and cultural institution.[1] However, although the topic of this section is the early struggles to 'place' film consumption, and so define its meanings as an activity, film consumption has never been finally defined or fixed, but has been in a constant process of contestation and transformation ever since.

None the less, for the first fifteen to twenty years of its history, film consumption was a far more heterogeneous affair than in later periods.[2] Films were consumed in a wide variety of public and private places and within a range of different contexts. Even by the late 1900s, when the first purpose-built venues began to emerge, places of film exhibition were rarely referred to as cinemas, but were more usually known as cinematographic theatres, electric theatres, picture palaces and picture halls. Within the different contexts of exhibition that predate these developments, films were not only consumed in different ways, but the very object being consumed was differently constituted. For example, films were first shown in London at a private performance to the photographic society and, in contexts such as this, it was not the films themselves that were the object of consumption but rather the spectacle of a new machine. In other places, such as the music hall, films were not consumed as discrete objects in themselves but simply as one feature within a broad programme of acts and turns. During this period, films were also shown in town halls, where people paid to see recordings of events such as local football matches. They were even shown in churches, where they were used to illustrate the clergyman's sermon.[3] Here, as in the fairground, they were incorporated within already established practices of performance. While the clergymen incorporated them into their sermons, showmen incorporated them into their shows in place of other spectacles such as the magic lantern or the ghost show.[4] In other words, there was no unified object of film consumption, but rather a period of fluidity, in which the meanings of film consumption were less dependent on the film as a text than on the location in which it was consumed.[5]

The importance of place can therefore be found from the very outset and it manifested itself in a number of ways. In Nottingham, for example, the first announcements of film showings in Nottingham make this evident through their description of it as 'London's Latest and Greatest Sensation'[6] or 'London's sensational Moving Pictures'.[7] Thus, while these exhibitions may have taken place within Nottingham, they were presented as the re-enactment of an essentially metropolitan experience. By consuming these films, it was implied, one was experiencing the life of the centre rather than that of the periphery. One could be *in* one location, without being defined by it; one could live in the provinces without being provincial. However, the place of film consumption affected its meanings in other ways too. Early film was often consumed in places of popular entertainment, such as amusement arcades, music hall and fairs, and the meanings of these locations affected the meanings of the activities within them. Similarly, the exhibition of films within churches provided an alternative set of meanings and identified them as instruments of education and edification.

If these meanings were opposed to one another, struggles over the meanings of film consumption also took other forms. The period saw a whole series of discourses through which various bodies tried to order and control film consumption.[8] In these cases, the control of film consumption was fundamentally concerned with the control of audiences but, at least until 1909, when the Cinematographic Act was passed,[9] the control of audiences was largely seen as a matter of controlling the places within which film was consumed. However, while a series of critics have claimed that this process came to an end around 1909,[10] and was replaced by an attempt to control the films exhibited rather than the locations of those exhibitions, this distinction was never as neat as such a claim may at first appear. The desire to control film texts is often little more than a concern to control the places in which they can be shown, and hence who sees them. Even those who claim that specific texts are a problem often display less concern if that text is shown in an art cinema than if it is shown in a popular venue. Each site of exhibition is supposed to have a very specific and distinct audience. Similarly, in the campaign over the so-called video nasties, despite the rhetoric of the campaigners, the attack was less directed at the films themselves than at preventing their availability for exhibition within the home where children might get access to them. The films banned on video could often still be shown within cinemas and even, in some cases, via television broadcasts. While television did not control the audience through the place of exhibition, it attempted to control it through the time of exhibition. While a video can be watched at any time, television broadcasts were supposed to prevent children from gaining access to 'inappropriate materials' through its time schedules: 'inappropriate materials' were shown after children were presumed to have gone to bed.[11]

Furthermore, as we shall show, the reason for the apparent decline in interest in the places of film consumption after 1909 may have been precisely because the Cinematographic Act provided the means of regulating these spaces. The regulation of these places still continued but such regulation did not need to be argued for to the same degree: it was already in active operation. While the law was reputedly designed to ensure that venues were safe from fire, the dangers of fire were often exaggerated. Even when fires did break out, few people were killed by the fires themselves, but rather by the panic which ensued. As a result, the Act did not simply ensure proper protection against the spread of fire, or even provide adequate exits to prevent panic or to eliminate its effects. The terms of the Act gave local governments the right to set *any* criteria for the licensing of venues and, as we will show, these powers were not only used to deny licences to places of 'ill repute' but also as a way of zoning the city. In Nottingham, for example, the Act was used to designate where film consumption could and could not take place, where it was appropriate and where it was inappropriate to watch films.

Class and the Cinema Audience

These struggles were often about issues of class, and cinema was often seen to be in need of control specifically because of its associations with popular amusements. However, it would be a mistake to present film consumption simply as an example of a radical sub-altern low culture that threatened existing cultural hierarchies. In America, for example, there has been a debate over the class composition of the nickelodeon. The traditional view was that the audience had been predominantly working class,[12] but this position has been hotly contested. For example, Robert Allen has provided evidence which sug-gests that the nickelodeon audience was much more middle class than had previously been acknowledged,[13] while Ben Singer and others have challenged this view with evi-dence of their own.[14]

One of the problems with this material is the particularly awkward status of the phrase 'middle class'. As Savage and his colleagues have argued: 'The middle classes, because they are in the middle, do not readily fit into the types of binary concepts so widely used in social science.' Most accounts of this class have therefore employed 'three ways of dealing with this problem': to 'squeeze them into binary oppositions by positing a set of links between the middle classes and either the dominant or subordinate social group'; to 'adopt a more descriptive approach [which fails] to explain the specificity of the middle class'; and 'to explore how the middle class might actually be social classes in their own right'.[15]

The first tendency can be clearly seen in both the claims that the nickelodeon audi-ence either was, or was not, middle class in nature. In both cases, the question is implicitly the extent to which it was resistant to, or incorporated by, the 'dominant' cul-ture. It can also be seen in Stephen Ross's claim that: 'Middle-class audiences certainly attended movies during these early years, but their numbers have been greatly exagger-ated because many contemporary observers, as well as recent scholars, wrongly classified all white-collar workers as middle-class.'[16] Ross's point is no doubt right, but his own response fails to specify the particularities of the middle classes. He fails to clarify the differences and distinctions that not only mark them off from both dominant and sub-ordinate classes, but also divide the middle classes themselves. He also replicates another problem: the tendency to use the concepts 'middle class' and 'bourgeoisie' as though they were simply interchangeable – a usage that is often entirely misleading. The term bourgeois is usually used to imply a reference to the dominant class that is defined through its ownership of the means of production, while those sections of the middle classes who attended the cinema were specifically those who, as Ross notes, were dis-tinguished by the lack of such property. However, Ross's solution is simply to use the fact that they did not own the means of production in order to imply that they were, in fact, proletarian or working class, a solution that just mirrors the problem.

For Savage and his colleagues, by way of contrast, the middle classes are specifically defined through their middle status between, on one hand, the owners of the means of production and, on the other, the proletariat or working classes. Savage and his col-leagues therefore define the middle classes in relation to three different forms of capital: property, culture, and organisational assets. The first of these capitals corresponds to the petit-bourgeois middle class of landlords and shopkeepers, while the second corresponds to the professional middle class, whose position is acquired through the accumulation of educational capital. The final capital – organisational assets – is therefore associated with the managerial middle class.

However, the relation to different forms of capital not only defines their class status but has also, historically, produced 'a deeply entrenched division between a professional middle class on the one side, and a petite bourgeoisie and managerial middle class on the other'.[17] One of the reasons for this is precisely that, as Bourdieu has shown, those sections of the bourgeoisie that are most reliant on cultural capital exist in a position of structural dependence upon those sections who are defined through their relation to economic capital. They are therefore forced into a position of antagonism in which they seek to raise the value of their cultural capital by asserting its autonomy from economic interests. The cultural middle classes therefore end up asserting their superiority to the economic middle classes and their interests. However, it is an assertion that is often directed at those sections of the middle classes with relatively low levels of cultural capital rather than at the owners of the means of production.[18]

Debates over the class composition of the early film audiences need to be understood within this context. Most of this work agrees that the audience was largely composed of the skilled working and the lower middle classes; the differences are largely how to define their social position. The poorer sections of the working class could not afford the cinema, while those who campaigned against its potential dangers were generally from the cultural middle class and the upper middle classes.[19] There was some opposition from sections of the petite-bourgeoisie middle classes but, as we will see, these were more specific complaints from trades people about threats to their business. As a result, the debate is less about who was going to the cinema than about how to position these groups: some critics want to present them as subordinate classes, while others want to present them as dominant classes. However, it is their very indeterminate status that is central: they 'do not readily fit into the types of binary concepts'.[20] They were neither simply subordinate nor dominant.

These issues can even be seen in current writings about early film consumption, and it is precisely a concern with its middlebrow status that is often at stake in the debates over the composition of its audience.[21] On the one hand, those who want to present the film audience as essentially working class in nature want to wrestle it from associations with the middle classes, a strategy that was also present in the period. Gunning, for example, discusses the reception of film by the early modernists[22] who saw the potential for a radical disruption of 'bourgeois' culture within it.[23] However, these modernists were themselves sections of the middle classes and it was therefore not 'bourgeois' culture that they wanted to disrupt, but those forms associated with the economic middle classes. Their supposedly oppositional cultural politics was, as Bourdieu has shown, not a challenge to 'bourgeois' society and culture itself, rather it sought to establish a distinction from, and superiority to, the legitimate culture through an identification with popular culture and oppositional politics.[24]

On the other hand, those who seek to challenge these romanticised views of early cinema audiences often end up simply making the case for their 'bourgeois' nature, in which they are damned precisely for their 'respectability'. For example, when May describes the supposed 'bourgeoisification' of film consumption with the emergence of the picture palaces, he describes it as 'a mass amusement ... clearly geared towards middle class aspiration'.[25] The picture palaces are condemned for their supposed incorporation within 'bourgeois' culture, but the culture associated with these venues is precisely not one that is the property of a dominant class. On the contrary, it was the property of a middlebrow, lower-middle-class culture that was defined through its association with the 'mass' rather than the elite, and exists in a state of 'aspiration', rather than security. It is a class that espouses democratic values, but reveres the 'symbols of high culture'.[26] In other words, it revered and aspired to legitimate culture precisely because it was excluded from it. This concern with the middlebrow is made still clearer in Chanan's account of the emergence of film consumption within Britain where he considers it in relation to the music hall and to 'the fluctuating relationship of popular culture, during the nineteenth century in Britain, to the decorum and propriety which bourgeois morals then demanded'.[27]

Gender, Space and Public Culture

However, the concern with these places of film consumption was not simply about issues of class. There were a whole series of concerns with the physical and moral safety of children which, as Pearson and Uricchio point out in the case of the United States, existed in a 'synechdocal relationship ... to the larger audience and its others, immigrants and women'.[28] Children were the group who most uncontroversially justified a call for paternalist control, but intervention that was supposedly made on their behalf could also result in the regulation of other social groups, such as women.[29]

The late 19th and early 20th centuries witnessed a profound series of changes both in women's social position in general and their relation to public space in particular.[30] While many have rightly analysed the ways in which public space has been defined as a masculine territory[31] and hence 'the ambivalent ways in which women could lay claims to new urban spaces',[32] Mica Nava has argued that a very different picture could have been drawn if these writers 'had been readier to focus on the expansion of women's cultural experiences in the city rather than on the constraints'.[33] For Nava, what is striking is 'the invisibility of women in the *literature* of modernity' rather than their actual absence from its public spaces.[34] In other words, women have been written out of accounts of the modern city, rather than being absent from them in the first place. Their presence was not only central to many attempts to regulate these public spaces but also operated as a kind of structuring absence in many accounts of the modern city.[35]

The presence of women within public space not only caused anxieties which led some to call for social reform and the regulation of social space, but it was also, at least in part, a result of their own involvement in movements for social reform and the regulation of social space. For example, as Judith Walkowitz and others have shown, many middle-class women were able to use the very discourses of domesticity to justify their involvement within philanthropic activities that not only sought to reform and regulate the public world but therefore required their active presence within the city and its streets.[36] However, the late 19th and early 20th century was a period which 'saw a destabilisation of

Victorian sexual mores'[37] through the emergence of two related figures: the new woman and the suffragette. While in no sense synonymous, both were connected to dramatic expansion in what was seen as appropriate for a respectable young woman.

In addition to a greater sense of licence with regard to their sexuality, a whole series of new spaces and public activities emerged which were not only acceptable for women, but actively courted them: exhibitions, amusement parks, galleries, libraries, restaurants, tea rooms, department stores and, of course, picture houses.[38] As Joanne Hollows argues, for some, the association between femininity and consumption that distinguished these places made them both doubly damned as trivial and insignificant[39] but, for others, their association is identified as a mechanism of women's oppression.[40] Women's association with consumption, it is suggested, produces a new form of cultural subordination. However, such judgments repeat the problems identified by Nava earlier: they emphasise the constraints associated with these places rather than the expansions of women's experiences that they enabled. Certainly, there are problems about the ways in which women have been associated with consumption, but many attempts to see consumption as a means through which women are controlled and regulated usually reproduce the masculine denigration of both women and consumption.[41]

Nor was it simply middle-class women whose experiences of public space were expanding during this period. As Kathy Peiss has shown in the American context, working-class women were also finding new places of leisure outside the domestic sphere. Here the situation was a little different: economic necessity often required working-class women to work outside the home so that they were probably never quite as constrained by the separation of the public and the private spheres as middle-class women. On the contrary, they may even, at times, have longed for the economic security on which a clear separation would have depended. None the less, while the public world of working-class leisure was still a largely homosocial, masculine space, the picture houses began to court female audiences actively and so provided the space for the development of a heterosexual culture, a place of relative respectability in which men and women could meet and mingle outside the home.[42] For some, this was clearly a source of concern and there were recurrent fears of female seduction, and even abduction, within these venues,[43] but the theatres themselves also actively encouraged female viewers in a bid for respectability. Women not only brought respectability but also, in the process, the potential for a larger audience. By making their establishments attractive to female viewers in general, film exhibitions also sought to attract the whole family as an audience.[44]

It was, however, this very bid for the female consumer which, as we have seen above, not only worried many critics at the time but was also used by many recent writers as proof of the cinema's middlebrow status. It is often precisely the attempt to make the cinema appealing to female audiences which is seen as a threat to its radical and transgressive potential.[45] As a number of commentators have noted, attacks on the middlebrow have often been gendered. The radicalism of modernist culture, for example, is often defined as masculine and its transgressions are usually directed at the values of domestic respectability that middle-class women were supposed to represent.[46]

Of course, for many women, the appeal of these places of film consumption was precisely that they offered a place outside the home where women could escape from the duties and responsibilities associated with the domestic sphere, while still remaining within a relatively safe environment where the dangers of harassment were minimal.[47]

Carnival, Heterotopia and Flânerie: The Dynamics of Public Life

We therefore need to be careful about the ways in which early film consumption has sometimes been figured. As we have seen, one of the crucial features that, for the modernists, were supposed to define its radical potentials and possibilities was its violently anti-bourgeois eclecticism. For many, the places of early film consumption were like other modern spaces of public life: places of chaotic intermingling. As Kirby argues, the cinema was therefore like the railway stations, trains and other modes of transport that so often featured in the films themselves. They were 'a condensed version of the commercial chaos of the city streets and marketplaces' which released one from the confines of identity.[48] Here, it is claimed, 'the juxtaposition of all social types entering and leaving, give [these places] an eclectic and, in a sense, undefinable character with respect to class and sex'.[49] It was for this reason, it is argued, so many of the films 'had more to do with deception and false identity than with common values or beliefs'.[50]

It is also for this reason that critics have turned to the concepts of heterotopia and the carnivalesque to describe the operation of these places,[51] and both these concepts are defined through their supposed difference from the places of 'normal' life. Unlike a utopia, which is an idealised place that does not have a real existence within the world – it is a non-existent place – heterotopic places 'have the curious property of being in relation with all the other sites, but in such a way as to suspect, neutralize, or invert the

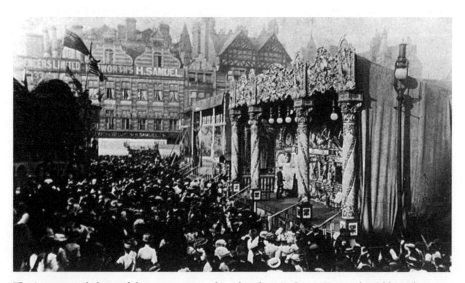

The 'commercial chaos of the city streets and marketplaces'? Goose Fair in the Old Market Square, City Centre

set of relations that they happen to designate, mirror, or reflect.'[52] In a similar way, the
carnival is supposedly 'a world turned upside down':

> It was characterized by the inversion not just of everyday rules and behaviour, but of the
> dominant symbolic order. As Bakhtin's study of Rabelais makes clear, carnival was a festival
> of *discrowning* in which the axial signifiers of medieval ideology were scandalously and often
> scatologically debased, tumbled down from heaven to earth, trampled over and sullied by the
> heavily material feet of the people's practice – as well as being opposed and overwhelmed by
> the 'popular belly' of carnival in its anticipatory celebration of a world of material surfeit.[53]

It is therefore significant that, as we will see, one of the key places of early film consumption was the fairground, which early modernists such Eisenstein used to establish
an association between early film and the supposedly anti-bourgeois aesthetic of avant-
garde art. As Gunning points out, the viewing experiences associated with early film
'relate more to the fairground than the traditions of legitimate theatre', and he therefore
describes early film as 'a cinema of attractions'. The term 'attraction' is drawn from
Eisenstein who made a similar link between the supposedly anti-bourgeois aesthetics of
early film and the fairground: 'Then, as now, the "attraction" was a term of the fairground, and for Eisenstein and his friend Yutkevich it primarily represented their
favourite fairground attraction, the roller coaster, or as it was known in Russia, the American Mountains.'[54]

These ways of understanding early cinema are also linked to the concept of the
flâneur that has become so popular within work both on the late 19th- and early 20th-
century city and on early cinema.[55] As Gunning argues, the cinema of attractions
prevents the modes of identification between spectator and film that distinguished the
legitimate arts and classical film. It has therefore been suggested that the modes of spectatorship associated with early cinema involved modes of visual perception that were
similar to those of the aimless, wandering flâneur who strolled the city while visually
sampling its delights in a detached but passionate way. As Catherine Russell claims, for
example, 'the cinema, as an extension of flânerie [the mode of visual perception associated with the flâneur], inverts this spatial mobility, rendering the interior of the theatre
an exterior space in which to wander'.[56] Anne Friedberg therefore links cinema with the
emergence of other spaces that transformed modes of looking and perception such as
the new modes of transport and new architectural forms that 'encouraged a pedestrian
mobilized gaze – exhibition halls, winter gardens, arcades, department stores, museums'.[57] These new modes of transport and architecture are therefore seen as
transforming modern urban perception into something akin to a form of flânerie. As
Friedberg puts it, 'just as machines of transport (from the railway to the *trottoir roulant*)
produced a new experience of distance and time, these architectural spaces were, in a
sense, machines of timelessness, producing a derealized sense of the present and a
detemporalized sense of the real'.[58] Friedberg therefore presents the cinema as a kind
of travelling time-machine, in which the audience was presented with a series of images
for visual consumption, a cinema of attractions, and one which is therefore also sup-

posed to rely on 'a converse instrumentalism, emphasizing mobility and fluid subjectivity' rather than restraint and subjection.[59]

However, as has been frequently noted, while the flâneur is often taken by critics such as Friedberg as emblematic of what urban space does to modern perception, the modes of perception associated with the flâneur were, on the contrary, the property of a very limited and restricted series of cultural positions. Flânerie was not the experience of modern life, but rather the experience of a very small and privileged social group and cannot therefore be extended to other social groups. Most obviously, as Friedberg and others acknowledge themselves, the flâneur was decisively male, and was dependent on a very specifically masculine experience of the city.[60] However, it was also classed and relies on the very fantasies and fetishisations of the popular that we have seen in figures such as Eisenstein. The flâneur relied on a position of authority and security within the city and its public places that was simply unavailable to those from the lower social orders, who would neither have had the leisure within, nor even access to, the arcades that were the haunt of the flâneur. Moreover, the figure is drawn from Baudelaire's writings as poet and art critic, a modernist adventurer who signalled his distinction from the 'bourgeois' through his association with the disreputable underbelly of the modern city. As Friedberg puts it, 'Baudelaire positioned himself in the midst of the nineteenth-century city, Paris (and later Brussels), wandering through its panorama of gaslit streets, cafes, theatres, brothels, parks and passages, collecting images that he would later record in newspaper reviews and prose poems.'[61] It therefore seems highly dubious to see this figure's experience as typical of modern visual experience and, on the contrary, the sense of distinction that it confers on Baudelaire strongly suggests that it *cannot* have been typical.

However, there are other problems associated with the concepts of the carnivalesque and the heterotopic, the foremost of which is their opposition to a vaguely defined and imaged 'normal' world. Hetherington, for example, rightly complains that 'the majority of this new theorizing of space has tended to focus on marginality and acts of resistance to the social order'.[62] However, he argues, without a corresponding analysis of the supposedly dominant social order, against which such acts of resistance are supposed to be opposed, the nature of their marginality cannot be properly understood. As Sarah Thornton has argued in a different context, this sense of opposition to, or difference from, the dominant or 'normal' (and they are not necessarily the same thing) eventually proves entirely contradictory, but it is necessary in order to provide a sense of marginality, and the distinction that can be made of such marginality.[63] In this context, then, 'inconsistent fantasies of the mainstream are rampant' in studies of marginality, and this is 'probably the single most important reason why . . . studies find pockets of symbolic resistance wherever they look',[64] and, by the same logic, why one can find incorporation everywhere, too.

Indeed, so many places are defined as heterotopic that it is difficult to imagine what could not be defined as a heterotopia. For example, in Shields' account of Brighton, he discusses it as a carnivaleque and heterotopic place precisely through its association with 'the new holidays [which] marked a collective release from the rationalised regimes of industrial labour',[65] while in his own discussion of heterotopic spaces, Hetherington includes the factory, the epitome of 'rationalised regimes of industrial labour'.[66]

The idea that pubic space enabled 'unmediated encounters with other individuals momentarily stripped of their social status' was always a myth. Goose Fair, overlooked by the Old Exchange Building, where the City Council had its offices

There is also a greater need for historical specificity here. The amusement parks and fairgrounds of late 19th- and early 20th-century America, Russia and Britain were not all the same: they had different cultural histories from one another. However, the one thing that they all did have in common was that the image of these fairgrounds was significantly different from that of the medieval carnival. In Britain, as we will see, the fairground had been remade as a public space during the 19th century, and by the time that films began to be shown there, these places were no longer seen as particularly disreputable and dangerous spaces. On the contrary, they actively courted middle-class audiences. As a result, the emergence of the cinematographic theatres may have spelt the end of the fair as a place of exhibition, but this process did not follow the trajectory that May claims.[67] The cinematographic theatres did not distinguish themselves from disreputable places of popular exhibition and convert the place of film consumption into a lavish, respectable place that appealed to the tastes of the middle classes. The fairground bioscopes were often huge and lavish affairs themselves. Far from being radical, popular performances for 'an audience not acculturated to the traditional arts' such as 'legitimate theatre',[68] the bioscopes gave their audience 'the illusion that they were sitting in an up-market theatre or variety hall, complete with upholstered seats, gaudy scenery and a two-tiered price system'.[69] The bioscopes overtly associated themselves with the legitimacy of the theatre and, as Toulmin has argued, 'The travelling cinema shows pioneered by the show people would have introduced their audience not only to the fantastical world of the moving image but also created an expectation of the surroundings in which they would see these films.'[70] The design of the cinematographic theatres was not a break from that of the bioscopes, but rather the legacy of these fairground venues.

It should also be borne in mind that the suggestion that these modern public spaces enabled 'unmediated encounters with other individuals also momentarily stripped of their social status'[71] was a myth that was developed by the places themselves, and later replayed in liberal histories of these places. As Hannigan argues:

> Increasingly working people had money and free time but as a group on their own, they were seen as neither a reliable market nor one which was particularly profitable. The middle classes represented a more desirable clientele but ... they were deeply nervous of the blue-collar crowds which they believed were prone to drunkenness and rowdyism. In order to attract the former market without losing the latter, leisure entrepreneurs needed to convince less affluent patrons that they were being transported to magical realms (the amusement park, the movie palaces) beyond the orbit of everyday constraints of class and gender, and at the same time reassure bourgeois pleasure-seekers that these new public amusements were safe and physically and morally 'clean'. To pull off this seemingly impossible task the merchants of leisure successfully constructed and marketed two concepts: 'democracy's theatre' and the 'good-natured crowd'.[72]

However, while these amusements were presented as democratic places where classes and genders mingled freely and social rank was temporally suspended, 'the lower strata of society were only admitted grudgingly to many of the new public amusement venues',[73] and were subject to various forms of control and surveillance. As we will see, while a wide range of classes may have gone to the cinema, they were often spatially segregated: they went to different cinemas, or were separated from one another by the ticket prices and the design of the auditorium.

Even when they did come together in the same place, such as the fairground, they did not simply shrug off their previous identities. On the contrary, their very presence in these places, and hence their consumption of them, was the result of very different interests. This is clear from the accounts that we have already seen, where some clearly consumed these places as representations of a culture to which they aspired, while others like the early modernists were clearly 'slumming it': they gained a pleasure from the supposedly low and disreputable status of these places.

The rest of Part Two will therefore be made up of two chapters. Chapter 3 discusses the first film showings in Nottingham and the meanings associated with the places within which these showings took place. It will look at the meanings of the theatres, music halls and fairgrounds and the ways in which they affected the reception of films in Nottingham. However, it will also examine the ways in which the medium of film and the content of the films themselves were bound up with issues of space and place. In other words, the reception of film was crucially bound up with the ways in which it changed people's relation to space and place. Not only could people see sights from other places and experience the illusion of travelling around the world without ever leaving their immediate locality, they were also able to re-examine their own locality through the eyes of the camera.

Chapter 4 then moves on to examine the introduction of the Cinematographic Act and its impact on Nottingham. In the process, it looks at the ways in which it was used to not only control audiences within the places of film consumption, but also produced a new place of film consumption: the cinematographic theatre. The chapter therefore examines the ways in which these new venues defined themselves and sought to establish their relationship to their local communities. Of course, the danger of using the word community is that it can imply a unitary, homogeneous and harmonious grouping. As a result, while the cinematographic theatres sought to establish relationships with their communities, their design and layout also sought to order and control the relationships between different sections of their audiences. However, while these issues demonstrate the importance of place to an understanding of film consumption, the chapter also examines the struggles over the placing of cinematographic theatres within certain locations in Nottingham. In other words, while these venues aspired to respectability, certain areas of upper-middle-class consumption fought to prevent the building of cinematographic theatres on the grounds that the presence of these theatres would threaten the meanings of these areas and the property values within them.

Notes

1. Chanan, 1980; and Musser, 1990.
2. For the classic account of these early years, see Low and Manvell, 1948; Low, 1948; and Low, 1950. For an account of these developments within the United States, see Browser, 1990; Koszarski, 1990; Musser, 1990; and Nasaw, 1993.
3. The Salvation Army were also involved in early film. They not only had their own film library but also made their own films, and their holdings were shown at public halls where they drew large audiences. See Rapp, 1996, pp. 157–88.
4. Toulmin, 1994, pp. 219–37; Toulmin, 1995, pp. 50–63; Toulmin, 1996; Toulmin, 1998; and Toulmin, 2001. See also Scrivens and Smith, 1999.
5. For more material on alternative exhibition practices and venues, see Musser, 1991b. However, it should be pointed out that this book concentrates on the United States. Indeed, much of the research on and debates about this period of film history has been focused on the United States and, for this reason, Part Two of the current study will make considerable reference to these studies. A word of clarification is therefore necessary: it is not supposed that the research on the case of the United States will simply *explain* developments in the United Kingdom in general, or Nottingham in particular, but rather that this research provides frameworks to be tested. After all, some of this research makes claims about early cinema that go beyond the national context of the United States, while other studies have stressed that the experience of the United States was not singular, but that cinema developed very differently in different localities. As we have seen, for example, Allen and Gomery have pointed out that many studies of the United States are actually studies of New York City or Chicago, and cannot be taken as typical of the experience of other cities, towns and rural areas.

In other words, research from the United States will be used to contextualise the case in Nottingham, and to examine how far it conformed to processes that have been analysed in the United States and elsewhere, and how far it differed from them. For example, the case of the United Kingdom, at least from our study of Nottingham, was different from that of the United States in two key ways. First, while class and gender were, as we will see, important to these processes, the issue of ethnicity was very different. Of course, the United Kingdom was an imperial nation and its cultural life was shaped by this fact. However, during the period of early film, the United States was understood as having a far more ethnically diverse population, and the collision between different ethnic groups was a central preoccupation of its cultural and political life. In contrast, the United Kingdom was less concerned with internal ethnic tensions than with its relation to ethnic groups beyond its shores. Second, while much of the research on early film in the United States has focused on the phenomena of the nickelodeon, the British equivalent (the 'penny gaff') seems to have provoked far less debate. None the less, despite this last difference, regulation to control these spaces was introduced at around the same time in the late 1900s, although the processes through which they were introduced, and the specific strategies of regulation themselves, were quite different.

6. NEP, 31 August 1896.

7. NEN, 31 August 1896.

8. Uricchio and Pearson, 1994, pp. 43–54.

9. The Cinematographic Act was supposedly introduced in order to protect audiences from threats such as fire, which could spread quickly due to the highly flammable nature of most film stock. However, as we will see later in Part Two, it was also used to regulate cinemas in other ways.

10. Kuhn, 1988; and, for similar claims in relation to the United States, see Grieveson, 1999, pp. 71–91 and Butsch, 2000.

11. Barker, 1984.

12. Jacobs, 1939; Hampton, 1931; Ramsaye, 1926.

13. Allen, 1979; Allen, 1996; and Allen and Gomery, 1985.

14. Singer, 1995; Singer, 1996; Higashi, 1996.

15. Savage, Barlow, Dickens and Fielding, 1992, p. 1. Indeed, the middle class has been a problem that has preoccupied historians and social scientists in recent years. See Blumin, 1985, pp. 299–338; Blumin, 1989; Horowitz, 1985a, pp. 239–58; Horowitz, 1985b; Mayer, 1975, pp. 409–36; and Ryan, 1981.

16. Ross, 1999, p. 94.

17. Savage et al., 1992, p. 36.

18. Bourdieu, 1984.

19. Although, as we will show, those richest in cultural capital often demonstrated their powers of discrimination precisely through the transgression of cultural hierarchies and the celebration of that which they saw as the popular tastes.

20. Savage et al., 1992, p. 1

21. As Leon Hunt has argued, 'it is the "middlebrow" – arguably always the real set of easy pleasures, in Bourdieu's terms – which has been recast as the low and indefensible'. See

Hunt, 1998, p. 160. For other work on the middlebrow see also Jancovich, 2001; Jancovich, 2002, pp. 306–22; Jancovich, 2000a; Jancovich, 2000c; Jancovich, forthcoming 2002a; Radway, 1997; and Ross, 1989.

22. Here and elsewhere in this book, the term 'modernist' is used to designate those cultural intellectuals who have been identified with modernism as a cultural movement.

23. Gunning, 1990, pp. 56–62.

24. Bourdieu, 1984.

25. May, 1980, p. 164.

26. Ibid., p. 166.

27. Chanan, 1980, p. 136.

28. Pearson and Uricchio, 1999, p. 74.

29. See Field, 1974.

30. Some clarification is necessary about the meaning of the term public here. Obviously, many of the places that women frequented, such as department stores, tea rooms, and picture houses, were privately owned and were not freely accessible to the public. On the contrary, they were places of commerce that often required some form of purchase as a condition of entrance. However, they are often referred to as public places due to their distinction from the private or domestic world. In other words, they were places where the people moved out of the private world of domesticity and interacted with one another in public. It is after all worth pointing out that the classic figure of the masculine public sphere, the 18th-century coffee-house, was also a privately owned and commercially defined place of congregation.

31. Woolf, 1985; and Woolf, 1990. However, this kind of critique is also, as we will see later, a powerful corrective to much theoretical work on the city, particularly that centred around theories of the flâneur. See Massey, 1994.

32. Rabinovitz, 1998, p. 182.

33. Nava, 1996, p. 41.

34. Ibid.

35. It should also be pointed out that these issues were also bound up with issues of class. For example, as Höher has pointed out in relation to music halls, while social reformers may have disapproved of working women attending these places, it was not necessarily considered inappropriate to those classes who made up much of their audience: Höher, 1986. In any case, while the 'division of spheres' was always an ideal rather than an actuality, most working-class women simply had no choice but to participate within the public sphere. The precise value of domestic privacy to the middle classes was based upon its rarity. It was through the ability to support their wives' retreat from the public world of work and commerce that middle-class males proved their own wealth and power.

36. Walkowitz, 1992; and Wilson, 1991.

37. Nava, 1996, p. 69.

38. Of course, gendered divisions within public space still existed, which suggest some of the ways in which women were supposed to behave in public. For example, in Nottingham, the Empire did not permit women in the bar area, while the Long Row Picture House had a smoking room that was also defined as a 'masculine' space.

39. Hollows, 2000.

40. Hansen, 1991; and Rabinovitz, 1998.
41. See Hollows, 2000; Huyssen, 1986, pp. 188–207; Nava, 1996; Slater, 1997.
42. Peiss, 1986.
43. Grieveson, 1999.
44. Gomery, 1992.
45. See, for example, ibid; and May, 1980.
46. See Grieveson, 2001, pp. 64–76; Hollows, 2000; and Huyssen, 1986.
47. Of course, these places were not free of harassment. On the contrary, their very function as a place to escape domestic surveillance meant that they were not only places of sexual adventure and experimentation, but also potentially places of sexual danger. While the dangers of harassment may have been relatively small, it was by no means absent.
48. Kirby, 1990, p. 50. See also Kirby, 1997.
49. Kirby, 1990, p. 52.
50. Harris, 1986, p. 49.
51. Indeed, many of the early modernists who celebrated these places would later go on to influence Bakhtin, the Russian literary theorist who developed the concept of the carnivalesque, and, as a result, the origin of this concept can even be directly linked to the modernist reception of these places. See Bakhtin, 1968.
52. Foucault, 1986, pp. 23–4.
53. Bennett, 1995, p. 243.
54. Gunning, 1990, p. 59.
55. The concept of the flâneur is drawn from the writings of Walter Benjamin, 1969; and Benjamin, 1999.
56. Russell, 2000.
57. Friedberg, 1993, p. 4.
58. Ibid.
59. Ibid., p. 16.
60. See, for example, Massey, 1994.
61. Friedberg, 1993, p. 29.
62. Hetherington, 1997, p. vii.
63. Thornton, 1995, p. 96.
64. Ibid., p. 93.
65. Shields, 1991, p. 85.
66. Hetherington, 1997.
67. May, 1980.
68. Gunning, 1999, pp. 59–60.
69. Toulmin, 1996, p. 8.
70. Ibid., p. 12.
71. Shields, 1991, p. 89.
72. Hannigan, 1998, p. 18.
73. Ibid., p. 19.

3

Novelties, Fairgrounds and the Exoticisation of Place

The first moving pictures shown in Nottingham do not seem to have been mentioned in the papers at the time, although it has clearly become a topic of considerable local interest since then. For example, while there is no contemporary evidence that Edison's Kinetograph was exhibited in Nottingham in 1895, a letter to the *Express Local Notes and Queries*, published 5 March 1920, described the event. It claimed that, in 1895–96, the Kinetograph was brought to an empty shop in Long Row that was tenanted by the printers Allen and Sons. The accuracy of this source is questionable, however, as it then goes on to make the erroneous claim that the first cinematograph was exhibited in January 1897 in Mr Caldwell's photographic gallery in Long Row. Alternatively, another letter to a paper in 1937 from an 'older timer' claimed that the first moving pictures were shown at Goose Fair and that 'vitagraphs' and Edison's moving pictures were shown in shops around the market.[1] As early as 1920, speculation about the history of film consumption within Nottingham was sufficient to justify a *Weekly Guardian Special*, 'How Did Pictures Get to Nottingham?', which claims that in 1897 a flick book, made up of eighty pictures from a fight, introduced moving pictures to Nottingham. The same pictures were also supposed to have been used in 'mutoscopes' that were exhibited in a Long Row shop.[2] Similarly, while Iliffe and Baguley, who printed the newspaper reports for most of the early showings, do not reproduce any report on the 1895 showing, they do mention the event.[3]

The first showing of the 'cinematographe' in Nottingham was reputedly July 1896. If it was, then it had taken about four months to reach Nottingham after the first showing in London in late February of the same year[4] or about six months after its first public showings in Paris.[5] This date puts Nottingham far ahead of most other towns in the East Midlands, as one might expect from a city that was concerned to present itself as the cultural centre of the region. Derby, for example, supposedly had its first showing on Monday 21 September 1896, while Leicester had to wait until November 1896.[6]

In Nottingham, however, there were adverts in the papers for 'living pictures' even before 13 July. In 1895, there was an advert for the Louis Tussaud's Exhibition at the Albert Hall which claimed that the exhibition also included 'Magnificent Tableaux Vivants or Living Pictures',[7] but even more interesting is an advert in 1896 for the Berlin Industrial Exhibition which supposedly had a 'living picture' of the history and development of Berlin.[8] This was obviously not at a local event, but an international exhibition, and the presence of such an advert within a provincial paper could not have been simply due to the large amounts of regional, national and international news that the Nottingham papers carried at the time. For an advert such as this to have been placed, it must have been expected that the film show would be a big enough draw to entice people to travel to Germany, although only the very wealthy would have been able to afford it.[9]

Film did, however, still continue to be shown in Nottingham after these first events, and these later screenings included the 'Lifeograph' at the Palace of Varieties in September and the 'Theatograph' which was also shown at the Palace around the end of September and the start of October.[10] Bostock and Wombwell also referred to 'Lions as living pictures' in their advert for Goose Fair of 1896, although none of the papers mention a film showing in their reviews of the menagerie. In addition, the Grand had a production in November in which dogs and ponies appeared in a series of 'Living Pictures' between two acts[11] and, in January 1897, the 'cinematograph' appeared both in the Grand's pantomime and at Caldwell's.

However, reports in the papers during this period need to be treated with some caution. As Audrey Field points out, while the London *Times* printed a report of the first film showings in London, it followed this with an eight-year silence, which was not due to the absence of film showings, but rather the paper's assumption that these showings were beneath its interest.[12] The first showing had featured an important new piece of technology, but later showings were not seen as being relevant to the paper's readership. Many film showings were therefore not reported in *The Times*. Similarly, while the local papers did carry far more coverage of film exhibitions than this national daily, there would still have been many film showings that would have passed beneath their notice.[13] For example, the 'penny gaff' was the name given to some of the earliest venues for the exhibition of moving pictures, which began to show single-reel films, but these venues were often little more than storefront amusements that received little or no coverage in the press.

Nor do the papers give much indication of who was going to see these film showings, and this is best gauged from the place of entertainment and the price of admission.[14] Between 1895 and 1897, films were mainly being shown in theatres or music halls, though the travelling bioscopes started at Goose Fair in 1897. The Theatre Royal seems to have been the most important theatre in Nottingham. In the press, it was usually at the top of lists of amusements and its productions generally appeared as the first reviews. However, it did not show films at all during this period, and this situation may have due to the fact that the theatre did not need to attract audiences and that it was nervous about the cultural status of films. Alternatively, the Grand nearly always followed the Theatre Royal in both the adverts and the reviews, but it had to make more effort to attract people. Its ticket prices also suggest that a wide variety of social classes attended its performances, although the way in which the theatre was designed ensured that these classes did not meet. For example, the pit had its own entrance to ensure that different classes of patron were not only spatially segregated within the theatre, but also that they did not mingle while they were queuing to enter.[15]

Only two music halls are recorded in *Kelly's Directory*, a directory of businesses, firms and many householders for 1895. The first, the Palace of Varieties, only had adverts in the evening papers and the NDG did not review its performances. The Palace's seat prices were less wide-ranging than the Grand's, although the latter's cheapest seats were less than the Palace's. The second, Coleno's Varieties Music Hall, is not mentioned in any of the papers either in reviews or advertisements. Music halls had been viewed with suspicion by many sections of the upper classes, who assumed that these places were frequented by prostitutes, thieves and those with the lowest occupations such as rag-and-bone men. This suspicion was further encouraged by the reports of a local newspapers columnist who visited working-class places of entertainment in the 1860s.[16] However, Caroline Knight and Anne Cockburn claim that by the end of the century music-hall-style entertainment was more acceptable, and that both the Empire (1898) and the Hippodrome (1908) were visited by the gentry. They do not mention the clientele of the Palace, but contend that it had been 'a centre of social entertainment' for many years.[17] Also, its status as a temperance musical hall made it more respectable than Coleno's, which was attached to the Crown and Cushion pub, and this may account for the adverts for the former that appeared in the evening papers.[18]

The Goose Fair Bioscopes

From 1897, however, one of the prime sites of film consumption was Goose Fair.[19] As we have seen, it is the association of early film with fairs that is often used as evidence of its anti-bourgeois character. However, Goose Fair was anything but a riotous place of popular subversion. It may have continued to have associations of the carnivalesque and heterotopic, but these fairs had been carefully redefined throughout the 19th century into relatively respectable places of entertainment.[20]

While there had been concerns with fairs at the beginning of the 19th century, when they were seen as places of drunken and riotous behaviour, which could also become sites of political agitation and even insurrection, this image had largely gone by the time of the bioscopes. During the 19th century, reformers had tried to 'wean the industrial operatives away from their customary pursuits – particularly animal sports – and the public house',[21] but the fair itself had not been subject to the same pressures. As Cunningham has argued, there were distinct financial benefits that fairs brought to local areas, which meant that they often had considerable support from elements of the respectable classes. Furthermore, the fairs were also reforming themselves during this period. For example, the showmen successfully distinguished themselves from the figure of the gypsy, and gained a relatively respectable image as economic entrepreneurs. They were no longer 'classed by magistrates as rogues and vagabonds and had become recipients of Royal patronage'.[22] This was also connected to changes in the nature of the fairs themselves, as market forces and the arrival of new forms of mechanised amusements encouraged the showmen to control the fairs and appeal to middle-class consumers. These changes, along with the introduction of the police force, who could provide better surveillance and crowd control, made it more trouble for the authorities to ban fairs than to leave them to die the natural death that most thought would be inevitable.[23]

These changes were also connected to changing views of the working classes, and in the late 19th century, there was a 'growing belief that the poor could be safely entrusted

The meaning of fairs had been carefully redefined throughout the 19th century into relatively respectable places of entertainment. The Goose Fair

to organise their own entertainment',[24] possibly because, as Steadman Jones has argued, the period also saw a remaking of the working class.[25] For Steadman Jones, working-class culture became a largely conservative culture that may have bemoaned class inequality but largely viewed it as inevitable. However, it was also a culture that rejected the killjoys who wanted to reform working-class entertainment and to make culture a means of education and spiritual improvement. Instead, its 'attitude was *a little bit of what you fancy does you good*'.[26] In the process, rather than a place of anti-bourgeois subversion, the fairground had become 'a relatively routine ingredient in an accepted world of leisure'.[27]

Even within this context, Goose Fair occupied a relatively privileged place. As a place of trade, it had a respected reputation and commercial significance for the city and, as a result, there was no campaign to move the fair during the 19th century, although other fairs of the period were not so lucky. Indeed, as we shall see in Part Three, the fair was only moved much later, in the 1920s, as part of a more general reconstruction of the city centre.

This perception of the fair can also be seen in the newspaper coverage. Certainly, letters to the papers showed that the shopkeepers or those with 'legitimate business' thoroughly disliked Goose Fair because it disrupted their trade,[28] and it was generally seen as a relatively low form of entertainment. There were also concerns about women's presence within it. For example, as a Roman Catholic bishop claimed about the fair in 1897:

it does not appear to me to be a modest or decent thing that young women should voluntarily allow themselves to be crushed up and carried along in a dense crowd of all people, nor can I believe that it can be otherwise than very dangerous to their purity. I fear many a girl owes her first fall into sin, and subsequent ruin, to the crowded rushes of Goose Fair.[29]

As a result, the NDE doubted whether the word 'superiority' could be associated with Goose Fair or the entertainment on offer there.[30]

However, other views were both more common and pervasive. For example, the NEP commented that:

The pleasures of the fair may not be elevating, but, on the whole, they are innocent enough, and that being so no one will feel inclined to strongly argue that the boisterous merriment and brazen music should give place to something more refined and elegant. To grudge the people what measure of satisfaction they can extract from a species of gathering, which, according to the predictions of many, should long ago have been a thing of the past, would be niggardly, and the spirit of the house is such that any attempt to abolish a time-honoured event must utterly fail.[31]

As this quote demonstrates, while certain sections may have disapproved of the fair, there was a more general sense that it was neither particularly dangerous nor disruptive. On the contrary, there is an almost affectionate tone here, which gives some sense of middle-class responses to the fair.

Rather than simply a working-class affair, the 'show people's proud boast was that they catered to all classes of the public; the Wadbrooke family would even claim that they had been patronised by no less a personage than Queen Victoria'.[32] Certainly there was still a residual sense of the fair as a place of low tastes, but the showmen who ran the bioscopes worked hard to dispel this image through the lavishness of their exhibits. Furthermore, this slightly disreputable image was also part of the fair's appeal for certain sections of the middle class. For example, Beckett notes that while Samuel Collinson complained in 1858 about 'the unusual assemblage of vagabonds of all sorts coming into town preparatory for the fair tomorrow', this complaint 'did not stop him from attending'. Beckett also notes that 'even a strict Methodist like George Harwood could not keep away' from Goose Fair, and that in 1861, 'his lace factory was closed for two days [while] he "went and my wife, children and servant, through the Fair and bought a few articles for amusement and use"'.[33] In other words, it was precisely their status as places of low tastes that made these places both horrifying and fascinating to the middle classes.

However, it would be misleading to see Goose Fair as simply a local amusement: it not only attracted people from the East Midlands but even from as far away as Liverpool. Indeed, in 1910, World's Fair claimed that as many as 200 to 300 special trains were laid on by the rail companies during the three days of the fair in order to cater for people travelling to it on excursions.[34]

The Reception of Film in Nottingham

Audience reactions are difficult to gauge, but none of the papers mention people who went wild at seeing the films, or tried to run away from the trains, or lifted their feet from the waves on screen. Franklin puts this down 'to the stiff, temperate nature of provincial journalism of the time',[35] but while the Nottingham papers used standard phrases to describe all entertainments, and so seemed rather stiff and formal, the discussions of the film exhibitions seems to have been extravagant and full of praise rather than 'temperate'. It is possible the papers wanted to ensure that exhibitors would continue to advertise in them, but although one occasionally finds a mediocre review (although not for the cinematograph), most reports described it as 'novel', 'diverting' or a 'success', even if it was not 'astounding'.

Indeed, the reviewers were highly impressed by the cinematograph and they discussed it in detail. On 14 July 1896, the NEN dedicated half an article to the cinematograph and, on 29 September 1896, a review in NEN also began with the cinematograph, although the article overall is much shorter. On 17 July 1896, the NDE had the same article as the NEN but then, on 29 September 1896, it spent the majority of a long review describing the films that were shown. On 14 July 1896, the NDG also devoted about half of a reasonably detailed article to the cinematograph, although it did not mention it again, not even when it was at the Grand in January 1897.

One reason that these reports were not as sensational as one might expect was that the Victorian period abounded with inventions and 'wonders of the world', and these reviewers seem to have viewed the cinematograph as yet another example of the 'great' age in which they believed that they lived. This is suggested by a quote in the NDE on the day after the first showing in July 1896. After describing the zoetrope, the article continued:

> Since those crude days, electricity and Edison have produced so many marvels that we cease to wonder even at the 'Kinetoscope' and its latest development, the 'cinematographe'.[36]

Victorians were so accustomed to new inventions that they expected improvement and were quite capable of imagining its possibilities. In the 1920 letter from Mr Race to the *Express Local Notes and Queries,* he commented on the films shown at Caldwell's:

> Of course, the elaborate dramas of today were quite unknown then ... Animated photography, twenty-three years ago, was naturally regarded as something wonderful, but no one could have foreseen the development of later years.[37]

However, he was quite wrong. An article in the NEN on 18 October 1894 – just after Edison came to London – suggests that these developments had been predicted from the start:

> In the kinetoscope Mr Edison has ... given the world what may be regarded as a natural corollary to the phonograph, inasmuch as it presents what the latter instrument fails to

convey – viz., looks and actions. For while the phonograph conveys sounds to the ear, the kinetoscope presents action to the eye, and it only requires the combination of the two instruments to reproduce, for instance, a whole play, with actors, acting and word complete.[38]

This is not to say that people did not find the cinematograph fascinating. They clearly did, and even though the NDE review claimed that people had ceased to be surprised at new inventions, it goes on to describe the cinematograph as 'astounding and delight-ful'.[39] The September showings were also described as a 'decided success' by the NDE, and even by the time of the October showings, the same paper described the Palace as being 'crowded by people anxious to see the fine series of animated pictures'. The fol-lowing week it also commented that 'one does not wonder that they are such an attraction'.[40]

The naive viewers who fled from images of trains or lifted their feet at the sight of waves were probably largely mythic. As both Hansen and Kirby illustrate, the films them-selves addressed sophisticated viewers and flattered them, presenting others as naive bumpkins who could not distinguish the film image from reality.[41] Hansen discusses the American film *Uncle Josh at the Motion Pictures*, which was itself a remake of a British import, Robert Paul's *The Countryman's First Sight of the Animated Pictures* (1901). In the American film, Uncle Josh sees three films and his 'transactions with each film demon-strate particular misconceptions about the nature of cinematic illusion'. For example, 'seeing a Parisian dancer, Uncle Josh jumps onto the stage and attempts to dance with her'.[42] In this way, Uncle Josh is meant to represent a type of naive viewer that audiences were not only supposed to recognise and laugh at, but also from which they were expected to distinguish themselves.

It is also interesting that this distinction has spatial connotations. Both Uncle Josh and the subject of Paul's original film are figures from the countryside – the rube and the bumpkin – and were distinguished from the sophisticated audiences associated with the urban world. As Hansen argues: 'The country rube was a stock character in vaudeville, comic strips, and other popular media, and early films seized upon the encounter of unsophisticated minds with city life, modern technology, and commercial entertainment as a comic theatre and a way of flaunting the marvels of that new urban world.'[43]

As a result, it is simply Whig history to assume, as Iliffe and Baguley do, that the reason that Victorian audiences found the cinematograph amazing was that they lacked sophis-tication.[44] Furthermore, although there were only a few references to specific films appreciated by audiences, these references demonstrate that the subject matter was important and that it was certainly not the case that as 'long as the picture moved, it hardly mattered what it was'.[45] For example, one reference to audience preferences notes:

> The pictures that found favour with the large and enthusiastic audience last evening were those of everyday scenes, such as street traffic near the houses of parliament, with its constant succession of vehicle and pedestrians; the arrest of a street betting man; and a domestic quarrel between a jovial husband and an irate wife.[46]

Another claims: 'the two that roused the audience to enthusiasm were representations of the last Derby, and the waves of the seashore'.[47] The interest in the traffic scene was possibly as much to do with seeing the Houses of Parliament, while others may have never seen the sea before. Alternatively, the fascination in seeing the Derby may have reflected the popular interest in sport and betting in the period. The papers were filled with sport news – of all kinds – and the NEN had a Saturday paper that was entirely devoted to football news and the NEP started its own in 1903.[48] Sport was an important element of 19th-century popular culture, as it continues to be today, but it may well also have been the case that this film was the first time that many people had seen the race on which they had been placing bets for years.[49] The showing of other sporting events also indicated that film-makers – like everyone else – were well aware of the enthusiasm for betting and sport, and some of the earliest films made were of football matches featuring local teams.

Projections of Place

These reports also suggest that issues of place were not only central to the location of film consumption, but also to the content of the films consumed. If one looks at the advertisements, one finds a continual preoccupation with images of other places, and this was one of the ways in which film was understood in the period. It collapsed distance so that not only were images of elsewhere brought to audiences but, in the process, it created the illusion of being able to travel elsewhere without leaving one's locality. This illusion was made explicit in exhibitions such as the one by Robert William Paul that is described to *The Era*:

> He had been reading the weird romance, *The Time Machine*, and it had suggested an entertainment to him, of which animated photographs formed an essential part. In a room capable of accommodating some hundred people, he would arrange seats to which a slight motion could be given. He would plunge the apartment into Cimmerian darkness, and introduce a wailing wind. Although the audience actually only moved but a few inches, the sensation would be that of travelling through space. From time to time the journey would be stopped, and on the stage a wondrous picture would be revealed – the Animatographe, combined with panoramic effects.[50]

A similar technique was also used for Hales' Tours, which came to England in 1906, and lasted in Nottingham until 1912, although it is not quite clear precisely when it first arrived in the city. The 'tour' featured an imitation railway car (complete with a ticket collector who blew whistles and waved flags) which was made to shake as though it were a real moving train. Within this space, travelogue films were projected that created the illusion that the carriage was travelling through some exotic locale such as the Rocky Mountains or the Swiss Alps.

In this way, these exhibits share with the other fairground amusements a sense of liberation from the body and the sense of spatial restriction that it necessitates. As Bennett argues, discussing the mechanical fairground rides at Blackpool's pleasure beach:

The pleasures offered by these rides are complex and diverse. In some cases, the dominant appeal is that of liberating the body from normal constraints to expose it to otherwise unattainable sensations. The Revolution, the Starship Enterprise (rather like the Ferris Wheel, except that the ride is placed on the inside of wheels and travels upside down) and the Astro Swirl ... all defy the laws of gravity. In releasing the body for pleasure rather than harnessing it for work, part of their appeal may be that they invert the normal relations between people and machinery prevailing in an industrial context.[51]

In a similar way, films allowed audiences to travel where it would be otherwise have been impossible for them to go, and they did so at a time when travel itself was becoming a leisure industry for more than simply the wealthy few. In Nottingham, for example, as John Beckett has noted: 'The introduction of the August Bank Holiday in 1870, together with the completion of the line to Skegness in 1873, enabled people to spend a day at the seaside. Ten thousand arrived in the town on August Bank Holiday 1874, and 20,000 in 1882.'[52]

Of course, this continues a long tradition in which fairgrounds would display the supposed mysteries of exotic places, and would therefore 'teem once or twice a year with stands, displays, heteroclite objects, wrestlers, snakewomen, fortune tellers, and so forth'.[53] However, again, we must be careful not to simply celebrate these objects as a rejection of the rationalising classifications of the museum or academy. As Chanan has argued: 'Film enabled Britain to export its spectacle, send it into the Empire itself and throughout the "civilized" world.'[54] However, it also allowed the inverse, the imaginary transportation of the 'civilised' world out into the Empire where it could see the spectacle of its own power. To put it another way, just as the expositions brought the fruits

The fair as a site for the consumption of exoticism. The Goose Fair

of Empire to the centre so that it could marvel in its own power, film images brought the spectacle of Empire to those who would otherwise have never travelled beyond the shores of Britain. One could consume the Empire as spectacle without ever leaving one's immediate locality.

Films also enabled 'the projection of the spectacle of the state' in other ways.[55] Many films were of state occasions, and so sought to create a sense of inclusion in, and reverence for, the imagined community of the nation. While it could not create the sense of simultaneity that is discussed by television analysts,[56] it did create a sense of close participation within national rituals that would otherwise have remained distant events of which one could only read second-hand reports. Even the experience of simultaneity was strived for by exhibitors and, according to Williams, special efforts were made to show film of the coronation of King George V on the same day as it occurred.[57]

However, despite this preoccupation with foreign places, the appeal of 'local views' such as football matches, crowds and local places does not seem to have been simply that they were cheap to produce. Musser claims that they 'would have elicited little reaction – except that they moved'[58] but their presence in advertisements and their persistence as a genre of film production seems to suggest otherwise. As Michael Hammond has pointed out, advertisements actively promoted the activity of coming to spot yourself, your loved ones and acquaintances within these images. For example, he notes that 'Pathe made this personal recognition the centre of their campaign for the Pathe Gazettes in 1915'.[59] One example features a young woman in a work smock with the caption: 'Oh yes, I always enjoy the Pathe Gazette. You see, it shows us pictures of our workshops and the girls just as they are. Besides I've seen Bert several times with his regiment.'[60] Another example showed a 'wounded Tommy' with the caption: 'I dunno about danger, but those Pathe Gazette chaps that take the pictures were in the thick of it. It's really grand to sit down and see the scenes that you've been in.'[61] As Hammond claims, 'The pleasure in these films is directed at personal, private expectation and couched within the interpellative form of direct address. *You* might expect to recognise someone, or even yourself, in these films.'[62]

As a result, the function of the 'local views' as familiar spectacles needs some explaining. The pleasure of watching these films (at least, the pleasure suggested by the advertisements that Hammond discusses) is precisely in the act of catching oneself, one's acquaintances or even one's familiar environment captured on film, and this thrill of recognition seems to be the product of two factors. On the one hand, there is the thrill of seeing one's self, one's acquaintances and one's locality through the eyes of others, of seeing it reflected back to one afresh. On the other, there is the thrill of seeing represented that which is usually deemed unworthy of representation, and the pleasure of obtaining a personal and private meaning from a public object.

According to Tom Gunning, the appeal of these local views was their 'lack of dramatic hierarchy [which] invites a different sort of gaze than the one we have learned from classical narrative cinema'. In these local views:

[new] centers of interest bob into the frame unexpectedly, while others depart beyond reclamation. The receptive spectator approaches these images with a global curiosity about its 'many interesting phases,' a curiosity that is being endlessly incited and never completely satiated. The street is filled with endless attractions.[63]

The pleasures of viewing were not connected to the desire to find a single or dominant meaning within the image that was itself part of a longer, overarching narrative pattern. Instead audience members ranged across the image, searching their own moments of interest and pleasure from within them.

However, the appeal of local views was also that they enabled the exhibitors to demonstrate the wonder of film technology. In other words, the familiarity of the local views demonstrated the visual accuracy of the camera. However, while the ability to recognise a face or place demonstrated the visual qualities of the camera, the camera also transformed the familiar. As Gunning put it:

> The motion picture intervenes on this scene, not by organising it, but by capturing it in a form which allows endless repetition, opening the way for a studied appreciation. Instead of an evanescent and immediate experience, the transfer to film allowed the city street to become another sort of spectacle, one mediated by an apparatus.[64]

The camera not only presented audiences with familiar images but also transformed the familiar in the process. It exoticised the familiar and made it into an object of fascination and interest – a spectacle of endless pleasures that could be endlessly rewatched and re-examined.

Right from the start, then, more was demanded of film images than simple movement. Within three months of the first film showing in Nottingham, films were already being shown in colour and this was considered to be a great improvement. Even by the end of September 1896, when films had only been in Nottingham for three weeks, a review appeared in the NDE that concerned the Palace's second set of exhibitions and explained why the 'theatographe' (theatrograph to everyone else) was so much better than the cinematographe:

> A really excellent entertainment is provided by Mr Carl Brennir this week, the programme concluding with yet another series of animated pictures – a series which easily eclipses any previously seen in town. The theatographe is unquestionably a great improvement on the cinematographe. Not only is there a greater variety of subjects but the duration of the pictures is longer, and in one or two instances, notably in the case of the two dancers, they are coloured. There is, of course, the inevitable 'Prince's Derby' and two or three seaside scenes . . .[65]

The reference to the 'inevitable' Derby film showed that the reviewer thought that people had probably seen enough of this film, which had already been shown in both July and September of 1896.

Films in Context

A final indication that the 'naive' and 'simplest stories' were not met with uncritical approval was that none of the films were shown alone, except for some twenty-minute films that were shown at Caldwell's photographic gallery. Films were not considered to provide enough entertainment on their own. In July 1896, *Trilby* was the main attraction at the Grand, and it was described as the 'Success of the Century', but in the Grand's adverts, the cinematograph was always second to the main play or pantomime. The 'Lifeograph' did head the bill at the Palace in August and September, as did the 'Theatograph' in September and October, but they were still part of a variety programme and they only remained at the head of the bill for their first week. By their second (and last) week, they were further down the bill, and the Theatograph was now second to the Dandurria Troubadours in adverts, despite being 'the Talk of the Town'.[66] Thus it was not until the films were longer and more elaborate that they were seen as an evening's entertainment in themselves. The move to narrative and to the feature film may not have been due to a desire to control spectatorship and so discipline audiences.[67] Indeed, the emergence of the story film, and even the feature film, were related to the emergence of new venues that demanded longer programmes and could showcase their attractions and, even in these venues, films were usually exhibited as part of a variety format.[68]

Notes

1. 'Which was the First Picture House?', unidentified cutting from 1 May 1937 in the Doubleday Scrapbook, Nottingham Local Studies Library, Vol. XIII, p. 83. It is claimed that the first bioscope was at the Palace of Varieties, which is incorrect.
2. Paul Jennings, 'The Rise of Cinema in Nottingham', *Weekly Guardian Special*, 23 October 1920, in the *Doubleday Scrapbooks*, Nottingham Local Studies Library, Vol. II, p. 143.
3. Iliffe and Baguley, *Victorian Nottingham: A Story in Pictures Volume 3*, 1971.
4. Atwell, 1980; Gray, 1996; Sharp, 1969.
5. Rhode, 1976, pp. 15–16. Franklin claims it was on 20 February: Franklin, 1996.
6. Ibid., p. 13; Williams, 1993, p. 2.
7. Reproduced in Iliffe and Baguley, *Victorian Nottingham: A Story in Pictures Volume 12,* 1974, p. 88. The term 'living pictures' was another term for moving images.
8. NDE, 14 July 1896; NEN, 7 July 1896.
9. It should also be pointed out that international exhibitions were all the rage at the time, and that the Midlands Industrial Exhibition was held in Nottingham in 1903. Also there was a close connection between these exhibitions and the cinema, and Dibbets and Convents argue that one reason that Brussels had so many more cinemas than Amsterdam during this period was that Brussels hosted five international exhibitions between 1900 and 1930. See, Karel Dibbets and Guido Convents, 2000.
10. NEN, 31 August 1896; NEP, 31 August 1896; NEP 28 September 1896. Iliffe and Baguley claim that the Palace showed films for over a month starting from 31 August 1896. This was not the case according to the papers: the Lifeograph was shown for the first two weeks of September and the Theatograph from the end of September to the first two weeks in October: Iliffe and Baguley, *Victorian Nottingham: Volume 3*, p. 44.

11. Programme for 'Signal Lights' at the Grand, 9 November 1896.

12. Field, 1974.

13. At a most basic level, the oral histories contain reminiscences of films seen in yards and sheds – events that were hardly likely to have been deemed worthy of comment in press reports. See example of watching early films in a stack yard in Nottingham oral history archive transcript A53/a–b/2: 27; and Roddis, 1993, p. 9.

14. Admission prices:

    The Theatre Royal: private box 10s 6d to £2 2s, dress circle 3s, orchestra stalls 2s 6d, upper circle 1s 6d, pit 1s, gallery 6d. Second price at 9p.m.: dress circle 1s 6d, stalls 1s 6d, upper circle 1s, pit 6d.

    Albert Hall: front reserved seats 2s, reserved stalls 1s 6d, balcony 1s, gallery, 6d.

    The Grand: boxes 21s, dress circle 2s 6d, second circle 1s 6d, stalls 1s, balcony/gallery 3d; pit 3d; gallery 3d.

    The Palace: 1s 6d, 9d, and 4d. Stalls 1s at 9 pm; pit and balcony 6d.

15. Hyson Green was a working-class suburb in the 19th century and so it probably housed the families of the lower middle class and well-off working classes. It was also adjacent to Forest Field, which drew on many of its facilities, and had a mixture of different social classes: professionals, skilled and semi-skilled workers, clerks and shopkeepers. See Weir, 1985, pp. 122–31.

16. Asmodeus, 'Revelations of Life in Nottingham', cited in Knight and Cockburn, unpublished paper, n.d., pp. 2, 10, 12.

17. Ibid., pp. 1–2, 17.

18. NEP, 1 September 1886.

19. Franklin claims that there were two big marquee entertainments at the 1897 Goose Fair: Collin's Living Pictures and Captain T. Payne's Electric Bioscope. Later there were a total of six of these shows that would move on to smaller fairs once Goose Fair had split up: Franklin, 1996, p. 19.

20. There are a number of histories of Goose Fair, such as Manning, 1994; Nottingham Historical Film Unit, 1973; 1989.

21. John Beckett, 'Leisure Recreation and Entertainment' in Beckett, 1997, p. 385. There is a wealth of material on the social process through which leisure was shaped during the 19th and 20th centuries. See, for example, Bailey, 1978; Clarke, Critcher and Johnson, 1979; Clarke and Critcher, 1985; Cunningham, 1980; Donajgrodski, 1977; Malcolmson, 1982; Mellor, 1976; Parker, 1976; Smith, Parker and Smith, 1973; van Voss and van Holthoon, 1988; Yeo and Yeo, 1981.

22. Cunningham, 1977, pp. 179–80.

23. Cunningham, 1988, pp. 99–107.

24. Cunningham, 1997, p. 179.

25. Steadman Jones, 1982, pp. 92–121.

26. Ibid., p. 108

27. Cunningham, 1977, p. 164

28. NDG, 30 September 1896.

29. Nottingham Archives (NA) M.24,480/A13.

30. NDE, 2 September 1896.

31. NEP, 1 October 1896.

32. Toulmin, 1996, p. 8.

33. Beckett, 'Leisure, Recreation and Entertainment' in Beckett, 1997, pp. 397–8. There are also several more examples in Iliffe and Baguley, *Victorian Nottingham: Volume 4*.

34. *World's Fair*, Saturday 15 October 1910.

35. Franklin, 1996, p. 16. The *Chichester Observer* did describe people leaping for cover as the galloping horses in *The Fire Brigade Call* approached the screen, so not all local papers were 'temperate' in this sense. *Chichester Observer*, 3 October 1897, cited in Eyles, Gray and Readman, 1996, p. 49.

36. NDE, 14 July 1896.

37. He continued: 'In one respect at any rate taste was better then, as the majority of the pictures reproduced were of current events and natural scenery, and were of a distinctly educational type.' This is interesting on two accounts. It first gives an idea of what he considered to be a 'better' taste in films – that is, educational. Second, it is a clear example of the attitude that the present is more progressive, at least regarding technology rather than the type of film.

38. Reproduced in Iliffe and Baguley, *Victorian Nottingham: Volume 3*, p. 39. According to Gray, the first known attempt to put sound to film was in 1889 when William Dickson synchronised the phonograph and Kinetoscope: Gray, 1996, p. 52.

39. NDE, 14 July 1896.

40. NDE, 2 October 1896; NDE, 6 October 1896.

41. Hansen, 1991 and Kirby, 1990.

42. Hansen, 1991, p. 25.

43. Ibid., p. 23.

44. 'The films as well as being short, were naïve and uncomplicated, actualities mainly or having the simplest of stories, but it is probably true to say that, in the early days at least, the mere movement of pictures was sufficiently enthralling to the unsophisticated audiences of the time.' Iliffe and Baguley, *Edwardian Nottingham: A Story in Pictures Volume 3*, 1980, p. 62.

45. Field, 1974, p. 15

46. NDE, 29 July 1896.

47. NDG, 14 July 1896.

48. Denison, unpublished paper, p. 3.

49. Betting was illegal during the period but it seems to have been extensive. Mark Clapson, for example, has argued that illegal book-makers were considerably aided from the 1870s by the expansion of the sporting press and the telegraph: 'The telegraph and the printed page transmitted the information which was vital to ready-money betting away from the course.' Clapson, 1991, p. 28.

50. 'An Interview with Robert William Paul', *The Era*, 25 April 1896.

51. Bennett, 1995, p. 238.

52. Beckett, 1997, p. 410.

53. Foucault, 1986, p. 26.

54. Chanan, 1980, p. 273.

55. Ibid.

56. Moores, 1993; Moores, 2000; Morley, 1992.

57. Williams, 1993, p. 69.

58. Musser, 1991a, p. 66. See also Musser, 1991b.

59. Hammond, 2000.

60. *Pictures and the Picturegoer*, 28 October 1915, p. 95.

61. *Pictures and the Picturegoer*, 4 November 1915, p. 115.

62. Hammond, 2000.

63. Gunning, 1997, p. 36.

64. Ibid., p. 35.

65. NDE, 29 September 1896.

66. This was the case for August; NEP, 31 August 1896; and NEP, 7 September 1896.

67. This is an argument made, for example, by Miriam Hansen in *Babel and Babylon* (1991). However, while some may have feared that 'the exhibition sites [of early film consumption] permitted too much interpretive latitude', narrative films do not prevent 'intertextually structured films' (Uricchio and Pearson, 1993, p. 53). Moreover, as Klinger has argued, there is no reason to suppose that inter-textuality and interpretive latitude were necessarily threatening to the film industry. On the contrary, it has often found them very useful. See Klinger, 1989, pp. 3–19. See also, Klinger, 1994; and Klinger, 1995/6, pp. 107–128.

68. In 1910, the cinematograph was being shown at the Empire and Hippodrome as part of a much larger act and it scarcely gets a mention in reviews.

4

Constructing the Cinematographic Theatre: Purpose-Built Cinemas, Community Relations and the Politics of Place

In January 1910, the Cinematographic Act became law, and it fundamentally changed the experience of cinemagoing. The Act was supposed to protect audiences from the threat of fire that was posed by the highly flammable nature of most films but, as we shall see, it was also used to control cinemas in a number of other ways. None the less, at the outset, few exhibitors opposed it. On the contrary, as Rachel Low has argued, initially 'no one pressed more urgently for these regulations than the showman himself',[1] and there were a number of reasons for this. First, while film itself had not been the subject of legislation up to this point, this 'did not mean that [showmen] were completely free of legal restrictions'.[2] A whole series of contradictory and conflicting local restrictions existed, and the showman hoped that the Act would rationalise this situation. Second, while the showmen 'vigorously denied that any but a small minority of shows would be found wanting',[3] they were worried that 'more and more places [were] completely without supervision'.[4] For the showmen, 'one death due to the carelessness of one irresponsible exhibitor was enough to damage the reputation of all the rest' and legal restrictions were seen as a way of enforcing responsibility among their own ranks and reassuring 'a suspicious public'.[5]

The Act required places of film consumption to apply for licences, which were only granted on the condition that they met adequate safety standards. As a result, after its introduction, many of the places in which films had previously been shown had little chance of obtaining a licence, and films were increasingly seen in buildings that were specially adapted to, or built for, film exhibition: the cinematographic theatres.[6]

However, while the Act was supposedly designed to protect the physical safety of the audience, it was used to control film consumption in other ways. For example, places were not simply denied a licence on the basis of the physical safety of the building, and it is significant that the Crown and Cushion, the seediest of the Nottingham music halls, was denied a licence. The Crown and Cushion served food and drink, and the Act was often used to enforce the separation of food and alcoholic drink consumption from that of film. The 19th century had seen a long battle over the presence of food and drink within places of entertainment, and their presence was clearly seen as problem.[7] The mixing of different forms of consumption not only suggested that a venue was lacking in respectability, but was also supposed to cause problems of discipline, particularly if alcohol was present.

Contested space: local petitions campaigned against the building of the Picture House, Long Row, City Centre

Cafés were seen as acceptable within the new cinematographic theatres, and the Long Row Picture House, for example, had three. However, the issue was not simply about the absence of alcohol. The Elite, as its name suggests, was concerned with cultivating an atmosphere of respectability, and yet it did serve alcohol in its cafés and restaurants. However, the food and drinks served in its cafés and restaurants could not be taken into the auditorium, and it was therefore able to maintain a respectable image because it ensured that its places for eating and drinking were kept quite separate from its places of film consumption.

This did not, however, prevent people from eating and drinking while they watched films. For popular audiences, the consumption of food and drink was strongly associated with the activities of leisure and entertainment, and many simply brought food and drink in from outside the cinema. Harry E. Crooks, for example, bought sweets from a shop up the road before he went to see a film,[8] while one woman, whose father owned a shop outside a cinema, remembers people coming in to purchase something for the show before they went into the cinema.[9] It was also common practice for children to be given fruit and nuts before a show,[10] while others made an evening of their entertainment by going out to eat afterwards. Kathleen Oakland, for example, claims that she went to the Empire every Friday evening: 'Before the First World War, my dad used to take mother and I to a show if there was anything special ... After the show we went across the road to Sandersons for Tripe and Mash.'[11]

However, the Act was not simply used to control the behaviour of audiences. While film consumption may have begun to establish itself as a respectable amusement, it was still too popular for some sections of the population. As a result, the Act was also used to control the locations of cinemas. Nottingham, like many other cities,[12] saw the development of a culture zone in which cinematographic theatres grew up at the intersection of traffic lines in the city centre and alongside theatres and shops and other places of entertainment and leisure. However, there were also concerted efforts by local businesses, the city council and the Watch Committee to keep film consumption away from certain areas of the city centre that were associated with upper-class consumption.

These new cinematographic theatres largely destroyed the old bioscopes but, as we have seen, it was not a process through which respectable houses drove out disreputable places of lower-class amusement. Not only was the lavishness of these new places of film consumption something that they shared with the bioscope shows, but this feature can be linked to the 'anticipatory celebration of material surfeit' that distinguishes the carnivalesque.[13] Certainly the design and décor was supposed to evoke a sense of respectability and made frequent reverential references to high culture, but it was also this lavishness that has been dismissed by others as simply a sign of vulgarity and excess.[14] These places may have desired respectability but their lavishness was specifically intended to create a fantasy world of abundance for audiences, many of whom would never experience such luxury outside the cinematographic theatre.

At this stage, the cinematographic theatres still looked for their inspiration to the theatre as a model of design, and it would not be until at least the 1920s that cinema would enter its most exotic phase.[15] None the less, these places did evoke a sense of exoticism and otherness, through which they offered to transport their audiences to other worlds and places, and this can not only be seen in the opulent décor, but also in their names. As Kathryn Fuller notes, the naming of places of film consumption 'provides a tantalizing glimpse into the impact of the moviegoing experience'.[16] Some theatres, for example, 'attempted to cement ties with their local communities by choosing names that created images of the movie theatre as a friendly, familiar gathering place close to home', while others drew on 'established entertainment traditions and local allegiances [by] retaining the name of the original building' such as 'the Town Hall, Opera House, Lyceum or Auditorium'. Names such as 'Superba, Ideal, Peerless, Elite, Bon Ton, and Unique assured sceptical neighbours of the high quality of the moving picture show and its appropriateness for family viewing'. Others emphasised 'the novelty of the new form of entertainment, such as the Electric Theatre, Arcade, Novelty, Theatorium, and Cameraphone'. Many cinemas also took the names of foreign places that evoked a sense of exoticism 'like Alhambra, Alcazar, or Valencia', while others 'dipped into a cache of names already popular with vaudeville and legitimate theatre owners to convey ideas of elegance, European grandeur, spectacle, and respectability, like the Royal, Queen, Princess, Regency, Rex, Empire, Empress, Monarch, Victoria, Strand, Palace, Rialto, Majestic, Lyric, Grand, Century, and Orpheum'.[17]

Demonstrating respectability: The Elite, as its name suggests, presented itself as a place of respectability and luxury. Illustration from the opening souvenir programme. The Elite, Parliament Street, City Centre

Most of these strategies were used in Nottingham. Local allegiances, for example, were emphasised by the Little John on Radford Road and the Robin Hood Electric on St Annes Well Road, both of which played on Nottingham's association with the legends of Robin Hood. Others such as the Elite sought to present themselves as high-quality entertainment. However, by far the most common were the names which fall into Fuller's last category of names that 'convey ideas of elegance, European grandeur, spectacle, and respectability', such as King's on Market Street (formerly the Palace of Varieties and later the Scala [1913]), the Empress on King Edward Street, the Empire on Upper Parliament Street, the two Palace cinemas on Main Street, Bulwell, and Vine Terrace, Hucknell, the Grand on Radford Road, and the Victoria Electric on Milton Street.

This last sense is also conveyed by the very name by which many cinematographic theatres became known: the picture palace.[18] As Denis Sharp points out, the effect of the Cinematographic Act was 'to force cinema owners to spend more on their buildings'.[19] It encouraged owners to convert their theatres into spectacular and respectable venues that would attract middle-class viewers who had more wealth and leisure time to spend on such amusements. However, this is not to say that after 1910 all cinemas were converted into picture palaces, nor could they have been. In the United States, for example, as Browser points out, despite the emergence of the picture palace, 'the old style nickelodeons continued to exist in large numbers', and if the trade periodicals gave the opposite impression, it 'was the task of the trade periodicals to promote the concept of improvement'.[20] Furthermore, as Gregory Waller has argued, despite the focus on the picture palace as a phenomenon, by definition, few cinemas actually conformed to this model. The picture palaces may have been, as Douglas Gomery claims, the theatres that reaped the greatest profits, but this was because they were first-run cinemas in the most prosperous neighbourhoods and could therefore demand a higher price of admission than other cinemas.[21] As Waller puts it, the 'large share of box revenue would not necessarily mean that a greater number of people saw movies at picture palaces than at other types of theatres'.[22] Indeed, few cinemas 'would have qualified as a picture palace, by Gomery's criteria'.[23]

For Gomery, picture palaces were places that seated over 1,500 people, but the size of cinemas in Nottingham was considerably smaller. Before 1930, the largest venue was probably the Mechanics Hall which had 1,750 seats, although this was not a full-time cinema. The 'Supers', cinemas with more than 1,000 seats, were definitely an inter-war development, and most of the cinemas built in Nottingham before World War I were small. The Midland Picture Palace had 450 seats, the Victoria Electric Palace had about 500 and the Long Row Picture House had about 600. There were a few that had near to 1,000 seats, such as the Regent's Hall, the Boulevard Electric, the Hucknell Empire and Leno's (also known as the Little John), while the Empress had as many as 1,500 seats. In contrast, however, none of the cinemas built in the inter-war period had fewer than 700 seats.

While the majority of cinemas were in central Nottingham and were mainly found around Theatre Square, either on Goldsmith Street or Milton Street (the Hippodrome, King's, the Victoria, the Mechanics, Hibberts, Goldsmith [Pringle's], the Empire), there were also other areas of town that were associated with entertainment. For example, three venues on the Radford Road showed films (Boulevard Electric, the Grand, Leno's/Little John) and some respondents to the Nottingham oral history archive remember walking to them from the city centre, where most residents still lived at the time. However, their location cannot be explained by their proximity to the city centre as all three were still quite far out, and it is best explained by a recognition that the new suburbs were in need of entertainment – a recognition that goes back at least as far as the 1880s when the Grand was built.

Locality, Community and Spatial Separation

Films were also being shown in other suburban cinemas and, between 1910 and 1912, cinemas were opened in Bulwell, Lenton, Hucknell, Netherfield and Arnold. Locality and community was therefore becoming increasingly important to many cinemas, and at the opening of the Midland Picture Palace, it was claimed that the cinema was 'intended to cater primarily for the inhabitants of the Meadows and West Bridgeford'.[24] The theatre owners also actively promoted an association between the theatres and their localities. Waller has claimed that, in the United States, theatre owners were encouraged by experts to make such associations. He quotes Harold B. Franklin's instructional handbook, *Motion Picture Theatre Management*, which was published in 1928, but would have drawn on practices and wisdom that predated its publication: 'a theatre, like a man, is a personality – for better or worse – by itself; and each one defines itself to its locality in its own way'.[25]

Nottingham cinemas also engaged in similar practices and one way in which cinemas established a relation to their locality was by providing a community service. For example, while the first children's matinee took place in a Derbyshire village in 1900, by 1910, these shows were well established, and they were timed to match the domestic rhythms of the period. In other words, they got the children out from under the feet of parents, but they also created loyalty among the young, for whom the cinematographic theatre became a central institution in the local community.[26] One respondent, who was born in 1902, describes going to the Scala (King's) to see children's afternoon matinees. Given that he refers to the cinema as the Scala, he is probably talking about the period just after 1913. He remembers there was a man each side of the door with a basket of nuts or oranges, which the children took as they went in:

> Well, people were cracking nuts and peeling oranges all over the floor. But it was nothing but Charlie Chaplin with his walking stick and his little moustache, you know, or cowboys and Indians, round and round the fort, galloping horses, and US cavalry on the, on the walls you know, shooting them down, and a girl at the front playing a piano ... and she used to suit the music to what she was watching on the film ... All children. No grown-ups whatever and there were thousands and thousands. We used to really enjoy it ... [in the evening] they'd still be silent pictures, of course, but the price would go up, and people didn't want all these thousand children screaming and yelling, you know ... everybody screamed 'look out', you know, when he were behind him, like this you know; 'Ey up!' It was like a mad house, but they didn't bother, the people that run the place. They knew what to expect. I expect they had to clean everything up after we'd gone because the floor was littered with orange peel and nut shells. The floors would be covered you know, and they'd be standing up, some of them. They says 'sit down', you know (laugh).[27]

There were competitions in the interval and children were called down to the front to do a 'turn'. This might also happen when the film broke and the managers needed to occupy the children while it was mended.

Also, as cinemas could not be used for profit on Sunday in Nottingham, many theatre owners held charity events, concerts or a mixture of the two on these days. For example, Leslie Spicer took part in one concert at the Palladium Picture House on the High Road, Beeston, which was held on a Sunday night in 1915 in aid of the Comfort and Troops Fund.[28] Although Sunday openings tended to be erratic, theatre owners used them to demonstrate that these venues were not only active participants within but also vital organs of the local community.

In this way, cinematographic theatres tried to create a sense of their centrality to the locality and its community, but they also used local media to promote themselves. There is evidence, for example, that they placed bills in local shops in return for free tickets for Monday nights,[29] and that they targeted the local area with fliers. As one respondent to the Nottingham oral history archive recalls, 'for cinemas there'd be about two thousand bills what would go all around the different districts within about a two or three mile radius from the cinema'.[30] The cinemas also used word of mouth and would announce forthcoming films at the end of shows. As a child, Leslie Spicer visited the Cozydrome Picture House, Beeston, and remembers that, on one occasion in 1911, the manager announced that the theatre had obtained, at great trouble and expense, the well-known story of 'The Doctor's Dilemmia'. Leslie Spicer could not recall anyone laughing at this mispronunciation, but he claims that it made him laugh – despite the fact that he was only seven.[31] However, this event only receives special mention due to its supposed comedy value: it was clearly normal practice to make this kind of announcement after the films.

Another way in which theatres sought to establish an association with their locality was through their programmes. In the United States, this technique was encouraged by Franklin's management handbook, where it is suggested that each cinema could construct a unique personality for itself through 'management style, architectural design, interior décor, booking policies and promotional strategies, as well as the theatre's civic and social role'.[32] However, this booking policy was not primarily about the films that it exhibited. As Waller points out, while the processes of economic centralisation in the United States during the 1910s and 1920s can be seen as producing 'a "mass", national product called the movies',[33] an alternative view can also be established: 'when we take into account, as does Koszarski,[34] not just the motion pictures screened but the whole "show", the multipart bill, the "balanced program," then moviegoing in this period looks far less homogeneous'.[35] As we have seen, this situation was also true of Nottingham cinemas, which provided other entertainments and attractions in addition to the films.

While films were usually shown as part of a variety programme, to which they often had a secondary role, theatres also used other techniques to distinguish themselves and the experience that they offered. The Mechanics Hall, for example, which became a fully blown cinematographic theatre around 1917, emphasised the presence of its facilities, such as the small hall, library and lecture theatres, and when the Elite opened in 1921, it distinguished itself through its cafés, restaurants, reading rooms, and so forth. The Boulevard Electric Palace, in contrast, held competitions, a practice that became even more popular in the 1930s.

In the process, the emergence of the cinematographic theatres transformed the image of film consumption as an activity. Although it had never been simply a working-class amusement, we have only found one reference that suggests that these places provided entertainment for 'the hard working classes', and this was not in any local source, but rather from an article in the *Law Times*. This article referred to a lawsuit by the London County Council over the opening of cinematographic theatres on Sundays, in which the magistrate had dismissed the case, a decision that the article claims would mean 'much to the hard working classes who have very little leisure: and to prevent them from enjoying themselves on the only occasions possible to many of them is extremely inadvisable'.[36] However, even here, the implication is not that these classes were the only classes attending but rather that Sundays might be the only leisure time available to the working class. In other words, it implies that the 'hard working classes' could not have been the majority of the audience.[37]

As we have seen, the design of the theatres has often been seen as evidence of their desire to attract middle-class audiences, but a closer examination of these designs actually gives a far more complex picture of the audience. The practices of providing varied ticket prices, different entrances and seating arrangements all suggest a far more diverse audience whose relationship to one another was not only spatially segregated between cinemas, but also spatially managed within them.[38] Unfortunately, there are no plans available of local cinemas for 1910, so it is impossible to verify whether the new cinemas in that year had different entrances for differently priced tickets. However, the Harwich Electric Palace, which was built in 1911, does have existing plans which illustrate these divisions well. The seating near the screen had its own entrance and box office down at the side of the cinema, so that these audiences would not be seen queuing at the front of house or frequenting the lobby area. The cinema was on one level, but the front seats were also divided from the back ones by a wall. In contrast, the seats at the back of the auditorium were accessed through the main doors, and they had their own toilets. There were also literal differences between the seats, in which some sections sat on benches and others on upholstered chairs.[39]

Descriptions of the Nottingham Hippodrome suggest that it too had a different entrance for those seated in the gods and, as we have already seen, this arrangement also seems to have been in practice at the Grand. Other cinemas also seemed to have used the same strategy and one respondent in the Nottingham oral history archive explained that when he went to the Scala as a child, 'you had to queue down a yard where the back is now at the top of King Street. Not at the front at all.'[40] He also went to the Hippodrome, where one had to queue up in Shakespeare Street for seats in the gods.[41]

The different types of seating in the older theatres and music halls were possibly a reflection of Victorian attitudes towards class and/or a reflection of the reduced working-class expenditure in that period. The Scala – the oldest cinematographic theatre which had been built around 1886 – still had benches in 1912.[42] Thus, these distinctions and their causes evidently lingered on into the Edwardian period, and the Hippodrome, which was built in 1908, only two years before the purpose-built cinematographic theatres, had only benches in its gallery.[43] The presence of benches in the gallery, however, suggests that it was primarily intended to be a live theatre, and in 'real' cinemas, the balcony tended to have the better seats than the gods because the view was better from there. The seats also got more expensive in the stalls the further they were from the screen. As one respondent in the Nottingham oral history archive remembered:

> when you were at school you see, it used to be a ½d on the front row you see and a 1d
> further back, the first three rows used to be a ½d and the others used to be 1d cos you could
> see better, you was looking up at it on the front rows you see ...[44]

The Long Row Picture House also had a balcony and tiered stalls, and its description in the NEP explained that the balcony had 'rather more luxurious seating' than the stalls.[45] The Boulevard Electric also had different types of seating.[46]

The differences between seating prices were also emphasised by the fittings and interior décor and the Scala Picture House at Ilkeston illustrates this well: the balcony had upholstered seats in blue that matched the Wilton carpet, while the stalls were red and had only linoleum on the floor.[47] However, most papers that described the opening of these theatres rarely discussed the differences between the seating, though they did make mention of the different prices of the seats. It may have been that the differences between the seats were not particularly obvious, or else that the emphasis on the luxuriousness of these theatres encouraged reporters to focus on the most expensive seating and leave it to their readers to deduce that the cheaper seats would be less well appointed. Indeed, special mention was made of the fact that the Victoria Electric had 'blue carpet and blue cushioned seats in every part of the house'.[48]

Zoning the City: Class, Place and the Containment of Film Consumption

It is therefore unclear whether certain cinemas were designed to reinforce class divisions or whether they just wanted to provide for all income levels. However, the existence of the wooden benches suggests that cinemas during this period were not intended to represent places of equality in the way that they came to do during the inter-war period when the benches in cinemas such as the Hippodrome were removed. Furthermore, the provision of different types of seating and different ticket prices shows that these cinemas were not solely directed to middle-class audiences. On the contrary, film consumption did not completely shrug off its associations with popular entertainment, and it continued to be the focus of protests from tradespeople, professionals and Christian organisations, all of whom objected to the building of cinematographic theatres, and to the entertainment that they provided, at one point or another.

For example, while film consumption had acquired a certain level of respectability, the protests over the building of the Long Row Picture House and Pringle's Picture House (also known as the Goldsmith Street Picture House) demonstrate that certain sections of society not only opposed cinema but also felt the need to control spatially the activities of film consumption and to designate certain spaces as inappropriate sites for these activities.

These struggles also demonstrate the complex ways in which local power and decision making worked and that there continued to be an assumption that if you paid a lot of rates, the Watch Committee and other sections of local government should not only listen to you, but act in your interests. For example, Brunts Charity – which owned much of Long Row – protested against the building of a cinema on the grounds that it was a street 'for a really high class trade, and the proposed license, if granted, would seriously depreciate the value of the property and the business of the tenants'.[49] The businessmen on Long Row also stressed that the street was a place of high-class consumption, and claimed that a picture house would have class connotations that were inappropriate in that part of the city. The Black Boy Hotel wrote to the Watch Committee pointing out that 'such an Entertainment would be undesirable in the immediate neighbourhood of a First Class Hotel',[50] and the tea dealers explained that many of 'our customers are ladies who would naturally avoid premises near to a place of this character'.[51] This reasoning was also behind the complaints of those who petitioned against Pringle's Picture House. The signatories on the petition were principally tradesmen and professionals, although the latter were more highly represented. However, not all members of the street were in the petition, and the reasons for these absences are simply unclear.

As a result, while film consumption was respectable enough for certain sections of the middle classes, it was still deemed vulgar by professionals and the upper classes. However, they did not object to film consumption itself, but rather to any 'place of this character', and indeed any place of entertainment which generated 'traffic'. It was felt that 'traffic' disrupted trade, although the term 'traffic' here meant pedestrians. In other words, they believed that their establishments appealed to those with their own transport, rather than to those who travelled by public transport or on foot. This meant that they saw their own clientele as upper class and that of the cinematographic theatre as working and lower middle class. By traffic, they meant crowds and the crowd still had decidedly lower-class connotations – a crowd was little more than a mob. However, these concerns about crowding contradicted another objection to the cinema: that there was already ample provision for cinemagoing public within the city centre.

For example, the letter from the Black Boy Hotel does not just object that 'such an Entertainment would be undesirable in the immediate neighbourhood of a First Class Hotel', but claimed that 'it could have a tendency to augment the congestion which already exists in that important promenade of the city'. Similarly the tea dealers, when fully quoted, show concern for the traffic that the cinematographic theatre would attract:

> we believe a place of this description will by reason of the noise, crowds etc., do serious damage to our business and also in all probability involve us in extra cost of insurance against fire. Many of our customers are ladies who would naturally avoid premises near to a place of this character and also the extra traffic of this nature would render it dangerous and inconvenient for carriage and motor traffic.

The concern over traffic is also the basis of the petition again Pringle's Picture Palace and it was claimed that:

> it will also be very detrimental and injurious to the professions and business of gentlemen who have acquired property in the neighbourhood, as, being comparatively free from noise and bustle, it was considered by them to be especially suitable for combined residential and professional or business purposes.

One resident explained these objections more fully in an individual letter of complaint:

> Talbot Street is a very busy thoroughfare for traffic, it is used by the Railway Companies and other carriers as being the easiest hill for their horses to climb in order to reach Alfreton Road, Radford, and the district beyond, nine carters out of ten being obliged to rest their horses at this point before proceeding up the hill. It is also in a direct line with the Victoria Station and Mechanics Hall, being used a great deal during the day and also at night for vehicular traffic.[52]

The complaints about traffic were therefore not simply about the volume of people, but also by implication the types of people: pedestrians signified different classes from those to whom these areas were designed to appeal.

Alternatively, one has to suppose that those seeking permission to build these theatres had chosen to locate them in these areas specifically due to their class connotations. For example, Provincial Cinematograph Theatres Ltd, the owners of the Long Row Picture House, aimed their chain of cinemas at the middle classes and its cinema in Leicester was known for its middle-class audience.[53] As a result, Provincial Cinematograph Theatres Ltd tried to situate its cinemas in localities that would either attract middle-class consumers or attract aspirational consumers from other classes for whom the connotations of these areas would lend prestige to the cinema. As a result, it was not simply that cinemas were associated with specific social classes, but also that the struggles over their location within the city were bound up with wider series of struggles over the control and definition of space and place within the city.

Provincial Cinematograph Theatres Ltd's response to these protests is therefore very telling, and it seeks to address the protesters' primary concerns: that crowds would lower the tone of the neighbourhood, scare off its most profitable consumers, and so lower its property values. The letter therefore tries to reassure the council that the cinema would not only fail to produce crowding in the area, but that it would also only attract the right kind of people:

> My Company's Theatres are entirely removed from the ordinary 'sluces' establishments such as at present exist at Nottingham and elsewhere. We cater for the best class and provide accommodation accordingly. The vestibule of our theatre on Long Row would consist of oak panelling and the entrance would be infinitely more refined in appearance than Lyon's Café next door to us.
>
> No nuisance whatever would occur. No queue would result, for we shall have a vestibule 70 or 80 ft long in which people could wait any time when special pressure took place on the accommodation.
>
> With regards to our programmes we most strictly eliminate everything of a suggestive nature or which could give rise to any objection to any portion of the audience. Our programmes contain a large element of moral/novel and educational pictures.
>
> We do not use posters: in fact we appeal first of all to the better classes, and to families for our connections.[54]

In the process, this letter makes it clear that the fear of crowds is not just about numbers of people, but also the types of people.

Christians also objected to the placing of cinema, particularly when they were built opposite their churches. They too complained that the 'traffic' going into the cinemas disturbed their congregations, although it is difficult to see how it would do so. For example, it was claimed of the cinematographic theatre in Ripley, which was to be built opposite the Wesleyan chapel, that 'the presence of large crowds entering such a theatre would be detrimental to reverent worship'.[55] The Church of England Men's Society also wrote to the Watch Committee to complain about the construction of a cinematographic theatre, and they were not just worried that the building work was being done on a Sunday but that 'this disgraceful sight, taking place as it did practically opposite St Paul's Church was particularly painful to worshippers there'.[56]

The professionals and tradesmen were mainly concerned with the effect that the cin-ematographic theatres had on their locality; what was shown in them was only used to signify the kind of people who were associated with these venues. The clergy on the other hand seem far more comfortable, and possibly felt more justified, in voicing their con-cern about the films being shown. The film of the Johnson–Jeffries prize fight, for example, caused a considerable commotion among the clergy who petitioned the Watch Committee and demanded that it would not be shown in Nottingham. The petition does not specify why they were against it, except that it was an affront to 'decency and good feelings',[57] although issues of race and sexuality may not have been entirely irrelevant. As Grieveson has pointed out, in the United States, Johnson and his cinematic depic-tion had been the focus of a series of moral panics over race, sexuality and the representation of masculinity.[58] Furthermore, as Hansen notes, boxing films had also produced anxieties about female spectatorship as they 'afforded women the forbidden sight of male bodies in seminudity, engaged in intimate and intense physical action'.[59]

It should be remembered, however, that Anglican clerical opinion was still powerful enough at this time that the Town Clerk was able to write to the Chief Constable with the suggestion that they should try and 'frighten' the exhibitors 'with some threats' in order to stop the show. In this particular case, given that the film was non-flammable, the Watch Committee actually had no power to stop the showing. However, the churches' condemnation of this and other films should not be seen as a wholesale con-demnation of the medium. On the contrary, the situation was essentially the same as in the United States, where, as Fuller notes, 'Jealous competition colored much of the reli-gious community's condemnation of the movies and film exhibitors.'[60] While the church complained about the cinematographic theatres, it was seriously trying to find ways to use the popularity of moving pictures for its own ends and it was quite willing to use the film showings to its own advantage.[61]

Notes

1. Low, 1948, p. 58
2. Ibid., p. 59.
3. Ibid., p. 58
4. Ibid., p. 59.
5. Ibid., p. 60.
6. As Richards points out: 'One game historians like to play is to try to identify the earliest purpose-built cinema. Denis Sharp opted for the Central Hall, Colne (1907), but more recently David Atwell has argued the case for the Haven, Stourport (1904).' Richards, 1984, p. 19.
7. Weightman, 1992. The Theatres Act of 1843 made a distinction between the 'legitimate drama house' and other venues which could sell drink in the auditorium but could not stage drama. In the 1890s, however, licensing laws became stricter and new halls were generally not allowed to sell drink. For example, of the twenty-nine halls that were run by Stoll, only eight had a liquor licence: Peter Bailey, 'Introduction: Making Sense of Music Hall', in Bailey, 1986, pp. ix, xii.

8. *Basford Bystander*, no. 30, Oct/Nov 1990.

9. Ibid.

10. Spicer, 1997.

11. *Bygones*, 3 July 1999.

12. See Gomery, 1992; and Staiger, 1990, p. 16.

13. Bennett, 1995, p. 243.

14. Atwell, 1980; Gray, 1996; Shand, 1930; Sharp, 1969; Stones, 1993; and Valentine, 1994.

15. Sharp, 1969.

16. Fuller, 1996, p. 51.

17. Ibid., pp. 51–3.

18. Gomery, 1992.

19. Sharp, 1969, p. 54.

20. Browser, 1990, p. 121.

21. Gomery, 1992.

22. Waller, 1995, pp. 195–6.

23. Gomery, 1992, p. 196.

24. NDG, 22 December 1911.

25. Franklin, quoted in Waller, 1999, p. 164.

26. The fact that children went to these shows without adult accompaniment suggests that most of the children lived locally, and this is further supported by the fact that it is unlikely that many children's pocket money would have stretched to a tram fare in addition to the entrance fee.

27. Nottingham oral history archive transcript: A94/a-j/2: 74.

28. Spicer, 1997, p. 5

29. Mrs C. A. Hawtin, *Basford Bystander*, November 1989.

30. Nottingham oral history archive transcript: A31/a-b/1: 2.

31. Spicer, 1997.

32. Waller, 1999, p. 165.

33. Waller, 1995, p. 217.

34. Koszarski, 1990.

35. Waller, 1995, p. 218.

36. NA: Town Clerk correspondence: CA TC 93/58/33: *Law Times*, 28 May 1910, p. 81.

37. Similar findings have also been made in relation to Birmingham, where David Mayall has found that, before World War I, cinemas were built for both working-class and middle-class audiences. The Birmingham Picture House, for example, was patronised by the 'Birmingham elite' (*Film*, 12 August 1915) and had a 'continuous succession of carriages and cars for the afternoon performance' (*Birmingham Weekly Mercury*, 15 February 1913). The Summer Hill Picture Palace had a 'well dressed audience' who were from the 'better-class' of families (*Birmingham Weekly Mercury*, 2 and 17 February 1912). However, in his conclusion Mayall claims that cinema 'was provided largely by the middle classes for the consumption of a predominantly working-class audience'. This suggests that while most sections of society went to the cinema, it had different meanings for these classes. While the middle class might attend the cinema, it was more important to the working classes, for

whom it was 'a central feature of working-class leisure'. In other words, the middle classes may have frequented the cinema but they also had a far wider choice of entertainment. See Mayall, 1985, p. 96.

38. This also contradicts Brigitte Flickinger's claim that 'by the First World War in front of the silver screen differences between upper-, middle- and working-class ceased to play a significant role'. Flickinger, 2000.

39. Strachan, 1979, pp. 7–8.

40. Nottingham oral history archive transcript: A94/a-j/2: 73.

41. Nottingham oral history archive transcript: A94/a-j/2: 75.

42. NEP, c. 1984, Letter from Mrs E. Daunt of Launder Street, The Meadows.

43. NDG, 28 October 1927. Roddis, 1993, p. 31. At King's Picture House (Scala) the main entrance led to the expensive seats that cost 4d and 6d. The admission prices for the side entrance were 2d and 3d.

44. Nottingham oral history archive transcript: A/10/a1b/1: 15.

45. NEP, 23 October 1912.

46. BBLN, 6 January 1911.

47. Roddis, 1993, p. 21.

48. NDG, 23 March 1910.

49. NA: Town Clerk correspondence: CA TC 93/57/32.

50. NA: Town Clerk correspondence: CA TC 93/57/34.

51. NA: Town Clerk correspondence: CA TC 93/57/44.

52. NA: Town Clerk correspondence: CA TC 10/93/57/35.

53. Williams, 1993.

54. NA: Town Clerk correspondence: CA TC 93/58/pt2.

55. NEN, 13 December 1910.

56. NA: Town Clerk correspondence: CA TC 93/59/120.

57. Petition from the Clergy of Nottinghamshire to the Watch Committee: CA TC 93/59/15.

58. Grieveson, 1998, pp. 40–72.

59. Hansen, 1991, p. 1.

60. Fuller, 1996, p. 85.

61. NDE, 10 October 1912: 'Sunday Cinemas: Bishops on their use for Moral Teaching'.

PART THREE

A Progressive City and its Cinemas:
Technology, Modernity and the Spectacle of Abundance

Introduction: Slum Clearance, Cinema Building and Differentiated Experiences

According to Maggie Valentine, the Depression hit the film industry hard in the United States, and studios 'could ill afford to spend money on building' new cinemas.[1] As a result, cinema construction declined during the 1930s, and those cinemas that were built 'were much smaller and simpler in scale than those of the previous decade'.[2] In Britain, however, the story was somewhat different. First, while the United States was building huge, lavish movie palaces in the 1910s and the 1920s, the cinemas built in Nottingham during this same period were, as we have seen, far smaller and, despite being lavish, there was no comparison with their counterparts in the United States. Second, while the number of cinemas built declined in the United States during the 1930s, this same period saw a boom in cinema building in Britain and the construction of the large 'supers', exotically designed cinemas with huge seating capacities that were comparable to the cinemas built in the USA during the 1910s and 1920s.

Size was a major feature of these new theatres. According to the 1921 edition of the *Kinematograph Year Book*, there were some 4,000 cinemas in Britain, 'not far short of the maximum number ever to operate in Britain, 4,900 in 1949'. However, the average seating capacity in 1921 'was around 600, much smaller than the 2,000- and 3,000-seater cinemas built during the heyday of the late 1920s and throughout the 1930s'.[3] However, it was not size alone that distinguished the cinemas of this period. As Sharp comments, the '"super" cinema was a direct result of the attempt of exhibitors and designers to provide the cinema-goer with greater "illusion", elegance and comfort in their buildings'.[4] Furthermore, as Atwell notes, this was the period that saw 'the first influx of American style atmospherics',[5] large cinemas that did not just signify luxury and extravagance but created the 'illusion' of exotic fantasy worlds in their design and décor. It was during this period that cinemas started to be designed not to resemble up-market theatres, but Moorish palaces, Egyptian temples and Gothic cathedrals.[6]

For Atwell, these cinemas were 'built in Britain to cope with the new phenomenon' of the 'talkies'.[7] However, the 'talkies' do not explain this building boom. On the one hand, no such boom followed the arrival of talking pictures in the USA. On the other, while it is certainly true that a limited number of cinemas could not be satisfactorily converted to sound and were therefore closed down, this was not a common practice. For example, in Nottingham only four cinemas closed between 1928 and 1932, and most cinemas made the transition to sound without many problems. However, Gray's explanation for the boom is no more convincing: 'there had been a moratorium on inessential building construction during the First World War, and it had taken exhibitors most of the decade after the end of the war to realise that it was possible to regularly fill a large cinema of 2000- or 3000-seat capacity'.[8] Not only did the moratorium fail to prevent continued cinema building in the late 1910s and 1920s, but also there is no explanation for this oversight on the part of exhibitors. American practices were familiar to British exhibitors and it is difficult to see why they would have missed the presence of such a large demand, if in fact it had been present.

The answer may therefore lie elsewhere, in developments within British society and culture more generally. As Peter Hall has argued, the nineteenth-century city came to be seen as a place of squalor and corruption, and this situation prompted a widespread concern with the reform of the city in the late 19th and early 20th century.[9] One particularly prominent exponent of reform was William Booth, the founder of the Salvation Army, who was born in Sneinton, Nottingham, and later claimed that he had been motivated by 'the degradation and helpless misery of the poor stockingers of my native town wandering gaunt and hunger stricken through the streets'.[10]

The pressure for reform was therefore particularly acute in Nottingham, which had been transformed during the 19th century from a 'garden town [to] an urban slum'.[11] Even by 'the early years of the nineteenth century visitors no longer went into raptures about Nottingham, and nor is it surprising: the population had tripled in sixty years without any appreciable expansion of the built-up area. The result was congestion'.[12] However, as the century progressed, the problems only intensified, and by 1919, 'nearly 9,000 houses were considered unhealthy'.[13]

Matters came to a head, however, when these problems were used as 'one reason why the corporation's application in 1920 for a further boundary extension was turned down by central government'.[14] The refusal was a blow to the Corporation and severely compromised the image of Nottingham that they had fought so hard to develop. It therefore prompted the Corporation to start 'a massive modernisation programme'.[15] In the years between the two wars, the Corporation built 17,461 houses which 'represented 65.5 per cent of the total addition to stock',[16] and this needs to be compared with a city such as Leicester, its nearest rival, in which the Corporation was only responsible for 35 per cent of the new housing stock.[17]

Urban Redevelopment and Cinema Construction

This modernisation programme created two immediate outcomes. On the one hand, it involved extensive redevelopment of the town centre in which the Old Market Square was redeveloped and a major new Council House was built. On the other, it led to a massive expansion of new suburban estates. As we shall demonstrate, the first of these processes was a highly contested one, involving the removal of both the market and Goose Fair from the Old Market Square and the building of a monumental neo-baroque Council House. This redevelopment was a conscious attempt to transform the identity of the city. The old exchange building was deemed no longer 'worthy of a progressive city'[18] and its demolition was therefore part of a process through which the Corporation 'came to identify civic pride and identity with big, sometimes grandiose municipal gestures'.[19] This process was therefore contested on two grounds.

A building 'worthy of a progressive city'. The Council House, Market Square, City Centre

First, it was criticised along the same lines as the City Beautiful Movement described by Hall, which was attacked by the likes of Lewis Mumford as a 'municipal cosmetic'[20] that he would later compare with the 'planning exercises of totalitarian regimes'.[21] In short, the City Beautiful Movement and its monuments were attacked for 'ignoring housing, schools, and sanitation'.[22] Similarly, there was a public outcry over the money spent on the Council House – money which, it was argued, should have gone into the housing programme in which the Corporation was also engaged.

However, the link with totalitarianism did not end there. Not only were these developments attacked for their arrogant neglect of the material conditions within which most people in the city lived, but they were also attacked as exclusionary. These developments mirror, almost too neatly, the processes described by Stallybrass and White, through which bourgeois respectability was constructed through the expulsion of the market, fair and carnival and the imposition of classical order.[23] It was a process through which the square was appropriated by the Corporation, who literally excluded the world of popular leisure in an attempt to redefine the area as one of high-income consumption. It was therefore unsurprising that so many felt excluded from the square. After all the process was clearly one in which the square was being redefined as a place that was literally 'not for the likes of them'. However, these matters were made still worse by the Corporation's decision to ban the public from the council building itself, shortly after its opening, on the pretext that they needed to protect it from vandalism.

As should be clear, however, this 'modernisation' of the town centre was directly related to the redefinition of the types of consumption appropriate to it. As Don Slater has argued, the 1920s 'promoted a powerful link between everyday consumption and modernization. From the 1920s, the world was to be modernized partly *through* consumption.'[24] However, of course, not all forms of consumption were appropriate. It is therefore interesting that, alongside the new places of consumption that flourished in the square, a new 'super' cinema also emerged. Indeed, it was not only permitted within this area but it was actively encouraged. As we have seen, cinema had been seen as inappropriate to places of high-income consumption in the early 1910s, when the Long Row Picture House was proposed but, by the late 1920s and 1930s, cinema was actively encouraged within such places. However, as we shall show, while it was built in a position almost directly opposite the new Council House, from the first, its image was directly opposed to that of the Council House for many sections of the population. While the Council House came to stand for the arrogance and authoritarianism of the Corporation, the new Ritz cinema became an emblem of democracy and classlessness.

The Ritz, however, was also tied to the second process of urban redevelopment in the 1930s – the Corporation's slum clearance programmes and the construction of new suburban estates – and it was this second process which was largely responsible for the dramatic boom in cinema building during the late 1920s and 1930s. Of the twenty-one cinemas that opened in Nottingham during this period, nineteen were in the suburbs. Thus while suburbanisation has often been seen as the cause of cinema's decline, it might be more accurate to see it as the reason for the phenomenal boom in cinemagoing from the late 1920s onwards, a period which saw the high point in cinema attendance and has therefore often been referred to as the 'age of the dream palace'.[25]

The 'age of the dream place'. The interior of the Savoy, Derby Road, Lenton

As our study of Nottingham will show, the problem with the new suburban estates was the lack of facilities and centres for communal leisure, and while the move to the suburbs has often been seen as a retreat from public life into the private sphere of the domestic home, there was still a strongly felt need for 'getting out', especially among those women who were not employed outside the home. Furthermore, the local influence of temperance organisations effectively blocked licences for public houses within these housing developments, and it was in this vacuum that the cinema was virtually the only form of local public entertainment and leisure available. In these communities, the 'local' therefore came to refer to the cinema rather than, as was traditional, the public house. As Richards puts it: 'The neighbourhood cinema had come to assume a place in the life of the community analogous to those other prime foci of leisure time activities, the church and the pub.'[26] Indeed, as we shall see, in most suburban estates, the cinema was usually there either before, or even in place of, these other two foci.

Differentiating Experiences: Cinemas and Their Meanings

As a result, cinemas not only advertised their locations as one of their major attractions, but many actively advertised themselves as 'local' in other ways. One of the key features behind the building boom of the period was the massive consolation and centralisation of major chains,[27] and many reports of cinema openings in the 1930s made a special virtue of the fact that they were run by local syndicates and not part of one of the bigger circuits. In the case of the Dale Cinema, for example, it was claimed, 'even in the cinema world, local enterprise can more than successfully compete with the combines'.[28] According to our estimations, three-quarters of the suburban cinemas built during the 1930s were run, or claimed to be run, by local syndicates.

Distinctions between cinemas were therefore still important and each cinema sought to foster its own unique identity. Even the big chains were well aware that people did not just go to see particular films, but that they selected between different cinemas that offered different 'experiences'. They tried to establish a balance between the corporate image and the image of the individual house. The Odeon chain, for example, became famous for its 'cavalcade of cinemas in the first totally recognisable house style that at the same time extended the frontiers of art deco design in the building'.[29] However, the 'house style' did not imply conformity. Each cinema was clearly individuated from other Odeon cinemas through its design and décor, even while these features were also used to associate it clearly with the company's more general identity as a brand.

Again, however, this boom in building only added to the stock of cinemas within Nottingham: it did not simply replace the existing stock. Nottingham cinemas of the 1930s can therefore be divided into three types, which in turn correspond to three very distinct geographical regions of the city. First, there were the city centre cinemas that were usually the most prestigious venues that almost exclusively attracted the first-run films. Second, there were the new suburban cinemas that did not attract the first-run films, and were considerably cheaper than the city centre venues. However, while they were less prestigious than the city centre cinemas, these local venues were accessible to many and usually extremely luxurious. Finally, then, the third group were the cinemas in what became known as the inner city. These were located in strongly working-class areas with old and often dilapidated housing stock and some local industries. These cinemas had the lowest status and were often old, dirty, uncomfortable and referred to as 'fleapits'.

However, while many people were now seeing films within the huge and spectacular suburban cinemas, many still continued to frequent these old 'fleapits'. In fact, few cities could not boast at least one fleapit, and rather than simply being forgotten hangovers of the past, these places also became central to people's mental maps of the urban landscape.[30] For example, it is significant that in both our interviews and in the mass observation studies of Bolton one finds similar mythologies and myths which construct specific cinemas as 'bad places', but 'bad places' that evoke a sense of frisson: a sense of repulsion, fascination and attraction.[31] For example, in his account of the cinemas of his youth, Leslie Halliwell comments on the Embassy in Bolton: 'It advertised itself as "Bolton's armchair cinema", but it was small and scruffy and the rumour ran that it was infested with rats; although I never saw evidence of them I was constantly on my guard for sharp teeth nibbling at my toes.'[32] We must therefore be careful not to make assumptions about where people watched films, because they clearly watched films in a number of different locations that were each supposed to offer very different pleasures. It is certainly true that, as Richard Maltby points out in the context of the United States, different audiences were classified according to the cinemas which they frequented. As Maltby puts it:

> In classifying theatres according to their hierarchical position in the zone-run-clearance
> system, the distribution divisions of each company also categorised their audiences, collecting
> a body of generic knowledge about them that was utilised in the generic assembly of movies
> to ensure that they contained ingredients appealing to different groups within the total
> audience.[33]

However, while cinemas needed to do this in order provide the type of entertainment that was associated with specific houses, this did not mean than audiences only ever went to one cinema or one type of cinema. They clearly went to numerous cinemas and the choice between them was not necessarily determined by the films shown, but the type of experience that was associated with each cinema.[34] The fleapits, and even the rumours of infestations by rats, could act as a draw for certain audiences who were attracted by the thrill of danger that was associated with these places, even while they might choose to visit the more lavish and up-market cinemas on other occasions and with an expectation of other pleasures.

Part Three will therefore examine the ways in which the meanings of cinemagoing changed from the late 1920s and throughout the 1930s. Chapter 5 examines the introduction of sound from 1929 onwards and, like the work of Allen and Gomery, it demonstrates that one cannot take the experience of New York as representative of this process elsewhere. It traces the processes of sound films' introduction and diffusion, and examines their reception within Nottingham. Certainly audiences responded positively to the novelty of sound but they also found sound films difficult in certain ways. Sound films also threatened certain of the appeals associated with the live aspects of silent film consumption. Although the move from silent to sound films may seem inevitable in retrospect, it was not a foregone conclusion.

Chapter 6 then moves on to examine the building boom of the late 1920s and 1930s, and the ways in which it was related to the Corporation's slum clearance programmes. It therefore considers the redevelopment of the Old Market Square, and it argues that while the Council House was seen as exclusionary by many Nottingham residents, the Ritz cinema, which was also built as a result of this development, was seen very differently. However, the chapter also examines the role of cinemas within the massive programme of suburban house building that was under way during the 1930s, and it argues that cinema became a central institution within these estates because it was one of the only amenities and places of communal congregation within them.

Chapter 6 will therefore look at the reception of the new cinemas through an analysis of the ways in which cinemas advertised themselves during the period, and of the stories about cinemas that featured in the local press. In both cases, however, it becomes clear that cinemas in the city had far more meanings and functions than merely as places where films were shown. Not only did cinemas differentiate themselves from one another by advertising facilities other than the films themselves, but also the reports of the cinema openings, which were a constant feature of press coverage throughout the period, usually discussed these places in terms of the technology and design that went into the construction of these buildings. In other words, these buildings were discussed as symbols of civic pride that represented Nottingham's status as a modern cosmopolitan city rather than a provincial backwater. The image of cinema had therefore changed considerably, and it had become an emblem of all that was positive about modernity. Reports of these openings conveyed a powerful sense of optimism about the future, and a confidence in the 'progress' and 'modernity' that these cinemas were seen as representing and which they supposedly conferred upon the city by association.

This transformation of image, however, was in no way total and Chapter 7 therefore concentrates on the ways in which cinemas still continued to be contested places. Morton P. Shand, for example, spent much of the decade lambasting these buildings as architectural abominations,[35] while concerns were still expressed over: the physical safety of cinemagoers from the threat of fire and/or overcrowding; the psychological effects of film viewing, particularly upon supposedly 'impressionable' groups such as the young; the cultural influence of American products upon British national identity; and the moral implications of Sunday opening. However, as will become clear, while debates over Sunday closing were an issue all over the United States and the United Kingdom, both the relative significance and the outcomes of these debates were determined by local conditions.[36]

Notes

1. Valentine, 1994, p. 90.
2. Ibid., p. 91.
3. Gray, 1996, p. 35.
4. Sharp, 1969, p. 104.
5. Atwell, 1980, p. 88.
6. Ibid.; Gray, 1996; and Sharp, 1969.
7. Atwell, 1980, p. 87.
8. Gray, 1996, p. 54.
9. Hall, 1996.
10. William Booth quoted in Beckett with Brand, 1997, p. 35. See also Booth, 1890.
11. Beckett with Brand, 1997, p. 35.
12. Ibid. Part of the problem was that Nottingham was unable to expand beyond its medieval boundaries until after 1845.
13. Ibid., p. 79.
14. Ibid.
15. Ibid.
16. Ibid.
17. Hayes, 2000.
18. NDG, 20 March 1926.
19. Chambers, 1956, p. 44.
20. Mumford quoted in Hall, 1996, p. 182.
21. Ibid.
22. Ibid.
23. Stallybrass and White, 1986.
24. Slater, 1997, p. 12.
25. It is for this reason that Jeffrey Richards' book on British film culture in the 1930s takes this as its title: Richards, *The Age of the Dream Palace: Cinema and Society in Britain 1930–1939*, 1984.
26. Ibid., p. 18.
27. Accounts of this process can be found in a number of places, most particularly Atwell, 1980; Eyles, 1993; Eyles, 1995; Gray, 1996; Richards, 1984; and Sharp, 1969. Similar processes were also taking places in the United States; see Balio, 1996; Crafton, 1997; Gomery, 1992; and Stones, 1993.
28. NDG, 27 December 1932.
29. Atwell, 1980, p. 122. See also Eyles, 1995.
30. Of course, some people could only afford the fleapits, or else could not afford to travel far for their entertainment. They were often dependent on a small locality, which helped foster a sense of community within them, and of affection and loyalty to them. These cinemas rarely advertised and so primarily appealed to a closed and established clientele who knew where the cinema was and when the programmes changed. Furthermore, the lack of advertising also suggests that these audiences either did not care what was showing or that they went past the cinema often enough to keep track of the changing programme, which would have been meant that they went past the cinema at least twice a week in most cases.

31. Tony, for example, recalled that the Vernon was known as the 'Vermin', but this name does not seem to have put him off going there. On the contrary, he remembers being in the audience while the staff doused the cinema with flea spray, but implies this was a regular and accepted occurrence (67, retired teacher, RM1). A similar story was also recalled by John, who remembers being sprayed by disinfectant at the King's (again due to bugs), but he describes the cinema affectionately as an attractive place that was warm and where you could snuggle up (John, mid-60s, retired, RK1).

Indeed, the similarity of these stories is worth noting. While we are not questioning the accuracy of these stories, it was striking that certain stories seem generic. In other words, they recur in different forms and in relation to different cinemas. In one such story people remember feeling something on their leg or foot and, in the dark, they either mistake it for a rat or do not realise that it is a rat. In one version, the narrator thinks that it is the cinema cat but it turns out to be a rat but, in another, the narrator thinks that it is a rat but it turns out to be a man touching her leg (Mrs Robey, 60+, retired, RM10).

The attraction of these places is best summed up, however, by the responses of the Clifton Women's Wednesday Club (age range from 60 to 80, KE25) who referred to the Moulin Rouge as a 'naughty place' that showed 'shady pictures'. Rather than simply condemning the place through these phrases, the group signalled their ambivalence about it, an ambivalence that was emphasised when one woman admitted, with a sense of embarrassment and titillation, that she had got engaged at the cinema. Furthermore, this admission was greeted by her friends with howls of laughter and with teasing, in which these women signalled the sense of danger and excitement that was attached to the place.

32. Halliwell, 1985, p. 110. See also Richards and Sheridan, 1987.

33. Maltby, 1999b, p. 25.

34. Bakersfield and Sneinton Women's Co-Op Guild (KE20). This group was made up of about thirty members that ranged in age from forty to ninety.

35. Shand, 1930.

36. A similar argument has also been made in relation to the United States although, in cases such as Virginia, these debates were resolved at a state rather than a local level. See Waller, 1995.

5

Translating the Talkies:
Diffusion, Reception and Live Performance

As Allen and Gomery have argued, one of the problems with histories of the talkies is the focus on one event and one location. As they put it, 'we are skeptical about the ability of one film, *The Jazz Singer*, to alter the course of history'[1] and 'New York City is not the entire country'.[2] To this we would also add that it is not the entire world either. Their argument is that the process through which sound was introduced to the cinemagoing public was much longer and more complex than is suggested by those histories that concentrate on the supposed overnight success of *The Jazz Singer*. Instead, they offer both an industrial history of the processes through which technologies were developed, tested and disseminated,[3] and a local study. As they argue, most 'historians of technological change in the cinema emphasize the origins of change' and it is rarely asked: 'How does the diffusion of technological change occur at the local level?'[4] It is not simply that the talkies arrived in cities outside New York at different times, but that the processes through which sound technologies were diffused were affected by the specific local conditions within which that diffusion took place.

First, the introduction of the talkies into Nottingham did not occur at the same time as the so-called overnight success of *The Jazz Singer* in New York. Although *The Jazz Singer* was released in New York in 1927, the talkies did not reach Nottingham until June 1929 when they were exhibited at the Elite. Moreover, the first show was not Jolson's performance in *The Jazz Singer*, but the film *Lucky Boy*, which was shown for two weeks. As the NEN observed, the film featured 'George Jessel, the original Jazz Singer, and a magnetic baritone, [who] wrote the story, and his attractive personality dominates the screen production'.[5] The first sound film to be shown in Nottingham that featured Jolson was *The Singing Fool*, shown at the Hippodrome in July 1929, two weeks after the screening of *Lucky Boy*.

As a result, by the time that the talkies reached Nottingham, they had already been preceded by numerous reports about them, and the adverts for these first showings exploited this fact. The first talkie was not a surprise sensation, but rather the final, long awaited arrival of a much-talked-about phenomenon. It was 'Hot from America' and 'the first presentation in the country, apart from the Regal, London',[6] and all references to *The Jazz Singer* assumed that everyone was already aware of the film. Consequently, the talkies were presented as something to which only the cultural centres of London and New York had previously been privy but which had now reached Nottingham and,

The talkies at the Bonington, Arnot Hill Road, Arnold

in the process, it was suggested that Nottingham had some special relationship to these cultural centres. The adverts claimed that the films had come straight to Nottingham after New York and London, and so presented Nottingham as close to the top of the cultural hierarchy of cities.

However, a review article on the event also made reference to other talking films that had been shown in England before this screening:

> The talking sequences came out well, the synchronisation being good, and the accents of the characters not too aggressively American, which has been the great drawback to some of the talking pictures sent over from the States.[7]

Thus, as Allen and Gomery have shown, *The Jazz Singer* did not mark the arrival of the talkies, and there had been numerous experiments that had been exhibited to the public prior to its release. However, these experiments were not always well received and it took some time to overcome various technical difficulties such as synchronisation and sound quality. Like the viewers of the first moving pictures, then, audiences for the 'new' talkies were not unsophisticated ones that simply marvelled at the talking images. On the contrary, the introduction of sound was the product of a lengthy process of trials and readjustments, in which the film companies sought to develop a product that audiences would find acceptable.

Furthermore, this first film showing did not herald the 'arrival' of the talkies. It was projected using a mechanism called 'Portable Talking Pictures' and the Elite promptly stopped showing sound films after its two-week engagement. The Elite had not been converted to sound but was simply staging a touring exhibition, and it did not show another sound film until February 1930.[8]

The Hippodrome was the first Nottingham cinema to show talkies on a full-time basis. It had been recently converted from a music hall in 1927 when it was taken over by Provincial Cinematograph Theatres Ltd and, in the process, the wooden benches were removed from the gods and an organ was installed. The newly converted cinema had 2,000 seats, and its size meant that it became Provincial Cinematograph Theatres' (PCT) premier cinema in Nottingham, displacing the Long Row Picture House from this position and closing it down. Like the Elite, the Hippodrome also reverted to silent films after a couple of weeks of showing sound films but it soon showed talkies again on the improved Western Electric apparatus. By June 1929, sixty-five cinemas in Britain had installed this equipment, and although the equipment did not reach Nottingham until 13 August of that year, the Hippodrome was still one of a small group of cinemas outside London to have acquired the technology. Other Nottingham cinemas also followed the Hippodrome's lead and, six months after the arrival of sound, the papers were advertising five cinemas that had been converted to sound.

However, while Nottingham was keen to present itself as the cultural centre of the region at this time, the picture is more complex. In April, the Victory cinema in Loughborough advertised that it was showing talkies, although the papers give no details as to what these films might have been. However, the claim that the films were British rather than American makes it unlikely that they would have been feature films. The first British sound feature, Hitchcock's *Blackmail*, was not shown until June 1929. Leicester, on the other hand, seems to have had its first sound feature at around the same time as Nottingham: on 20 June, the Palace Variety House gave a presentation of *The Singing Fool*.[9] However, it was a little ahead of Nottingham when it came to the matter of equipment and, on 24 June 1929, the Western Electric Sound was installed at the Picture House.[10] This cinema was owned by PCT, which also owned Nottingham's Hippodrome. In contrast, sound came to Lincoln sometime later. The first sound on disc film (*The Donovan Affair*) was shown on 12 August 1929, and the first sound on film was shown on 23 September 1929: the Grand showed *Showboat* while, at the same time, the Central was showing another sound film.[11]

The Reception of Sound Technology

The reception of sound films is difficult to assess. Reviews of the first talking picture in Nottingham claimed that 'the film, and the novelty of its sound effects obviously delighted the crowded audience'[12] and there were also reports of record audiences for the talking pictures shown at the Hippodrome in July.[13] However, journalistic reports are not always a reliable gauge of audience reactions. For example, the *Nottingham Journal* claimed that the audience at the Hippodrome was critical of the synchronisation and the music, but it also claimed that 'there is no denying the wonderful combination of movement and speech' and that the audience 'were startled into silence' when Al Jolson started to sing.[14] Also, as we will see later, many press accounts of the new talking pictures objected to the American accents present in these films but these objections were not shared by many sections of the audience, nor was this situation unique. Journalists often sought to establish a clear and appreciable distinction between their own responses and what they saw as the responses of the 'ordinary' cinemagoer, and one reason for this was that, as Klinger has argued, reviews:

> signify cultural hierarchies of aesthetic value reigning at particular times. As a primary public tastemaker, the critic operates to make, in Pierre Bourdieu's parlance, 'distinctions'. Among other things, the critic distinguishes legitimate from illegitimate art and proper from improper modes of aesthetic appreciation.[15]

It was precisely by distancing themselves from what they saw as the responses of 'ordinary' cinemagoers that journalists asserted and established their own legitimacy.

However, so long as we remain aware of these dangers, and test journalistic accounts against other evidence whenever possible, press coverage has much to tell us about the reception of the talkies.[16] For example, comments in the reviews also suggest that it took some time for audiences to get used to the new sound films:

> The Western Electric Apparatus resulted in a rich and mellow sound from the four 'receivers' (or loud speakers) behind the special screen and it was satisfactory reproduction. The voices (especially the male) were at times a little overwhelming, but little fault could be found with the music which accompanied the silent periods.[17]

In this instance the audience found the best parts to be the 'silent' sections. The managing director of the Elite also talked to one reporter about his 'shock' at seeing the talkies in America and at the lack of 'silent relief'.[18] A second article echoed this sentiment:

> But the fact remains unchanged that the talking film is a quite different form of entertainment from the silent. It makes greater demands on the attention of the audience, which had to key up two senses instead of one [and] while that increases one's capacity for enjoyment it makes the 'talkie' much more physically tiring than the silent film.[19]

Indeed, contrary to Horkheimer and Adorno's claim that the sound film simply increased the illusory realism of film and created greater passivity on the part of the audience,[20] the evidence from Nottingham suggests that audiences did not find the sound film easy to consume. The consumption of the sound film required considerable adjustment and could even be an uncomfortable experience.

Of course, at one level, cinemas almost always had some form of music to go along with the silent films, and the problems were partly due to the types of sound technology that were available. Another reviewer, for example, commented that the viewer had to adapt to appreciate the talkies because the 'voice reproductions are a bit artificial'.[21] This opinion might also explain why, although talkies proved popular, they did not simply replace the silent films in the public's interest.

At any rate, the transition to sound could not have taken place overnight, despite audience interest: cinemas needed to be converted and studios needed to switch over to sound production. However, the silent film did not become an inferior object overnight. Both the Elite and the Victoria Picture House not only continued to show silent films, but actively and unembarrassingly identified themselves as 'The Silent House' in their adverts and listings in the papers. Furthermore, on 29 October 1929, one silent film shown at the Elite was described as being a 'sensation in London even at the height of the "talkie" boom'.[22] It should also be remembered that until the opening of the Ritz in 1933, the Elite remained Nottingham's most prestigious movie palace, and even in cinemas that had been converted to sound, silent films continued to be shown, although in many cases they were used to support the talking pictures.

Where the reviewers did register problems with the new talking pictures was, as we will see later, with the American accents of the actors. They also objected to the plots of many of the early films. The NEN, for example, comments on the unvaried subject matter of the talkies: 'The Melody of Broadway does not depart from the talking film habit of being about chorus girls and the night life of Broadway' while Broadway Babies, showing at the Hippodrome in January 1930, was described as having the 'inevitable Broadway as its background'.[23] By the end of October, however, the NEN felt that the audience was beginning to become more critical: 'The talkies having lost their novelty, the public naturally are paying more attention to quality of acting, singing and humour.'[24] Another reviewer was happy with The Great Gabba not only because the stage screens were 'magnificent, but at last chorus girls have not been allowed to entirely dominate the plot'.[25] Furthermore, when Blackmail was shown at the Hippodrome, the reviewer in the NEN was delighted, and considered it to be 'genuine drama' and the best talkie production yet seen in Nottingham.[26] It is, however, unclear quite how much this praise was due to the film's status as the first British talkie, given the general disdain for American products in the press.

Music, Variety and Live Performance

There were also other worries about the impact of talking pictures. Music had always been an important part of silent films, especially in the big central cinemas such as the Elite and the Hippodrome that had large orchestras. However, even the smaller local cinemas generally featured some form of musical accompaniment, usually a pianist but sometimes a small band on special occasions. Given that many of the working classes could not afford gramophones or radios before the 1930s, cinemas and dance halls were often the only places where they could hear professional performances.[27] In a reminiscence of early theatregoing in the local press, Kathleen Oakland therefore spoke for many of her generation who considered the music to be an important part of an evening at the theatre:

Each week I used to book for a Friday evening performance second house for my young man and myself. I always asked for front seats as I enjoyed watching and listening to the orchestra as much as the stage performances. There was a special cello player who always gave us a smile as we went to our seats.[28]

In another account published in the local press, N. Hall even claimed that the music was his primary motivation for going to the cinema. As he explained, he had spent many 'contented hours' at the Picture House because the orchestra there was particularly good. His preference for the music over the films themselves is also demonstrated by his choice of an end seat in the balcony, a seat that no one else wanted due to the poor view of the screen but from which he could see right into the orchestra pit. In addition, he remembers that the conductor was a Belgian who liked French music, and that he would buy the 'piano conductor's' copy of the score as a souvenir of the show.[29]

In his study of Lexington cinemas, Waller observes that there was a great deal of concern about the possible effects that the talkies might have on the nature of the music in cinemas,[30] and similar anxieties were also present in Nottingham:

> Since the advent of the talking film in Nottingham, many picture-goers have had plenty of cause for nursing a grievance because the orchestra at the cinema concerned, which to many was the centre of attraction, had been dispensed with. The 'canned' music that has been associated with the 'talkies' yet shown in the city has not been the slightest compensation for the loss of a fine orchestra, for without exception it has borne a very striking resemblance in the harsh, strident, unmusical noises which issued from the now obsolete phonograph and the very first gramophones.[31]

In this situation, one reason for the continued appreciation of silent films was that these film showings were still associated with the presence of live music. As one review commented:

> it seems that although the talkie has become very popular in this city, the silent film is still attractive when presented under such ideal conditions. The Elite orchestra is very fine. There is something about the human player that sometimes seems an indispensable part of the showing of a film, and certainly a very large number of people think so, judging by the audiences.[32]

However, this reviewer also went on to explain that the sound film being shown that week was the first example in which the music was 'pleasing to the ear', and he concluded that, if the music in the talking picture continued to improve, 'the cloud which hangs over the "talkie" in the eyes of the music-loving section of the films' goers will be lifted'.[33]

However, it was not only the presence of live music that was threatened by the talking pictures, but the variety format, too. *Movietone Follies of 1929* was almost just a film version of a music hall revue but had 'the additional advantage of going through without the intervals of waiting inseparable from the stage show'.[34] It was also the case that, as Murphy argues, sound had the advantage of providing a cheap alternative to live performances, not only for those cinemas that already had live acts, but also for those cinemas that depended on gramophones.[35] The coming of sound therefore hastened the demise of the music hall and the variety show, and cinemas became less dependent on live entertainment. However, the decline of the music hall had already started before the arrival of sound, as the conversion of the Hippodrome to a cinema in 1927 indicates. None the less, Priestley blamed the lack of live acts in Leicester on the presence of films and, although there was not such a striking absence of live entertainment in Nottingham, his comments are indicative of the impact of sound films on live shows:

> In the whole of Leicester that night there was only one performance being given by living players, in a touring musical comedy. In a town with nearly a quarter of million people, not without intelligence or money, this is not good enough. Soon we shall be as badly off as America, where I find myself in large cities that had not a single living actor performing in them, nothing but films, films, films. There a whole generation has grown up that associates entertainment with moving pictures and nothing else; and I am not sure that as much could not be said of this country.[36]

Although Priestley does go on to say that he liked films, he felt that they did not provide any inside knowledge of a town.[37] These concerns therefore pick up on a more general fear of Americanisation in the period, and the loss of national and local identity that it supposedly caused.[38] However, although there were certainly local acts and performers associated with the variety show, many were also touring players, often from abroad, and it is difficult to see why they, any more than the recordings of American performers and performances, would provide an inside knowledge of a town in which they appeared.[39]

Of course, the arrival of the talkies did not completely shut down the presence of live acts either within the cinema or within culture more generally. The Empire remained open as a music hall until the late 1950s; the Playhouse was opened in an old cinema in 1942; and the Theatre Royal continued to function as a prominent and respected institution. Even in the cinemas, as we shall see, live performers continued to be a major draw with figures such as Jack Helyer, the organist at the Ritz, often being a more important draw than the films shown.

Notes

1. Allen and Gomery, 1985, p. 116.
2. Ibid., p. 196.
3. See Crafton, 1997; Gomery, 1992; Stones, 1993.
4. Allen and Gomery, 1985, p. 194.
5. NEN, 25 June 1929.
6. NJ, 24 June 1929.
7. NDG, 25 June 1929.
8. The first sound films were shown in February 1930, but on 1 January, a screen voice did wish the patrons of the cinema a happy new year.
9. Williams, 1993, p. 200.
10. Ibid., pp. 200–1.
11. Clarke, 1991, pp. 12, 15.
12. NJ, 25 June 1929.

13. NEN, 9 July 1929.

14. Ibid.

15. Klinger, 1994, p. 70.

16. For a more detailed discussion of the dangers and uses of journalist reviews, see Jancovich, 2000b, pp. 33–44.

17. NEN, 13 August 1929.

18. NJ, 25 June 1929.

19. NDG, 4 February 1930.

20. Horkheimer and Adorno, 1979.

21. NJ, 25 June 1929.

22. NEP, 29 October 1929.

23. NEN, 22 October 1929; NEN, 4 January 1930.

24. NEN, 29 October 1929.

25. NEN, 3 December 1929.

26. NEN, 5 November 1929.

27. Some may have had instruments of their own, and even been members of formal or informal bands.

28. *Bygones*, 3 July 1999.

29. NEP, 7 April 1970.

30. Waller, 1995.

31. See article 'A serious Crisis has Arisen in German Musical Circles Owing to the Arrival of the Talking Film (Says Berlin Wire From the Exchange)': NEN, Tuesday 18 June 1929.

32. NEN, 15 October 1929.

33. NJ, 23 September 1929.

34. Ibid.

35. Murphy, 1984, p. 45. According to Murphy, from 1926, 'Kine-Variety' was a popular form of entertainment, and it involved live acts supporting the main film programme. However, the smaller cinemas, which could not afford expensive variety acts, 'were helped by the fortuitous arrival of the electric gramophone'. British Brunswick, for example, claimed that, by 1928, it had installed over 1,000 gramophones in cinemas. 'Sound films were envisaged as fulfilling a similar function to the gramophone in providing a cheap alternative to live performers.' Gomery also makes a similar point in his study of movie exhibition in the United States; see Gomery, 1992.

36. Priestley, 1994 (originally published 1933), p. 121.

37. Ibid.

38. For work on Americanisation debates, see Hebdige, 'Towards a Cartography of Taste', in *Hiding in the Light*, 1988; Morley and Robins, 1995; and Webster, 1988. See also Higson, 1995.

39. According to Crump, unlike the North East and Lancashire, the success of early music hall in Nottingham and Birmingham 'needs to be located in the context of early integration into a national circuit based in London rather than a regional tradition'. As a result, music halls in the Midlands never really were a reflection of local identity. See Crump, 1986.

6

The City Centre, the Suburbs and the Cinema-Building Boom

Urban Redevelopment, High-Class Consumption and the Construction of the Ritz

If the Ritz cinema showcased the talents of its organist Jack Helyer, it was also seen as a showcase for the city itself. It was built as a result of the 'massive modernisation programme' that the Corporation embarked on after 1920, when its bid for a boundary extension was refused. Alongside its substantial house-building programme, the Corporation also undertook a monumental remaking of the town centre, the fulcrum of which was shifted to the Old Market Square and a new council house opposite which the Ritz was eventually built.

An 'aristocratic attitude': the official opening of the Council House, 1929

However, the cost of the project caused a public outcry. Estimated at half a million pounds, it was seen as a waste of money when there were more pressing civic responsibilities. Surprisingly for a period in which the local papers tried to maintain a sense of civic consensus, controversy raged in the local press over issues of public space and social exclusion that continued well into the 1930s. Opposition did not stop the construction work but, even in reports of the official opening of the Council House by the Prince of Wales in May 1929, there was still a concern about the exclusion of the public concealed within the rhetoric about the greatness of the city. The NDG noted, for example, that:

> A modification of the arrangements affecting the general public had to be made at the last minute. It was originally intended to permit spectators to utilise the Processional way [which occupied the space of the old market and stood directly in front of the new council house] shortly after the Prince had passed along but the main parade was not in readiness for general use, and the public was not permitted to pass the barricade.[1]

The concrete beneath the slabs, it seemed, had not set properly, and although it was firm enough for the ceremonial party to walk along, it supposedly had not set sufficiently for the public to walk on and they were kept behind barricades.

Controversy also resurfaced only a few months later when the viewing permits allowing members of the public to look around the Council House were withdrawn, apparently due to the damage that they were causing to the interior of the building. Numerous letters of complaint flooded into the local press, and the general tone of these is captured by the quote: 'Each time I see the building the more I hate it, and those people connected with it.'[2] Correspondents were incensed that, as ratepayers, they had financed the building and yet were prevented from entering it. They also objected, as before, that the Corporation had spent so much money on a building for its own aggrandisement rather than on other projects to benefit the public more generally.

For the Corporation, however, the Council House was its most impressive building and it was actively promoted. Indeed, its very construction was an act of self-promotion, designed to present Nottingham as a modern, progressive city. It was therefore accorded considerable space in the *Nottingham Official Handbook*, a volume produced by the Corporation to attract people and investment to the city. Under a singularly inappropriate heading, given the circumstances, 'The Principal Public Buildings', are four pages on the Council House, while other buildings are given about a page each.[3]

In this way, the Council House functioned as a synecdoche for the Corporation more generally, and it became the focal point of both criticism and praise for its activities. For example, the image of the Council House was used to illustrate both a newspaper article on a week of national radio programmes about Nottingham,[4] and the cover of the city's official handbook.[5] However, in 1933, the Corporation also took out a libel case against a national magazine which had contrasted the luxury and beauty of the Council House with the city's poor housing and economic decline.[6]

The Council House was therefore a contested image, but it also functioned as such on account of the ways in which it was produced out of a more general contestation of urban space. The plans for the Council House not only involved the construction of a building, but the redefinition of the whole of the Old Market Square which became the site of the processional way and formal gardens. In the process, this redefinition of the square required the removal of the daily open-air market and the annual Goose Fair, both of which had been on the site for centuries. The outdoor market was converted into an indoor market that was located within a purpose-built site that stood adjacent to the new bus station to the north of the city centre, while Goose Fair was moved to the Forest Recreation Ground, well away from the city centre. In some ways, this move eventually benefited the fair, enabling it to expand, but it also changed its meanings in significant ways.

Their removal was necessary to the Corporation, who believed that they conveyed the wrong connotations. Their presence in the centre of the city, it was argued, made Nottingham look like a provincial market town rather than the modern and progressive city that the Corporation wanted to promote, and this was made clear by the language that was used to describe the site in the *Nottingham Official Handbook*: 'the Old Market Square, formally tenanted by a picturesque medley of canvas stalls, is now laid out in broad marble pavements'.[7] The word 'picturesque' conveys the image of a quaint, old-fashioned and probably rural small town while the 'broad marble pavements' imply a grand, imposing city, suggestive of the classical polis.

Newspaper reports, however, suggested that the removal of the market would lead to the economic decline of the area, and the Corporation had to work hard to ensure its economic prosperity. In 1930, the NEP reported plans for a series of concerts that were to be held in the square and for more buses to use it as a terminus. Previously, most buses from the north of the city had terminated to the north of the square and, as we have seen, it was partly for that reason that cinemas and other places of leisure, entertainment and consumption had formed a culture zone there. By 1933, however, all but three of the Corporation's bus routes (or at least those serving the local area) terminated in the Old Market Square,[8] and this demonstrates the Corporation's determination to shift the focus of the city.

Prior to the construction of the Council House, the square had functioned as a central location within the city, but it did so in different ways and for different social groups after 1929. In addition to the market, the square had previously been the site of the old exchange building which housed small shops and the Council Chamber. There was also a shambles, where the butchers' shops were located and, according to the NDG in 1926, these 'open shops in the Shambles ... have long offered good taste'.[9] This mix of shops meant that the area addressed the needs of a general public. However, the cost of the new Council House was in part offset by higher rents in the spaces that replaced the old exchange building, and only the National Provincial Bank, Stapletons the Drapers, and Burtons High Class Food Shop remained in the new building.[10] Most of the other stores had been offered accommodation, but found the rent prohibitively high, and they all relocated.

The notable exception here were the butchers who were not offered accommodation in the new building. Their absence meant that the only remaining food shop in the square was an exclusive one, with very different connotations and customers from those who had used the square to purchase their daily provisions. These developments therefore opened the way for the area to be colonised by new types of shops and facilities, and this had been clearly factored into the Corporation's plans for the redevelopment of the square. The new exchange building had been designed to house a large number of shops, and at one stage of the planning process, the Estates Committee of the Council had even proposed that the new building should house only shops. This proposal was roundly criticised in both the editorials and the letters pages of the local press and, eventually, the Corporation rethought its plans and reinstated the mayoral rooms and the Council Chamber into their designs. However, the provision for shops was still very different to that of the old exchange building. The new shops were housed in an arcade in the Italian piazza style, which was designed to convey an impression of elegance and high fashion.

The square was also home to a department store, Griffin and Spalding, which strengthened its appeal as a place of high-income consumption. The department store is mentioned in the *Nottingham Official Yearbook* for 1937, where it is described as 'the shopping rendezvous of the East Midlands. It is at this store fashionable Nottingham assembles to do its buying'.[11] This clearly identifies the store's status and image as a place of upper-class consumption not only for the city, but also for the region as a whole. Indeed, it implies that Nottingham and the East Midlands were virtually synonymous. Other stores around the square were also designed to attract these groups and there was a preponderance of drapers, milliners and high-class grocery shops.

This redevelopment was also connected to the Corporation's slum clearance programmes, particularly towards the north-western area of the square which was to become the site of Nottingham's premier 1930s' cinema, the Ritz. Located just off the Old Market Square, the site was in a prime location for commercial development. In addition to nearby bus routes, the construction of the Council House had produced a locus which would not only be conducive to the presence of a luxury cinema, but would also be enhanced by its presence. As a result, in 1931, plans for the Ritz were put forward by S. W. Gibbons, a local businessman who owned a large amount of property in the area condemned under the new slum clearance programme.[12] However, Gibbons did not own all the property in the area, and his original plans had to be scaled down. None the less, these initial plans had been extremely ambitious, and referred to as 'a transformation ... within a stone's throw of the heart of the city' that would seat 3,000 people and provide car parking for 1,000.[13] The car parking alone indicates that Gibbons hoped to attract wealthy audiences.

Gibbons' plans were put before the Corporation two weeks after the reports of these plans in the local press in late November 1931. In December 1931, the Housing Committee agreed to take the area out of the scheme in the light of the proposal for the new cinema, although they had approved the slum clearance plan in March of the same year. The rescinding of the clearance order demonstrates that, unlike the Long Row Picture House in the 1910s, the Ritz was not seen as a threat to the image that the Corporation envisaged for the square. On the contrary, it was considered a very valuable addition to this image that was actively supported and encouraged.

Although Gibbons' original ambitions had been scaled down, the Ritz still became Nottingham's premier cinema when it opened. In the 1920s, the Elite on Upper Parliament Street had fulfilled this function, but was quickly eclipsed by the Ritz. In part, this was due to the fact that the Ritz belonged to a local chain, County Cinemas, while the Elite was independently owned. In a 1935 article on the falling profits of the Elite, it was claimed that independent cinemas would soon be forced by economic necessity to merge with the big syndicates. The scaled-down Ritz still had 2,500 seats (rather than the original 3,000), and there was no other cinema in the city with a larger capacity. The Ritz also had its own café, restaurant, ballroom, crush halls and rotunda for around 700 people. The pretensions of the building were also demonstrated by its design, for which Gibbons had hired the London architects Verity and Beverley, rather than using local firms as was common at the time, and by its ability to host theatrical productions and a full orchestra.[14] The Conacher organ was claimed to be one of the largest in the country, and the internal décor was deemed to be tasteful and artistic: 'the dominant tones in the auditorium are green and gold and lend a light, airy aspect to the building'.[15]

However, as we shall argue, while the construction of the Council House was seen as the product of an arrogant and oppressive Corporation, the Ritz was seen very differently. The Council House was claimed to be based on an 'aristocratic attitude'[16] but the Ritz, like other cinemas of the period, despite the fact that it was so clearly designed to appeal to a wealthy upper-class audience, was also seen as a democratic space that not only welcomed the public, but was actually also made for them.

Coming to Terms with Suburbia

The Corporation's ambitious five-year slum clearance programme which provided the impetus for the building of the Ritz also created the conditions for the extraordinary level of cinema building in the period. The programme ran from 1929 to 1934, resulting in the host of new suburbs that sprang up around Nottingham.[17] It is common to think of the 1950s and 1960s as 'the suburb's golden age'[18] but the process of suburbanisation can be traced back about 200 or 300 years.[19] The development of rail and tram networks in late Victorian England, however, prompted their most decisive establishment and enabled the upper and lower middle class and skilled artisans to distance themselves from the social dangers associated with the 19th-century city.[20] By the 1930s, these suburban developments were not simply for the middle classes.[21] Slum clearance resulted in the relocation of working-class families to the suburbs, although the largest single group to inhabit council estates were the more respectable working class, themselves displaced by ex-slum dwellers.

Despite its centrality to the transformation of the city in the 20th century, Silverstone argues that 'Suburbia has remained curiously invisible in accounts of modernity.'[22] However, this supposed 'invisibility' needs some unpacking. Rather than being simply 'invisible', suburbia has instead been a continual source of anxiety and discomfort in accounts of modernity, almost a repressed 'other' that structures the discourse. Even this would be somewhat inaccurate: rather than being repressed, it has actually repeatedly returned to trouble critics.[23] As Hall notes, suburban developments 'were all universally

derided and condemned', although he tempers the term 'universal' with the acknowl-
edgment that 'the prosecutors were all upper-middle class and the offenders were mostly
lower-middle class'.[24] The common complaint against the suburbs, apart from the simple
accusations of bad taste that frequently surface in these accounts, is one of cultural
decline. Fishman and others, for example, have represented suburbia as a flight from the
public, political life of the city,[25] while Harris and Larkham argued that it is characterised
by 'a singular search for ... privacy and control'.[26] The result, it is claimed, is a retreat
from socially minded public notions of politics to a 'politics based on self-interest and
grounded in defensive anxiety'.[27]

This opposition also underpinned the modernist obsession with the public spaces of
the city, such as those represented by Eisenstein (see Part Two). Here the modernist
avant-garde not only identifies with a fantasy of the 'popular' to oppose the middlebrow,
but also identifies with a fantasy of urban public spaces for the same ends. In other
words, they privilege urban public spaces over suburban domesticity, which is frequently
presented as the epitome of a feminised, middlebrow culture. These oppositions also
feature in the numerous accounts that associate suburbia with consumption and conformity. For many critics, the suburban experience is, as we have seen, one of anxiety,
which its inhabitants seek to solve through consumption: 'Private property and fresh
air'.[28] Anxious about their position in the world, the suburbanites are also supposed to
be anxious about their identities and they look to commodities to secure a sense of identity. However, this solution is not only supposed to be illusory but the debate frames the
problem in such a way that residents of the suburbs cannot win. As Vance Packard
observes, in these debates, suburban residents are placed in an impossible dilemma in
which they are simultaneously accused of displaying status panic *and* conformity.[29] No
matter whether they try to fit in or to distinguish themselves, they are seen as equally
contemptible by most critics.

It also important to acknowledge the extent to which these conceptions of suburbia
present it as a gendered space, a space that is defined as feminine through its opposition to the masculine world of the urban public sphere. However, the politics of this
gendering of suburban space needs some unpacking. While some feminist critics have
seen suburbia as part of a political process designed to contain women within the domestic sphere of the home and the bourgeois nuclear family,[30] others have emphasised the
complexity and contradictions of the suburban experience of women. They have
analysed the active ways in which women produced new modes of sociality within these
locations and *through* consumption.[31] It is also worth remembering the extent to which,
as Joanne Hollows has noted, early feminist accounts of both femininity in general, and
suburban femininity in particular, often reproduced the masculine values of the mass-
culture critics discussed above.[32] In short, femininity itself was seen as a problem to
which masculinity was often presented as the solution, and the horror with which many
critics, whether feminist or not, viewed the suburbs was often specifically due to the
sense that it was a space dominated by women and domestic values.[33]

In other words, suburbia was demonised precisely through its association with femininity which can been seen in every stage of the attack: it is a withdrawal from the

The Metropole,
Mansfield Road,
Sherwood: 'luxury in
suburbia'

masculine public sphere into the feminine private sphere of the domestic home; and, like femininity, it is associated with the supposedly 'trivial' world of consumption rather than the active masculine world of production. Indeed, it is a space that is, as Fishman claims, 'founded on the primacy of the family and domestic life',[34] and it is this very feature that is seen to prove its status as a flight from the public, political life of the city. However, rather than seeing this world as apolitical, it might be worth bearing in mind the old feminist adage that 'the personal is political', and not simply because it is that to which women are confined and within which they are oppressed. For example, in another context, while Elsaesser has criticised melodrama as a form on the grounds that it has 'resolutely refused to understand social change in other than private contexts and emotional terms [which results in] a lamentable ignorance of the properly social and political dimensions of these changes and their causality',[35] Angela Partington has roundly criticised this position on the grounds that the supposed depoliticisation that Elsaesser so deplores is only 'a consequence of the critic's class and gender-specific notions' of politics. As Partington puts it, for critics such as Elsaesser: 'The experiences of working-class women, in which conflict and change are inevitably "private and emotional", are relegated to the realms of "escape", rather than reconciled with the "properly social and political".'[36]

As a result, these critiques of suburbia were not limited to the modernist avant-garde and the mass-culture critics. As Hollows has pointed out, it remains deeply ingrained not only within certain varieties of feminism but also cultural studies, and particularly its conception of subcultural resistance. In most cases, the supposedly 'dominant' culture from which these subcultures are differentiated is not that of the owners of the means of production, but rather the suburban domesticity of their parent cultures.[37] Indeed, these criticisms of suburbia can even be found in the origins of cultural studies. For example, as Silverstone has argued, Raymond Williams claimed that suburbia 'depended on developments in media technologies, pre-eminently radio, television and the telephone, to compensate for loneliness and distance, as well as to make mobilization possible'.[38] Williams can be read somewhat differently[39] and the position that Silverstone describes can be seen as putting the chicken before the egg. Silverstone starts from the assumption that suburbia was founded upon loneliness and isolation to which media technology offered some consolation, but it could also be argued that suburbanisation took place exactly because the presence of transportation and communications prevented loneliness and isolation from ever being a factor in the first place.

At least, this claim can be made of the suburban developments of the late 19th century. What is interesting here is that most of these attacks are not directed against the suburbs *per se*, but rather at the cultures and values of those who willingly moved to them. Although loneliness was not a condition for those who had been able to move to suburbs in the 19th century, it was a condition for the working classes who moved to Nottingham's new suburban estates as a result of the slum clearance programmes.[40] It was the latter group who needed communications systems such as cinema to offset this sense of isolation and loneliness.

Constructing an Identity in Suburbia: Slum Clearance and Communal Space

As Turkington argues, the major problem with the public housing programmes of the inter-war period was that 'the local authorities gave little time or attention to the provision of amenities and to the development of a sense of community on the new estates'.[41] This is also borne out by the evidence from T. Cecil Howitt, the architect of the Nottingham estates.[42] His priorities were primarily aesthetic, and he carefully planned the houses to be as spacious and light as possible. He incorporated existing mature trees into his schemes, as well as differing land levels, and he tried to ensure that there was as much greenery and open space as possible. However, there was no sense that the estates were created to form a community. Space was sometimes allocated for a parade of shops, which were designated as a 'special feature' on which surrounding roads converged. However, Howitt does not refer to any other indoor facilities. At the Sherwood estate, a shopping centre was introduced part of the way through the building programme, but on some estates there do not seem to have been any shops. The experience of Nottingham therefore supports Turkington's claim that 'in the early stages of municipal housing the general opinion seems to have been that all that was necessary was to transfer people to new estates where they could live in labour saving homes, and spend their time in their gardens'.[43]

All the estates had a planned recreation ground, space allocated for allotments and some of the larger ones incorporated a school. The estates were therefore clearly planned as a reaction to the housing that they replaced, namely high-density housing with only tiny yards or a street outdoors. They were also designed as a response to certain notions of the 'urban' and therefore included an attempt to integrate the benefits of the rural world of 'nature' (gardens, green spaces and allotments) but little in the way of modern, urban amusements or leisure activities. However, despite being cramped and unsanitary, the old urban developments did foster a sense of community: their residents often lived within one local area most of their lives and consequently developed strong relationships and support networks. It seems that this loss of community was not a concern to the Corporation's inter-war planners, if indeed these suburbs were not specifically designed to transform the cultural lives of these groups. The national initiative to revolutionise housing was part of a major cultural shift, and the way of life that the new estates sought to foster was not one based on notions of community, but one that placed the domestic and familial at its centre. As Turkington puts it, 'Community development was to remain the poor relation of Corporation suburbia throughout the inter-war years.'[44]

In retrospect, the Council has claimed that 'Great care was taken in planning the [Aspley] estate and provision was made not only for houses but for all those other things that are required to make a complete town – such as churches, shops and places of amusement.'[45] However, there was no mention in the original plans of either a church or a cinema, and this was true of all the Corporation-built estates of the 1920s and 1930s. The most significant absence, however, was the lack of public houses, which were actively excluded. In the 1930s, many sections of the middle classes still identified alcohol, and particularly the public house, as a social threat. As a result, despite being the traditional centre of community life, and probably even for this very reason, there were few licensed premises on the new estates. Turkington, for example, states that pubs were banned from the inter-war Corporation estates in Liverpool[46] and, in Nottingham, a major battle raged over whether licences should be granted for the new estates. An NEP article in February 1931, for example, makes it clear that the Aspley estate had no facilities for drinking alcohol, and that even an application for an off-licence had been refused, although there were already 1,900 houses on the estate and plans for another 700.[47] Another example was the Wollaton Park estate where an application for an off-licence was refused on the grounds that it would 'encourage secret drinking'.[48] In this particular instance, the Church of England Temperance Society and the British Women's Temperance Association were lined up against the licence, and their argument appears to have been about issues of class. Wollaton Park (the Corporation estate) was not granted a licence but an area of private housing, Trowell Road, Wollaton, did receive one.[49] The argument that 387 houses had been built within a mile of it and that more were planned contrasts vividly with the situation in Aspley, which had a considerably greater number of homes but was denied a licensed premises. One argument that was used against the granting of licences was that West Bridgford (one of Nottingham's most up-market suburbs) did not have any slums because it had no licensed premises, an argument that now seems entirely self-serving. However, temperance associations fought against licensed premises in many of Nottingham's suburbs throughout the 1930s, and the local press contains numerous accounts of licences being refused, sometimes despite the presence of petitions from local residents who supported the application.

Other facilities such as libraries, public buildings and doctors' surgeries were also absent from the original specifications, and some of these gaps in provision were documented by the local press. For example, a 1936 article recounts plans to open a public library in Aspley some six years after people had begun to live on the estate.[50] Residents on the Lenton Abbey estate complained about the school, in which overcrowding was resulting in class sizes of over fifty; classes were being held in makeshift huts; and the playground was in a poor condition.[51] At the Aspley estate, it was difficult to see a local doctor, and the NEP reported that insurance-panel doctors were unable to obtain surgery accommodation there, despite the fact that it was a city council estate.[52] Transport was also a problem, and although the estate had opened in 1929, it was only in May 1930 that the NEP announced that a bus service was finally scheduled to stop there. Nor was this problem unique to Aspley, and it appears to have been common practice for transport on all the new estates to have lagged behind the house building. Thus, evidence in the local press suggests that residents of the new estates faced severe problems in the first few years due to absence of necessary facilities.

Within this context, cinemas became a significant presence within the new estates. Although they were still not classed as an amenity by the Corporation and, as we have seen, were not factored into the original plans, they did not encounter the same kind of resistance that was faced by the public houses and cinemas built within these estates during the 1930s. We found no evidence of opposition to the construction of cinemas, nor were any building applications for cinemas refused. As a result, these cinemas filled a significant gap within the cultural life of these suburbs. For example, while building on the Aspley estate began in January 1929 and the cinema did not open until December 1932, the cinema was still there before the estate had any shops and this meant that it was the only significant local amenity or communal space.[53]

The tone of articles on these proposed cinemas was therefore either warm or neutral. For example, a NDG article on plans for the Aspley Cinema described it as a 'facility' for the estate,[54] and newspaper accounts of the opening of suburban cinemas often presented them as a vital part of the suburb's infrastructure and social fabric. For example, an account of the opening of the Savoy claimed: 'With the exodus of people from the city to housing estates in the suburbs the need is being felt for amusement facilities in these areas.'[55] In these articles, then, each suburb was seen as a separate entity with its own need and even 'right' to entertainment, and it was an unspoken assumption that entertainment meant cinema. Certainly, no other forms of entertainment were prevalent in the 1930s' suburb: cinema was quite simply the only game in town.

Another reason that the suburbs were supposedly in 'need' of cinemas was their distance from city-centre amenities. The newspaper accounts of the opening of the Aspley cinema states confidently that: 'It has been realised that for residents in these areas to spend an evening "at the pictures" has often meant a lengthy bus journey.'[56] As a result, the appeal of the 'local' cinemas was often presented as precisely their location, and the implication that they were firmly tied to their community. This is clearly evident in the ways in which they were discussed and promoted within the local press, and the following quotes, for example, are typical: 'Carlton's own luxurious cinema';[57] 'luxury in suburbia';[58] 'Radford's luxury cinema';[59] and 'Bullwell's premier cinema'.[60] One account even tried to present the local as a threat to the city centre and claimed that the Aspley 'must be counted a serious rival to the houses in the centre of the city'.[61] Indeed, these local cinemas frequently offered more luxury than most of the city-centre cinemas, many of which were around twenty years old. However, the city-centre cinemas also had other attractions, one of which was precisely that they were in the city centre.

In other words, the suburbs changed the meaning of the city centre for those who moved out to them. Previously most people had lived and worked in close proximity to the centre, but once in the suburbs, they had a different relationship to the centre. For those in paid employment, the move to the suburbs usually placed their home at some distance from their place of work, and the resulting journeying between the two meant that few were inclined to travel into the city centre for an evening's entertainment, at least during the week. Instead, weekday leisure tended to be organised close to home. However, once the town centre was no longer convenient and local, it could also come to be seen as special and different, somewhere divorced from one's everyday surroundings. It therefore became, for many, the place of weekend entertainment and other special events, and the effort of travelling into town simply added to the sense of occasion through its distinction from the everyday.

Notes

1. NDG, 23 May 1929.
2. NDG, 8 October 1929.
3. *Nottingham Official Handbook*, 1932.
4. NEP, 4 December 1933.
5. *Nottingham Official Handbook*, 1932.
6. NJ, 5 December 1933.
7. *Nottingham Official Handbook*, 1932.
8. NEP, 1 July 1933.
9. NDG, 20 March 1929.
10. NDG, 20 March 1929.
11. *Nottingham Official Handbook*, 1937, pp. 154–5.
12. NDG, 26 November 1931.
13. Ibid.
14. It should however be noted that the frontage of the Ritz was very different to that of the Elite. While the Elite had an ornate white frontage that evoked a classical marble monument, the Ritz had a much more streamlined and modern appearance. However, the difference between the two was also a difference of period. Built in the 1920s, the Elite was still mimicking the classical pretensions of many high-class theatres, while the design of the Ritz no longer felt the need to pay homage to the legitimacy of such buildings. Its lines may

have been more streamlined but it was this very feature which announced, and celebrated, its modernity – a modernity that promised glamour, luxury and abundance.

15. NDG, 4 December 1933.

16. NDG, 24 October 1929.

17. This was also a response to the Town and Country Planning Acts of the inter-war period discussed by Cherry, 1996.

18. Silverstone, 1997, p. 22.

19. See Fishman, 1987; and Silverstone, 1997. However, the history of suburbs in Nottingham is somewhat shorter. According to Christopher Weir, it was not until after the 1845 Enclosure Act that Nottingham could expand beyond its medieval boundaries. Lenton, New Basford and New Radford were the result of industrialisation, but it was only with the 1877 Borough Extension Act that Basford, Bulwell, Sneinton, Radford and Lenton were absorbed into Nottingham: Weir, 1985, p. 122. The park was also a 19th-century development: Brand, 1984, pp. 54–75.

20. As Leonore Davidoff and Catherine Hall point out, the middle-class images of suburban life were based on the image of a 'rural idyll', and the removal of these classes to the suburbs was designed to enable the separation of spheres and produce a 'domestic idyll'. It removed the domestic sphere from the supposedly corrupting influence of the city and its public life. See Davidoff and Hall, 1987.

21. Judy Giles has pointed out, however, that there were conflicts and tensions between those who considered themselves to be respectable council tenants and those whom they felt were not clean and decent and hence were undeserving of a council house. Giles, 1995, pp. 85–89.

22. Silverstone, 1997, p. 4.

23. For accounts of these concerns, see, for example, Hall, 1996, and Carey, 1992. Accounts of modernity in the America during the 1950s and 1960s were particularly preoccupied with the problem of suburbia and the conformity that it is supposed to represent. See, for example, Keats, 1957; Reisman, 1961; and Whyte, 1956. A similar argument is also implied by Jürgen Habermas, 1989.

24. Hall, 1996, p. 79. Oliver, Davis and Bentley also provide some good examples. D. H. Lawrence, for instance, described the suburban semi as 'horrid little mantraps'; Antony Bertram, whose book *Design* (based on his radio talks 'Design in Everyday Things') was published by Penguin in 1938, described the supposedly 'indiscriminate sprawling of our towns through ring after ring of shoddy suburb, to ribbon development and the commercial exploitation of our countryside'; William Howell, a fan of Le Corbusier and member of the design committee for the Roehampton slab blocks, claimed that they wanted to turn back the tide of suburbanisation and that 'we wouldn't want to go and live there because everything from the bright lights to art galleries, the continental restaurants, in short "life", the things one goes to the city for – it didn't seem to be happening in the suburbs'. All cited in Oliver, 'Introduction' in Oliver, Davis and Bentley, 1994.

25. Fishman, 1987.

26. Harris and Larkham, 1999, p. 10.

27. Silverstone, 1997, p.12.

28. Ibid. It should also be noted, however, that many English suburbs were not made up of private properties but rented council housing, although the growth of the inter-war suburbs did create more home-owners than ever before. Between 1919 and 1939, 28 per cent of the total houses built nationally were council houses, and this figure was even higher in Nottingham. This means that suburbia was composed of a variety of different classes, a large number of whom were not home-owners.

29. Packard, 1959.

30. See Spigel, 1992.

31. See, for example, Alison J. Clarke, 1997; and Alison J. Clarke, 1999. See also Attfield, 1989; Attfield, 1990; and Attfield, 1995.

32. See Hollows on Betty Friedan's feminist classic, *The Feminine Mystique* (1963), in Hollows, 2000. See also Meyerowitz, 1994. Indeed, as Alison Light has shown, similar positions were also present in the 1930s when many upper-middle-class women began to dissociate themselves from the domestic femininity of the working and lower middle classes: 'Not surprisingly it is the "suburban" woman who is inveighed against most violently by conservatives and progressives alike, earning the scorn of both a Jan Struther and a Vera Brittan.' Light, 1991, p. 218.

33. Wylie, 1956, pp. 51–2, 77–9; and Wylie, 1958, pp. 23–4, 50, 79.

34. Fishman, 1987, p. 3.

35. Elsaesser, 1973, p. 4.

36. Partington, 1991, p. 51.

37. Hollows, 2000.

38. Silverstone, 1997, p. 10.

39. See Williams, 1974.

40. It should, however, be pointed out that inter-war council housing had a very different image from post-war council housing, if only because the rent tended to be much higher than for inner-city housing and the council regulated behaviour. Giles also stresses that, according to women's testimonies of living in suburbia, it is evident that '"A home of one's own", whether it was privately rented, purchased on a mortgage or a council tenancy, was different from renting rooms.' Giles, 1995, p. 95.

41. Turkington, 1999, p. 59.

42. T. Cecil Howitt, (n.d.g.).

43. Turkington, 1999, p. 67.

44. Ibid., p. 59.

45. City of Nottingham Education Committee, 1952.

46. Turkington, 1999, p. 62.

47. NEP, 13 February 1931.

48. NEP, 13 February 1931.

49. NEN, 5 April 1934.

50. NEP, 2 June 1936.

51. NEP, 16 October 1929.

52. NEP, 26 April 1930.

53. NDG, 1 December 1932.

54. NDG, 8 July 1932.
55. NDG, 8 November 1935.
56. NDG, 12 December 1932.
57. NEP, 17 June 1936.
58. NEP, 17 June 1936.
59. NEN, 28 November 1936.
60. NEP, 12 April 1939.
61. NDG, 1 December 1932.

7

Consuming Cinemas: Technology, Modernity and the Spectacle of Abundance

Selling Cinema

As cinemas became bigger and more spectacular, individual cinemas became objects of consumption as much as the films that they showed, and the cinema advertisements of the period made this quite clear.[1] Certainly many cinemas advertised the films that they showed but in all cases the cinema itself was foregrounded as a major attraction and, in many cases, it was presented as *the* major attraction. Even though the city-centre cinemas almost exclusively attracted the first-run films, which were not shown in the sub-urbs until up to a year later, it is significant that there is little reference to this asset in the advertising of the period. Adverts were far more concerned with distinguishing cin-emas from one another through their use of the full programme. Most cinemas in the period featured a double bill but they also showed cartoons, newsreels, trailers and some-times a serial. The Ritz, for example, made the best promotional use of its full programme and its policy was to regularly present details of the entire programme – a policy that made the cinema programme appear far more substantial than its competi-tion, but also appealed to a wide number of different potential audiences. As Thomas Doherty has pointed out, one of the key points about the full programme was that the different parts were meant to appeal to different sections of the audience so that there would be 'something for everybody'.[2] The following example from a 1937 advert for the Ritz is typical: 'Sydney Howard in *Chuck*, also Eddie Quillan and Chic Sale in *The Gentleman from Louisiana*, Jack Heyler radio organist and *Three Blind Mouseketeers*, silly symphony.'[3]

Furthermore, as the decade wore on, an increasing number of cinemas advertised their newsreels, which had become a standard feature of the cinema once sound was introduced. This was no doubt partly due to growing concern about international affairs and crises in the build-up to World War II,[4] but it was also that these newsreels provided a sense of event and spectacle. For example, the King died in 1936 and while the royal funeral was covered by the local papers, the Hippodrome offered 'special pictures of the Royal Funeral'[5] and the New Empress went one better by announcing that it had the 'Royal Funeral Official Film'.[6] Newsreel footage of sporting events also featured in the adverts for some cinemas.

However, while these aspects of the adverts emphasised the films shown, the adverts also highlighted other features of the cinemas themselves and some adverts made no reference to the programme. These other features can be divided into three main areas of promotion: technology, facilities and location. Obviously one of the most important aspects of technology in the period was the presence of a sound apparatus, although, as we have seen, some cinemas also made a point of advertising themselves as 'The Silent House'. Other silent cinemas also tried alternative methods of attracting customers, such as the Victoria Picture House, which highlighted the presence of a 'brilliant musical interlude by the Victorians' as part of its programme.[7]

The appeals of sound were not, however, advertised in a uniform way, and cinemas used the presence of sound not only to distinguish themselves from silent houses, but also from other houses with sound. The first adverts, of course, simply advertised the novelty of sound so that the Hippodrome announced an 'all talking, all singing, all dancing' programme[8] and the Elite referred to *Careers and Love's Test* as 'all talking, all drama'.[9] However, as talking pictures became more established, the refinements in sound technology came into play. For example, the Tudor promoted itself as 'the house with sound system supreme'[10] and the New Empress claimed that it was 'the house with perfect sound'.[11]

A cinema's facilities also represented another means of differentiation in the adverts. In the early 1930s, adverts for the Elite regularly mentioned its restaurants and cafés, and even referred to the availability of particular menus. An advert in the NDG even promoted businessmen's lunches,[12] which also served to advertise the high-class, successful clientele that the Elite supposedly attracted. However, these adverts were not just aimed at these sections of the population, but also those who aspired to the sense of class and grandeur that this clientele implied. As a result, the Elite described itself as 'the most elegant public building in the town', which featured 'a French menu in true French style', and it also claimed that 'nothing differs between our presentations and that of the London theatres'.[13] Here décor and facilities become the markers of class, but also the markers of a truly metropolitan experience, rather than a mere provincial one.

When it opened in 1933, the Ritz soon superseded the Elite's role as Nottingham's leading cinema, and it too emphasised its restaurant and décor. However, the Ritz had a further attraction that distinguished it from the rest of Nottingham's cinemas: a monumental organ played by the well-respected organist Jack Heyler. Indeed, Heyler was such a local cinema phenomenon that his name is still being used today for his association with the cinema. A recently released video of Nottingham's cinema history not only mentions him during the video, but uses his name on the cover as a selling point.[14] However, in his day, he was also a major selling point as is clear from the following advertising copy: 'Jack Heyler at the console of the Ritz wonder organ. Hear the latest and most marvellous addition to the Ritz organ.'[15] His significance is also underlined by the adverts that not only listed the times of the films but also the times of his performances. The coverage accorded to Heyler in the Nottingham Archives also provides further evidence of his significance. As radio ownership in the decade increased from 1 per cent of English households in 1922 to 71 per cent in 1939,[16] Heyler came to be promoted as a 'radio organist' who was not only a local celebrity but one that appeared on national radio.[17]

A 'dream come true'! Illustration in the souvenir programme from the opening of the Ritz, Angel Row, City Centre

In other words, he was seen as a figure of national renown. He 'was never a superstar, but to Nottingham and to wireless listeners further afield, he was a household name', and one who put Nottingham on the map by 'frequently broadcasting for the BBC from the cinema'.[18]

Furnishings, décor and design were used to advertise a cinema's luxuriousness. This was particularly true, as we have already seen, of the new suburban cinemas of which the following claims are representative: 'Nothing has been spared to ensure complete comfort';[19] 'a luxury cinema ... with artistic green and gold interior decorations and furnishings';[20] and 'there is little doubt that the patron will be sensitive to a feeling of modern liner luxury'.[21] The last quote also demonstrates the ways in which luxury and modernity were seen as almost interchangeable terms in the period, and many of the cinemas sought to claim that they were 'the most up-to-date in every respect'.[22]

For example, from the mid-1930s onwards, certain cinemas began to include a phone number in their adverts, along with an invitation to book seats by phone. However, as few people had access to a phone at this time, the management was probably less concerned to advertise the convenience that this technology supposedly offered than to suggest an association with a wealthy upper-class lifestyle to which others might aspire. The same is also true of the many cinemas that advertised the availability of car parking. Car owners were a small minority in 1930s' Britain, yet all the suburban cinemas advertised their parking facilities.[23] The parking facilities at these cinemas were derisory

The 'architecture of pleasure'. The interior of the Adelphi, Bulwell

by present-day standards – parking for 200 cars was normal at a cinema seating between 1,000 and 1,500 – but even in terms of their parking facilities, cinemas sought to distinguish themselves from one another. The Astoria, for example, promised a 'large, floodlit car park' for its patrons' use.[24]

On a more down-to-earth note, other forms of transport were also prominent in cinema advertising. Many suburban cinemas included adverts for bicycle sheds, which clearly had a considerable resonance – in the mid-1930s, 1.5 million bikes were sold each year.[25] Adverts also included details of bus numbers and their departure point from the city. The implication was that some people would travel some considerable distance, possibly on two buses, to visit these cinemas. Location and transport were not so heavily promoted by the city-centre cinemas which were well established and could rely on the fact that most residents of the city would already know of their location and how to travel to them. The New Empress did take out a large box advert, separate from the main cinema listings, to announce that it was 'near the new market and central bus station'.[26] However, this was designed to draw attention to the cinema's place within the new layout of the town centre after the redevelopment of the market square and its resulting impact on the area within which the cinema was located.

Mediating Modernity: Cinema Buildings and the Local Press
Many of these concerns were also evident in the newspaper articles that announced the openings of the new cinemas during this period but, as has already been claimed, these articles tended to concentrate on the modernity of these buildings and convey a power-

ful sense of optimism and confidence in the 'progress' that these cinemas were supposed to represent. In a report of the opening of the Ritz, for example, special mention is made of 'a singularly happy speech' that 'referred to the wonderful age in which we live, and mentioned the momentous consequence that followed the first flight, thirty years ago, by the American inventor Orville Wright'. In other words, the speech, and the newspaper's account of it, directly associated the opening of the cinema with a narrative of human progress.[27] Similarly, the Astoria Cinema in Lenton Abbey opened in 1936, and the report of its opening in the NEP presents its supposed modernity as being its main attraction, rather than the films that it would show. Noting its 'many novel features', the article uses these to support the claim that 'it is the most up-to-date [cinema] in the country', stressing that the cinema had, to its advantage, harnessed the latest techniques and technologies: 'For the first time in any cinema in the kingdom plastic mural photography has been introduced into the decorations' and a constant temperature was ensured by the use of 'robot-fed boilers'. In this account then, modernity is equated with a positively presented progress that supposedly creates an environment that is comfortable, secure and well regulated. Extractor fans 'draw off foul air' and an automatic battery back-up meant that the cinema would never be entirely dark, even in the event of a power failure.[28]

This positive representation of modernity is also reproduced in most, if not all, accounts of the cinema openings in this period, and it extends to aspects of architecture, design and technology. The report of the opening of the Savoy in 1935, for example, claims that it 'demonstrated how really beautiful modern architecture can be',[29] while the account of the Curzon's opening in Carrington is especially effusive in its welcoming of modernity to the city. This 'modern stream-lined cinema' is an 'outstanding demonstration of progress' that benefits from 'modern furnishings' and 'up-to-date technical equipment'. It features 'the latest hygienic silent action seats' and even its brickwork is of 'the most modern type'.[30] Similarly, the souvenir programme of the opening of the Ritz made special mention of the use of electricity, and the cinema, it was claimed, 'functions almost entirely on this mysterious agency', which powers all the elements that 'are necessary to run the theatre efficiently'.[31] As a result, this modernity was praised largely for its supposed ability to create order, harmony and balance, an assumption that was crucial to the accounts of these cinemas' architecture and design. In the construction of the Ritz's café, it was claimed, every 'detail has been considered to give the atmosphere of harmony and rest',[32] and an account of the Aspley's opening in 1932 commented on its 'dignified and elegant structure',[33] while the Roxy was praised for its 'Plain, simple lines which blend harmoniously with its surroundings'.[34]

Indeed, a sense of balance was continually emphasised. For example, several accounts of suburban cinemas allay worries by stressing that this modernity and streamlined design does not go 'too far'. It was therefore claimed that the Dale Cinema in Sneinton had been built 'on the most modern lines' but 'without embarking on futuristic design'. Here homeliness and modernity had been harmonised so that 'cosiness has been achieved without cramping design'.[35] Similarly, the Plaza Cinema, Trent Bridge, was designed in 'the Continental modernistic style', but also gives 'an impression of warmth and cosiness'.[36] These suburban cinemas therefore had to balance their claims to modernity with the reassurance that they were in keeping with both the existing low-rise architecture and the culture of domestic comfort within which they were located. Their success in doing so was also highly significant. Many of the articles presented these cinemas as valuable contributions to the sense of pride and identity of the communities within which they were located. The Ritz was even claimed to be a major contribution to the history of the city.[37] Slightly more modestly, it was claimed of the Curzon that it 'adds to the appearance of the neighbourhood',[38] while the Majestic was supposed to have 'provided Mapperley with one of its finest buildings'.[39] In this way, these reports suggest a strong sense that each suburb should have its own sense of identity, and that cinemas were an intrinsic element in the production of that sense of identity.

However, while this careful balance of modernity and cosiness is evident in the articles on the suburban cinemas, in the city centre, it was the most up-to-date look that was valued. The Ritz did make special mention of the comfort offered by the cinema: the lighting provided a 'comfortable glow' and the auditorium had 'just the amount of light for your comfort'. Similarly, the café had 'plenty of room for the comfort of taking meals', and employed 'Rayred heating panels [to] maintain an even temperature designed to add to the comfort of patrons'.[40] None the less, on 4 December 1933, the day of its opening, the Ritz received a full page of editorial and advertising in the NDG, the city's most up-market newspaper, which was aimed at the business and professional class, and it concentrates almost exclusively on issues of strength, steel and destruction. The article states unequivocally that 'it is difficult to acquire a site for a theatre capable of holding an audience of 2,500 in a commanding position in the centre of an ancient, commercial and industrial city like Nottingham, and this has only been possible by the ruthless demolition of existing property'.[41] However, this 'ruthless demolition' is not presented negatively but as necessary for the creation of a modern, progressive building. Furthermore, alongside the editorial are advertisements by the various contractors who worked on the project, including Hawley Brothers, the demolition contractors, who state with pride that they 'removed 150,000 cubic feet of earth'.[42]

The article also concentrates on the structure of the building and the engineering skills that were required in its construction. In the process, there is an abundance of references to steel: we learn that the whole of the shell of the theatre is made of steel; that both the auditorium and the stage are completely steel-framed; and that the construction as a whole involved the use of 650 tons of steel. A couple days later, the NJ also carried a short article exclusively on the steelwork of the Ritz, which was apparently the work of the builders of the Sydney Bridge, a fact that was seen as 'sufficient evidence of the strength of the structure in every part'.[43]

The scale of the enterprise was therefore a key feature in its promotion and this extended into other areas. For example, it was claimed that 'no question of expense has been considered but everything possible has been done to ensure perfect reproduction' in both sound and picture quality.[44] However, it is probably the Conacher organ that is most often used to signify scale: the NDG claimed that it was 'one of the largest cinema organs in the country',[45] while the NJ went so far as to maintain that it was 'the second largest in Europe'.[46] More recently, a letter to the NEP on the closure of the cinema in 2000 claimed that the writer could 'recall being struck by the sheer width of the Ritz stage and the height of the proscenium'.[47]

However, despite the focus on luxury and distinction within these reports, the grandeur and spectacle of these cinemas was continually presented as anti-elitist. Many cinemas associated themselves with a life of leisured luxury, but they also presented themselves as places where all could, at least for a time, enjoy such a life. For example, Rita Dove remembers that, when she worked at the Ritz, the door commissionaires 'always had to wear white gloves no matter what' and that 'Barbara Mason who used to be in the foyer to greet the customers ... always dressed in a black evening gown'.[48] Similarly, the NDG claimed: 'Reminiscent of the first night at the opera would perhaps be a fitting description of last night's opening ceremony of Nottingham's super-cinema, the Ritz in Angel Row.'[49] However, despite its high-class associations, the music played at the cinema clearly identified its intended audience. At the opening ceremony, a full band 'gave a selection of popular music', and Jack Heyler's organ performances would later include an eclectic mix of styles, which 'always included ten minutes of jazz and classics, a waltz and – to finish – something light'.[50] Furthermore, while these cinemas stressed the luxury that they offered, they especially mentioned the fact that their prices were 'extremely modest'.[51] In other words, it was implied that luxury was available to all without distinctions of class. All benefited, for example, in a place where 'the system of no tipping is in vogue'[52] and where 'Every part of the theatre now affords a comfortable seat'.[53] This was also the period, as we have seen, when benches were removed from many cinemas in order to remove the class distinction that they signified, even though classes still tended to be distinguished geographically between cinemas and spatially within them. As a result, these cinemas represented a modernity that brought security, comfort and luxury to all. Cinemas such as the Aspley provided a spectacle of abundance, but at 'a low price',[54] and so promised a world in which progress would obliterate class distinction and provide affluence for all: a life beyond the demands of necessity.

The irony was, of course, that luxury was often signified through the service provided. While these places announced their anti-elitism, they offered their clientele the opportunity to experience the ministrations of a servant class; the opportunity to be the recipients of service rather than servants themselves.[55] In this way, these cinemas presented themselves as places of fantasy in which the social relations of the outside world were momentarily neutralised or inverted. They presented themselves as places in which a 'dream [can] come true' and, in the NJ report on the opening of the Ritz, the newspaper even went so far as to suggest that the construction of the cinema itself was the realisation of an impossible fantasy: 'A few years ago a Nottingham man, Mr S. W. Gibbons, had a vision, a vision of a super cinema. Everyone thought he would never succeed. The difficulties were too great ... But what was a dream 25 weeks ago was an accomplished fact today.'[56] Cinemas were not just places to show films; they were celebrated as spectacles of consumption in themselves and, as a result, *The Kinematograph Year Book* of 1932 commented on 'the advance made in this country in what has been termed "the architecture of pleasure"'.[57]

Cinema, Nation and Locality

However, not everyone viewed these spaces in these ways. Throughout the late 1920s and 1930s, Morton P. Shand attacked 'the appalling taste of English cinema designers'.[58] Given that this position can be found in his book, *Modern Theatres and Cinemas*, which was only published in 1930, some of his vitriol was clearly directed against designs from the first significant wave of cinema building in the 1910s and 1920s. However, he did not stop his attacks as the 1930s wore on and his identification of Julian Leathart as 'our foremost cinema architect'[59] clearly demonstrated his opposition to the values on which most of the cinemas of the late 1920s and 1930s were built. Shand saw himself as a modernist, but unlike the democratic modernity discussed above, Shand supported a style of cinema building that drew on 'the Modern Movement and the progress its pioneers had made on the Continent'.[60] Instead of the democratic spectacle of abundance, the buildings that Shand called for were 'austere and controlled'.[61] Instead of celebrating the sensual world of 'gratuitous luxury and conspicuous consumption' that Bourdieu associates with the world of popular tastes, Shand's aesthetic asserted 'its superiority over those who . . . remain dominated by ordinary interests and urgencies'.[62] Drawing on classicism, it did not aim to indulge the body but to order it,[63] and hence remained 'a systematic refusal of all that is "human"'.[64] As such, it remained tied to the aesthetic of the pure gaze, which, as Bourdieu demonstrates, is directly dependent on the economic situation of the bourgeoisie. It was a refusal of 'simple' and 'natural' pleasures and it relied on 'a distance from necessity': it involved a privileging of form over function that was the result of 'an experience of the world freed from urgency'.[65]

However, there is little sense that Shand's views had much effect on the locality of Nottingham. They were usually published in *Architectural Review* and were therefore directed at another audience: an elite of the metropolitan, professional architects. As a result, they would have only been representative of the tastes and practices of a very small minority in Nottingham, although it would have been a vocal and powerful minority.

The same is also true of many other campaigns against cinemas and films throughout the period.[66] For example, as we have seen, the cultural influence of cinema had also been a matter of concern since the origins of cinema, and while cinema had become far more respectable by the 1930s, it was still a contested form of entertainment. The 1930s and 1940s saw a series of social surveys, newspaper articles and pressure groups warning of the potential ill effects of film viewing.[67] Some were specifically concerned with issues of content, and claimed that the representation of sex and violence on film would influence behaviour, particularly among 'impressionable' groups such as women and children. Others were more concerned about the supposedly insidious effects of films as a whole: the 'drip, drip' influence of a diet of sentimentality and woolly thinking.[68] Indeed, as these terms make clear, many objected to the cinema's association with both women and the young. Manvell, for example, argued that cinema should be more 'mature', and saw the fact that cinema was most popular with women and youngsters as proof of its low status.[69] Others clearly discussed film consumption in terms of sickness and addiction,[70] and Mayer not only complained of the 'sentimental shows for an emotionally empty metropolitanized population'[71] but also claimed that instead of producing the 'katharsis' of Aristotelian theatre, the cinema was more like the circuses that were used to pacify the Roman mob.[72]

These kinds of criticism often came from professional groups, particularly 'teachers and educationalists', who, like the clergy, saw the cinema as a threat to their cultural authority.[73] However, while this situation led some to challenge and oppose the cinema, it also led others to attempt an appropriation of the cinema, as the clergy had done in the 1900s and 1910s. This period, for example, saw the publication of *The Film in National Life* (1932),[74] a report by the Commission of Educational and Cultural Films, which called for a series of initiatives that would become the responsibility of the British Film Institute when it was formed only a year later in 1933. As the title of the report makes clear, part of the anxiety here was precisely the effect of films on the *national* culture, and particularly the effect of American films.

However, while this led some to call for a strengthening of an indigenous British film culture against the supposed domination of American cinema, the newly forming film societies called for a more cosmopolitan celebration of films from around the world.[75] Roger Manvell, for example, repeatedly exhorted people who were serious about the cinema to set up their own film societies but also struck out against the censorship that made so much foreign cinema unavailable.[76] The contradictions of the movement are, however, best summed up by one of its founder members and spokesmen, Sir Ivor Montagu, the Communist aristocrat, who opposed censorship for the enlightened classes who could appreciate the foreign films that were championed by the film societies, but also conceded that 'mass audience films needed stricter censorship than those for the educated minority'.[77]

However, of the three main concerns about cinema in the period – physical danger, cultural influence and the moral implications of Sunday opening – the concerns over cinema's cultural influence seem to have stimulated the least local reaction in Nottingham, except for the concern with American films and Americanisation. This concern was most in evidence with the arrival of the talking pictures, and many of the reviewers found American accents not only difficult to understand, but unpleasant to hear. Furthermore, they assumed that the audience would also think that 'the voices are not exactly pleasing to English ears, and the accent unfamiliar'.[78] Alternatively, another reviewer wrote:

> It was even possible for a typically English audience such as that of Nottingham, to give credence to a motley assembly of American-speaking characters, one of whom said 'Can't yer be jus a fren' ter me?' with a gloriously foreign accent. The illusion of the 'talkie' has been achieved but is it too much to hope that before long we may be addressed by English speaking heroines and heroes, to which Broadway is unknown.[79]

These sentiments were repeated in several articles, but it is unlikely that they were representative of the majority of the viewing public. While some believed that the 'poor' accents of the Americans would actually lead to English dominance in the talkies due to the superior elocution of English actors,[80] the truth was that the accents of most English actors were as alien to much of the English audience as those of the Americans. Indeed, there is ample evidence that English audiences generally preferred American films to British films. The Mass Observation studies in Bolton, for example, found that 63 per cent liked American films while only 18 per cent preferred British films.[81] As Andrew Davies has explained: 'the majority of British productions with the upper-class "society" settings and "Oxford accents" had little appeal'.[82] As a result, the American chorus girl may have seemed less distant to many sections of the audience than the British upper-middle-class heroine. Interestingly, the only real exception to this rule was that Bolton's favourite films concerned working-class people in Northern towns who had Northern accents, films that starred the likes of George Formby and Gracie Fields.[83]

Debating Sunday Closing

While concerns over physical safety and the cultural influence seem to have had only a limited impact on local politics within Nottingham, the debate over Sunday closing lasted throughout the 1930s. However, even here the outcome was the result of local political conditions, rather than a simple reflection of a larger national picture. It would also be wrong to see the debate in isolation from debates over other forms of entertainment on Sunday. For example, in 1930, there was a dispute over a proposed circus performance,[84] and even the North Nottinghamshire Symphony Orchestra was prohibited from holding concerts on a Sunday.[85] In the early 1930s, cinemas were already forbidden from opening on a Sunday but a number had started to open illegally and were prosecuted as a result. However, the existing law was not considered to be enforceable, and this problem, combined with a public opinion that was supposed to be in favour of Sunday opening, led to the passing of the Sunday Entertainments Act in 1932. This Act gave local authorities the power to sanction cinema opening on Sundays, with the proviso that a proportion of the takings went to charity and no employees were forced to work more than two Sundays in three.

In Nottingham, however, the Corporation rejected this opportunity and, in January 1932, the local branch of the Cinematograph Exhibitors' Association (CEA) made an abortive attempt to pre-empt the Corporation's decision at a meeting that was attended by a number of local councillors, the Lord Mayor and the Sheriff. The CEA representatives advocated Sunday opening and made claims for the 'educational' nature of films.[86] In July 1932, the NDG also entered the debate, and ran an editorial on 'the leisure problem' in which it urged people to develop healthy hobbies that would enrich their life, but argued that Sunday should also be a day of rest.[87] This position was also shared, rather unsurprisingly, by the clergy who were generally against Sunday openings for cinemas, although one parish priest in Nottingham did present Sunday evening cinema shows after his evening service. However, he would only show British films, which, it was strongly inferred, were morally superior to Hollywood productions.[88] From 1932 onwards, the local press also covered numerous accounts of towns and cities around the country that were debating Sunday opening as a way of trying to establish some sense of perspective on the local debate.

The debate came to a head, however, in 1939, when the Watch Committee recommended that cinemas should be able to open on Sunday evenings after 7.45 p.m.

Their report was provoked by an alleged 400 per cent rise in juvenile crime during the decade and, according to their report, a high proportion of this crime was committed on Sunday as the result of boredom. It was also claimed that towns in which cinemas were open on a Sunday had fewer problems with crime on this day. Indeed, there was considerable local concern with the groups of young people who loitered around the city 'looking for trouble', and the response of the Nottingham police was typical of the national picture. Richards claims that throughout the 1930s, the police were generally pro-cinema and believed that cinema was a major factor in the reduction of drunkenness that characterised the period.[89]

The debate that ensued in the local press was a low-profile one that was largely restricted to the letters page. There were no leader columns on the subject and few follow-up reports in the week between the recommendation by the Watch Committee and the relevant council meeting. From the evidence of the local press, the debate did not seem to have engaged the passions of the local community, outside the ranks of those who opposed Sunday opening. The NDG did enter into the debate obliquely through a misleading headline which stated 'Sunday Cinemas Not Favoured', but this headline merely referred to a short item on the views of the Forest Women's Conservative Association. Of course, the headline, combined with the fact that these were the only views that were represented by the paper, does give some indication of the paper's position in the debate.[90]

The arguments against Sunday opening were numerous: it commercialised Sunday; cinema workers would be condemned to work a seven-day week; and it would more generally erode family life and family values. Interestingly, the arguments for Sunday opening also tried to base themselves in morality. If those against Sunday opening saw cinema as a corrupting influence, those in favour saw it as a method of social order and control that would clear youths from the streets and remove them from 'the moral dangers inseparable from the street parades'.[91]

However, despite the advice of the Watch Committee, the bill was defeated by thirty-four to twenty at the City Council meeting of 3 April 1939. Alderman Green made this an issue of national identity and claimed that 'England did not want a continental Sunday.'[92] However, there is no sense that England as a nation was against Sunday opening. Sunday opening was permitted at the discretion of the local authority, and a number of cities had already taken advantage of this national legislation. Birmingham and Coventry, for example, had both introduced Sunday opening, and it seems to be that the Nottingham bill had failed to get passed because only the anti-Sunday campaigners felt strongly enough about the issue. References were made at the council meeting to the leaflets and letters from those opposed to Sunday opening, but there were no references to similar publicity from those in favour of Sunday opening. The local media seemed to want to ignore or distance themselves from the debate, and even the local cinema owners did not campaign vigorously for Sunday opening.

Sunday opening only became a reality in Nottingham due to World War II. Although it had been denied to local people, when the army requested Sunday opening in 1940 in order to entertain the troops that were stationed in the area, their request was duly granted. Post-war Sunday opening, however, was only retained on the basis of a referendum,[93] and this gives some indication of the relative value given to the leisure time of the civilian community in peacetime and the armed forces in wartime.

Notes

1. Of course, it should be remembered that not all cinemas advertised in the press, and it was rare for the 'fleapits' to do so. The audiences to which a cinema wanted to appeal would not only determine whether they advertised or not but also in which local papers they placed their adverts if they did decide to advertise.
2. Doherty, 1999, pp. 143–63.
3. NDG, 3 April 1937.
4. Filmed records of major events had been an attraction from the very earliest days of film and, even in the early 1920s, adverts for the Long Row Picture House claimed that the programme included the 'latest news in pictures'.
5. NEN, 31 January 1936.
6. NEN, 1 February 1936.
7. NEN, 1 July 1930.
8. NDG, 7 January 1930.
9. NDG, 1 March 1930.
10. NEP, 25 February 1932.
11. NEN, 5 July 1930.
12. NDG, 2 March 1931.
13. NJ, 2 December 1926.
14. *Nottingham at the Cinema*, Viewpoint Video, 1999.
15. NEN, 2 April 1934.
16. McKibbin, 1988, p. 457.
17. NDG, 1 April 1937.
18. NEP, 16 October 2000.
19. On the opening of the Savoy; NDG, 8 November 1935.
20. On the opening of the Aspley; NDG, 1 December 1932.
21. On the opening of the Capital; NJ, 17 October 1936.
22. On the opening of the Savoy; NDG, 8 November 1935.
23. By our calculations about 2 per cent of the total population had a car, although this does not account for those who were too young to drive. In 1930, there were 1,050,000 registered cars for a population of 46,040,000 (1931 census). If the average family size at the time was about four, then 9 per cent of families had a car, assuming of course that each family only owned one car, which would have been unlikely.
24. NEN, 28 November 1936.
25. McKibbin, 1988, p. 379.
26. NEN, 5 July 1930.
27. NJ, 5 December 1933.
28. NEP, 8 June 1936.
29. NDG, 11 November 1935.

30. NDG, 1 August 1935.

31. Souvenir programme, the opening of the Ritz.

32. Ibid.

33. NJ, 17 October 1936.

34. NDG, 12 December 1937.

35. NDG, 27 December 1932.

36. NEP, 13 May 1932.

37. The souvenir programme opens with a two-page history of Nottingham which tries to establish both its national and international significance, after which is added the following: 'Today, December 4th, 1933, the Ritz Theatre … opens its doors, girded by the hopes of its sponsors that they will have given to the City a building, and with it entertainment, worthy of the fair fame and traditions of the City of Nottingham.' (The souvenir programme from the opening of the Ritz.) The cinema is therefore seen as the fulfilment of Nottingham's history and as a major contribution to its identity as a modern, progressive city.

38. NDG, 1 August 1935.

39. NJ, 12 June 1929.

40. Souvenir programme, the opening of the Ritz.

41. NDG, 4 December 1933.

42. Ibid.

43. NJ, 6 December 1933.

44. Souvenir programme, the opening of the Ritz.

45. NDG, 4 December 1933.

46. NJ, 5 December 1933.

47. David Rippon, letter to the NEP, 4 November 2000.

48. Rita Dove, letter to the NEP, 30 October 2000.

49. NDG, 5 December 1933.

50. NEP, 27 January 2001.

51. Souvenir programme, the opening of the Ritz.

52. NEP, 8 June 1936.

53. NDG, 8 November 1927.

54. NDG, 1 December 1932.

55. The souvenir programme from the opening of the Ritz devotes a special section to the service on offer in the cinema and states that any suggestions 'from patrons as to any manner in which their comfort and convenience can be studied still further, will be welcomed by the Management and, if found to be practicable, will be put into operation'.

56. NJ, 5 December 1933.

57. This is taken from a discussion of S. L. Rothafel's visit to England. Rothafel or Roxy was then 'chief of "Radio City," the proposed huge amusement centre in New York'. *The Kinematograph Year Book*, 1932, p. 209.

58. Sharp, 1969, pp. 92–4.

59. Shand quoted in Sharp, 1969, p. 94.

60. Sharp, 1969, p. 92.

61. Ibid., p. 94. For other work on modernism in 1930s' Britain, see Peto and Loveday, 1999.

62. Bourdieu, 1984, p. 56.

63. Stallybrass and White, 1986; and Nead, 1992.

64. Bourdieu, 1984, p. 4.

65. Ibid., p. 54.

66. For example, there was a major news story in the local Nottingham papers about a cinema disaster in Paisley, Scotland, on New Year's Eve 1929, in which a fire broke out and seventy children were killed in the resulting stampede. However, despite the prominence of this story in the Nottingham press, it does not seem to have sparked a major concern with local cinemas. On the contrary, it gave the local press the opportunity to claim that the superiority of local cinemas would make any such event unlikely in the extreme. The NDG, for example, reassured readers that Nottingham cinemas were very safe and regularly inspected by the fire brigade: NDG, 2 January 1930. One reporter also noted that, despite the disaster only the week before, there were still as many children attending the cinemas in Nottingham as ever: NG, Saturday 4 January 1930.

67. See Richards, 1984.

68. Ibid.

69. Manvell, 1944. A similar argument is also made by Gilbert Seldes in the context of the United States: see Seldes, 1950. As existing research demonstrates: the young went to the cinema more than older sections of the population; women went more than men; the working classes went more than the middle classes; skilled and clerical workers went more than unskilled workers; secondary modern pupils went more than grammar school students; and people from the North were twice as likely to go as people from the South. See, for example, Box, 1946; Moss and Box, 1948; Corrigan, 1983; and McKibbon, 1988.

70. This language turns up repeatedly in the responses of respondents in Mayer's study of film audiences, and this demonstrates the prevalence of these terms within the period. See Mayer, 1948.

71. Ibid., p. 6.

72. Ibid.

73. Richards, 1984, p. 48.

74. Commission on Educational and Cultural Films, 1932.

75. For a history of the film society movement, see Samson, 1986.

76. See, for example, Manvell, 1944.

77. Richards, 1984, p. 100. However, the cinema owners were frightened of alienating viewers and therefore saw things differently. As the Nottingham Guardian put it, 'Cinema Owners Want Cleaner Films', and they reported on a discussion at the Nottinghamshire and Derby Branch of the Cinematograph Association of Great Britain and Northern Ireland about whether a third certificate should be granted: NDG, 19 September 1929.

78. NEN, 19 November 1929.

79. NDG, 12 August 1929.

80. NDG, 24 September 1929.

81. Richards and Sheridan, 1987.

82. Davies, 1994, p. 274.

83. Sedgewick, 1998, pp. 333–51.

84. NEP, 7 May 1930.

85. NEP, 10 February 1931.

86. NDG, 14 January 1932.

87. NDG, 5 July 1932.

88. NJ, 1 January 1938.

89. Richards, 1984, pp. 60–61.

90. NDG, 30 March 1930.

91. NDG, 31 March 1939.

92. NEP, 4 April 1939.

93. Hill, 1997, p. 538.

PART FOUR

Cinema Closures, Post-War Affluence and the Changing
Meanings of Cinema and Television

Introduction

In the United States, during World War II, there was a boom in cinema attendance that was followed by a rapid decline in cinema attendance in the immediate post-war period. In Britain the pattern was quite different. In 1946, cinema attendance reached 1,640 million, which meant that 'three-quarters of the population attended at least once a year, and one-third once a week or more'.[1] This moment represented the peak in cinema attendance in Britain, and although it gradually declined thereafter, it was ten years before cinema figures declined significantly. When the decline came, however, it was dramatic. Between 1946 and 1956, the audience dropped from 1,640 million to 1,101 million – a loss of 500 million and nearly a third of attendances – but in the next four years alone the audience 'plummeted by another 600 million to 501 million'.[2] Thus, within the fourteen years after 1946, cinema attendance had fallen by over two-thirds.

Between 1950 and 1968, thirty-eight cinemas were closed out of the seventy-two that had opened in the Nottingham area since 1910,[3] and a smaller number closed between 1970 and 2000 (see the graph at the end of the chapter for details). Furthermore, the majority of the cinemas that closed in the post-war period were in the suburbs, with only four suburban cinemas remaining open after 1968: the Savoy (still open today); the Sherwood Metropole (closed 1973); the Classic, Lenton Abbey (closed 1975); and the Byron, Hucknall (still open). This meant that in the 1970s and 1980s, cinemagoing once again became a city-centre experience.

There were two main periods of cinema closure: 1957–59 and 1968. Six cinemas closed in 1959 alone, and in 1968 another five were closed. According to the National Board of Trade statistics, 1957–59 was a particularly bad time for cinemas all over the country. Between 1957 and 1958, the number of cinemas fell from 4,194 to 3,996, a fall of 5 per cent but, during this same period, there was also a 17.5 per cent fall in admissions and gross box-office takings fell by 10.2 per cent. However, there were significant regional variations in the statistics. The London and South Eastern region suffered the least with only an 11.3 per cent decline in gross box-office takings, while the Northern region suffered the most with a 27 per cent decline. The North Midland region fared a bit better, and its takings fell by 17.6 per cent, which was close to the national average.[4]

The size of the cinema also affected the rate of decline. Larger cinemas did better than smaller ones: the takings of cinemas with less than 500 seats fell by 22.5 per cent whereas the fall for those cinemas with between 1,501 and 2,000 seats was only half as much at 10.4 per cent. However, the audiences for cinemas with more than 2,000 seats declined by 14.9 per cent, which suggests that there was a point at which size was no longer a virtue.[5]

Although many cinemas closed between 1957 and 1959, nationally the years between 1960 and 1962 were actually far worse. Between 1961 and 1962, the total number of cinemas declined by 11 per cent – twice as bad as the decline between 1957 and 1958. However, this was not the case in Nottingham where 1961–62 actually saw a fall in the number of closures. There were also differences between Nottingham and national figures in 1968: while Nottingham witnessed another spate of closures, nationally the number of cinemas closing levelled off.

Part Four will therefore be divided into four further chapters, the first of which will examine the reasons behind the dramatic decline in cinema attendance during the 1950s. While television has been blamed for cinema closure in contemporary research, Chapter 8 will demonstrate that, during the 1950s, television was only held responsible for cinema's decline towards the end of the decade. Rather, there were several other reasons given by cinema owners for the closure of their cinemas during the decade, of which heavy taxation was the most prominent.

Chapter 9 will therefore consider the contextual factors related to the decline of cinemagoing in the period. In the process, it will examine the 'age of affluence' from 1955 onwards, and the ways in which this changed many people's leisure habits. For example, the political promotion of home ownership at this time meant that many made the home the focus of both financial investment and leisure activities. At the same time, however, the dramatic increase in car ownership also did much the same. As a result, people's conception of their 'local' area changed as they both spent more leisure time in the home and travelled further and further for their entertainment.

Chapter 10 then moves on to look at the development of television as a leisure activity. Although television was not initially intended to become a form of 'home cinema', television did develop and change between the mid-1940s and the early 1970s and, by the end of this period, more films were watched on television than at the cinema. However, this process should not simply be seen as a competition between television and the cinema but as a far more complex process through which both media changed in relation

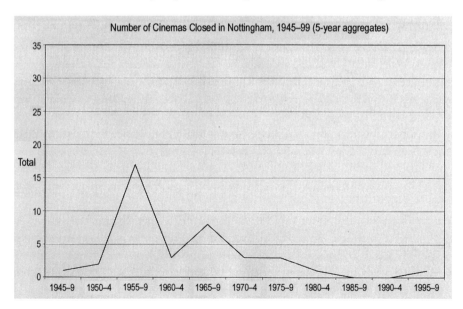

to one another. For example, while television gradually integrated more and more films into its overall programme, the cinema gradually jettisoned more and more of the programme and concentrated on the individual feature film. In addition, this chapter will also examine the processes through which televisions were acquired by households as consumer items; the conflicts that they generated; and the range of uses and meanings that they acquired within the home.

Finally, Chapter 11 will examine the changed meanings of cinema, and will demonstrate that, while it was seen as a symbol of modernity in the 1930s, by the 1950s, it had come to be seen as a nostalgic object that represented community and tradition. In the process, the chapter will look at press coverage on the closing of cinemas from the 1950s onwards, and at our respondents' memories of cinemagoing. Finally, it will demonstrate that the cinema and television are not straightforward rivals, but that each is associated with different activities and experiences. In other words, television is not simply a domestic replica of the activity of cinemagoing, but rather has very different meanings and functions precisely because of its location within the domestic realm rather than within public places outside the home.

Notes

1. Docherty, Morrison and Tracey, 1987, p. 4.
2. Ibid., p. 15.
3. This figure of seventy-two included those which were opened or were converted to full-time cinemas after 1910.
4. *Board of Trade Journal*, 16 October 1959, p. 537. Nottingham was included in the North Midland region according to the *Census 1951 England and Wales: General Report*, London: HMSO, 1958, p. 224.
5. *Board of Trade Journal*, 16 October 1959, pp. 536, 538.

8

Contemporary Understandings of Cinema Closure

Accounting for Closure: Taxes, Levies and the Local Press

In 1962, John Spanos studied the dramatic decline in cinema attendance and concluded that it was television that was responsible. According to Spanos, there were three phases of decline. In the first, prior to 1955, the majority of television sets were owned by higher-income groups that were not a core cinema audience, and therefore it was the second phase, between 1955 and 1958, that was most decisive. During this phase, working-class families had begun to acquire television sets and he argues that not only were these families a core cinema audience, but that they also tended to have larger families and 'an age composition which led to high cinema scores'.[1] In short, they had more family members aged between fifteen and twenty-four. In the third phase, however, he claims that the impact was much less severe. Although televisions were selling at roughly the same rate as that between 1955 and 1958, after 1958, the families that acquired these new sets not only tended to have smaller families, but also to have members that were older.

While competition from television has been a popular explanation for the decline of cinema in the post-war period, as we shall see, this explanation has been severely contested by current research. Moreover, within the period itself, it only emerged as an explanation relatively late in the day. From our analysis of local papers, it was clear that in the 1950s the decline of cinema was attributed to a number of factors, and that it was only at the very end of the decade that the blame shifted towards television. For most of the 1950s the main complaint was against the various taxes and levies placed upon cinema. In 1955, for example, the secretary of the Nottinghamshire and Derby Cinematograph Exhibitors' Association (CEA) was reported as saying that the main problem facing cinemas was the 'high rate of entertainment tax',[2] while an article in the Guardian Journal (GJ) claimed that the entertainment tax was five times as high as it had been before the war.[3] Certainly, for much of the 1950s, it was the entertainment tax which concerned most exhibitors, and they campaigned against it most vigorously. The reason for this can clearly be seen when one looks at the figures involved.

In the early 1950s, the industry was paying approximately 35 per cent of the gross box-office takings in entertainment tax. Although this had fallen by 1957, after its reduction by the government, it still stood at 29.9 per cent and at 18.7 per cent a year later in 1958.[4] It was eventually abolished after intense campaigning, but not before it had effectively pushed up ticket prices. In June 1956, the average price of cinema seats in Nottingham was increased from around 3d to 5d, and the explanation for this rise was the Chancellor's refusal to reduce the entertainment tax.[5] This 60 per cent increase eroded the cinema industry's claims to being among the cheapest forms of entertainment, and it was particularly hard on the small, local cinemas whose main attraction was their cheapness. However, the removal of the tax did not help many cinemas. By that time, the cinemas that had most needed the reduction had already closed.

The entertainment tax was not the only financial burden that was being imposed on the exhibitors, and there were two further financial demands. The first was the British Film Production Levy, which had started as a voluntary fund from box-office takings in the period of high entertainment tax. Although it was small compared to the entertainment tax, it was gradually increased as the entertainment tax was reduced. An article in the GJ, after the entertainment tax had been reduced to 30 per cent in 1957, noted that the amount paid to the Production Fund had increased from £2.5 million to between £3.5 and £5 million.[6] Thus, although the reduction in tax would save cinemas approximately £6.5 million, the increased contribution to the British Film Production Fund meant that there was in fact only £5.25 million left over which had to be shared among 4,000 cinemas,[7] and again this largely helped the larger cinemas with over 8,000 patrons a week which charged middling prices. The levy remained after the entertainment tax had been removed altogether and, in 1968, £4.2 million was still being paid to the fund.[8]

The Windsor today, Hartley Road: a victim of taxation?

The second financial demand was the Sunday Levy, although it received far less attention in the local press. After the war, the local prohibition on Sunday opening had ended,
but local authorities were still able to impose a levy of their own choosing on venues that
opened on the Sabbath. This levy was donated to charities and, in 1956, a letter to the
GJ from the Nottingham and Derby Branch of the CEA explained that it affected cinemas in Nottingham particularly badly. It noted that the Watch Committee not only
refused to set the levy at the minimum amount but had also collected over £30,000 that
it was as yet unable to decide how to spend:

> Last week, a national newspaper published a letter written by a local exhibitor, who states
> that he is prepared to sell his modern cinema for any industrial purpose. This man, like
> others, is being forced out of business by heavy Entertainment Tax. At the same time, he had
> also paid a few hundred pounds towards that £30,000.[9]

For the CEA, the committee's insistence on setting the levy at a higher rate than in other
regions was 'an outstanding indication of legislation at its worst'.[10]

Other Threats: Age of the Cinema, Operating Costs and the Shortage of Films

Another reason given for cinema closure was that many of the buildings were now considered inadequate and out of date. While cinemas in the 1930s had been seen as places
of modernity and luxury, these same buildings had changed in meaning. During the war
and its aftermath there had been a ban on inessential building, which included cinemas,
and by the 1950s many cinemas were either in disrepair or just seemed old and out of
date. The age and discomfort of the Netherfield Cosy and the Palace at Bulwell were
therefore cited as the reason for their closure in the same week in April 1955: 'Both these
houses were built in the days of silent films. After showing pictures for 30 years they are
now out of date by modern standards.'[11] This reason was also used to explain the decline
in theatre attendance. The chair of the trustees of the Nottingham Playhouse, for
example, believed that the only way to get people away from the television was to give
them theatres that they would want to go to regardless of the play that was being shown.
He maintained that people wanted to go to exciting new theatres, and if Nottingham
was to have a repertory theatre, it needed to have an adequate building.[12] He also noted
that the Playhouse was one of the five or six top theatres in the country, but its building
was the worst: it was housed in what had once been Pringle's Picture Palace, which again
demonstrates how perceptions of cinema buildings had changed.

However, it was not just a matter of perception. In the 1930s, some cinemas had closed
because they could not be adapted to sound and, in the 1950s, cinemas that could not
adapt to the new technologies of this period faced a similar fate. Hollywood, in a bid to
compete with the supposed threat of television in the United States, introduced a range
of technologies that were designed to emphasise the superiority of cinema over television
by stressing the spectacle of cinema: forms such as widescreen and CinemaScope.
Unfortunately, in some cinemas, the proscenium arch meant that the screen necessary

The Cavendish today, Wells Road: 'out of date by modern standards'

for CinemaScope could not be accommodated. This was the case with both the Roxy in Daybrook and the Capitol.[13] As the NEP put it, 'The introduction of sound, colour, cinemascope and cinerama had put the small cinema owner at a tremendous disadvantage.'[14] The key problem was therefore the size of these cinemas rather than simply their age. As we have seen, the cinemas built before World War I were generally far smaller than those built in the late 1920s and 1930s and smaller cinemas were also more likely to close because they could not compete.

However, there are other reasons which suggest that the age of cinemas cannot be seen as a principal reason for their closure. During the period, some of the older cinemas were 'extensively re-decorated' and modernised, but closed none the less. The Boulevard in Hyson Green, one of Nottingham's first purpose-built cinemas, and the Beeston Palladium, which had been built for silent films, were both examples. Despite having been renovated, they were both forced to close. On the other hand, the Scala and the Hippodrome, which were both far older than either of these two cinemas and had been converted from theatres, had still not closed by the end of the 1960s. By 1971, however, even the Hippodrome (by then the Gaumont) was considered out of date and it was claimed that if it was reopened as a venue for other types of entertainment, 'it would have to be modernised on a large scale'.[15] By the 1970s, the meaning of what was 'up-to-date' had changed: a cinema was now seen as 'old fashioned' if it could not be converted into a multi-screen.

However, neither the age of the cinema nor its inability to adapt to new technologies was ever seen as being responsible for a cinema's closure itself: the entertainment tax was usually seen as far more important. For example, the manager of the circuit that owned the Netherfield Cosy and the Palace at Bulwell maintained that the main reason for their closure was due to the entertainment tax, rather than the limitations of the buildings.

The remaining reasons the local press gave for cinema closure were the increasingly high operating costs, the lack of films available, and other demands upon the location. In the first case, it was argued that the post-war period saw an escalation in the operating costs that seriously threatened profitability. The manager of one of the largest Nottingham cinemas, for example, claimed that by the mid-1950s cinema running costs were three times what they had been in 1939. Fuel and power prices had risen due to high taxation and workers' wages had increased in proportion.[16] Again this problem was particularly acute for the smaller cinemas and, in a NEP article announcing the closure of the Boulevard, Hyson Green, the manager explained that, like many other smaller cinemas, they 'were finding it impossible to carry on with wages and all other overheads constantly rising'.[17]

A shortage of films created competition between cinemas. The Odeon (formerly the Ritz) tended to get films first

Another manager believed that one of the main problems facing the cinema industry was that the quality of films available was not good enough, and that patterns of cinemagoing were changing: 'People today are shopping for their films ... They are only going for a particular film.' He continued to explain that the cinema industry 'has given us superlatives, but failed to live up to them. What has been hailed as a great film often squeaked like an old mouse.'[18] However, it was not the quality of the films that was the primary problem, but rather the quantity. The 'shortage of film' was, for example, given as another reason for closing the Rank-owned Gaumont. The problem here was also that the three-screen Odeon, Rank's premier cinema in Nottingham, got the key films first, but it was also a more general phenomenon. As film audiences fell, fewer films were made; as fewer films were made, competition for films increased between cinemas; as competition increased, some cinemas were forced out of business; as some cinemas were forced out of business, audiences fell; and so a vicious cycle was established.[19]

However, not all cinema closures were blamed on the above trends. Some cinemas claimed that they were not closing due to falling attendance, but rather that the building's lease had expired or that they had been offered incentives to sell the property. In 1962, for example, the director of the Highbury in Bulwell maintained that the cinema's closure was not due to bad business but that a generous offer had been made for the building by the Co-op.[20] However, it is doubtful that the cinema would have accepted the offer if it had been doing well.

The Perceived Threat of Television

As a result, it was only quite late in the day that the papers started to see television as the main threat to cinema. Indeed, it was only once the entertainment tax was removed that television started to be seen as a major problem. In 1961, for example, the sale of six cinemas from the Levin's Circuit was blamed on the combined factors of television, crippling costs and the late removal of the entertainment tax.[21] The cost of cinemagoing was also seen as a major contributing factor. Once the initial investment had been made, television was relatively cheap: there were no food or transportation costs; no need for a babysitter; and the whole family could watch it together at no extra cost. As a Mrs Dorothy Jackson commented in a letter to the *TV Times*, 'To go to the cinema where I live, to see a decent film, costs £1.25, including bus fares. What we get from ITV in one week would add up to much more.'[22] However, as this quote makes clear, it was not television *per se* that was seen as the threat, but rather commercial television, which began in 1954. Rank's chairman, for example, already believed that this was the case as early as 1956 when he stated:

> having regard to the impact of commercial television during the year, which extended its coverage from London and South to Midlands and Northern counties – it is not surprising that cinema attendances have declined and that profits from exhibition are lower.[23]

He was correct to be more afraid of commercial television than of the BBC. It had overtaken the BBC in the ratings within two years of its launch, probably because, unlike the

BBC, it did not have the educational, highbrow image which alienated so many of the cinema audience. However, commercial television also spurred the BBC into making 'exceptional efforts ... with the result that our theatres and cinemas have to meet additional competition, not only from an ITV that can hardly be described as youthful and struggling, but of a hotted-up BBC as well'.[24]

There were also a further four reasons why television was seen as the main threat by the beginning of the 1960s. First, there was the reduction in the price of televisions. In 1956, the GJ reported that tax on television tubes and radio valves had been reduced which meant that television prices fell. For a 21-inch television, the new price for a cathode ray was £26 8s 6d (plus purchase tax), which was a reduction of £5 10s 1d.[25] Second, after 1960, the number of films on television increased. The four main film trade organisations had introduced a levy of a quarter of a penny on cinema seats, which was used to fund the Film Industry Defence Organisation (FIDO), an organisation that aimed both to persuade film producers not to sell their films to television and to buy the rights to classic films.[26] However, by 1960, this initiative had failed, and the number of films on television began to increase dramatically.

The third reason that television was seen as a threat was the introduction of colour TV which, the industry believed, would remove one of the central advantages of cinema over television – its spectacle. This was the reason given for the closure of the Windsor in 1963,[27] but it seems highly unlikely that colour television would have had any effect on cinema attendance at this time. Colour television was not introduced until 1967, and

Television was only used as an explanation for the decline of cinema from the late 1950s onwards. The Metropole today

even then most programmes were still shown in black and white. Indeed, in 1971, in a letter to the *Radio Times*, P. Pascoe complained about this problem, and made special mention of its relation to sport. In reply, it was explained that the BBC often had to depend on sports coverage from countries that did not yet have colour television, and that many 'excellent and entertaining feature films were made in black-and-white. Their intrinsic quality is sufficient to claim a place for them in the schedules'. The response also claimed that about 90 per cent of programmes were broadcast in colour and that this percentage was increasing.[28] The reference to colour television in relation to the closure of the Windsor was therefore probably due to the fact that colour television was a 'hot topic' at the time, and the main reason for the closure of the Windsor was actually the expiration of its ground lease.

The fourth and final reason that television was supposed to present a threat to the cinema was due to its sports programming. Since sport was largely seen as a male interest, and men had greater purchasing power, sports programming was used as an incentive for men to buy a TV and, as we will see, these decisions caused considerable tension in some families. Sport had always been a rival to the cinema as far as male audiences were concerned, but the decision to televise sport on Saturday nights was considered to be particularly damaging. The general secretary of the National Association of Theatrical and Cine Employees sent a telegram to the Football League asking them to abandon their proposed agreement with ATV. In this message, he claimed that Saturday night football matches would dramatically affect attendance at provincial cinemas, many of which depended on their Saturday night takings. The telegram also claimed that these televised matches would hit the whole of the cinema industry and might lead to a complete breakdown in British film production. However, in 1956, both the ATV and the BBC offers were rejected by the Football League, which feared that the televised sport would both lead to a decline in gate takings and adversely affect minor sports which would not get televised.[29] However, this decision was soon reversed and, until the 1970s, only sports-related programmes could be televised on Saturday mornings and early afternoons.[30]

Conclusion

As we have seen, for much of the 1950s, the decline in cinema attendance was largely blamed on the high taxation the industry faced in the form of the entertainment tax, which was compounded by other factors relating to the condition of the film industry itself. It was only towards the end of the 1950s that television was seen as a major threat. The meaning of television, however, was itself related to wider changes that were taking place in British society during the 1950s. The 'age of affluence' altered many people's leisure habits and these changes are the subject of the following chapter.

Notes

1. Spanos, 1962, p. 22.
2. NEN, 29 April 1955.
3. GJ, 26 June 1956.

4. *Board of Trade Journal*, 22 August 1958, p. 388.

5. GJ, 26 June 1956.

6. GJ, 25 April 1957.

7. GJ, 18 April 1957.

8. *Board of Trade Journal*, 16 July 1969, p. 158.

9. GJ, 10 July 1956.

10. Ibid.

11. NEP, 29 April 1955.

12. NEP, 19 October 1959.

13. They both still managed to show films in CinemaScope but, as Hornsey pointed out, a screen of 15 by 20 did not show the technology or the cinema off to their best advantage: Hornsey, 1994, p. 9.

14. NEP, 10 February 1957.

15. NEP, 6 January 1971.

16. GJ, 26 June 1956.

17. NEP, 21 May 1956.

18. NEP, 22 October 1959.

19. See Spanos, 1962.

20. GJ, 2 March 1962.

21. GJ, 26 August 1961.

22. *TV Times*, 22 July 1971, p. 45.

23. NEP, 12 September 1956.

24. GJ, 16 April 1959.

25. GJ, 30 June 1956.

26. Buscombe, 1991, p. 202.

27. NEP, 9 March 1963.

28. *Radio Times*, 11 March 1971, p. 57.

29. GJ, 21 July 1956.

30. *TV Times*, 21 January 1971, p. 53.

9

Locality, Affluence and Urban Decay

Beyond the Threat of Television

As we have seen, television was only introduced as an explanation for the decline of cinema at a relatively late stage after the most significant decline in cinema attendance and, consequently, many critics have suggested other reasons for the post-war fate of cinema. For example, as Docherty, Morrison and Tracey put it, television was not the guilty party but, on the contrary, it 'was framed; the real culprits were Elvis Presley, expresso coffee, the Town and Country Planning Act of 1947 and the sclerosis of the British exhibition industry'.[1] That is, they claim that cinema attendance was threatened by the development of new forms of entertainment, particularly for the young, and most importantly by the removal of large sections of the population from town centres to new suburban developments:

> The Town and Country Planning Act of 1947 completely transformed the conditions for a successful film industry. The Act led to the clearing of slums, the growth of new towns, the rebuilding of city centres and, crucially, the resiting of large sections of the working class. Between 1931 and the 1970s the inner cities lost around one-third of their population while the number of people living around the edges of the cities grew by around one quarter ... The population which sustained the cinema in the inner cities moved out.[2]

Docherty, Morrison and Tracey argue that this problem was compounded by a miscalculation on the part of the film industry, which 'believed that its fight was with an alternative technology for delivering moving pictures', the television, and therefore 'struck back at the technological level' by offering bigger and better spectacle, rather than by 're-siting the cinemas and following the audience to the new housing estates'.[3]

There is some local evidence to support this case. When St Ann's was cleared and many people were dispatched to out-of-town estates, the local cinemas in the area lost their patrons. The loss of audiences due to slum clearance was also identified as the reason for the closure of the Orion, Alfreton Road, although the entertainment tax and rising overheads were also mentioned. According to the circuit spokesman: 'the cinema was in a slum area with houses coming down and the regular patrons leaving for other districts'.[4] The exodus to the suburbs was also given as the reason for the fall in the membership of the Mechanics Institute.[5]

However, the problem was not simply supposed to be geographical relocation. The move to the suburbs also involved a change in domestic routines. It took longer for those in work to get home, and this not only made the evenings shorter but thereby created less time to go out. The impact that the new estates had on city-centre entertainment was explained in detail by one respondent in the Nottingham oral history archive, who had been a tram conductor during the period:

> When people got to Clifton, well they didn't want to come to the Theatre Royal, to the Empire, to the Odeon, to the Gaumont or the other places of amusement, only on rare occasions or when there was something that was highly sensational, so you got a fall off in your attendances at cinemas and theatres and so on, and you got a fall off in traffic, y'see and the pubs and other places of entertainment not on the same standard as what were in the City were introduced at the Aspley's and Bilborough's and the Sherwood's and the Bestwoods estates. The people didn't want, after they'd gone home, they didn't want to go out, particularly on Monday to Fridays, Saturday and Sunday were a different kettle of fish ... the central means of leisure were being limited or curtailed or reduced and so was your pubs and other places that were ... and there, they were either stopping at home then you got television come in, that a person who'd been at work, had been transported three miles from the centre of the city, got home, wanted to go three miles to the pictures when he could look at the television or go to the pub which was being set up ... in the area where he lived ... particularly you've got outside areas ... Mansfield was developing its own type of entertainment ...[6]

A letter from a woman who wanted to see *The Ipcress File* demonstrated some of the difficulties involved in getting to the cinema that resulted from a change of domestic rhythms. She had a car and therefore transport was not a problem for her. However, the timing of the films did not fit in well with her domestic routines; it was difficult for her to get to the film for 5.40 p.m. because her husband returned home from work at this time, and she did not want to go to the late showing which made a trip to the cinema into a major event and meant that she returned home too late.[7]

There are, however, significant problems with the claims of Docherty and his colleagues. On the one hand, as we saw in Part Three, there is no reason why suburbanisation in and of itself should have produced such a problem. Indeed, it was the inter-war programmes of suburbanisation that created the conditions for the peak years of cinema attendance and, during this inter-war period, the industry followed the audiences out to the suburbs without any difficulties. On the other hand, as Martin Barker and Kate Brooks have argued, the evidence simply does not support the suburbanisation thesis. As Barker and Brooks put it:

> The suburbanisation thesis would predict that the city centre cinemas would be hardest hit. In fact, the opposite is the case! Of the 22 cinemas that died in the key decade only 4 were city centre cinemas, while 18 were suburban. They provide the basis for our alternative explanation. Cinemas died because for a complex of reasons people discontinued the idea of the 'family night out'. Where they did, they tended to 'do it properly' by going into town – hence the disproportionate survival of city centre cinemas. This was the beginning of the process by which city centres at night became mainly the preserve of young people.[8]

'The suburbanisation thesis would predict that city centre cinemas would be hardest hit. In fact, the opposite was the case!'. The Majestic today, Woodborough Road, Mapperley

The trouble with Barker and Brooks' account is that it only alludes to, but does not detail, this 'complex of reasons'.

However, despite its problems, the account provided by Docherty avoids the privatisation thesis present in many accounts of the decline of cinema. As we saw in the last chapter, many accounts of suburbanisation present it as part of a retreat from the public world of urban life into a privatised world of the suburban family, and television is often used as the key signifier in this process.[9] However, as Shaun Moores has pointed out, 'while television and radio have contributed to a domestication of popular entertainment – part of a larger process of "withdrawal into interior space" (Donzelot 1980) – they have also opened the household up to electronically mediated public worlds'.[10] He therefore invokes Williams' concept of 'mobile privatisation'[11] but emphasises both sides of the process. It is not simply about a retreat into the private but, on the contrary, this concept also suggests that 'the walls of the home are now more permeable, and far away events can be witnessed on TV virtually at the time they happen'. Nor was it simply that people were increasingly able to witness the outside without ever having to leave the home, but also that many were becoming ever more mobile. At the same time as television was supposedly keeping people indoors, cars and package tours were increasingly taking them further and further afield. Rather than a retreat into privacy, this period saw a major transformation of many people's experience of space, which profoundly affected the experience and meaning of locality.

As a consequence, a 'night out' increasingly meant a night in town rather than a night in what had previously been seen as the 'local' area, and our findings clearly show that, since the 1950s, people have been prepared to travel even further for a night out at the pictures. As we will see, not only do many people today come into town from all over the region for a night at the pictures from places as far afield as Loughborough, Derby and Southwell, but also many Nottingham residents stated a preference for cinemas outside Nottingham, particularly the ABC Mansfield. In other words, people's understanding of what constitutes their 'local area' changes with greater mobility.

However, as Doreen Massey points out, greater mobility for some frequently leads to less mobility for others,[12] and as a car culture developed throughout the 1950s and 1960s, public transport was increasingly cut back by government, a move that limited the mobility of others. Most significantly, as John Giggs has noted, the local train services that linked many Nottingham suburbs 'closed before the 1960s',[13] a move that not only limited the mobility of many Nottingham residents but also fundamentally transformed the geography of the city. These local rail lines had circled the city and allowed for movement between suburbs but, as they closed, public transport was increasingly organised on a radial pattern with the city centre as its hub. Thus closure of the local railways cut suburbs off from one another and movement between them increasingly required a journey into the city centre and another journey out again.

For Docherty and his collegues, the decline in cinema attendance and the rise of television viewing are connected, but not in the way that is often suggested:

> Rather than asserting a causal connection between cinema and television it is more accurate to say that the rise in television was caused by the same process underlying the decline in cinema attendance. Just as the conditions for the cinema emerged during one phase of industrial capitalism, which created a working-class concentration in large industrial conglomerations, with increased leisure time and a financial surplus; so the conditions for television were created by a rise in real wages, comfortable homes and the emergence of the nuclear family, which was concurrent with the sense that the working-class extended family was breaking up.[14]

While cinemagoing had been associated with luxury, affluence and social mobility during the inter-war period, it was the home, the car and the television set which became the key symbols of affluence in the post-war period.

Affluence and Leisure

One factor that might explain the vast disjunctive between the experience of British and American patterns of cinemagoing in the ten years after World War II was the continued presence of rationing in Britain. While there were initial fears that America might return to Depression at the end of the war, it in fact experienced a period of virtually unrivalled prosperity. This situation created new symbols of affluence and new fantasies of abundance that displaced cinema from the position of centrality that it had enjoyed during the inter-war period. In Britain, however, the debts of the war created an 'age of austerity', and rationing continued well into the 1950s. The rationing of tea, sugar, sweets, butter, meat and cheese, for example, were only phased out between 1952 and 1954. Therefore, 1955 was a critical year that symbolised the dawning of a new 'age of affluence'. This change resulted in what Stuart Laing has described as an embourgeoisement thesis: not only did the television and the car become symbols of the new affluence but also it was claimed that the new prosperity that they symbolised had brought an end to class divisions. Thus, the old working classes were not only becoming affluent, but they were becoming indistinguishable from the middle classes: they were becoming bourgeois.[15]

This new affluence, and the patterns of consumption associated with it, were also clearly organised around the 'domestic unit of consumption'. Central to this process was the political promotion of home ownership. While the inter-war and the immediate post-war periods saw a massive programme of slum clearance and house building, the assumption was that many of the new buildings would be rented out, whether by local councils or private companies. In 1953, however, a White Paper on housing shifted the emphasis to owner occupation 'as Conservative rhetoric switched away from the number of houses built to the importance of owner-occupation by the individual family'.[16] This shift was significant in a number of ways. It not only allowed the Conservatives to direct the issue away from the quality of the existing housing stock, it also operated ideologically. Owner occupation became a sign of the increasingly middle-class or classless nature of British society, but it was also believed both by left and right that owner occupation would actually create a nation of Conservative voters. Once committed to home ownership, it was believed, the values of working-class people would become indistinguishable from those of the middle class.

Home ownership also had other implications. It helped consolidate a 'domestic unit of consumption', a unit of consumption that was not the individual but supposedly the family itself, and the emergence of this unit enabled the development of 'consumer durables' that were directed at the home as a unit of consumption. In this context, the car and the television acquired special significance, and as Laing puts it:

> While car ownership spread less quickly than that of many domestic consumer durables it was more important in the imagery of affluence precisely because of its unavoidable visibility. The car out the front (or, even better, in the drive) together with the television aerial above symbolised the new way of life within. Television was, of course, the defining symbolic object of affluence. In 1951 there were still only 650,000 sets in Britain; by 1964 this had increased to 13 million – a rate of increasing outstripping every other domestic appliance.[17]

On the one hand, home ownership was associated with a notion of affluence of which the television was also a symbol but, on the other, home ownership for some also led to a greater importance of the home as a site for leisure and consumption.

As Garnham has pointed out in another context, the larger an investment is as a proportion of income, the more likely it is that this investment will become the focus of future investment. As Garnham argues in the case of television:

> consumption in cultural goods and participation in cultural practices increases in range and amount over virtually the whole spectrum of activities (except TV viewing) as income rises. This is hardly surprising. It is just normally ignored in discussions of cultural policy. The higher level of TV consumption among the poorer sections of the community is attributable to the higher proportions of their total discretionary expenditure tied up in the relatively fixed investment in the TV set and licence. Once this investment is made, subsequent consumption is virtually free, making them a captive audience.[18]

In this situation, not only is most leisure time invested in the watching of television, but most future financial investments are made in relation to the television, investments that will extend and enhance the original investment, such as investments in video players or in cable and satellite subscriptions.

In much the same way, for many of the new home-owners, the initial investment in the home not only encouraged people to centre more and more of their leisure time around this major financial investment, but it also encouraged them to make the home the recipient of further financial investments that might raise its value. As a result, the period not only saw a boom in leisure within the home but the amount spent on improving their homes also increased.

As a result, Mark Abrams, the managing director of Research Services Ltd, claimed that private consumption – expenditure on food, housing, fuel, light, household goods, private motoring and foreign travel – had increased markedly between the late 1940s and the late 1950s. He also believed that the trend would continue and that 'the average British consumer would spend more of his increasing affluence on making his home cleaner, warmer, brighter and better equipped'. This was in contrast to the amount spent on alcohol, tobacco, clothing and 'public' entertainment, which had all suffered a relative decline.[19] W. G. Bennett, a Nottingham cinema manager, also claimed at the Mechanics Institute Debating Society that TV, the do-it-yourself craze, home hobbies and the growing number of car owners had helped to keep thousands of people away from cinemas.[20]

Although car ownership created an opposite trend by taking people out of the home, it was still a family-centred activity. According to Mark Abrams, the biggest relative change in spending during the period was in relation to the motor car and, in 1959, one in four families had a car, a trend that heavily affected attendance at public entertainments. Once an investment had been made in a car, there was an incentive to realise the value of that investment by making it an alternative focus for leisure activities, such as a day out or a family caravaning holiday. The running costs of a car also made other forms of entertainment less affordable. The car also posed another problem for the cinema: parking in town became increasingly difficult, and those with cars became increasingly resistant to leisure activities that required them to use public transport.

However, it is important not to overstate the extent to which leisure time became more home-centred. Working people and especially their children had always felt an attachment to home, and while it is true that they had a less materialistic experience of home than the middle classes, this does not mean that they did not value domestic objects.[21] Furthermore, while architectural historian Alison Ravetz claims that DIY 'did not gain full momentum until the later 1950s',[22] the working class had always done their own repairs and decorating. This took a considerable amount of time but, unlike post-war home improvements, was designed primarily to save money rather than to increase the financial value of the home. Another difference in the post-war period was that certain sections of the middle classes started to do work on their own houses, rather than paying others to do it for them and, in the process, home improvements started to acquire new meanings. Increasingly, home improvements came to signify not only the material upkeep of the home, but also increasingly expressed the individualised lifestyle of the family.

Furthermore, demographic changes meant that there was more space for domestic leisure activities. Working-class leisure had traditionally taken place outside the home because there had not been enough space for it, not because they did not 'feel at home'. The lack of space was partly to do with house size and partly due to the lack of central heating, which meant that the use of rooms was restricted for much of the year. It was also a result of large families which meant that children and adolescents had to spend more time out of the home. Once the size of families fell from a national average of 4.5 in 1911 to 3.4 in 1951,[23] more space was available in the home. Children might get their own room, where they could read or do homework without interruption, and fathers felt less pressure to visit the public house as a way of escaping noisy children or bath night in front of the fire. Heating, of course, remained a problem into the 1960s and 1970s, and working-class families still had less space and more people per house. For example, as Pearl Jephcott found in her 1967 study of three towns in Scotland, one-third of adolescents had six or more people living in the home.[24]

Thus, there was both a perceived and real increase in the amount of time spent at home. This was reflected in the local press which reported that more people were drinking, reading and even playing guitars in their homes.[25] In 1959, D. Fry of the Nottingham and District Off Licences Protection Association claimed that TV and foreign travel had increased wine drinking 'to an unprecedented level' and that TV 'must surely have helped if it has encouraged drinking in the home'. He explained that there had been a 50 per cent rise in sales between 1950 and 1957.[26] The Nottinghamshire Education Committee also reported that the number of readers borrowing books from its county libraries had gone up by a third and that the number of books issued had risen by 50 per cent in the five years prior to 1958.[27] In 1959, the director of Allen and Unwin claimed that there had been a six-fold increase in book sales since 1939, and that he believed that this was the result of rising education and higher incomes,[28] although the introduction of Penguin paperbacks in 1935, which sold at about 6d, probably had a greater impact on book ownership.[29] These contemporary articles contradict historian Arthur Marwick's claim that people were actually reading less and that book sales were

The new affluence created a whole series of new leisure forms that competed with the cinema for the population's leisure time, displacing cinema from the centre of people's leisure. The Ritz today

lower in the 1960s than they had been in the 1930s.[30] Halsey's figures, on the other hand, support the contemporary evidence and he argues that book sales had in fact increased by 90 per cent since 1939.[31] Another problem with Marwick's position is that it does not take into account the number of books that were being borrowed from libraries, which almost doubled between 1932 and 1963 from 247,335 to 460,504.

In other words, the new affluence created a whole series of new leisure forms that competed with the cinema for the population's leisure time, displacing cinema from the centre of people's leisure. While the town centre became the prime location for 'a night out', the town centre itself was now in competition with the motor car as well as the home as the focus of leisure activities.

The Changing Meanings of the City Centre

In the process, the meaning of the town centre was also changing. By the 1960s, as with many other cities, the migration of people from the town centre led to its decline and decay and, for many people, it was seen a dangerous and alien place.[32] Several letters to the local press complained about the roughness of the town centre and claimed that it put people off making trips into town, particularly after dark. Women in particular felt threatened and two young women wrote to the local press to express their outrage when one of them was 'seized' by two 'drunken louts'. They also claimed to have witnessed 'several violent incidents' in which bus conductors had been attacked by youths. They demanded: 'How can a decent young woman enjoy an evening in the city if the present state continues?'[33] These fears were also fuelled by the bus drivers' strike in 1965, which was organised in protest against the number of violent attacks made upon them at night: there were reputed to have been fifteen such attacks in 1965 alone.[34]

Cinema was particularly implicated in this process. As early as the mid-1950s, Teddy boys had caused disturbances in the cinemas, giving the impression that cinema had been appropriated by troublesome teenagers. However, another letter blamed cinema and television for 'Saturday night hooliganism', and claimed that the root of the problem was 'the lower moral standards generally accepted' which were 'largely the result of a sustained programme of X-films, kitchen-sink [drama] and such things as the BBC deletion of "Lift Up Your Hearts" programme'.[35] As audiences changed, many cinemas turned to the X-rated feature to stay in business, a move that alienated certain audiences still further but also came to be blamed for the very sense of urban decay of which they were the product.

One reason for this sense of decay was not a lack of investment, but ironically the exact opposite. As an NEP article of 4 December 1962 noted, 'Britain's cities of the Sixties are becoming just a man-made hell'. It was claimed that 'in an economy where there is full employment and a steady level of prosperity coupled with high rents, it becomes profitable to pull down city centres and erect tall buildings'. As a result, the town centre was converted from a place of residence into one of office buildings. This process accounts for some of the concerns above. A city centre dominated by office workers empties out after work and can have a desolate and threatening atmosphere at night.

However, the article also complained about the effect on the city-centre environment during the day: 'Nobody would dispute that part of the city mystique is busyness and bustle, but nowadays this quality has become frantic, with hordes of people neurotically hurrying from place to place, breathing petrol fumes, and becoming almost the quarry of the metallic monsters that belch out the smoke.' While some of these machines are clearly seen as those 'ripping old buildings to pieces and replacing them with huge office blocks', the car was particularly singled out as a major cause of the city centre's problem 'which is forcing renewal'. The article therefore quoted Mr Thomas of the Town and County Planning Association, 'a "pressure" group which has as its objective "decent living conditions and the opportunities for a full life"'. According to Mr Thomas, the car was increasingly determining the agenda of city redevelopment. As he puts it, 'We have to keep it moving ... park it, and prevent conflict between pedestrians and cars.'

However, despite the 'high profit to be made by putting [money] into the redevelopment of town centres', the article stressed that the same is not true of residential housing. It quotes Mr Thomas who rather prophetically claimed that 'the tragedy is that we are still building thousands of substandard houses and will bitterly regret it'. As he went on to add: 'There is a clear conflict between the commercially advantageous rebuilding of city centres and what is desirable for civilised standards of living.' His solution was to scale down the size of cities and develop new towns where the scale and pace of life would not create 'the miserable conditions in which people are being forced to live' at the present. Thus, as the article noted, while the 'age old choice has been between city life and that in rural surroundings … even the enthusiasts are beginning to find that cities in the sixties are fast becoming unbearable'.[36]

Similar concerns were being voiced in other cities and other countries. Indeed, 1962 was also the year that witnessed the publication of Jane Jacobs' classic critique of urban planning and redevelopment, *The Death and Life of Great American Cities*.[37] In it, she articulated a growing sense of opposition to the transformation of the urban landscape by government and developers and the 'demand that local communities should have greater say in the shaping – and especially the reshaping – of their own neighbour-hoods'.[38] Similar arguments were also being made about the clearance of the East End slums. For example, as Laing has pointed out, best-selling sociological studies such as *Family and Kinship in East London* and *Education and the Working Class* 'ultimately offered a defence, and even a celebration of certain "traditional" working-class life-styles and values which became easily lost in the move to more modern, expansive and mate-rially comfortable ways of life'.[39] They therefore presented a critique of the developers and educationalists who sought to impose their own order upon this class, rather than accepting and developing 'the best qualities of working-class living'.[40]

Notes

1. Docherty, Morrison and Tracey, 1987, p. 5.
2. Ibid., pp. 25–6.
3. Ibid., p. 28.
4. NEN, 10 April 1959.
5. NEP, 20 April 1959.
6. Nottingham oral history archive transcript: A35/a–b/1: 19–20.
7. EPN, 1 June 1965.
8. Barker and Brooks, 1998, p. 189.
9. See Silverstone, 1997.
10. Moores, 2000, p. 5.
11. Williams, 1974.
12. Massey, 1994.
13. Giggs, 1997, p. 460.
14. Docherty, Morrison and Tracey, 1987, p. 25 (although we would point out that the nuclear family long predates this period).
15. Laing, 1986, p. 17.
16. Ibid., p. 26.
17. Ibid., p. 29.
18. Garnham, 1990, pp. 124–5.
19. NEP, 18 November 1959.
20. NEP, 22 October 1959.
21. See Faire, 1998, p. 178.
22. Ravetz, 1995, p. 169.
23. *Census 1951 England and Wales: Housing Report*, London: HMSO, 1956, p. xxiii.
24. Jephcott, 1967, p. 104.

25. According to the EPN, 'Beatlemania has brought such a demand for guitars ... that thousands are having to be imported from abroad.' One of Nottingham's biggest guitar shops claimed that they sold sixty guitars a week, and they would sell more if they were available: 'With wages in the city factories high, Nottingham's young people can often afford the best in six-stringed music, and they buy it': EPN, 11 December 1963.

26. NEP, 20 October 1959.

27. GJ, 9 July 1958.

28. GJ, 29 October 1959.

29. Clarke, 1996, p. 212.

30. Marwick, 1982, 1996, p. 136.

31. Halsey, 1972, p. 565.

32. EPN, 17 July 1965; EPN, 31 July 1965.

33. EPN, 21 July 1965.

34. EPN, 23 July 1965.

35. EPN, 27 July 1965.

36. NEP, 4 December 1962.

37. Jacobs, 1962.

38. Hall, 1996, p. 262.

39. Laing, 1986, p. 46.

40. Jackson and Marsden, 1966, p. 224. See also Young and Wilmott, 1957.

10

From Cinemagoing to Television Viewing: The Developing Meanings of a New Medium

Changing Places: Film and the Transformation of Television

While television is often seen as responsible for the decline in cinemagoing, most people consume cinemagoing and television as different, rather than rival, experiences. Indeed, one problem with seeing television as the major threat to cinema is that this claim is usually made in retrospect, and hence ignores the extent to which the meaning of each activity is defined in relation to the other.[1] In 1948, for example, during its negotiations with J. Arthur Rank, the BBC had maintained that: 'It is no part of the Corporation's intention to convert the BBC Television Service into a home cinema, showing mainly commercial films. It has a far more serious responsibility.'[2] This attitude had already been noted by Rank in 1946, and he believed that it was responsible for driving young people into the cinema.[3] Since the BBC displayed a contempt for films and believed that it had a far loftier educational mission, it was often seen as dull and didactic, particularly by the young. This partly explains why the BBC averaged only one feature film per week in the 1950s, although it was also due to the pressure of the exhibitors, who were trying to prevent films from being sold to television. As a result, the ATV schedule was not much different and, although TV schedules varied from week to week, the ATV schedule that we looked at for 1956 did not have any films at all.

This situation meant that if people were staying at home rather than going to the cinema, they were probably not seeing as many films as before, and they were certainly not getting the choice offered by the local cinemas. The films that they did see would also have been quite old, and probably from before 1938. However, from 1960, the number of films shown by the BBC increased dramatically. By July 1966, there were six films shown in the second week of July, although this may not have been representative as it was during the World Cup. In February 1971, the number of films per week had increased to fourteen, and this was about standard for the next decade with seventeen films being shown in the same week in February 1976 and fifteen in the same week in February 1981. The main difference between 1966 and 1976 was that ITV was showing films on weekend afternoons, and there were occasional films on Saturday mornings for children. By 1976, there was also a film every day of the week, which had not been the case in 1966 and 1971, and ITV and BBC were showing films in competition. There were also special weekly slots for certain types of films – the Western being a classic example. By the 1970s, then, television had become the primary site of film consumption. More people consumed more films via the television than at the cinema, and while this change was due, in part, to FIDO's failure to prevent films from being sold to television, it was also due to a more general change in the meanings of both television and the cinema.

Indeed, when one refers to 'films on television', one needs to be careful. The figures above are actually for 'feature films', but it is worth stressing that it was only with the advent of television that the term 'film' came to mean 'feature film'. Early on, the BBC's use of the term 'film' did not refer to feature films alone, but anything that was recorded using film or which might have composed part of an evening's programme at the cinema. Hence, *The Magic Roundabout* was a 'French film', and there were also documentary films, as opposed to documentary programmes, and 'film series' such as *Bewitched* and *Dr Kildare*.

One of the problems here is that it was only during this period that a night out at the cinema became predominantly about watching a single feature film rather than a full evening's programme. Critics have often opposed cinema and television specifically through assumption that cinema viewing was concerned with a bounded text (the feature

The decline in cinema-going was related to the changing meaning of town centres, which were increasingly seen as dangerous and alien places. The Ritz today

film) while television was predominantly about sequence or flow.[4] However, it was only in the 1950s and 1960s that people started to see films in separate performances.[5] Prior to this, cinema had also been about the sequence and flow of the programme but, as television started to schedule feature films, the meaning of cinema was reconstructed as one almost solely about the viewing of a single feature film. As cinema became less a habit and more of a special event, the feature film became the focus of that event and the rest of the programme fell away. In other words, the programming of feature films on television was part of the process through which the meaning of a night at the cinema changed.

This change, however, was highly significant, and needs to be understood in terms of the changing nature of the film audience. During this period, the cinema audience was becoming predominantly middle class, or rather a process was taking place by which the cinemas were not only losing their working-class audience, but cinema was gaining in respectability in the process. As Garnham has pointed out, as forms of popular entertainment lose their traditional popular audiences, they become a rare taste, which enables and encourages their appropriation by the very classes that had previously despised them.[6] The focus on the individual film was therefore not only closer to the consumption patterns of pure and legitimate taste, but it was a strategy already associated with the art cinema.[7]

The meaning of cinema also changed in other ways. As Barbara Klinger has pointed out, it was during this period that the cinema of the 1930s and the 1940s came to be reconstructed as 'classics'. As the cinema audience dwindled, film societies and repertory cinemas began to spring up in Britain and America that specialised in reruns of 'classics' of the 'Old Hollywood'.[8] Television was also participating in the process. In order to make old films desirable events, they had to be recontextualised as 'classics' rather than simply outdated relics of a bygone medium. Television not only featured Western series, but also showed 'matinees' and 'the Saturday Night Movie', all of which alluded to, and worked to create, a notion of a golden age of cinema. These processes also worked to construct a profound sense of nostalgia for the cinema in which 'the "Old" in many cases appeared better and more authentic than the "New"'.[9] The very films that had been seen as the epitome of shoddy inauthenticity came to be redefined through their opposition to a supposedly shoddy and inauthentic present.

Consuming Television: The Cultural Meanings of a Material Object

However, the television was not simply the programmes that it showed, just as the cinema was not only the films that it projected. The television was also a material object and, as Shove and Southerton have argued, one should not isolate and abstract individual household objects 'from the contexts and circumstances in which they are acquired and used'.[10] For example, the acquisition of the television set was shaped by a series of different factors. In 1950 about 3.2 per cent of wired households had a television, but by 1960 this had increased to 73.7 per cent and, by 1970, 93.4 per cent of households had a black-and-white television and 3.6 per cent had a colour television.[11] In 1954, the *Daily Mail Ideal Home Book* claimed that the peak audience was around

8 million and that the majority of viewers were in families earning under £12 per week.[12] This was possibly a 'popular' conception of TV viewers and Needleman showed a quite different pattern of ownership in the *National Institute Economic Review* in 1960. According to Needleman, in 1956 (only two years after the *Daily Mail* article) 50.5 per cent of middle-class homes had a television as compared with 35.5 per cent of working-class homes. By 1958, this gap had closed, and 53.4 per cent of middle-class homes had a television compared with 51.1 per cent of working-class homes.[13] This pattern was different from some parts of the USA, where the middle classes seemed to be more reluctant to buy televisions.[14] The highbrow image of the BBC was probably partly responsible for this difference, and the middle-class attitudes of the management were reflected in TV scheduling such as the 'Toddler's Truce' which was designed to fit the daily rhythms of middle-class households.[15]

Gender was also a significant factor in the acquisition of the television. As Tim O'Sullivan found in his oral histories, men were usually 'ultimately responsible for the decision to buy the set',[16] and this position is confirmed by Sue Bowden and Avner Offer's analysis of sales figures. They conclude that 'time-using goods', such as televisions and radios, were bought before 'time-saving goods', such as washing machines, because men had greater purchasing power within the home, and 'time-using goods' were seen to benefit the whole family unlike 'time-saving goods' which were considered only to benefit their wives.[17] Van Zoonen and Wieten also found a similar pattern in 1950s' Netherlands where television was 'hardly ever a result of the needs of women in the family'.[18] Also, since hire-purchase forms had to be signed by the head of the household,[19] the set was generally seen as belonging to the man of the house who was also considered the legal owner. In 1960, when Margret Ward's ex-husband broke into her home and took the television set, the police told her that she had to let him take it because he had bought it.[20] This remained the situation until the Matrimonial Property Act of 1970, when it was decreed that household goods that were paid for by a husband were also partly owned by his 'non-working' wife.

Male ownership of the television set also had implications for its use. On a domestic level, some men felt that they had the right to decide how it should be used. They made the decision about when and what to watch, and this created conflict between couples. In a letter to the *TV Times*, one woman complained that her husband, who was the one who usually switched on the television, would go to bed without switching it off. Furthermore, she also claimed that, when the alarm sounded at shutdown, she was the one that was expected to leap out of bed to turn it off.[21] An extreme example from the NEP was one husband who would remove the plug from the television to make sure that his wife did not watch the set while he was out and, in this case, the wife filed for divorce on the grounds of cruelty, and won.[22]

A Matter of Taste: Conflicts over Television Programming

Television programming and content was another reason for discord between couples, and these clashes over taste were more likely to make it into the letters page than conflicts over usage. For example, Mrs Challender wrote to the *Radio Times* and complained about the clash between *Elizabeth R* and *Sportsnight*:

I can foresee six weeks of argument with my husband. He is addicted to *Sportsnight* with
Coleman (BBC1), whereas I don't wish to miss the new series *Elizabeth R* (BBC2). This
conflict must arise in a lot of families. Please do not tell me to get two television sets. Do
change one of these programmes to another night or time.[23]

The assumption of both Mrs Challender and the BBC was that it was the wife who would
have to give way. Some women also felt that the programmers were responsible for this
conflict. They believed that the programmers were aware of who had the domestic purchasing power and therefore geared television towards the tastes and interests of men.
In 1976, two letters to the *TV Times* complained about this. As the first put it:

I live in a man-less household and we have for years criticised the way both channels cater
for men's sports programmes on Saturday afternoons. BBC2 put on a film but is always a
man's film. Us females can lump it.

It ended by commenting: 'I suspect that the powers-that-be are all men.'[24] The second
letter also wanted to know 'Why is it that only men are catered for on television?' and
felt that this bias was demonstrated by the fact that, while 'manufactured women, made
to look excessively exciting' were continually on television, there was no equivalent for
women.[25]

However, while there seems to have been a bias to male tastes and interests, this
should not be overemphasised. The reply to Mrs Challender's letter stated that the '"sex
war" which the conflicting attractions of *Sportsnight* and *Elizabeth R* had provoked . . . is
without precedent'. In the previous year, they claimed, the BBC had shown *The Six Wives
of Henry VIII* at the same time as *Sportsnight* 'which met with almost no complaint and
attracted a very high audience to BBC2'.[26] Furthermore, analysis of the programmes on
BBC in 1955–56 reveals that sport got only slightly more coverage than light entertainment and comedy: 11.9 per cent of programmes broadcast were on sport compared with
13.2 per cent on light comedy and entertainment, although there were another 9.3 per
cent on news and sports news. Children's programmes also made up 15.6 per cent of
the schedules, which was the second highest coverage after documentaries, which made
up 21.7 per cent. Between 1955 and 1989, the percentage of programmes on sport
remained the same – around 12–14 per cent – while the number of light entertainment
and children's programmes fell to around 6–8 per cent. This decline also coincided with
an increase in the number of films shown which seemed to fill the gap left by light
entertainment.[27]

However, gender conflicts were not the only tensions that surrounded the television.
There were also conflicts between the different age groups. While Barclay's survey of
Scottish adolescents claimed that teenagers were allowed to watch pretty much what
they liked on TV,[28] the report also noted that there was a great deal of argument between
teenagers and parents over what to watch, and that parents usually won. Those teenagers
who remained at school were more likely to have their viewing regulated – which suggests that regulation was more class-based since middle-class children tended to remain

at school longest. However, conflicts between different age groups were not confined to the family, and there were public complaints over the amount of programming devoted to teenagers. One pensioner complained:

> ITV should devote less time to teenagers and a little more to old people. There is already 45 minutes of *Thank Your Lucky Stars* and now *Ready, Steady, Go* is back again. Couldn't this half hour be given to pensioners?[29]

However, as one teenager responded:

> Does Mrs Hobbis know that there are about 65 hours (I counted) of television in one week? One hour and 15 minutes of this is for teenagers, and about six hours and 15 minutes of it for children, leaving 57 hours and 30 minutes for adults. I don't mind pensioners having a half-hour to themselves, but could they have it out of adults' time instead of that of teenagers?

The lack of programmes for teenagers may explain why the Governor Director of Sales Consultants believed that teenagers were not that interested in TV and that, when they did watch it, they did so at particular times of the day: 'Television is not so much use in selling teenage products ... They're never in to watch it except in the early or late evening.'[30] The lack of teenage programmes could have been one reason why cinema continued to be popular with this audience throughout the 1960s when adults were staying away. However, it was more likely that there was little provision on television for teenagers because teenagers were resistant to television viewing as an activity. Teenagers preferred the cinema because it was not subject to parental surveillance, while television's location within the home made parental surveillance virtually inevitable.

The Uses of Television

While it may have been the centre of various familial conflicts, the television was also seen as a way of bringing the family together through laughter or by provoking discussion.[31] As one letter writer to the *TV Times* put it: 'Who said that "the box" has killed the art of conversation? In our house it has the opposite effect. Without the television we read in silence, but watching it revives memories, stimulates discussion and leads to many witticisms.'[32] Another asked for a blank screen after each programme 'for three to five minutes to allow family talk and discussion of what has been seen'.[33] There were also quite a number of letters to the *TV Times* that asked for information to resolve family disagreements that had arisen while discussing TV programmes.[34] Furthermore, the association between television viewing and family life was demonstrated in 1956 when miners at Bolsover Colliery went on strike until the Coal Board would agree to their request to end their shift fifteen minutes early at 8.45 p.m. so 'that they could have more time in the evenings to be with their families and to watch TV'.[35]

Television viewing also had other familial uses. Both O'Sullivan and Goodman, for example, have referred to the way in which television was used as a way of rewarding children for good behaviour,[36] but it was also used as a form of childminder. In his study of radio and domestic routines, for example, Shaun Moores has argued that in the 1930s the BBC attempted to plan its radio schedule around everyday routines, so that there were children's programmes at lunchtime and when they came home from school, and that the news was on at night after adults had returned from work.[37] He also noted that 'children's hour' was scheduled to coincide with the preparation of the evening meal when housewives were less inclined to listen to the radio, and would have welcomed getting the kids out from under their feet.[38] Many of these issues were also applicable to the TV schedules – especially in the early days when children's television was between five and six in the evening.[39] One Nottingham woman with ten children explained how useful the television was as a childminder: 'I never have time to watch it myself, of course, but I like it because it keeps the children amused and lets me get on with odd jobs which I don't have time to fit in during the day.' The interviewer also observed how, in this instance, television helped people manage their time: 'Whoever called television the greatest time-waster in the world should meet Mrs Lane.'[40] Nor was Mrs Lane alone in valuing television as a childminder:

> This is a cry from the heart! Please, please could some children's films be shown on Saturday mornings, during the winter months, when children are indoors?
>
> I know of many mothers who feel the same, getting to absolute screaming point trying to cope with chores and squabbling children.
>
> Waiting until the afternoon for a children's programme is a nightmare, not to mention having to wait through an afternoon of sport before there's anything suitable for young children.[41]

However, it was not only adults who were aware of the childminding benefits of the television. One twelve-year-old suggested: 'Why not put on more children's programmes in the mornings and afternoons, particularly during school holidays? It would give mothers the chance for a bit of peace.'[42]

The television was not only used to keep children away from their mothers, but also as a form of company for those living on their own. Lesley of the *TV Times* responded to one letter about an old woman who was using her TV as company by explaining that: 'From the many letters I receive from both young and elderly people living alone, I know that the television does give them companionship as well as entertainment.'[43] However, it was not just people who lived alone who used the TV for company. For example, O'Sullivan suggested that women used TV as an 'antidote against domestic isolation'.[44] Furthermore, one letter to the *TV Times* demonstrated that this isolation or loneliness was not confined to the daytime:

> My husband has recently started to work on a night shift at the factory where he is employed and I am sure that there are many more wives who like me would welcome the idea of ITV showing a late programme, perhaps a film or a repeat of a popular series during the week. It would certainly make the nights seem shorter![45]

Alternatively, another woman, who was stuck in her bedroom after the birth of her baby, was cheered up considerably when her husband brought the television upstairs so that she could watch it.[46]

The Contexts of Viewing

As this later point makes clear, we need to be careful about the presumed context of television viewing. While much research has benefited from its presumption that the cultural politics of the domestic living room was the primary social context for the analysis of television viewing, not all television viewing takes place within the home and, even when it does,[47] the living room is not the only location within which television is watched. Televisions were, and still are, kept in a variety of rooms. In the 1950s and 1960s, they were generally in sitting rooms, parlours and living rooms, but if a television was kept in the sitting room or parlour, it would have been used differently from those located in the living room. The latter was often the place where people sat and ate, and it was therefore easier to watch television while eating the evening meal. Also television viewing in the living room may have been more communal, although it could also create conflicts. This room was used for a range of other activities, and this made it harder to follow programmes. However, if the set was located in a sitting room or parlour, this location would have changed the nature of television viewing considerably. The sitting room, for example, was rarely a feature of working-class homes, but in those homes that did have one, it had a very different function from the living room. It was not a room in which one ate but, unlike a parlour, it was used on a regular basis, if only for sitting. As a result, in homes where the television was kept in the sitting room or parlour, the television might be watched by certain members of the family or at specific times such as weekends. The functions of these rooms have, of course, changed since the 1950s, and the functions of the living room and the sitting room have converged. However, televisions are also found in a number of other rooms, and the activity of watching television in the kitchen, your own room or someone else's room have quite different meanings.

Even in 1960, there was also a range of places outside the home in which people watched television, such as the club, pub, friends' homes and even in cafés. The Scottish adolescent survey, for example, found that, after the home, the next most popular place to watch television was at a friend's house, which meant that the television viewing was never an activity that was limited to the private, nuclear family. On the contrary, in the early days, television was a novelty and people with televisions would often invite their friends and neighbours over to watch the television. Rather than a retreat into privatised space, it was the focus of communal activities.

Furthermore, despite their stated preferences, few people faced the choice between cinema and television as a straight or exclusive choice, and therefore most people continued to engage in both forms of film consumption. The choice between these two had always been a choice between different types of experience, but experiences whose meanings were defined in relation to one another. 'Going out' is therefore the inverse of 'staying in', and while some people may state a general preference for staying in, most would also go out on specific occasions. Similarly, while some may state a preference for

As films began to be shown on television, cinema was reconstructed as a nostalgic and glamorous object. The Elite today is no longer in use as a cinema but has a preservation order on it

a night out, they would still value a night in every now and again. In other words, the choice between these activities was never simply a matter of straightforward preference but a choice between different social activities with different meanings that can be appropriate or inappropriate at different times. Even those who rarely go to the cinema often have ritual periods when they do go: many, for example, saw cinema as a 'treat', something that they would do at Christmas or for someone's birthday;[48] while others see the cinema as the best place for a first date.[49]

Even those who watch television in the home sometimes try to recreate the 'cinema experience' in their own homes, although there are a number of different ways in which people actually define the 'cinema experience'. When Valerie Avery's mother bought a television around 1955, for example, the family were the first in the neighbourhood to have one and Valerie describes how they tried to recreate the cinema experience. First, the room was normally oriented towards the fire rather than the television, so the family would rearrange all the furniture around the set before the 'performance' started. This ritual also shows that they were trying to construct television viewing as a special and concentrated event. In this example, the television was also kept in the front room, which was reserved for special occasions. Thus the front room and the television added to each other's importance: the television was special and therefore kept in the front room, while the fact that the television was watched in the front room also bestowed status on this room. In addition, the family always switched off the lights while they were watching, and her grandmother would bring a bag of sweets whenever they watched the Sunday night play. The absence of lights is particularly significant as it was one way in which the

Although cinema itself
came to be seen as
nostalgic and
glamorous, many
cinemas acquired new
and less glamorous uses.
The Capitol today

event was marked off from other domestic activities and concentration was demanded of the viewer. It removed the differences that many people use to justify their preference for television – the ability to do other things while the television is on. It also created the conditions that most people associate with the cinema – the lack of distractions. It is therefore significant that many respondents still described similar rituals that they would perform before they watched a film on television: arranging furniture; putting the answer machine on; turning the lights off. In so doing, they actively sought to construct film viewing as distinct from 'normal' television, and to privilege this activity as a specific event or occasion that was separate form the 'ordinary' or 'everyday'.[50] Valerie's family also watched the entire evening's programme of about three hours, which made it not unlike going to the cinema when it consisted of more than a main feature. When television shut down, however, all the furniture would be moved back into its daytime position.[51]

Conclusion: Contrast and Comparison

However, while some tried to recreate the cinema experience in their own homes, others considered the two media as incompatible. For example, Buscombe cites one commentator who believed that the two experiences were completely different and required different types of programming:

> It is doubtful if there exists a cinema film of any appreciable length that is ideally suited to the television screen. In the first place, the commercial film is made essentially for a mass audience, not a group in the sitting-room. Secondly, because it is for a mass audience its tempo is much faster, with quick-cutting technique that can be disturbing when viewed at home.[52]

The differences between cinema and television were also discussed by Joyce Crammond in 1976:

> Although, superficially, [cinema and television] seem alike, there are several differences in terms of context, availability and content. Television viewing takes place in the home where one can move around; it is freely available and provides a wide range of programmes. On the other hand, at the cinema there is no opportunity to move around, there are few distractions, visits must be planned with the available times, and some effort made to get there; also there is, in the main, only fictional content.

She also compared the use of television and radio:

> Television and radio are more alike in terms of context, availability and content. Radio has the added advantage of being portable and provides at any time a wider selection of programmes ... The aspect which makes it less attractive, of course, is its non-visual format and is perhaps for some consumers, particularly children, less absorbing.[53]

Although the majority of the adolescents in the Scottish survey preferred cinema to television, those who preferred TV gave a variety of reasons for their choice, many of which would have applied to all age groups. For example, some preferred TV because their homes were not cold, dingy and smoky, while others liked watching television because they did not have to keep getting up to let people get to their seats.[54] While Sheldon may have affectionately remembered the experience of being continually disturbed throughout the film, many at the time found it thoroughly annoying.[55] TV was also preferred because there was no queuing and no cold bus journey home. One teenager even claimed that he found home to be more relaxing and much quieter: 'you can put your feet up in comfort. In the pictures you can hardly hear the film for the usherettes shouting at people'.[56] Adolescents also liked the freedom of being able to move about and talk as much as they liked, or to be able to watch in silence. They also liked being able to switch off without thinking that they had wasted their money by doing so.[57]

Notes

1. As Jane Stokes has argued, the perceived rivalry between the cinema and television often meant that films represented television in specific ways and television represented the film industry in various different ways. See Stokes, 1999. However, although these 'on-screen rivalries' did affect the meanings of each medium, the following discussion is not concerned with the ways in which they represented one another but rather other ways in which they changed meaning in relation to one another.

2. Quoted in Buscombe, 1991, p. 202.

3. Cited in ibid., p. 200.

4. These latter terms originate in Williams, 1974.

5. See Williams, 1994, pp. 14–17; and Hawkins, 2000b, pp. 13–30.

6. Garnham, 1990.

7. Hawkins, 2000b.

8. Gomery, 1992; Mark Jancovich, 2002b.

9. Klinger, 1994, p. 84.

10. Shove and Southerton, 2000, p. 303.

11. Bowden and Offer, 1994, pp. 745–6. See also Bain, 1962, pp. 145–67.

12. Black, 1954, p. 220.

13. Needleman, 1960, p. 27.

14. Saxon, 1956, p. 94. The Netherlands was more like Britain in that TVs were at first bought by the better-off: van Zoonen and Wieten, 1994, p. 647.

15. Faire, unpublised thesis, 1998, p. 167.

16. O'Sullivan, 1991, p. 164.

17. Bowden and Offer, 1994, p. 740. See also Gray, 1992, p. 61.

18. Van Zoonen and Wieten, 1994, p. 649.

19. This situation was made painfully apparent to Joyce Storey when she wanted to buy a washing machine in 1952. See Storey, 1995, p. 39.

20. Ward, n.d. p. 35.

21. Letter from Mrs M. S. Bowen to the *TV Times*, 7 October 1971, p. 20.

22. GJ, 20 November 1957.

23. Letter from Mrs A. Challender to the *Radio Times*, 4 March 1971, p. 58. The fact that the BBC took two columns to reply to this letter suggests that the issue was considered to be an important one, despite the claim that there had been 'almost' no complaint in the previous year.

24. Letter from Mrs P. Burton to the *TV Times*, 18 March 1976, p. 30.

25. Letter from V. B. Saunders to the *TV Times*, 18 March 1976, p. 30. There were also a couple of letters which complained about the lack of women on programmes such as *This is Your Life* and on TV panels.

26. Robin Scott, Controller of BBC, reply to A. Challender's letter to the *Radio Times*, 4 March 1971, p. 58.

27. BBC Yearbook and Annual Reports/BBC Handbook and Report and Accounts, 1950–1990.

28. Barclay, 1961, pp. 36, 40.

29. Letter from Mrs S. Hobbis to *TV World*, 7 April 1966, p. 22.

30. GJ, 23 March 1959.

31. Lynn Spigel has demonstrated that, in America, the introduction of television was directly connected to constructions of the domestic ideal. See Spigel, 1992.

32. Letter from Eileen Fielding to *TV Times*, 8 July 1971. As with early cinema, it was often the cultural middle classes who believed the opposite. For example, Cleethorpes schoolmaster Mr W. B. Cockerill told Lindsey Education Committee that too many children were forced to be quiet while the rest of the family watched TV and that this resulted in them starting school with speech difficulties. NEP, 7 April 1962, p. 9.

33. Letter from Dorothy Camfield to the *TV Times*, 2 July 1976, p. 19.

34. For example, letter from R. E. Row to the *TV Times*, 20 May 1966, p. 25; and D. Smith of Nottingham in *TV World*, 7 April 1966.

35. GJ, 9 July 1956.

36. O'Sullivan, 1991, p. 175; Goodman in Morley, 1986, p. 26.

37. Moores, 1988, p. 36.

38. Ibid., pp. 33–4, 37.

39. O'Sullivan, 1991, pp. 167–71.

40. Peggy Conroy, NEP, 28 October 1959.

41. Letter to *TV Times*, 21 January 1971, p. 53.

42. *TV World*, 10 March 1966, p. 22.

43. *TV Times*, 20 May 1976, p. 25.

44. O'Sullivan, 1991, p. 176.

45. Letter from Mrs Diane Fulleylove to *TV Times*, 10 April 1969, p. 55.

46. *TV World*, 26 January 1967, p. 20.

47. McCarthy, 2001.

48. Nina, 30, bus-driver (RSQ).

49. Julie, 31, playscheme co-ordinator (KE34).

50. Many respondents liked to have a drink while watching a film on television. For example, when Sharan (33, nurse/tutor, KE35) watches Sky Box Office, she likes to open a bottle of wine and treat it as a night in. Another respondent claimed that 'If it's sunny outside and if we've got a video on, mum will pull the blinds and we'll sit there in semi-darkness watching the film. It's just like being in the cinema again.' (Joy, 45, occupation unknown, member of Nottingham Young Disabled People, RM20.)

51. Avery, 1980, pp. 62–4.

52. Smith, 1950, p. 186. Cited in Buscombe, 1991, p. 201.

53. Crammond, 1976, p. 273.

54. Scottish Educational Film Association and Scottish Film Council, 1961, p. 44.

55. Sheldon, unpublished 1999, p. 4.

56. Scottish Educational Film Association and Scottish Film Council, 1961, p. 44.

57. Ibid., pp. 58–9.

11

Negotiating Nostalgia:
Modernity, Memory and the Meanings of Place

As we already have seen, not only was the rise of television related to changes in the meanings of the home, but the meanings of the city centre were also changing. However, while these changes certainly made the city centre unappealing to some, they also made it attractive to others. As Joanne Hollows has pointed out, it was specifically in these decaying inner-city areas during the 1960s that the cult movie started to flourish. The image of these places 'worked to confirm the heroic masculinity of its male fans' and their opposition to the supposedly feminine world of domestic consumption associated with the home and the television.[1] Furthermore, as Miller and his colleagues point out, attitudes to places are 'related to perceived changes in the local social and cultural fabric'.[2] In their study of Wood Green's Shopping City, for example, they found that the supposed 'loss of "community spirit" was frequently related to the racialised nature of neighbourhood change due to the influx of people from ethnic minority backgrounds with which the construction of the Shopping City coincided'.[3] This chapter will therefore consider how the changing meanings of cinema were also related 'to perceived changes in the local social and cultural fabric', through an analysis of nostalgia for cinema in popular memory and public discourse.

Coming to Terms with Closure: Modernity and Tradition in the Local Press

As we have seen, the local newspapers often devoted a considerable amount of space to reports of cinema openings in the 1930s, sometimes as much as a full page of coverage, and this is an indication of the importance these sites once had for the city's sense of identity. However, the closure of many cinemas also received considerable space, between a half and a full page in most cases, and this space was not simply a result of the local media's need to maximise all local stories as their emotional tone indicates. While a strong sense of civic pride was evident in reports on the opening of cinemas, an equally strong sense of regret can be found in most reports on the closure of cinemas.

As we have seen, in the 1920s and 1930s, reports on the opening of cinemas had conveyed a powerful sense of optimism about the future and confidence in the 'progress' that these cinemas were seen to represent. However, the reports of their closure presented a very different attitude to both modernity and these cinemas. While still bound up with notions of civic pride and local identity, these cinemas were seen as representatives of tradition rather than modernity, and their closure was presented as the tragic destruction of this tradition by a modernity which was now seen as far from benign.

In other words, these news reports express the dialectic of modernity that Marshall Berman so brilliantly captures in the opening of his book, *All That is Solid Melts Into Air*:

> To be modern is to find ourselves in an environment that promises us adventure, power, joy, growth, transformation of ourselves and our world [but] at the same time threatens to destroy everything we have, everything we know, everything we are.[4]

As a result, by the time of their closure, these cinemas were no longer seen as symbols of a modernity that brought harmony and order, but as symbols of a dying traditional way of life. They were still viewed just as favourably as they once had been, but now modernity was presented as a destructive force that was represented by the bingo halls, warehouses and supermarkets that were taking over the disused cinema buildings.

The emotive tone found in all the articles is particularly strong in an NEP story of 26 October 1960. This story begins with a discussion of the closing of the Apollo, Berridge Road, but extends to a lament for all the recently closed cinemas in the city and those still under threat: 'The Apollo adds its name to the gloomy list of cinemas being made into furniture stores, frozen food depots and warehouses, or waiting gaunt and derelict, to be pulled down and cleared for car parks and petrol stations.'[5] The elegiac tone is redolent throughout, with much use of highly charged language: 'gloomy', 'gaunt',

Cinemas that once announced their modernity came to be seen as relics of a golden age of tradition and community. The Futurist today, Valley Road

'derelict', 'doom'. Under the subheading, 'Death Roll', the paper also lists other recent cinema casualties and those under threat from closure. This theme is also reproduced with varying degrees of ardour in all the articles about cinema closures. A 1963 item on the Windsor Cinema, for example, is headlined, 'Death of Another Cinema',[6] while the NEN item on the closure of the Commodore (formerly the Aspley) frequently refers to the 'danger' facing other cinemas.[7]

Cinemas had therefore changed their meanings significantly. An article on the demolition of the Astoria, for example, no longer presented this cinema as 'the most up-to-date in the country' as the papers had done on its opening in 1936. By 1994, the cinema represented tradition, decline and folk memory. An article in the NEP at the time referred affectionately to 'Nostalgic film fans' before interviewing local residents who remembered the tuppenny rush, visits with gangs of friends and courting in the double seats at the back.[8] The article also recounts the history of the Astoria which was closed in 1975, projecting a sense of nostalgia for the cinema's heyday, coupled with a sense of the tawdriness and tackiness of modern life. The Astoria had previously had an 'imposing and very attractive exterior', 'fin-like corners suggesting just a hint of Egyptian influence' and a 'bold red neon sign',[9] but it had been forced to close in 1970 for renovation so that it could 'attract audiences which by now had gone into decline'.[10] However, although it reopened the following year 'with the luxury of armchair seating', refurbishment had done little to halt the cinema's decline and, after its final closure as a cinema in 1975, the building became a bingo hall and then a snooker hall. Plans to turn it into a drive-through McDonald's and a car part showroom had failed and eventually led to its final demolition. Its increasing redundancy is also demonstrated by its post-1975 history. At the time of its demolition, 'The site's future [was] in limbo ... no further application had been submitted.'[11]

There is no a sense in this article that bingo and snooker were worthy successors to the cinema, or could hope to hold the same place in people's affections. The cinema is presented not just as a building but as the embodiment of a culture and a way of life. The personal accounts of childhood and courting also give a sense of the importance cinema once had as the site for these rites of passage. The demolition of the Astoria is not only meant to represent the destruction of a building but a part of the city's past as it is experienced both collectively and personally.

Indeed, there is a strong sense that the importance of cinema lay in its social and community function as much as, if not more than, in the films that it presented. As we have already observed, cinemas in the city have had far more meanings and functions than merely as places to show films. This is particularly evident in the news reports of the 1950s and 1960s, and can clearly be seen in an article on the closure of the Metropole, Mansfield Road, which makes special mention of the 'flourishing children's film club' that was established there in 1948 and 'whose members [had] put on anything from fancy dress contests to conker championships'.[12] As a result, the destruction of cinemas was seen as representative of a loss of community, a loss that was supposedly caused by the motor car as a representative of modernity. The perceived modernity of cinemas in the 1930s was sometimes presented as quaintly old-fashioned, and hence positive, through its association with a different period of the car's history. For example, the NEP article on the closing of the Astoria comments on its car park, which had been a feature given special importance in the reports of its opening, in a way that contrasts the significance of the car in the 1930s with that of the car in the present. The car park had been for 'the few people who had wheels in those days, a far cry from the site today as six lanes of traffic roar across the A52 Derby Road'.[13]

The numerous reports on cinema closures and their emotional tone seem to demonstrate that these places have had particularly deep significance. In order to assess this significance, we compared these reports with the coverage of both the cinema's immediate predecessor in mass entertainment (the music hall) and its immediate successor (the bingo hall). The demise of bingo halls is reported in very different language to that of cinemas. First, coverage of the subject was minimal. A general piece written in 1961 did discuss 'the bingo craze which is the biggest social revolution since television'.[14] However, the article comments on a number of halls in a factual rather than emotional account of its popularity. The same factual, unemotional tone was used in the closure of bingo halls. The following excerpt is typical: 'A chain of four bingo clubs – two in the Nottingham area – has shut down because of falling attendances.'[15] The only emotive account of the closing of a bingo hall is that concerning the Adelphi Bingo Hall (formerly the Adelphi Cinema) which is reported in the *Hucknall Dispatch*, and included the line: 'Tears filled some eyes down for the last session at the popular Adelphi Bingo Hall.'[16] However, even here, most space is devoted to a personal memoir of the Adelphi Cinema, which had closed down thirty-four years before. An NEP article about the demolition of the Adelphi later in the year also concentrates almost exclusively on the history of the Adelphi Cinema, with only a very few lines on the building's years as a bingo hall.

Press coverage of the music hall was also limited, with only three accounts of halls opening or undergoing refurbishment. This dearth of material when compared to cinema indicates the greater importance of the cinema to Nottingham city life. Accounts of the opening of music halls, like the cinemas, claimed that the buildings were 'in every respect up-to-date',[17] and also emphasised their décor and luxury: 'marble mosaic', 'a handsomely appointed waiting room' and 'one of the finest galleries in the country' were all supposed to be in evidence at the Hippodrome.[18] However, there is far less sense that these sites were symbols of modernity like the cinema. There are certainly no accounts that suggest that the music halls could be seen as symbols of the city as the Elite cinema was seen on its opening[19] or as a 'Sign of National Recovery' as the opening of the Curzon was described.[20] Particularly noteworthy in terms of these comparisons is that we have found few accounts concerning the closure of music halls. Many halls were converted into cinemas in the early part of the century, and yet there are no nostalgic articles that presented these conversions as a sign of cultural decline, and this is in sharp contrast to the coverage concerning the conversion of cinemas into bingo halls forty years later.

So significant were these cinemas that there was even a debate over whether the council should take over the responsibility for running them. For example, a 1959 article on the recently closed Tudor in West Bridgford discussed a petition signed by 945 residents, which asked for the council to reject an application to demolish the building so that a series of shops and offices could be built on the site. However, the local residents also wanted the council to take over the running of the cinema as a local amenity, presumably in much the same way as it was responsible for other forms of leisure such as swimming pools and libraries. The social significance of the cinema was also emphasised through its relation to the elderly:

> The position of old people was stressed in the letters and petition. The committee was sympathetic to the general view which regretted that the cinema could not carry on. They particularly sympathised with the old people.

However, it was stressed that the petitioners 'could not prove that the Council could carry on a cinema any more economically than a private undertaking' and that 'a substantial rate subsidy would be needed'.[21]

Memory and its Meanings: Recalling Cinemagoing

None the less, the focus on the elderly in the above article is telling. If these changing meanings of the cinema were related 'to perceived changes in the local social and cultural fabric', it is hardly surprising that age plays such a crucial role in the distinguishing attitudes to cinemas. As a result, the teenagers that we interviewed largely valued the most modern developments in film consumption, such as the Showcase, Nottingham's local multiplex.[22] Others also believed that new technologies such as DVD and the internet would eventually do away with cinema altogether and presented this process positively as progress.[23] The elderly, on the other hand, tended to feel most alienated from these developments. Most expressed extreme hostility to the Showcase, and tended to prefer older cinemas such as the Savoy and the Odeon (formerly the Ritz).[24] However, even these cinemas were marked by their relationship to progress. Among those who tended to favour the Odeon, there were those who clearly suggested that they had stopped going to the cinema once it was converted into a twin screen in 1965. For these people, this event transformed the building from one with which they felt a connection into one that represented developments from which they felt excluded and to which they were opposed.

Thus, while the young generally seemed to regard progress as creative and positive, the elderly seemed to experience it as largely destructive and negative, as a process of loss. One therefore needs to be careful when analysing memories of the past because they are never simply recollections of what once had been. On the contrary, as Lynn Spigel argues:

> popular memory is history for the present; it is a mode of historical consciousness that speaks to the concerns and needs of contemporary life. Popular memory is a form of storytelling through which people make sense of their own lives and culture.[25]

In other words, memories are always reconstructions that tell us as much about perceptions of the present as they do about the past. However, it is this that gives them their

People who are hostile to recent developments such as the multiplex tend to claim that they prefer the Savoy, Derby Road

value and importance: they not only speak about the past, but also use that past to comment on the present.

As a result, while most of the elderly people that we interviewed viewed cinema as representative of a golden age from which the present was seen as a decline or fall, they reconstructed the positive features of that golden age in different ways. For example, while most of our elderly respondents made it clear that different cinemas had different social significances, and were tied to different kinds of social interaction, they also privileged specific aspects of cinemagoing, depending on their specific feelings of loss and disenchantment in the present.

While most respondents would initially claim that they went to particular cinemas not because of the place images of those cinemas, but simply to see a particular film, when asked about specific cinemas most almost immediately reconstructed an account of their week in which different cinemas were clearly positioned within specific social routines. For example, they might have gone to one local cinema with their family on a Tuesday, another local cinema with a group of friends of the same sex on a Wednesday where they might have encountered and flirted with groups of the opposite sex, yet another local cinema with their best friend on a Friday, and then to a city centre cinema on a Saturday night, where they met a member of the opposite sex for a date.[26] Here specific cinemas were clearly seen as appropriate or inappropriate to specific social activities. There were certain cinemas that one might go to with one's family, and others that one might go to with one's friends. The Ritz, on the other hand, seems to have almost universally been favoured as a place one went to when on a date.

However, while cinema may have represented the location for all these different types of social interaction, most respondents associated the cinema with specific forms of social interaction dependent on their own specific feelings of loss. Many, for example, saw cinemas of the past as representing a period of community. One respondent, for instance, remembered the Bonington Cinema where he went as a child, and claimed that everyone knew one another in the cinema. He also recalled one local character, Johnny, for whom the cinema would reserve a specific seat because he was disabled.[27] This story conveys a sense of intimacy and community where people not only knew one another but also looked after one another.[28]

For others, however, the image of community was far less central than that of the cinema as a family event. Indeed, the numerous elderly respondents who stated their preference for the Savoy as a cinema often referred to it as a 'family cinema'.[29] What is interesting here is that this phrase works to conflate two different meanings. On the one hand, these respondents often praised the Savoy as the last remaining 'family owned' cinema, where each member of the family has a different role in the organisation – ticket seller, concessions stand, usher, etc. However, this meaning is also conflated with the sense of the cinema as a place where families could feel at home. Ironically, most also stated that when they did go to the cinema now, it was usually when they took their grandchildren to the Odeon or the Showcase.[30] None the less, the notion of family is very important here and it represents an image of closeness and intimacy that many felt was missing in their present circumstances. Many lived on their own, their partners deceased, and only saw their children and grandchildren relatively rarely. Indeed, many distinguished between the family when they were younger and the family today, and presented the family of their past as one of closeness and connection as opposed to the family of today which they saw as uncaring and from which they felt excluded.

For others, the fondest memories of the cinema were of going there with friends. Many of these people missed the close bonds of friendship that they associated with their youth, and this relates to a general experience of isolation that was often related to the death of friends or the immobility of themselves or others. One respondent, for example, claimed that up until a few years ago she still went to the cinema regularly with a friend, but that she had to stop when her friend's health had declined significantly and forced her into care.[31]

One of the most common memories of cinema is, of course, as a place of courting, romance and sexual experimentation.[32] Indeed, a large number of people remembered the cinema as either a place of sexual awakening[33] or as a place of sexual threat and harassment.[34] There were repeated stories about the Moulin Rouge, which many women claimed was occupied by the 'dirty mac brigade'. However, while most women said this was one cinema that they did not frequent, other women clearly did go there,[35] although one respondent claimed that she always took a hat pin to see off 'the gropers'.[36] The cinema was also associated with more pleasurable romantic and sexual encounters. For some, these cinemas evoked memories of partners that were now dead, and placed these relationships back into their idealised early stages. However, for others, these cinemas were not about specific romantic relationships, but rather a period of excitement and vitality, a period that was contrasted with the supposed absence of these features within their present lives. For others, these cinemas clearly evoked an idealised sense of themselves. They saw this period of courting as one in which they were attractive to the opposite sex in a way that they no longer felt themselves to be, but it might also be that this was a time in their lives when the expression of sexual feelings was seen as less incongruous and inappropriate. It is unclear how many remembered this period so intensely because they did not feel that they had the opportunity to express these feelings in the same way in their present.

If people's memories of the cinema differ, it is also the case that specific cinemas have different meanings for different people. Thus, while many female respondents claimed that the Moulin Rouge was frequented by the 'dirty mac brigade', others had very different perceptions of the place. The features that made this cinema sordid and disreputable to many also defined it as a place of distinction for others. One respondent, for example, clearly identified European culture with quality, and praised changes in Nottingham that he believed made it more like Europe, and particularly Brussels. He also talked quite openly of his preference for the Moulin Rouge as a cinema, which he remembered as a place where he saw good foreign films.[37] The very qualities that made it seem dirty and seedy to some were precisely the qualities that marked it as a place of distinction for others. As a number of studies have demonstrated, the European art film was often marketed through its sexual content, which was often supposed to signify its adult and serious nature. However, it was these features which also associated it with 'obscenity and perversity'.[38] Indeed, as we saw in Part Three, it was this content which Manvell and others valued and led them to oppose censorship, at least for certain audiences. Similarly, the Savoy was seen very differently by different sections of the population. While many elderly respondents stated a preference for the Savoy, which they saw as an old-fashioned, traditional cinema, others saw it as a student hangout from which they felt alienated.

Even the very same feature could acquire markedly different meanings within different social contexts. For example, many elderly respondents complained about the noise in contemporary cinemas.[39] Sometimes this referred to the volume of the soundtrack and sometimes the activities of the audience, but in most cases the two were conflated together. However, the meaning of noise frequently slipped and changed. Some regarded noise as a sign of the vulgar and brash present that they contrasted to a more restrained and dignified past, and some even claimed to prefer watching films in the afternoons when it was quieter.[40] Others considered noise to be a sign of the shared experience that they thought was missing in contemporary culture. It was a sign of active enjoyment and communal interaction.[41] Some even slipped between the two in their comments: they complained about noise but also saw it as essential to a sense of shared experience and atmosphere,[42] a sign of the very thing that distinguished cinema from television viewing and defined it as superior.

Differentiated Activities: the Meanings of Cinemagoing and Television Viewing

As Chapter 10 demonstrated, rather than presenting a straightforward threat to the cinema, television provided a different kind of experience. Of course, this experience offered an alternative to cinema, but only to the extent that any other leisure activity would. In his history of BBC audience research, Silvey therefore refers to Professor Wilbur Schramm's claim that 'when TV comes in *functionally similar* activities will be replaced, whereas functionally different ones will not',[43] and he clarifies the meaning of the term 'function' as follows:

> The primary function of the nightly visit to the local may for one man be social and for another the need to quench thirst. One man may garden primarily for exercise and another primarily for the prestige of producing the prize-winning vegetable marrow. Viewing television performs different functions for different people – and for the same person at different times. One child may be glued to the screen because of the need to satisfy an appetite for vicarious excitement; another because he knows he cannot keep his end up when he plays with his peer group.[44]

As a result, while television may have screened similar types of entertainment, its domestic location made its function quite different to that of the cinema. As we have seen, a night at the cinema was about more than the entertainment viewed and different cinemas served different functions for their audiences. In much the same way, then, television and the cinema were less rivals than alternative experiences that served different functions.

Thus, while Silvey claims that 'the habit of family cinema-going, which was primarily for the entertainment it offered, had a function similar to that of [television] viewing and, as every circuit knows, has shrunk severely since television's advent', he also acknowledges that the location of these different activities also changes their function: 'significantly adolescent cinema-going, the function of which was to provide an escape from the family if not an opportunity for necking in a dark warm environment, has been much more resistant to the inroads of viewing'.[45] In other words, television did not offer the same pleasures as cinema within the comfort of one's own home; rather it offered a completely different kind of experience precisely because it was in the home.

As a result, when our respondents were asked whether they preferred watching films on television or at the cinema, and why, we found that cinemagoing and television viewing were evaluated in quite different ways. Many claimed to prefer cinema because of 'the big screen'. Here the preference was for a sense of spectacle with which television is unable to compete, but it was also related to a much more general sense of the difference between television and cinema. Both those who preferred cinema and those who preferred television justified their preference by referring to the cinema as 'overwhelming'.[46] Here the pleasures of cinema were related to a sense of the cinema as 'more absorbing than TV',[47] as something that demands and controls one's attention. Those respondents who preferred cinema to television therefore claimed to do so because it

had 'no distractions',[48] and allowed one to 'block things out'.[49] Morley found that concentrated viewing in the home was often associated with male viewers, precisely because
they had a different relationship to the home from women.[50] However, the desire for an
intense and concentrated experience was not simply the preserve of male respondents.
It was often articulated by female respondents who saw a trip to the cinema as a 'night
out', a sense of occasion that took them away from the home where they often felt
assaulted by numerous different demands and unable to indulge themselves without a
feeling of guilt.[51] The cinema was therefore seen as a protected and nurturing space
closed off from the world outside.[52] As one respondent claimed, he felt 'cocooned in the
cinema'.[53]

However, this feeling of guilt also accounts for the exact opposite response. Many
respondents, for example, claimed that they preferred television exactly because they
could get on with other things at the same time.[54] Rather than demanding and controlling their attention, television provided 'freedom' and 'control'; rather than cutting one
off from the outside world, television could be fitted in and around other activities;
rather than a sense of spectacle and occasion, television provided the pleasures of the
'cosy' and the everyday. People repeatedly explained their preference for television
through its association with the 'cosiness' or 'comfort' of the home.[55] Thus, while some
saw the cinema as a cocoon separated from the outside world, many saw the home as a
comparable space, a place of warmth and comfort in which they could 'snuggle up' in
security and intimacy.[56] Indeed, numerous respondents referred to television viewing as
an 'intimate' experience.[57]

The word 'intimacy' here is particularly interesting and it came up a number of times
in connection with both the home and the cinema. On the one hand, certain cinemas
were distinguished from others through their supposed 'intimacy'. For example, some
contrasted the Odeon and the Savoy to the Showcase by claiming that the former were
'intimate'.[58] In these accounts, 'intimacy' not only stood for the respondent's sense of
community within, and shared experience with, the audience, but it was also distinguished from the supposedly 'impersonality' of the Showcase in another sense.[59] The
Showcase's 'impersonality' not only signified a lack of communal or shared experience
but was also opposed to the 'personality' of cinemas such as the Savoy and the Odeon.
In this way, the 'personality' of these cinemas represented a sense of identity and individuality, which, as we will see in more detail later, was distinguished from the supposedly
mass-produced nature of the Showcase experience.

While those who preferred television viewing claimed that it did not require effort,
for those who preferred the cinema, the effort was often a vital element of the pleasure.
Many people had rituals and saw 'dressing up as part of the experience' of going to the
cinema,[60] while television viewing was often seen as an opportunity to 'slob out'.[61] In
other words, part of the pleasure of cinemagoing was as a reclamation of the body as a
source of pleasure and identity, while the pleasures of television were often seen as a
opportunity to release the body from regimentation and control. However, it was not
simply the effort of getting ready that was important. Many others stressed that the effort
of going out was also important, and maintained that travelling to the cinema was part

of the adventure of cinemagoing.[62] Several respondents actually claimed that they used to travel all over Nottingham in order to visit and explore different cinemas.[63] Similar findings have also been made in the United States where Janna Jones has shown the ways in which the audience members of the Tampa Theatre actually identified the difficulty involved in getting to that cinema as one of the key features that made their cinemagoing superior to those who visited the more accessible and convenient multiplexes.[64]

Conclusion

In other words, the activities of film consumption associated with television and the cinema are distinguished by their different locations. The meanings of television viewing are shaped by its domestic setting, while the meanings of cinemagoing are defined through their freedom from the domestic. Alternatively, the meaning of cinemagoing is defined through its association with public space, while the meanings of television viewing are defined as a retreat from the demands of the public.

Notes

1. Hollows, 'The Masculinity of Cult', forthcoming.
2. Miller, Jackson, Thrift, Holbrook and Rowlands, 1998, p. 49.
3. Ibid., p. 50.
4. Berman, 1983, p. 15.
5. NEP, 26 October 1960.
6. NEP, 9 March 1963.
7. NEN, 11 July 1963.
8. NEP, 2 February 1994.
9. *Beeston Gazette*, 20 May 1980.
10. NEP, 2 February 1994.
11. Ibid.
12. NEP, 20 October 1973.
13. NEP, 2 February 1994.
14. NEP, 29 May 1961.
15. NEP, 16 January 1961.
16. *Hucknall Dispatch*, 28 February 1997.
17. *City Sketches*, 1899.
18. NEN, 3 April 1908.
19. NDG, 23 August 1921.
20. NEP, 2 August 1935.
21. 'Council Sorry, But They Can't Run Tudor', NEP, 4 November 1959.
22. See, for example, Tarnjit, 16, student (RMQ); Dalbir, 14, student (RMQ); Subaigh, 11, student (RMQ); Suroop, 10, student (RMQ); Harprit, 18, student (RMQ); Harjot, 10, student (RMQ); Bikrumjit, 14, student (RMQ); and GCSE English Class, 14–15, Minister School, Southwell (KE17).
23. See, for example, Andrew, 14, student, (KE27); Stefan, 25, unemployed teacher (KE19); and Delma, 40, teacher (KEQ).

24. See Chapter 13.

25. Spigel, 1995, p. 21.

26. John remembers going with family to certain cinemas, friends to others and his 'young lady' to yet another (mid-60s, retired, RK1). Kath remembers going between four and five times a week before she was married, but she had set nights on Monday, Thursday and Saturday (70, retired, RSQ), Similar patterns were also common among the members of the Bakersfield and Sneinton Co-op Women's Guild (KE20).

27. John and Julia, mid-60s, retired (RS1).

28. An article on the closure of the Grand mentioned a woman who had sat in the same seat all her life, and who was offered the seat by the cinema when it closed. GJ, 22 May 1956.

29. John and Julia (RS1) made special mention of the fact that the Savoy was family run, a feature that distinguished it from other cinemas and made it friendly. At the Savoy, they claimed, people recognised them and said 'hello' as opposed to the city centre and the Showcase, where, it was felt, the staff simply took their money but never even looked at their faces. Michael (58, lecturer, KE9) also believed that the closure of cinemas was due to the destruction of local communities.

30. These interviews were held before the closure of the Odeon in 2000. Betty (69, retired office worker, KE11), for example, took her grandson to see *Star Wars*, and most of the women from the Bakersfield and Sneinton Co-op Women's Guild took their grandchildren to see films at these cinemas (KE20).

31. Iris, 72, retired teacher (61). One respondent remembers cinema as a place where you would arrange to meet up with one's friends (member of the 'Something Different for Women Club', ages ranged between 60 and 75). Another claimed that the cinema evokes memories of security and friendship, qualities that she feels are absent in society today (Barbara, 40, headteacher, KEQ).

32. Members of the Bestwood Park Women's Club claimed that thinking about cinema brought back memories of courting (age range from 40 to 75, KE31), and this was certainly true for many members of the Bakersfield and Sneinton Co-op Women's Guild, too (KE20).

33. For example, one respondent claimed that, for her, the most memorable experience associated with cinemagoing was: 'Early discovery of sexual feelings (with partner rather than thro' images on screen!)' Anonymous female, health information advisor, 36 (KEQ). However, while this puts it particularly bluntly, most accounts of courting also make it abundantly clear that, for many, the cinema was a place of sexual experimentation and adventure – which could also tip over into sexual danger.

34. As we have already seen, stories of women being groped are common (see, for example, Mrs Robey, 60s, retired, RM10), and there were also complaints about flashers (National Council of Women, Nottingham Branch, KE36). However, possibly the most distasteful story is that of the woman who claims that her most memorable experience of cinemagoing was 'watching *Jurassic Park* while man in next seat masturbated!' (Anonymous female, cleaner, 30, KEQ.)

35. As we have seen, one woman even got engaged there (Clifton Women's Wednesday Club, age range from 60 to 80, KE25).

36. Member of the 'Something Different for Women Club'. See also Bestwood Park Women's Club (age range 40 to 75, KE31); Joan (a member of Chrysalis, a friendship group for those who have suffered bereavement); Kath, 70, occupation unknown (RMQ).

37. Ken, 67, retired maths teacher (KE29).

38. See Wilinsky, 2000, p. 37; Schaefer, 1994; and Schaefer, 1999.

39. For example, Sheila claims that she finds the cinema 'often too loud' and that, as a result, she 'ends up with a headache' (60, lecturer, RM19).

40. Many found the town centre 'intimidating', particularly at night (John and Joan, early to mid-60s, retired, RK1). They were not only frightened of mugging (Robert, 64, occupation unknown, RS13) but also of being knocked over by the young who, it was felt, dominated the town centre at night (Anthony, 57, lecturer, RM16). They were frightened partly because the young tended to move around in large groups and at great speed but also because, with brittle bones, the elderly were not only aware that, if knocked over, they were likely to break a bone, but also that such a injury could result in a complete loss of independence thereafter: many old people never become fully mobile again after such an injury (Betty, 69, retired office worker, KE11).

41. George, for example, recalls: 'Oh, it was murder: "Look out behind you!" "Look over there!" "Go on, get him, get him!" Oh, it was scream anything.' However, this is remembered affectionately, rather than critically (80, occupation unknown, RS15). Similarly, another person remembers that, at the Boulevard, 'everyone would sing during intervals – a happy atmosphere', while another recalls that, even from outside Leno's, 'we could hear the kids shouting and screaming' (both members of the Thursday Disabled Club which had about 12 to 14 members of which all but one were aged between 71 and 90, RM13).

42. This was evident, for example, in the responses of a meeting of the National Council of Women, Nottingham Branch, whose members were aged between 41 and 78 (KE36).

43. Professor Wilbur Schramm quoted in Silvey, 1974, p. 156.

44. Ibid., p. 157.

45. Ibid.

46. Catherine, 25, student (RMQ).

47. Ibid.

48. Brian, 46, probation officer (KE16).

49. Melanie, 34, information officer (RM7).

50. See Chapter 1 but also Morley, 1986.

51. For example, Jo claimed that watching films on television was a waste of time and that she felt guilty about the jobs that needed doing (22, receptionist, KE1).

52. Margaret, for example, claimed that she preferred cinemagoing to watching films on television or video because it 'is dedicated time' where she is 'not tempted to do anything else e.g. household chores' (45, occupation unknown, KEQ).

53. Simon, 23, trainee solicitor (KE18).

54. Stuart, 32, student (KEQ).

55. Whitegate Mothers and Toddlers Group (KE13); and Bestwood Park Women's Club (age range 40 to 75, KE31).

56. Stephanie, age unknown, occupation unknown (RMQ).

57. Rowena, 56, housewife (RMQ).

58. Barbara, 40, headteacher (KEQ). One respondent even claimed to 'love' the Savoy (Helen, 40, project worker, RM18).

59. Catherine, 25, student (RMQ).

60. Judith, 39, probation officer (RM3).

61. Phillip, 32, carpenter (RM2).

62. Marc, 25, student (KE15).

63. Betty, 69, retired (KE14).

64. Jones, 2001.

Beyond Cinema:
Film Consumption in the Information Age

Introduction

While the post-war period witnessed a dramatic decline in cinema attendance and the closure of numerous cinemas, these processes did not spell the end for film consumption. On the contrary, over the past two decades, film consumption has been central to the promotion and consumption of a whole range of new media technologies that have proliferated after the advent of television.

Part Five therefore examines the emergence of these new media technologies and the modes of film consumption that have become associated with them. Chapter 12 concentrates on the emergence of the video recorder as a domestic object. In the process, it not only examines the ways in which this object was seen by some as a threat to the integrity of domestic space, but also the way in which it was used by others specifically to control and regulate domestic life. It therefore looks at the video alongside other 'hypermodern convenience devices' such as the freezer, the microwave and telephone answer machine, devices that 'neither save time nor compress time but rather allow the re-ordering of sequential use of time'.[1] As a result, it demonstrates that the video cannot be seen simply as a product of increasing privatisation, and that the uses and meanings of the video are not only shaped within specific social relations but can also be used to establish and order social relations with others.

While the video has been related to processes of privatisation, Chapter 13 examines the emergence of the multiplex and the ways in which it has figured in debates over the changing nature of public space. In other words, while the multiplex has been central to a regeneration of cinemagoing during the 1980s and 1990s, there have been concerns about these venues that relate them to other out-of-town developments, such as shopping centres. This chapter, however, demonstrates the ways in which responses to these places were often the product of class-specific dispositions, and it also examines the different ways in which images of America figure in these debates, and the ways in which these spaces come to represent a series of concerns with modernity and mass culture.

Those who expressed greatest concern over the multiplex were usually those who most identified with the art cinema as a venue, and Chapter 14 moves on to examine the emergence of the Broadway Media Centre from its earliest origins in the film society movement of the 1950s. It examines the ways in which the Broadway not only emerged out of the changing function of culture within city economies but also out of the changing organisation of media industries within the 1980s. During this period, it will be shown, cultural and media industries were increasingly seen as central to economic growth, particularly for declining city economies, but it was also a period in which older liberal notions of culture gave way to a more entrepreneurial concern with the economic uses of culture. In other words, the Broadway had to balance the preservation of a legitimate culture from the supposed barbarism of the market with a more businesslike concern with the economic 'bottom-line'.

This tension also created problems for its image in other ways. From the earliest days of the film society, there had been accusations of elitism directed at the art cinema and its audience and, again and again, the film society and its heirs rejected these accusations by presenting themselves as the champions of diversity. However, while diversity was often used to imply open access to all, it was also used to distinguish itself from the figure of the supposedly homogeneous mass audience of popular culture. In other words, diversity was used to deny elitism at the very same moment as it asserted its distinction from, and superiority over, popular cinema and its audiences. This rejection of popular tastes was recognised both by those who identified with the cinema and those who avoided the place as 'not for the likes of us'.

Finally, Chaper 15 concerns the proliferation of new media technologies: satellite, cable, home cinema and the internet. It not only assesses the predictions that are often made in relation to these media technologies – predictions that are similar to those that we have seen time and again over the course of the 20th century. The chapter also examines the growing importance of film to the promotion and consumption of these new media technologies, and demonstrates that, rather than them spelling the end of film consumption, film is now often seen as the premium and privileged content that is used to justify investment in these media technologies. However, as it will also show, these new media have once again redefined the meanings of film consumption in very specific ways.

Notes

1. Warde, 1999, p. 522.

12

Regulating Reception:
Legislation, Time-Shifting and the Sociality of Video

Just as television was seen as a threat to film consumption, the introduction of video was also widely viewed with suspicion by the film industry. It was believed that its presence would deplete cinema audiences still further and spell the final end of cinemagoing. However, the video again effectively demonstrates that cinemagoing and domestic film consumption are not rival but alternative activities. Moreover, as video ownership increased, so did the cinema audience for the first time since World War II.[1] Indeed, as Phil Hubbard has argued, 'the most frequent cinema-goers are also those most likely to own satellite TV and/or rent videos on a regular basis'.[2] As Docherty, Morrison and Tracey put it: 'video did not poach the cinema audience … cinema and video are parallel entertainments, not strict competitors'.[3] It is even widely believed that video helped the industry. First, the industry was able to use video as another means of reaping profits from film. Film companies once operated the zone-run-clearance system. This was a release pattern in which films were premiered in metropolitan centres, such as the West End of London, before being distributed to the first-run houses in other city centres and then, only in the last instance, were released to local cinemas. Today, similar release patterns are still employed but for different formats. Films are usually first released at the cinema, then on video, then on cable and satellite, and finally, in the last instance, on terrestrial television. Second, video reawakened people's interest in films, so that film consumption has once again a central role in many people's leisure activities – even if cinemagoing remains marginal for many.

Like television, the video is an item of domestic technology that needs to be understood within the total package of domestic technology and domestic relations. Its meanings have changed and developed over time, but they are crucially bound up with the relationships into which they are inserted. For example, one of the reasons why film consumption was able to reacquire a position of centrality within people's leisure activities was due to video's position as an adjunct to the television. It has, for example, been noted that video ownership grew more quickly and became more pervasive in Britain than in other Western countries and the reason for this may be due to the place of television within British culture. The presence of the licence fee, which has long been used to fund the British Broadcasting Corporation, means that television ownership not only required a significant investment for the poorer sections of the population but that, once this investment has been made, 'subsequent consumption is virtually free, making them a captive audience'.[4]

As a result, not only has television become central to the leisure activities of the poorer sections of the population but, in an attempt to optimise their initial investment, most other leisure spending tends to be made in relation to the television. However, the centrality of the television is not limited to the poorer sections of the population, and there has been a concerted effort:

> to turn the domestic TV set into a multipurpose visual display unit, the core of a home entertainment and information processing centre, by offering a range of plug-in peripherals or enhanced facilities such as videocassette recorders, videodisc players, teletext and viewdate decoders, home computers, etc. Efforts are concentrated upon the TV set in part because it now occupies between 30 and 40 per cent of most people's available free time, is their major source of information and entertainment and absorbs about 25 per cent of household leisure expenditure. It also provides people's main point of entry into other sections of the entertainment industry and the arts.[5]

Film consumption has reacquired a position of centrality within people's leisure activities through its integration within forms of domestic leisure that were centred on the television, not through competition with the television set.

Technology, Domesticity and the 'Video Nasty'

However, this process was not a straightforward or unproblematic one. Although the video recorder was initially seen as an expensive technological toy for the connoisseur,[6] for the reasons discussed above, it took off among poorer sections of the population. This situation created problems for the image of the video – a situation that was made still worse by the film industry. It feared that the video would finally destroy the cinema once and for all, and it was therefore reluctant to release its major films on video, a reluctance that created a gap in the market. This gap was quickly filled by the release of an eclectic mix of materials often from marginal sections of film production, and many of these films came to be known as 'video nasties'.

The 'video nasties' were the product of a campaign that was itself the product of a conjunction of factors: first, there was the disreputable image of the video that was created through its association with a popular audience; second, there was the seemingly lurid nature of the films that were available; and third, these issues became caught up in a wider debate about liberal values, particularly in relation to the home.[7] As Barker and others have shown, certain right-wing pressure groups, sections of the press and the Conservative government claimed that the video threatened the sanctity of the family and particularly the innocence of children within it. Using a repeated concern of both left and right, that new media threatened to blur the division between the public and the private sphere and lead to a corruption of the latter by the former, the 'video nasties' campaign argued that censorship was needed to police video materials that would be available in the home.[8]

However, in her study of the response to video within Nottingham's local press, Kate Egan found that local debates were not simply identical to those that preoccupied the

The 'video nasties' were
an eclectic mix of
materials from marginal
sectors of film
production but were
most usually associated
with horror and
pornography. Even
today horror is an
important genre within
the video market.
Hollywood Video,
Hucknell Road

national press. Thus she found that 'Nottingham Evening Post's "nasty" articles demonstrate [the] need to "minimise and maximise" dominant national discourse – to
simultaneously support and contribute to national legislation and discourse, but also to
pre-empt it, or frequently, oppose it'.[9] As she demonstrates, on the one hand, the local
press drew upon public discourses to position itself as a player within a major political
process but, on the other, its local allegiances led it to 'promote local business and
demonise threats against it'. As a result, while it endorsed the views of councillors and
teachers who were opposed to the 'video nasties', it also condoned 'a "laissez-faire" attitude to video censorship'. It therefore sought to defend the rights of the new video
consumer who wanted diversity and choice, and those of 'legitimate' video businesses
as local entrepreneurs. In the process, the local press not only expressed 'a great diversity of opinion' when compared to the national press,[10] but redrew the terms of the
debate. Instead of the straightforward opposition between those 'ordinary people who
know "instinctively" that these videos are an embodiment of evil' and those whose failure to be 'grossly offended' defines them as 'unreasonable',[11] the local press presented

the consumer and the mainstream trader as 'reasonable' and opposed them to the illegal 'backstreet' trader who was supposedly linked to organised crime through 'video piracy'.

However, despite these variations between local and national levels, the struggle over the video and its regulation has parallels with the struggles over early film. Initially, videos were available primarily on rental from 'video libraries', 'often hastily converted small shops' that were 'a feature of almost every high street'[12] but, in both Britain and America, these stores not only became subject to regulation but were increasingly replaced by a series of corporate video chains of which Blockbuster became the most prominent.[13] These stores sought to dispel the disreputable image of their predecessors through a series of strategies. First, their design worked to present a sleeker, clearer and more corporate image. Second, they directed themselves at a family audience and made promises about the types of material that they *would not* stock. In contrast to the supposedly violent and pornographic materials that were the mainstay of the older video libraries, chain stores such as Blockbuster built their reputation and success on supplying more mainstream Hollywood products.

Ironically, of course, this very development also alienated many from the video as a medium. On the one hand, a whole subculture of fandom developed in relation to the video nasties which was directly opposed to the supposedly conformist nature of mainstream film and video. On the other hand, many of our respondents declared their lack of interest in renting films because of the supposedly 'mainstream' nature of the product,

Corporate chains such as Blockbuster, sought to dispel the disreputable image of their predecessors. Blockbuster Video, Mansfield Road, Sherwood

and these respondents were specifically those who tended to see themselves as discerning viewers who identified with the art cinema.[14] As a result, one respondent complained about the 'lack of choice' in video stores. For this respondent, it was not the number of films available that was at issue but rather the range of 'types' of films. There was no choice because the films were all too mainstream and offered little sense of diversity.[15] Ironically, others criticised the video stores for having too much choice on the grounds that they felt overwhelmed by the range of titles, or believed that choice creates 'passivity'.[16] Although choice is often supposed to provide diversity and to allow for discrimination, the implication here was that choice actually prevents discrimination: that it encourages people to simply select from what is on offer rather than actively seek out that which is rare, exclusive and inaccessible. It was similar to the complaint that people go to multiplexes without any idea about what they are going to see. The implication is that people are not actively seeking out a particular aesthetic experience, but simply selecting from a predetermined menu of options.

Control, Choice and Time-Shifting

It was not only those who criticised video who discussed it in terms of choice. On the contrary, the provision of choice was usually seen as the primary positive feature of the video. However, choice here was not simply restricted to the range of materials that can be seen but more commonly it was associated with the contexts of viewing, particularly in terms of the scheduling of viewing. In other words, for many, the video's major benefit was that it enables people to decide when they watch programmes and hence to organise their time more efficiently. Rather than be confined to the schedules of cinemas or broadcasters, video enables people to hire videos that they can watch when they choose or else tape materials off-air and 'time-shift' them – play them back at another point in time from that of the original broadcast. As a result, people claimed that video is more 'convenient', that it provides 'freedom', and allows one to 'adjust the schedules to myself'.[17] Not only does video enable one to 'watch when one likes' but it also enables one to stop and start the video when one likes.[18] One respondent, for example, claimed that she taped materials so that she could watch them while ironing,[19] while another never watched television live but controlled her viewing by taping whatever she wanted to see.[20]

However, one needs to be careful of terms such as 'choice' and 'control'. Some have argued that these terms really amount to little more than the 'consumer sovereignty' championed by the New Right,[21] while others have pointed out that control and choice in consumption is no compensation for exploitative labour relations. Indeed, the increasing concern with choice and control outside work may itself be the product of an increasing loss of choice and control within the labour process.[22] However, while we might accept the second of these arguments, as Sonia Livingstone has demonstrated, choice and control have different meanings for different people and it cannot therefore simply be reduced to a concern with the sovereign consumer.[23]

A different way of understanding many of these references to choice and control is by reference to Alan Warde's work on convenience foods. For Warde, these foods need

One of the key features associated with the video is its convenience and, as a result, video stores are usually located in local neighbourhoods. Hollywood Video, Hucknall Road

to be understood in relation to processes of de-routinisation in which the management of time becomes increasingly problematic. As a result, he notes that 'it was only in the 1960s that convenience came to be associated in any sense with time, and importantly with the re-ordering of time'.[24] He therefore links the video with a range of other 'hyper-modern convenience devices', such as the freezer, microwave, answer phone and electronic mail, that do not operate by saving time but 'rather allow the re-ordering of sequential use of time'.[25] They are about 'timing rather than time'.[26]

Thus, while eating is still seen as a 'social event' and 'eating alone is rarely the pre-ferred option', convenience foods 'permit a form of juggling necessary in a world where the problem is "getting together"'.[27] In this way, hypermodern devices can be 'as much a cause as an effect of de-routinisation', but they can also be used as ways of enabling moments of togetherness through time-shifting. The video, for example, allows one to tape programmes so that busy people can watch them at a time when they can all get together in one place. Alternatively, one may choose to tape a favourite programme so that one can watch it on one's own when others are not around. Choice and control are not simply trivial distractions from the real issues of production but, on the contrary, may be fundamental concerns with the organisation of everyday life.

However, it was not only control that was an issue here but also priorities. Another respondent, who was elderly and felt isolated, claimed that she always watched things on video so that she could put them on pause if the phone rang. For this woman, the phone had a far higher priority than the programmes that she watched: it represented a contact with the outside world which was far more rare and hence far more precious.[28] Other elderly respondents used the video to time-shift films shown in the afternoon into the evening.[29] These viewers felt alienated from contemporary television and films but found old films, that were usually shown in the afternoon, were far more to their liking. Time-shifting therefore allowed them to reorganise the television schedules and redefine shows that had been relegated to marginal spots as central and important events in their evening's entertainment.

For many parents, however, the video was something that existed for the children's use,[30] and they hired videos that would satisfy their children's tastes, rather than their own.[31] For these parents, the video was used to manage familial relationships in a number of different ways. First, it could be used as a childminder, something to keep the children entertained while other domestic chores were undertaken, such as cooking the tea. Second, it could be used as an element in familial bargaining in which it might be offered as an incentive or a reward for particular behaviour. Finally, it could also be used as a way of spending time together, of defining quality family time in which one or both of the parents spent time with the kids. However, these issues are not simply limited to domestic arrangements but may also involve the construction of other senses of communality and identity. Gillespie, for example, has written about the ways in which the video has been used by Asian families to create a sense of cultural and linguistic heritage through the consumption of Bollywood cinema.[32] It should also be borne in mind that time-shifting can be used to create a quite different situation. For example, one family used the video to time-shift programmes so that the parents could share quality time together in peace and quiet after the children had gone to bed. In this way, the video was also used to create a sense of occasion and event that was marked off from other domestic rituals and routines.

However, one of the problems with analysing contemporary uses of video is that, unlike the period in which Ann Gray did her research,[33] the video has become such a 'normal' part of television viewing that it was considered hardly worthy of comment for many of our respondents and had become virtually transparent to them. Some even predicted an end to simultaneity within television viewing, and envisioned an age in which technologies such as the video and the TiVo would mean that everyone watches programmes according to a completely individualised script. These predictions are distinctly premature and other indications suggest that viewers still crave moments of simultaneity. For example, as the phenomenon of *Big Brother* demonstrated in 2000, there is still a desire not only for simultaneity but live viewing,[34] a desire that can also be seen in the attractions of news coverage, live football matches and soap operas.

Social Events

If news, sports and soap operas are among the least time-shiftable programming, film is among the most time-shiftable. While channels do try to create a sense of event through the announcement of 'movie premieres', the problem is that films are rarely genuine premieres but have usually been shown at the cinema, and released on video for rental, long before they are shown on satellite and eventually reach terrestrial television. However, this means that different media can have very different connotations. One respondent, for example, casually remarked that he saw satellite as halfway between video and 'normal' television.[35] Here video was the privileged object, a special event that existed in opposition to television. While one was simply freely available, the other requires an investment of time and effort in taping, hiring or possibly buying a video, and it can also be augmented by other ritual and activities.[36] While 'normal' television viewing was seen as an everyday activity, many people reserved the hiring of videos for a special occasion. One family restricted themselves to one film a week as a way of making that event special,[37] while another achieved the same effect by only renting videos on Friday and Saturday nights.[38] Another respondent explicitly stated that he rarely rented videos so that when he did rent them, it was clearly defined as an event or a special occasion.[39] Others used a range of rituals to mark video viewing off from 'normal' television viewing – rituals such as turning off the lights or having a special drink, such as a bottle of wine, while watching the video.[40] In this way, the experience could be marked as a special event, and one respondent even stated that she used video viewing as a personal indulgence.[41]

However, while this respondent used video as a kind of personal treat, video can also be used to produce or maintain social relations with others. While video has been claimed to represent the retreat into privacy, video has also been used to produce and maintain a whole series of different kinds of sociality. As we have seen, some used the video as a way of doing things 'as a family' or 'as a couple', but others used video as a

Video stores not only display their videos to suggest that they offer choice but also place them alongside other goods, such as popcorn and ice cream that can be used to mark the hiring of a video as a special event. Hollywood Video

way of getting together with friends.[42] One respondent stated that she and her friends often used it for 'girlie nights',[43] but it was not simply private groupings that used video to produce and maintain a sense of sociality. For example, one organisation, Chrysalis, a support group for the bereaved, regularly held video showings for its members in order to create a focus for the group, and to generate a sense of collective activity and belonging.[44]

However, video is about more than simply the programmes viewed: it is also important to remember that videotapes are themselves material objects with meanings that exceed those of a mere recording. As with records, for example, one copy of a particular recording is not necessarily equivalent to all the other copies of that same recording. For example, an original pressing of a rare single will be worth more in both symbolic and financial terms than a mass-produced compilation that contains the exact same track. As a result, videotapes can be used to construct relationships. For example, it has become common practice to give videos as presents on birthdays and at Christmas,[45] but these are usually pre-recorded videos. It would usually be seen as 'cheap' to simply give an off-air recording on such an occasion. In contrast, however, one family specifically used off-air video recordings to establish relationships of intimacy and care. Thus while the elderly grandfather did not have satellite or cable, he claimed that he did not feel a need for them because his daughter taped things for him and provided him with a selection of the best films.[46] In this way, the exchange of videos was used to demonstrate care for the recipient and so made the recordings meaningful as more than simply copies of films, but as labours of love.[47]

This distinction between videos as mere recordings and as cultural objects in themselves can also be seen in other ways. One respondent, for example, refused to use his machine to tape off-air and would only watch pre-recorded videos.[48] Given that this practice was much more expensive, it is clear that for this respondent the meaning of a pre-recorded video was somehow seen as superior to that of an off-air recording. This choice may have been due to the supposed quality of the recording, but it may have also involved other pleasures. For example, one of the ways in which the value of a tape can be constructed is through the practice of video collecting. As Hollows has demonstrated, this practice is often used in fandom as a way of distinguishing between the implicitly male fan and the imagined other of the feminine consumer,[49] and she quotes Saisselin who argues: 'Women were consumers of objects; men were collectors. Women bought to decorate and for the sheer joy of buying, but men had a vision for their collections, and viewed their collections as an ensemble with a philosophy behind it.'[50] Hollows is not implying that the collector is necessary biologically male, but rather that 'different modes of collecting can be seen as a means of constructing or performing gendered identities'.[51] As a result, collecting is not simply an individualised activity: different modes of collecting are ways of not only constructing and performing identities but also of producing and maintaining specific forms of sociality. For example, as Straw argues, 'male practices of accumulation share in an ongoing relationship between the personal space of the collection and the public discursive systems of ordering or value [that] tie each male's collection to an ongoing, collective enterprise of cultural archaeology'.[52] In other words, the material culture of collecting provides 'the raw materials around which the rituals of homosocial interaction take place'.[53] Similarly, while women's collections have frequently been claimed to be more personal and intimate, it is through these characteristics that their collections operate to construct and perform gendered identities. Far from being outside social and cultural relationships, these are the very characteristics that are usually associated with femininity.[54]

However, while the video is usually seen as providing convenience, freedom and control, it is also the case that it is not 'a totally responsive device' but one that has 'a script of its own'.[55] This is not to imply that design directly determines use but simply to stress that it can impose demands of its own. For example, one elderly woman said that she could not use the video to tape films and other programmes because her poor hearing made her dependent on the subtitles on teletext, subtitles that the video does not tape.[56] Similarly, while video is often used to solve familial conflicts when two shows are on at the same time, conflicts can also arise over which should be taped and which should be watched. It is also the case that in some homes conflicts occur between those who want to use the video to record a programme and those who want to use the video to watch a recorded programme.

This situation is also related to the types of programming associated with the video. For many, certain films are seen as more or less appropriate to different modes of presentation. For example, one woman claimed that with most films she waited until they can be rented on video or appear on satellite before she saw them, but this statement also implied that there were certain films for which she would not wait.[57] As we noted in Chapter 11, many believed that big-budget spectaculars were best seen at the cinema, and a large number of elderly respondents, many of whom had not been to the cinema in decades, turned out to see *Titanic*. However, these choices are still a matter of the experiences that one values and the relationship that one wants to establish to a particular type of film. This can be seen through the seemingly contradictory views of two respondents. While one stated quite definitely that horror films were best seen in the cinema, another stated, equally definitely, that they were best seen on video. For the latter, the appeal of the video was that he could stop the video at the scary bits, giving him a measure of security and control over the film. However, for the former, it was precisely the unstoppable and uninterruptible nature of cinema presentation that made it the perfect venue for watching horror films. For this respondent, the pleasures of watching horror in the cinema were bound up with a lack of control.

Notes

1. Hubbard, forthcoming.
2. Ibid.
3. Docherty, Morrison and Tracey, 1987, p. 2.
4. Garnham, 1990, p. 125.
5. Ibid., p. 118.
6. A similar process can also be seen in relation to the current emergence of 'home cinema' and is discussed brilliantly by Barbara Klinger in *Fortresses of Solitude: Cinema, New Technologies, and the Home*, forthcoming.

7. See Barker, 1984.

8. The contradictory status of the family can most clearly be seen through the contrast between two campaigns at the time. The video nasties campaign called for experts to police what would be available in the home and so take the decision out of the hands of parents who, it was claimed, were in some cases too liberal in their values to be trusted. However, in roughly the same period, a campaign led by Victoria Gillick and others also attacked liberalism but called for the right to prescribe the pill to young girls to be taken out of the hands of experts such as doctors, whose liberalism meant that they could not be trusted, and required that they obtain the permission from parents before the pill could be prescribed. In both cases, sanctity of the family is invoked, but it is not the family that is valued, but specific values. In one case, the family is equated with permissiveness and experts are required to police it and, in the other, experts are associated with permissiveness and the family is required to police them. See Barker, 1984.

9. Egan, forthcoming, unpublished PhD thesis.

10. Franklin and Murphy, 1992, p. 10.

11. Barker, 1984, p. 23.

12. Gray, 1992, p. 217.

13. For a history of the rise of Blockbuster see Gomery, 1992.

14. Stefan, 25, unemployed teacher (K19).

15. Tracey, 37, solicitor (KE4).

16. Stefan, 25, unemployed teacher (K19).

17. Ms Caine, 41, teacher (RMQ); and Mrs Gee, 62, retired (RMQ).

18. Catherine, 25, student (RMQ).

19. Anne, 46, learning support assistant and teacher (KE28).

20. Sharan, 33, nurse/tutor (KE35).

21. McGuigan, 1998.

22. This argument was recently articulated by Nicholas Garnham at a one-day event at the LSE hosted by Nick Couldry: 'Media Research: New Agendas, New Priorities?', 14 May 2001.

23. Livingstone, 1992, pp. 113–30.

24. Warde, 1999, p. 520.

25. Ibid., p. 522.

26. Ibid., p. 521.

27. Ibid., p. 523.

28. Betty, 69, retired office worker/home help (KE11).

29. Mrs Calder, 72, retired teacher (KE22).

30. Whitegate Mothers and Toddlers Group, members between 20 and 40, occupations unknown (KE13).

31. Anne, 46, learning support assistant and teacher (KE28).

32. Gillespie, 1989, pp. 226–39; and Gillespie, 1995.

33. Gray, 1992.

34. It should be pointed out that, in the case of *Big Brother*, the desire for simultaneity was also augmented by the ability to view events in real time on the computer via the internet.

35. Mark, 25, student (KE15).

36. Chris, 52, lecturer (RM5).

37. Whitegate Mothers and Toddlers Group (KE13).

38. James, 15, schoolboy (KE23).

39. John Straw, 55, occupation unknown (RS2).

40. Stefan, 25, unemployed teacher (K19); unnamed female, 41, registered general nurse (KEQ).

41. Joanne, 25, human resources administrator (KE5).

42. Tracey, 37, solicitor (KE4).

43. Donna, 30, clerical officer (KE3); and Keith, 35, clerk (KEQ).

44. Sheila, 61, teacher and secretary of Chrysalis (RM19).

45. Celia, 62, retired cleaner (KE6).

46. Massey, 1994.

47. For work on care and consumption see Warde, 1997; and DeVault, 1991.

48. Michael, 58, lecturer (RM9).

49. Hollows, forthcoming.

50. Rémy Saisselin cited in Belk and Wallendorf, 1994, p. 241. See also Straw, 1997, pp. 3–16.

51. Hollows, forthcoming.

52. Straw, 1997, p. 6.

53. Ibid., p. 5.

54. Hollows, 2000.

55. Shove and Southerton, 2000, p. 314.

56. Bakersfield and Sneinton Co-op Women's Guild (KE20).

57. Donna, 30, clerical officer (KE3).

13

'The Splendid American Venture on the Ring Road': Multiplexes, Americanisation and Mass Consumption

If the video helped place film consumption back at the centre of people's leisure activities, another development also compounded this situation: the emergence of the multiplex. However, the multiplex has not been straightforwardly celebrated for its regeneration of cinemagoing but, on the contrary, it has been a highly contested institution. Part of the problem has been its association with the blockbuster. As Gomery has noted, the success of multiplex cinemas was specifically their ability to use their multiple screens to reap maximum profits from blockbusters. Describing the strategy of Cineplex, a 'Canadian enterprise [that] significantly altered the standards by which North America judged "going to the movies"',[1] Gomery writes:

> Cineplex began booking first-run Hollywood films and developed a formula: open a popular, well-advertised film on three or four of its screens, and then slowly cut back the number of auditoria as the popularity of the film waned. Maneuvering auditoria was perfected to a science. What Taylor and Drabinsky hoped, however, was for the opposite problem. If an *E.T.* or *Top Gun* came along, they would move it into a half-dozen of their largest auditoria, accommodate surging crowds, and not miss a single possible customer.[2]

While this association between the multiplex and the blockbuster has proved financially profitable, and also stimulated renewed interest in cinemagoing as an activity, both remain objects of considerable criticism. For example, Martin Barker and Kate Brooks have argued that these cinemas are 'for unashamed indulgence in trash'.[3]

In other words, cinemas become associated with, and come to represent, specific forms of consumption that are hierarchically ranked and valued, and this has specific implications for cultural policy. For example, in the draft business plan of the East Midlands Region Media Agencies Partnership (EMRMAP), the strategy for exhibition policy draws on a specific metaphorical distinction:

> The terms 'specialist cinema' or 'cultural cinema' indicate cinemas which predominantly screen films whose language, form or subject matter tends to result in it obtaining only a limited release in the UK. Like the restaurant sector, specialist cinemas offer a different menu and a different ambience compared to the 'fast food' multiplexes.[4]

This distinction is not peculiar to the EMRMAP and, as we shall see, it draws on a series of discourses and associations that surround the multiplex more generally.

The Place of Consumption

However, the multiplex is not only criticised for the types of film consumption with which it is associated, it is also criticised for its relationship to, and effects upon, the city more generally. It is often linked with the growth of other out-of-town developments such as the shopping mall, and is subject to very similar debates.[5] According to Miller and his collaborators, the 'often contested meanings of these shopping places'[6] can be divided into two main concerns. On the one hand, these shopping malls are seen as a solution to the problems of the inner city. As Miller and his collaborators put it:

> the privatisation of space within shopping centres and malls provides a solution to the now
> widespread fear of public space, with closed-circuit television and other visible means of
> improved personal security adding to the sense of risk-free shopping (at whatever cost in
> terms of social and spatial exclusion).[7]

These fears of public space are also expressed, according to Miller and his collaborators, in 'highly racialised terms … sometimes mediated through notions of dirt and pollution'.[8]

If the shopping centre is viewed positively in these terms, there are others who display 'fears about the increasingly "artificial" nature of contemporary shopping', and such fears 'are as much about the social context of shopping as they are about the physical setting of the shopping centre or mall'.[9] Certainly these fears do reflect a sense of unease at the forms of social exclusion on which these places are based, but they are often as much the product of a largely middle-class desire to distance oneself from the figure of an undifferentiated mass:

> When people yearn for a return to 'personal service' or support current trends for opening
> up enclosed shopping centres to 'natural light', we suggest that they are at least as concerned
> about the increasing artificiality of their social relationships (and in particular the perceived
> materialism of their children) as they are about the physical environment itself.[10]

Middle-class nostalgia for an 'authentic' and 'natural' world of consumption cannot therefore be explained with reference to the past. As Miller *et al.* argue, 'what is seen as "natural" today' is best explained not through reference to 'historical knowledge', but through 'a distinctly modern and rapidly developing reconceptualisation of what is being projected backwards as having once been the traditional "community", or what can be termed the imagined community of creative nostalgia'.[11]

As a result, Miller and his colleagues not only discuss the campaigns to open up Brent Cross Shopping Centre to natural light but also the preference among certain sections of the middle classes for a shopping area called Ibis Pond, that was perceived as 'more of a community'.[12] On the one hand, these consumers are clearly engaged in an attempt to distinguish themselves from the 'ordinary' consumer through a sense of themselves as discerning and distinctive people who reject the commercialism and homogeneity of mass consumption. The desire for diversity is therefore not necessarily an appreciation of others but rather a way of differentiating oneself from the mass. On the other hand, Miller and his colleagues also stress that these 'shoppers act to ameliorate the negative feelings that they have about shopping as an act of materialism ... by situating the shopping act within some other concern'.[13] One of the reasons for the preference for natural light is that it creates 'a potential ambiguity between going shopping and going for a walk'.[14]

These strategies are also related to a different understanding of the nature of consumption. Having little experience of the shop as a place of work, these sections of the middle classes tend to view shopping in moral terms: 'In particular, they are concerned with the conflict between an idealised notion of community and the idea that materialism has been the main force which destroyed this mythical state.'[15] In this way, materialism becomes the cause of all contemporary social ills and they are therefore 'concerned to use the ambience of the shop to resolve the constant sense of ambivalence and contradiction which they experience' in relation to shopping.[16] They seek out modes of consumption that can be associated with their fantasies of community rather than their fears of materialism. In this way, the experience of shopping places was closely related to class identifications:

> Many middle-class informants identified with Ibis Pond as an imagined ideal community
> redolent with nostalgia which assumed how communities used to be, though bolstered also
> by the genuine experience of meeting other shoppers that they knew. In the case of Wood
> Green this was replaced by a community of personal association built up largely through an
> identification of working-class people with those who continue to work as shop assistants.
> The symmetry of the two class positions becomes more acute when the relationship between
> shoppers and shop assistants is taken into account.[17]

While the middle classes perceived Ibis Pond as a place of community, few middle-class shoppers came 'to know any of the shop assistants where they shopped'.[18]

These concerns were also related to other features of the shopping centre and the multiplex. These developments were largely outside the city centre and were often specifically seen as a solution to traffic congestion within the city centre. However, this feature created two related concerns. First, these spaces reinforced their patrons' dependence on the motor car. The success of these developments was precisely that they were geared to customers who not only had access to cars, but had also largely deserted consumption in the town centre due to the problems of parking there. Similarly, while the old picture palaces had been built at the intersection of public transport systems in the city centre, the new multiplexes were usually built near major road intersections on the outskirts of the city, and were therefore able to draw on patrons from a wide area. These multiplexes drew upon the changing perceptions of locality that a car culture produced, and people not only came from as far away as Grantham to use the

Showcase, Nottingham's multiplex, but many Nottingham residences stated their preference for the ABC in Mansfield or the UCI in Derby.[19]

However, as we have seen, the car has increasingly been seen as symbolic of the destruction of the city. Its demands tear up neighbourhoods and pollute the environment, but it also creates social exclusion. As car ownership has increased, public transport has not only been cut back but has become increasingly associated with the poorest sections of the population. Out-of-town developments are, in part, seen as safe exactly because only certain sections of the population have the transport necessary to gain access to them, but these locations are also haunted by the social exclusion on which they were based.

The second concern is that these developments have only increased the decline of the town centres. As leisure and consumption have increasingly moved out to these developments, town centres have declined still further, and these developments have therefore also become important symbolically. Unlike America, where they were produced out of the processes of urban sprawl, most of the British shopping centres and multiplexes have been built on 'redundant industrial land ... in the Midlands and the North of England where the multiplex has established itself easily'.[20] In this way, these developments have come to symbolise the transformation of the city from a place of production to one of consumption.[21] They represent the literal replacement of industrial factories with cathedrals of consumption and have therefore created a 'tale of two cities': a landscape of increased luxury and prosperity for some and extreme poverty for others.[22]

Selling the Multiplex

Nottingham's first multiplex, the Showcase, was opened on Thursday 16 June 1988 and it had eleven screens – more than any other cinema in the country at the time. There was also space for another three screens.[23] Bowden Wilson of Leicester, the company that had acquired the site, were planning to build a garden centre, a DIY store, a car accessory store and either a public house or a restaurant.[24] However, the area became a centre of leisure and entertainment rather than retail, and the multiplex was soon joined by the Megabowl and Isis nightclub.

As with earlier periods of cinema building, the promotional and publicity materials all stressed the new cinema's modernity and comfort. An advert in the NEP claimed that the Showcase would be 'very upmarket',[25] while the press claimed that it combined 'Comfort ... Convenience ... Luxury' with 'the healthful comfort of perfectly controlled air-conditioning'.[26] Also like earlier cinemas, it was 'yet another "first"' and demonstrated that Nottingham was fully up-to-date.[27] Not only was it 'the only one of its kind in the Midlands',[28] but it was also 'Britain's newest and largest cinema'.[29] Furthermore, it would be part of 'one of the most exciting leisure areas in Europe'.[30] Nor was this simply local exaggeration: *The Independent*, a major national newspaper, also believed that it was one of the largest in the country.[31]

The cinema's claims to being modern and innovative were also consolidated through its presentation as an 'an all-American operation'. According to the 'American' manager,

The Showcase multiplex: 'The splendid American venture on the ring road'

American National Amusements (the company that owned the Showcase) was 'bringing American standards of quality to Britain in an industry which has a great future'.[32] The NEP also added to the sense of the building as positive in its foreignness: 'the 11-screen cinema is nothing like anyone remembers; nothing like anyone in this country has ever known'. It was 'entertainment in the grand style' with 'spacious surroundings', 'luxurious comfort' and 'the highest quality of presentation'. The NEP 'comment column' also referred to it as 'the splendid American venture on the ring road' and the *Nottingham Trader* and *Nottingham Recorder* were similarly positive. In short, the 'American invasion of the city' was definitely presented as a 'good thing'.[33]

These reports worked to construct an imaginary America that was consumed through the practices of cinemagoing.[34] For the NEP, the rocking chairs summoned up images of '"sitting" on the old front door' and an interview with the manager (who actually came from Preston but had emigrated to America) sought to define the '"all-American" outlook on life',[35] which was encapsulated in the words 'movies', 'corporate images', 'concession stands', 'multiplex concepts' and 'quality customer service'. Something else that was associated with America was the supposed glamour of the place. Its 'glittering celebrity opening'[36] had 'a grand reception in grand American style' that gave the guests a 'taste of Hollywood'.[37]

However, the company was also concerned that some Nottingham residents would not appreciate the fact that an American company owned the cinema or that the company had brought over its own management. As a result, press releases and interviews tried to alleviate these concerns, or at least to convince the NEP's readers that they would benefit from the 'American way'. For example, a spokesman for National

Amusements stressed that while the cinema's American style was synonymous with quality, the company would not ignore Nottingham as a place:

> Our theatres, with more comfort, more space and more attention to detail, are recognised as the finest in the United States – and that's the standard we're bringing to Nottingham ... The addition of this kind of enterprise serves as a magnet for and contributes to the development of a myriad of other business enterprises, with the resulting additional employment and revenue to the community. We aim to play a significant role in not only the civic but also the economic affairs of the communities in which we operate.[38]

Also when National Amusements flew Tercon Management Systems over from Kansas to train their staff, John Bilborough of National Amusements was aware that this might upset people, and he justified the move by explaining: 'We're not saying British cinemas aren't run well, but we just like to run our business in a certain way.'[39]

It was not only through its supposed 'Americanness' that National Amusements tried to sell the Showcase. The cinema also marked its distinction from more traditional cinemas in other ways. For example, it had a car-parking space for 850 cars and it was therefore claimed that everyone would find car-parking space, not just a few customers. It was designed in ways that, as can be seen from the comments above, were clearly supposed to signify spectacle, comfort and luxury, although as we shall see, others have read the multiplex as bland and functional. The 'product' was also different: there were no adverts, no smoking, no double features, no interval and no ice-cream lady.[40] However, there was a massive concession stand that dominated the central foyer which one had to pass to gain access to the cinemas. As James Lyons has argued, food was therefore central in the construction of the Showcase's image, and the selection of foods clearly associates the cinema with the pleasures of America and the mass-produced abundance that it represents.[41] It is therefore significant that National Amusements made special mention of the two types of popcorn that were available and that the management felt 'really account for a lot'.[42]

The cinema management was also very concerned to emphasise that for the first time Nottingham audiences could see films at the same time as the West End of London, a feature that symbolically relocated Nottingham as a central place. The Showcase, it was implied, gave one direct access to Hollywood cinema and, as a result, Nottingham was no longer marginal to London but was as up-to-date as anywhere in Britain.

Despite this concern with its newness, there were several features of the Showcase that were not new, and which question Nottingham's claim to being at the cutting edge of cinema. First, while the Showcase was the first cinema built by American National Amusements in Britain, and the first cinema with eleven screens, it was certainly not the first multiplex. The Point in Milton Keynes was opened in 1985 by American Multi Cinemas (AMC), predating the Showcase by three years. The Salford Quays then followed the Point in 1986 and by the end of 1988 there were fourteen multiplexes in Britain. Even if we accept that the Showcase was probably the first in the Midlands, as it claimed, it did not maintain this advantage for very long. By the end of 1988, Derby had two multiplexes, one of which was built by AMC and the other of which was built by National Amusements.[43] Even within Nottingham, the Showcase's claim to being the first multiplex was contested. Ernest Frisby, the manager of the Canon (formerly the ABC), thought that, as the manager of a multi-screen cinema, he already operated a multiplex.[44] Nor did the Showcase ensure that Nottingham had more choice in venues or screens: there had been more screens in the 1930s and 1940s.

Indeed, while the Showcase's management made claims to the cinema's newness and modernity, it also associated the cinema with this earlier era. The advertising played heavily on nostalgia for the glamour of the Hollywood past, even though it sought to assert the Showcase's superiority over that past in other respects. In short, it tried to negotiate a relationship between the past and future. In a similar way, Lynn Spigel has claimed that her students were able to maintain both a nostalgic desire for the past and a sense of the present as progress from that past, and that they did so by imagining the future as an idealised time in which they could reconcile the pleasures associated with both past and present. As she claims: 'Nostalgia in this regard is not the opposite of progress, but rather its handmaiden. Like the idea of progress, nostalgia works to simplify history into a time-line of events that lead somewhere better.'[45]

The management even enlisted the veteran local film critic Emrys Bryson to endorse the cinema by dedicating an auditorium to him. The report of this event places particular emphasis on both his age and his professional status. It begins by quoting the plaque commemorating the critic: 'Emrys Bryson, Critic Emeritus, for his outstanding contributions in the field of film commentary'. This quote is then followed by the paper's own words: 'For 38 years, Emrys Bryson shared his wit and wisdom with readers of the *Evening Post*, while he steered them in the direction of what and what not to see at the cinema. And to his fans he was, indeed, outstanding.'[46] The majority of the article then proceeds to provide Emrys with the opportunity to recollect nostalgically a golden age of cinema and to lament the closing of many old cinemas, before he finally endorses the Showcase with the claim:

> I was worried at first about the effect the Showcase would have, but in fact it cleared out a lot of dead wood and it put the other cinemas on their mettle ... I think that the multiplexes have actually done a great deal for the cinema industry.[47]

While he acknowledges certain anxieties about the multiplex, he ultimately condones it as embodying both the best of the past and the best of the present.

The Meanings of the Multiplex

These perceptions of the Showcase were shared by a great many of our respondents. Many saw it as the best of the Nottingham cinemas,[48] and associated it with America in ways that were wholly positive.[49] For these respondents, the Showcase was a distinctive and spectacular building that was often described as 'overwhelming'.[50] Here the term overwhelming was a positive one, implying sensorial abundance even to the point of dizzying overload. This abundance was not, however, limited to the scale of the building or the provision of food, but also to the range and choice of films on offer. As a result, one respondent liked the cinema because one had more chance to catch a specific film there than anywhere else. It was particularly popular with the groups of Asian youth and with the youth of Southwell, for whom it represented something that was clearly divorced from what they regarded as the provincial location of their everyday lives.[51] Parents often claimed that their young children loved the place, and that they frequently felt pressure to take them there.[52] However, while some parents were clearly ambivalent about their children's attachment to the place, its success as a cinema is also closely tied to its function as a 'safe environment' for youth. Many parents used the place as a kind of teenage crèche at which they would drop off their teenagers, in the knowledge that the location of the multiplex made it difficult for them to go anywhere else, while the security systems also meant that they were free from dangers associated with the town centre. Parents implied that they felt that the security prevented their kids getting into other sorts of trouble, such as petty crime and drug taking. Safety was an issue for disabled respondents too, who stressed that the Showcase was distinguished by its provision of level access.[53]

However, many adults also saw the cinema as an unappealing and alienating space,[54] and it is significant that those adults who did like the place often had an association with it through a teenage intermediary. Some elderly respondents, for example, took their grandchildren there, and the positive experience of spending time with their grandchildren also coloured their feelings about the cinema more generally.[55] Another respondent who liked the Showcase had a point of access as a result of her son, with whom she often went to films.[56] In these ways, the Showcase was seen as a place where the family could do something together, although this situation does not necessarily imply that they occupied the same auditorium. Several respondents said that one of the advantages of the multiplex was precisely that one could go out as a family together, but watch different movies. In other words, the family would travel to the cinema together and then split off to see different movies before meeting up again after their respective shows.[57]

For these respondents, the cinema was also described as welcoming,[58] and with friendly staff.[59] For others, however, the cinema was a deeply unpleasant and even repellent place whose audience was a mindless mass who were simply duped by marketing.[60] For these respondents, the Showcase was not a spectacular and visually impressive building but a characterless and even 'placeless' place.[61] However, it was not simply the building that was being discussed here but a more general sense of the building's cultural meanings. Thus while some described the showcase as 'soulless',[62] 'clinical'[63] and 'like an airport',[64] these descriptions also suggested that it is 'impersonal'.[65] These terms therefore had two implicit meanings: on the one hand there was a sense of this place as somehow lacking in identity, but on the other this was associated with a sense of functionality and rationality – with technology, materialism and commerce. Furthermore, while Miller and his colleagues found that concerns with the supposed 'artificiality' of Brent Cross Shopping Centre were frequently framed through concerns with the lack of 'natural' light, from its first opening, similar concerns about the Showcase were framed in relations to its 'atmosphere'.

The air-conditioning units that had been used to sell the place as a well-regulated space became the target of criticism almost immediately, when customers complained that they found the cinema too cold. The managing director, speaking from the United States, said that they had to turn up the heating on the grounds that 'it must be a lot colder over there and we got a few complaints'.[66] However, our questionnaires and interviews demonstrate that many people still found the cinema too cold. This was more than simply a complaint about the temperature, and complaints about the coldness of the building were often metaphorically related to a generalised criticism of the cinema. Most obviously, many respondents claimed that the cinema had 'no atmosphere' by which they meant again that it lacked personality, character and was emotionally cold and empty.[67] However, other complaints about the air also emerged time and again in other contexts. One respondent, for example, complained that the cinema 'smells funny',[68] while another experienced a feeling of revulsion at the smell of popcorn which, they claimed, permeates the cinema.[69]

As this reference to popcorn makes clear, this visceral intolerance to the air of the cinema was actually related to broader cultural meanings. One respondent condemned the cinema as 'popcorn city',[70] and so associated it with low and debased cultural forms and activities. Popcorn has become a symbol for negative evaluations of the Showcase as an American place and, by implication, as a place of popular amusements and 'unashamed indulgence in trash'.[71] This is made clear by the frequent references to the cinema as

In opposition to the supposed 'sterility' and 'commercialism' of the multiplex, many fan cultures associate themselves with the non-commercial through a celebration of the shabby, seedy and sleazy. Forbidden Planet, Broadmarsh Centre, City Centre

'vulgar'[72] and 'brash',[73] and to the claims that the cinema was part of a process of Americanisation[74] – a process which, as Duncan Webster has pointed out, is often claimed to
involve 'invasion', 'colonisation' and 'homogenisation'. In this way, as Webster points
out, Americanisation is used to displace anxieties about modernity through a deflection
of its effects onto an alien invading other. Thus, America comes to signify the negative
features of materialism and mass production in a way that not only lets Britain off the
hook but is 'mediated through notions of dirt and pollution' even if this process is seen
in terms of nation rather than race.

Thus, when people complained about the corporate image of National Amusements,
they associated it with a pushy and materialistic American culture.[75] These issues were
also related to complaints about being 'herded'[76] or 'treated like a number'.[77] Here the
complaint was not just about a materialistic and commercial system but one that turns
its customers into mere product to be processed. It evoked the imagery of people as
mere mass product – cattle – and asserted the common distinction between the crowd
and the authentic community. It was also a common claim that the Showcase provides
no place to interact with one another or talk about the film afterwards.[78] These accounts
of the Showcase also presented it as a place in which there was a confusion between the
audience as those who consume and those who are consumed. This can also be found
in references to the Showcase's 'pile em high' attitude.[79] The audience here were discussed as the commodities not as the consumers of those commodities. It is also for this

Many respondents saw the choice provided by the multiplex as no real choice, but only
homogeneous and standardised fare, a position that leads many fan cultures to celebrate the
weird and wacky. Forbidden Planet

reason that while those who identified with the Showcase used the term 'overwhelming' positively, those who disliked the place referred to it as 'overwhelming' too.[80] For these people, it was too big, too overpowering and hence inhuman. These people complained about the crowds, but also the range of choice which, as we have discussed in relation to video, was assumed to produce passive and undiscriminating customers who had no idea of what they are going to see before they arrived at the cinema.[81]

The Multiplex and City-Centre Cinemas

This concern with the undifferentiated mass also shaded over into concerns about the effect of the multiplex upon the city centre. For example, the planning officer, Dick Blenkinsop, claimed that he was afraid that the public's choice would be reduced, rather than increased, by the presence of the multiplex, if its presence forced the city-centre cinemas to close.[82] However, the NEP displayed considerable optimism in their claim that there would be plenty of customers for the city-centre cinemas, and that the Odeon was 'meeting the challenge not with moans and groans about competition but with typical enthusiasm and verve'. The presence of the multiplex was therefore read as 'healthy competition' in which the 'customer invariably wins'. Moreover, the newspaper claimed that 'the quality of production, direction and acting has never been higher' in feature films and that this situation, together with the presence of 'breathtaking new technology and techniques', would ensure high attendance at all cinemas.[83] This view was even supported by the Odeon manager who believed that there was enough 'product' around to justify the presence of the existing cinemas.[84] However, the NEP also believed that Nottingham was a unique case; that the city was such a vibrant centre of leisure and culture that it could easily sustain another large cinema: 'No other city outside London offers so much and no other city buzzes with people and activity during the leisure hours in the way that Nottingham does.'[85]

While this might sound a lot like boosterism, which it no doubt was, it also seems to have been partly correct. Ironically, it was not the Showcase that killed off the Odeon and the Canon/ABC. In the late 1990s, as we will see, there were growing concerns about the impact of out-of-town leisure and retail developments and, in response, new developments were encouraged to site themselves within the city centre. One such development was the Cornerhouse, a large leisure complex that boasted '18 catering outlets and 14 screens'.[86] As the NEP commented,

> Two thirds of a century after opening as Nottingham's biggest talkie palace, the Odeon tomorrow becomes the city's hottest development site. Across Chapel Bar, along Market Street and over Theatre Square, the scaffolding has come off a ritzy new leisure emporium. Multiplex cinemas have come in from the trading estates, and it was the imminent opening of Warner Village at the £50m Cornerhouse that led Odeon Cinemas to tear up their ticket.[87]

The Odeon and ABC had been 'able to overcome the national box office crisis of the mid-1980s and the arrival ... of National Amusements' edge-of-town Showcase complex', but it was the Cornerhouse that was the 'straw [that broke] the camel's back'.[88]

However, no other city in the region fared in this way. Nottingham's presence as the centre for consumption, leisure and culture within the region meant that it was able to sustain a more diverse film culture than other towns in the region. In Derby, for example, the presence of a multiplex resulted in the removal of all cinemas from the town centre with the exception of a small regional film theatre, the Metro.

None the less, the Showcase did have an impact on the Odeon. The management responded to its presence with a renovation programme that cost £65,000.[89] Furthermore, in the weeks leading up to the opening of the Showcase, the NEP contained adverts for the Odeon which referred to it as 'Nottingham's first multi-screen cinema' which presented 'cinema as it was meant to be' on the largest screens in the city. These adverts also announced the introduction of 'executive' seats which were installed in the Odeon, possibly in response to the 'rocking chairs' that were such a feature of the Showcase.[90]

The Showcase also had an impact on attendance at both the Odeon and the Cannon, and in July 1988 both managers admitted that their attendance had fallen.[91] In 1997, the manager of the Odeon also described the long-term impact of the Showcase: the sorts of people who went to the Odeon had now changed and were largely those who could not afford a car, such as students, and certain types of families.[92] None the less, despite the prevailing tendency elsewhere, the opening of the Nottingham Showcase did offer people more 'choice'. People could either go to the cinema in the car without having to brave the supposed dangers of the city centre, or they could use the city-centre cinemas as before. It also provided more screens and could therefore screen a wider range of films than was available at the Odeon or the Canon/ABC combined. None the less, many respondents saw the choice provided by the multiplex as no 'real' choice, but only a homogeneous and standardised fare. For these respondents, the supposedly 'non-commercial' cinemas provided a more meaningful degree of choice.[93]

Notes

1. Gomery, 1992, p. 105.
2. Ibid., p. 107.
3. Barker and Brooks, 1998, p. 195.
4. East Midlands Region Media Agencies Partnership, *Draft Business Plan*, February 2001, p. 23.
5. This link is made clear by the title of William Paul's essay, 'The K-Mart Audience at the Mall Movies', 1994, pp. 487–501. See also Gomery, 1992; Jones, 2001; Hanson, 1999; and Hubbard, forthcoming.
6. Miller, Jackson, Thrift, Holbrook and Rowlands, 1998, p. ix.
7. Ibid., p. xi.
8. Ibid., p. x.
9. Ibid., p. xi.
10. Ibid.
11. Ibid., p. 123.
12. Ibid.

13. Ibid., p. 133.

14. Ibid.

15. Ibid., p. 131.

16. Ibid., p. 121.

17. Ibid., p. 126.

18. Ibid.

19. Sharan said that she regularly met her friends from Grantham at the Showcase, although she also stated that she generally went to the ABC Mansfield on other occasions (33, nurse/tutor, KE35). Lisa (29, teacher, KEQ) also stated that she tended to go to the ABC Mansfield.

20. Gray, 1996, p. 129.

21. See for example, Hannigan, 1998; David Harvey, 1989a; and Zukin, 1995.

22. Hannigan, 1998, p. 53.

23. *Nottingham Recorder*, 23 June 1988.

24. NEP, 13 February 1987.

25. NEP, 4 February 1987.

26. Advert in NEP, 17 June 1988.

27. 'Post Comment', NEP, 17 June 1988.

28. NEP, 13 December 1987.

29. NEP, 17 June 1988. Earlier articles described it as 'one of the biggest of its type in the country': NEP, 12 May 1987.

30. NEP, 1 October 1987.

31. *The Independent*, 5 August 1988.

32. NEP, 13 May 1988.

33. NEP, 15 October 1987.

34. Webster 1988. See also Morley and Robins, 1995.

35. NEP, 15 October 1987.

36. *Nottingham Trader*, 22 June 1988.

37. NEP, 17 June 1988.

38. NEP, 14 October 1987.

39. NEP, 14 June 1988.

40. NEP, 23 May 1988.

41. Lyons, 'Food Consumption and the Cinema', unpublished manuscript.

42. NEP, 7 July 1988.

43. Franklin, 1996, p. 156.

44. NEP, 15 October 1987.

45. Spigel, 1995, p. 29.

46. NEP, 25 June 1998.

47. Ibid.

48. Dalbir, 14, student (RMQ).

49. Tony, 67, retired teacher (RM1).

50. Ibid.

51. See Tarnjit, 16, student (RMQ); Dalbir, 14, student (RMQ); Subaigh, 11, student (RMQ); Suroop, 10, student (RMQ); Harprit, 18, student (RMQ); Harjot, 10, student (RMQ);

Bikrumjit, 14, student (RMQ); and GCSE English Class, 14–15, Minister School, Southwell (KE17).

52. Donna, 30, clerical officer (KE3); and Whitegate Mothers and Toddlers Group (KE13).

53. GCSE English Class, 14–15, Minister School, Southwell (KE17); and Joe, 36, volunteer and part-time student (RM22).

54. One respondent even claims that it is a place for gangs and couples! Stefan, 25, unemployed teacher (KE19).

55. One respondent said that she had taken her grandson to the Showcase a number of times and felt that the cinema is much better when you go there with young people ('Something Different for Women Club', age range from 60 to 75, KE37).

56. Another elderly woman thought that the Showcase was marvellous and that she went there all the time with her son (Clifton Women's Wednesday Club, age range from 60 to 80 KE25). Another respondent, who also went to the cinema regularly with her son, also viewed the Showcase positively and goes there every Monday night with a friend (Judith, 39, probation officer, RM3).

57. Donna, 30, clerical officer (KE3).

58. John, 55, lecturer (RK1).

59. Charlotte, 16, occupation unknown (KEQ).

60. Stefan, 25, unemployed teacher (KE19).

61. In a similar way, Marc Auge discusses a range of 'placeless' places or 'non-places', such as airports, motorway service stations and the like. See Auge, 1995.

62. Anonymous female, 30, occupation unknown (KEQ).

63. Lynnette, 26, clerical assistant (KE30).

64. Helen, 40, project worker (RM18).

65. Catherine, 25, student (RMQ).

66. NEP, 7 July 1988.

67. Bakersfield and Sneinton Co-op Women's Guild (KE20).

68. Dorothy, 61, occupation unknown (RS4).

69. Vic, 59, part-time teacher, and Christine, 60, retired secretary (KE8); and Judith, 60, administrative assistant (KE24).

70. Anonymous female, 41, nurse (KEQ).

71. Barker and Brooks, 1998, p. 195.

72. Jackie, 49, part-time student advisor (KE12).

73. John, 75, retired (RMQ).

74. Stefan, 25, unemployed teacher (KE19); Neil, 55, welfare worker (KE32).

75. For example, one respondent claimed that although it was 'comfortable', they disliked its 'corporate/business image'. Anonymous female, 40, careers advisor (KEQ).

76. Helen, 40, project worker (RM18); Marc, 25, student (KE15).

77. Marc, 25, student (KE15).

78. Brian, 46, probation officer (KE16). More recently the Showcase has integrated such an area as part of its reaction to the new inner-city multiplex, the Cornerhouse.

79. Tracey, 37, solicitor (KE4).

80. Catherine, 25, student (RMQ).

81. Stefan, 25, unemployed teacher (KE19); Gray, 1996, p. 131.

82. NEP, 12 February 1987.

83. 'Post Comment', NEP, 17 June 1988.

84. NEP, 15 October 1987.

85. 'Post Comment', NEP, 17 June 1988.

86. NEP, 'Weekend', 27 January 2001.

87. Ibid.

88. Ibid.

89. NEP, 15 October 1987.

90. NEP, 16 June 1988.

91. NEP, 7 July 1988.

92. NEP, 15 March 1997.

93. A similar argument is also made by Hanson, as demonstrated by the title of his essay, 'Spoilt for Choice?' (1999).

14

Cultural Capitals: Culture, Diversity and Legitimacy

From Film Society to Media Centre: A Short History of the Broadway

The Broadway, Nottingham's regional film theatre, is seen as a 'non-commercial' alternative to the multiplex, but its identity has always been shaped through the changing economics of film and television production, distribution and exhibition. It emerged out of the film society movement, which was largely formed in opposition to the emergence of cinema as a form of popular entertainment and was concerned with appropriating cinema for the cause of art and education.[1] In 1950, the Nottingham Film Society consisted of a small and select group with 256 members who met in the Adult Education Centre in the centre of town and whose president was Mr B. L. Hallward, the vice-chancellor of Nottingham University. At this point, the society largely specialised in showing the European art cinema of France and Italy, which were seen as 'one of the encouraging signs' within contemporary cinema, despite the perceived threat of television.[2] However, the society's educational remit was also clearly signalled not only by its meeting place and choice of president, but also by its study group and by its 'library which contained some 85 books on films and allied interests'.[3]

However, despite the society's reported concern over the threat of television, it was actually falling cinema attendance that was to prove the making of this organisation. As the cinema audience declined, cinema became an increasingly rare taste, and was therefore open to appropriation and legitimisation by the cultural middle classes. As a result, not only did the membership of the society increase to over 600 as the 1950s progressed,[4] but it began to receive official public endorsement and support. While the council had resolutely refused to financially support the Tudor, by the 1960s, plans were under way to support a series of regional film theatres around the country. In Nottingham, the old film society was converted into the Nottingham Film Theatre that was launched in 1966, and was supported by the British Film Institute. At this point the membership was 'mostly made up of students' and the theatre stated its intention to 'include films from the silent era, experimental and educational films, musicals, war films and a whole range of Continental films'.[5] Thus, while the cinema continued to remain committed to the foreign art film, the Film Theatre was also keen to emphasise its commitment to the revival of Hollywood 'classics' from the golden age, the very films to which the original film societies were supposed to have provided an alternative. As a result, these cinemas can be seen as not only the product of the changing meanings of the cinema, but also as actively transforming the meanings of the cinematic past.

However, the system of support was still precarious, and in 1969, the *Sunday Times* reported on 'a crisis in the establishment of regional film theatres which touches almost every corner of Britain'. This crisis was due to the government's failure to honour its promise 'to supply capital for this type of venture ... [leaving] the British Film Institute, the intermediary which shares out the capital, powerless to help'.[6] The report used Nottingham to illustrate the significance of this situation: 'There the local authority withdrew its support and the BFI was forced to pull out as well. In that case, a complete shutdown was avoided when Players, the cigarette manufacturers, put up £3,700 to promote an increase in membership.'[7] However, the crisis was short-lived and the BFI was able to secure government support that stabilised and institutionalised the regional film theatres.

However, while these cinemas helped to transform the meanings of earlier periods of popular cinema, they were still opposed to the meanings of contemporary popular cinema. The justification for their financial support by government was precisely to protect a selective tradition of legitimate culture from the values of the market. As John Huntley, regional controller at the BFI, argued state funding was needed 'to spread the distribution of films not seen generally on the commercial circuits. It's the only way Birmingham and Edinburgh, say, can catch up with the Antonionis of this world.'[8] In this way, the cinema was organised around a notion of the 'alternative' and 'oppositional', which was also central to its association with cult cinema,[9] which emerged out of cinematic modes of exhibition in the USA and in which 'the phenomenon of the midnight movie in the 1970s' marked its 'apex'.[10] It is hardly surprising that in 1973, the Film Theatre also followed suit through the introduction of 'a monthly late night show'.[11]

The revival of cinemagoing in the 1980s as a consequence of the rise of video and the multiplex transformed this situation. Not only was cinemagoing popular once more, but government philosophy had shifted from the liberal values that encouraged state funding of cultural institutions to 'the politics of Thatcherism' in which cultural institutions were under pressure to render themselves efficient, and to reorganise themselves as businesses that relied on market profitability and corporate sponsorship rather than government 'handouts'.[12] In television, the BBC, for example, was threatened with the removal of its licence fee and, while this did not actually take place, the Peacock Report (1986) 'subjected [the corporation] to greater financial discipline' and required it to become far more reliant on 'commissioning material from independent sources' along the lines of Channel 4.[13]

Channel 4 was also influential in other ways. One of the key ways that it distinguished itself as a channel was through its film showings. It not only became famous for showing European art-house films and revivals of Hollywood 'classics', but it also became instrumental in the supposed renaissance of British film production in the 1980s through its financing of film production. By supplying funds for British films, Channel 4 ensured that it had the television rights to these films and this finance helped to regenerate film production in Britain. However, the films that were financed were those that suited Channel 4's image as a quality channel directed at discerning and marginal audiences.

In this context, the Nottingham Film Theatre was replaced by a new media centre that was funded through investment from the BFI, East Midlands Arts and the European Economic Commission and it hoped to 'combine entertainment for the general public with production facilities for independent film and video makers [and a] media training course'.[14] As the *Evening Post* put it: 'With Government demands on BBC and ITV that 25% of their programmes should come from independent producers, Mr Allen [of the Nottingham Media Consortium] expects a massive expansion in local media production.'[15]

City, Culture, Capital

This situation was also shaped by the growing importance of culture to the new economic situation of the 1980s. This period had seen a dramatic decline in traditional industries and the Thatcher government saw the service industries and communications technologies as the key to economic development. Furthermore, as capital became more global and fluid, cities and regions also found that they had to compete with one another for investment and finance and that, in this situation, a city's culture and image was not only one of the crucial factors in attracting investment, but the main commodity that cities had to sell.[16] In a discussion of Nottingham's successful bid to host the 1992 Bouchercon, an international crime-writing festival, in association with the Broadway's own annual film festival, Shots in the Dark, the NEP commented: 'As traditional industry slips away, a city becomes raw material from which to profit. With a little gloss here and there, Mark [Alexander of Conference Nottingham] has confidence in his product':[17] the city itself. The importance of attracting Bouchercon was therefore primarily financial:

> Mark has done the sums: 'We're looking at about three-quarters of a million pounds in direct revenue from accommodation, the banquets and the initial spend, not to mention the spin off . . . It's a proven fact that the largest spending visitor to the city is a conference delegate. They're going to buy presents, meals, use taxis and see the attractions. We expect Nottingham to find itself a lot busier when they're here.'[18]

In this new economic situation, tourism was central and this was one of the key attractions of the new media centre itself when it was announced: 'A deal on a new media centre attracting hundreds of thousands of visitors to Nottingham every year loomed nearer this week.'[19]

However, the benefits of Bouchercon and the media centre were not simply financial. Indeed, there was a reciprocal relationship between economic and cultural factors. In attracting tourism and conference delegates, Nottingham not only benefited financially but also culturally. As a result, in his description of Bouchercon, Adrian Wootton, then head of the Broadway, stated: 'What you'll have is a really sparkling and exciting event. The people of Nottingham will see these writers and stars. It's going to enhance the city's image nationally and internationally.'[20] However, by benefiting culturally, it was argued that Nottingham would also be able to attract more finance. Indeed, the mutual interrelationship of the two is perfectly captured by Wootton's own words: 'The centre will

'Shots in the Dark' at the Broadway: 'a really sparkling and exciting event ... It's going to enhance the city's image nationally and internationally.' The Broadway, Broad Street, City Centre

in the long run bring undoubted economic and cultural prosperity to the city.'[21] Here the term 'cultural prosperity' perfectly captured the sense of culture as a form of wealth or capital.

In this way, the media centre was produced out of, and participated within, the city's need and desire to compete within regional, national and international markets where its image was central. The media centre was frequently presented as 'a major resource for media training, tourism and job development in the East Midlands',[22] but also an institution that would 'place Nottingham on the map', making it ideologically central to these regional, national and international contexts. Regionally the paper's claim that 'Nottingham looks set to become the Hollywood of the Midlands'[23] used the centrality of Hollywood to signify Nottingham's regional centrality. However, it was in the national and international arenas that Nottingham's ambitions primarily lay. David Puttnam was quoted as claiming that 'Nottingham is fast becoming one of Britain's premier cities and this centre will add to its already growing list of attractions',[24] while the media centre was described as 'one of the country's top three independent film centres'.[25] These claims were then used to place Nottingham in a competitive relationship with London, which clearly operated as the national centre, but in which Nottingham was not seen as simply marginal to it: 'No longer do we need to look to London as the centre of film excellence – Nottingham people now have excellence on their own doorstep.'[26] The media centre was therefore supposedly intended to 'prevent the drain of many of the city's talented young film and video producers to the South'.[27]

However, the media centre's ambitions were also international and its aim, as Wootton put it, was 'to put Nottingham on the world media map of the 1990s'. Indeed, he went so far as to state: 'I hope that one day we can hear a voice floating down through the ether on a satellite link asking "Would that be Broadway New York you are wanting – or Broadway Nottingham?"'[28] He therefore claimed that 'any realistic map of the world today should show radio reception areas, phone links and satellite footprints' and that, in this context: 'We want to put Nottingham onto the new media map. Locally we have some of the most advanced and best equipped production studios in Europe ... Broadway's primary role is to provide a confident focus for that burgeoning media industry.'[29] In this endeavour, the media centre also positioned itself as the potential centre for a European assault upon the American market: 'Europe wants English language products as it's the only way to break into the American market. After 1992, access to the USA will be through Britain ... We've got the best technicians in the world. Spielberg doesn't come here to make Indiana Jones because he likes our scenery. It's because he can't get the skilled technicians in America.'[30]

This desire for centrality has also been a feature of Shots in the Dark, the Broadway's film festival. This festival was described as 'Britain's first-ever international festival dedicated to crime and mystery' and was 'held in the city as part of the Nottingham Festival', a festival of the arts that the city hosts each year both to attract tourists and enhance its reputation as a cultural centre. This film festival was first held in the early 1990s and it included 'an extensive programme of old and new films ... special retrospectives, writers' evenings, a photographic exhibition, theatre activities and television events'. It also featured a 'gala preview' of *The Silence of the Lambs*, 'the most talked about movie thriller of the year', which represented 'the film's British public premiere'. Television was also represented in the figure of 'Britain's most popular detective, Inspector Morse, or at least his creator Colin Dexter, who will be discussing his novels before being joined by the producer of the cult television programme and one of the show's major scriptwriters'. The festival was also to include another 'real coup' in the form of '"Criminal Acts", a theatre event written by Nottingham-based international scriptwriter, Michael Eaton (*Fellow Traveller, Shoot to Kill* and *Why Lockerbie?*)'

Thus, the festival, and the press coverage that concerned it, was preoccupied with emphasising the ways in which it made Nottingham the centre of an international media culture, in which the references to *The Silence of the Lambs* and *Inspector Morse* are particularly significant. On the one hand, the crime and mystery 'genre' is one that harks back some of the central images of the Hollywood 'classic' and its appropriation by art cinema: most particularly in the form of film noir, Hitchcock and the gangster film. Thus the festival was also to include 'old favourites including *Bonnie and Clyde, Vertigo* and the classic thriller, *Psycho*'. It is therefore not without significance that both *The Silence of the Lambs* and *Inspector Morse* represented two of the most respected and revered examples of, respectively, Hollywood cinema and British television in the early 1990s. Furthermore, they were also works that were based upon novels, a feature that is emphasised both through the presentation of *The Silence of the Lambs* as 'the first of three cinematic tributes to Thomas Harris, one of America's most successful and yet mysterious novelists' and the presence of Colin Dexter.[31] There have also been repeated tributes to novelists such as Donald E. Westlake, Graham Greene and John Harvey.

During its ten-year life, both the festival and its press coverage were also obsessed with the presence of the international 'players' who have passed through the festival. Quentin Tarantino created the greatest stir and was even made an honorary patron of the conference. As Adrian Wootton recalls in an article to commemorate his departure from the Broadway: 'I had spotted a very small review of *Reservoir Dogs*. It said something like "ultra-violent gangster thriller". I thought: That's right up our street.' He therefore tried to contact the director before eventually meeting him at an Italian film festival, where they:

> hung out, saw all the films and drank a bit ... He was really enthusiastic about Shots and came to the festival that summer. He stayed for the whole ten days ... He was staying at the Rutland Square Hotel. I remember us being up until three in the morning most nights in the bar arguing about movies. Every evening he would make calls to LA about the casting of *Pulp Fiction* ... He had the *Pulp Fiction* script in this room. He was still finishing it off ... He came over with the print of *Pulp Fiction* to Shots in 1994. He just liked hanging out in Nottingham. We had two great years with him at Broadway but in 1995 everything went nuts for him. He won an Oscar and the media pressure grew so much he couldn't go out. He became a recluse ... We had the best of him in Nottingham – just before he became famous ... And it helped raise the profile of the festival and Broadway.[32]

Indeed, it was not only the local papers that made reference to Tarantino's presence at the festival. As *The Times* also wrote: he 'hangs out in the café bar of the two-screen Broadway centre in the middle of Nottingham – the festival's major venue'.[33]

However, the association with Tarantino also presented problems for the Broadway. The cinema had to protect itself from 'anti-violence lobbyists' and it did so through 'its insistence on an active audience'.[34] In other words, a whole series of strategies was used to create an educational context around the films that were 'designed to provoke a more intellectual response to more disturbing films'. Consequently, a distinction was drawn between the 'mindless violence' of popular films (or more particularly the tastes of the popular audiences that they are supposed to attract) and the 'intellectual responses' of the Broadway audience. As *The Times* put it:

> So knee-jerk reaction is not encouraged and Shots features none of the Terminator-style mindless violence. As Adrian Wootton, the festival director, puts it: 'This is not a splatterfest.'[35]

However, at the same time, the association with crime and mystery was useful to the Broadway specifically because of their ambiguous status between popular and elite forms. On the one hand, they are genres with a long heritage of popular associations,

but on the other, as we have seen, they are also precisely those popular genres that have
been more taken up by legitimate culture in both its middlebrow and avant-garde mani-
festations.[36]

Diversity and Distinction

In this way, the crime genre helped to negotiate one of the most fundamental problems
for these cinemas, the accusation of elitism. From the start, the Film Society was concerned with disavowing any elitism as a letter published in the 1950s from H. F. Darking,
the Honorary Secretary of the Nottingham and District Film Society, demonstrates:

> Correspondent 'Philomel' would be well advised to check his facts before making a
> statement. The Nottingham Film Society does not charge an admission fee for each
> performance. The subscription covers all performances including lectures and sub-standard
> shows. Far from being 'twice that of the dearest cinema seat in Nottingham', the average
> cost of each performance, based on last season's shows, was under two shillings and
> sixpence. Surely, in view of the present cost of inferior entertainment, no fair-minded student
> of cinema art can consider this charge excessive.[37]

Of course, this letter tries to have it both ways, both denying the accusation of elitism
implicit in references to the cost of admission while also justifying this cost on the
grounds that popular cinema is simply 'inferior entertainment' that a 'student of cinema
art' would naturally reject.

Accusations of elitism were still in evidence in the mid-1980s when the Film Theatre
marked its twentieth anniversary with the 'appointment of its first professional co-ordinator', Paul Scully: 'One of his first jobs is to dispel the elitist myth of the Film Theatre
movement: the popular misconception that the FT is all about subtitles, precious people
with pretensions to radical insight and tedious "art house" movies.'[38] Even in 1992, when
further updating of the cinema was announced, the Broadway was concerned with
emphasising that 'the "enthusiasm and interest of people on the street" will prevent the
Media Centre from becoming an elitist body'.[39] Also, when the Bouchercon deal was
reported, the cinema stressed: 'We're very much part of the city. We've always said we're
not exclusively directed to people who like French movies and we've begun to demonstrate that.' In the process, they wished to distance themselves from assumptions about
their staff and patrons. They not only claimed that the 'hippy arts worker is no more'[40]
but also stated that they wanted to attract 'ordinary everyday folk'. Moreover, they
wanted to dispel the perception that 'Media centres, arts cinemas and the like seem to
have a knack of enticing professional trendies from advertising agencies and the like
who'd rather discuss the concealed light in the offices than pushing Nottingham into the
spotlight.'[41] As a result, the Broadway management argued that the cinema was not just
directed at the 'media-literate' but 'the community at large', and that they offered 'events
that are accessible to all'.[42] Class was therefore particularly central to the Broadway's
concerns and it has repeatedly stated that 'We don't want the Media Centre to become
a place for middle-class, middle-aged film buffs.'[43]

These quotes also suggest that a narrative of progress was constructed in which the cinema's 'elitism' was projected into the past as something that the cinema was in the process of transcending for the future: 'Two years ago, there was undoubtedly an alternative flavour to Broadway. The audience was largely made up of academics – either students or lecturers – and young professionals. But Broadway is broadening.'[44] In this way, it was claimed, while 'it used to be just a small elitist film theatre . . . it has evolved to become a vibrant centre recognised as one of the top three or four film theatres in the country'.[45] However, despite this rejection of its elitist image, the cinema also holds onto its image as an 'alternative' place. This is achieved, ironically, through the same language of accessibility and diversity that it used to counter the accusations of elitism made against it.

For example, accessibility is used to imply the diversity of its audience. This can be seen in the cinema's concern to present itself as accessible to marginalised groups such as the disabled. As a result, the cinema was rightly proud to announce that 'Features for the disabled have won Nottingham's Broadway Media Centre special recognition in the Lord Mayor's awards for urban design.'[46] However, the supposed diversity of the cinema's audience is also specifically set up against the supposedly homogeneous and undifferentiated nature of mass culture and its audiences. In one article it was argued:

> Patrons who visit the Broadway Media Centre have a tendency towards long skirts and/or beards, belong to minority groups and only eat wholefood. True . . . They are students. True . . . They are middle-aged intellectuals with a degree in philosophy. Probably true as well . . . But they are also old age pensioners, schoolchildren, factory workers, professional executives, shoppers . . . just ordinary people like you and me, in fact . . . The truth is that times, they are a-changing at the Broadway Media Centre and its appeal is extending to an increasingly wide audience.[47]

If the Broadway's concern has been to present itself as addressing a diverse public, this public is opposed to the supposedly undifferentiated public that frequents the 'mainstream' cinemas. In this same article, it was claimed that when Wootton 'arrived from Bradford four years ago there was no "alternative" film activity in Nottingham' and that his brief was to create an 'alternative'.

This opposition to the 'mainstream' is clearest in claims about its programming policy and from the start it was this opposition that, as we have already seen, not only justified the presence of the cinema but also its funding by government and other bodies. For example, in 1969, when the BFI was fighting to secure government funding for the regional film theatres, it was claimed that the Film Society 'is continuing with its policy of showing films which have never been on general release, or have not been on release for some time'.[48] In a *Sunday Times* article on the subject, it was claimed that funding for these cinemas 'was intended to spread the distribution of films not generally seen on the commercial circuits'.[49]

However, as the cinema moved into the 1980s, this position had to be carefully tempered. As we have seen, Thatcherite economics meant that the regional art cinemas could not present themselves solely as alternatives to the commercial market but neither could they present themselves as simply part of that market without losing their claim to special treatment. They had to claim that they provided that which the market could not support while also presenting themselves as hard-nosed commercial businesses with a close eye on the 'bottom line'. However, this position also allowed them to enhance their claims to diversity. For example, in an interview with Paul Scully on the twentieth anniversary of the Film Theatre, it was claimed:

> 'We are a focus for movies which might otherwise not be seen outside London and also for films which were perhaps screened in Nottingham for a week and then disappeared.' ... The 20th season demonstrates clearly this mix, with first-run movies and films like the excellent *Brother from Another Planet* and *Once Upon a Time in America* which the commercial cinema flirted with and then discarded ... The balance between providing both 'populist' and 'minority' movies is a delicate one for the new co-ordinator, whose box office is complemented by funds from the British Film Institute, East Midlands Arts and the City Council ... 'People forget that even though we are funded, we still have to keep a very close eye on the box office, and that means showing plenty of films that plenty of people want to see,' says Paul ... 'It's all about striking a balance between commercial films and minority ones, old and new, English and foreign language. That's why our programmes are so varied.'[50]

This position is stated even more directly by Wootton, when he distinguishes the modern Broadway from the image of the 'hippy arts worker': 'As subsidy slips away, it's impossible to run a show without doing the business. The Media Centre walks the tightrope between artistic integrity and financial health. You just can't do that in Jesus sandals.'[51]

None the less, Wootton was also keen to point out: 'There's certainly no way that we're in competition with the city centre mainstream cinemas ... I just can't conceive of us showing *Jurassic Park* for instance.' However, he then qualifies this remark in an interesting way: 'not unless we were doing a season on special effects films, or we got Steven Spielberg over to do an introduction to it'.[52] It is therefore not so much the films that distinguish the Broadway from the mainstream but rather the context within which they are placed. *Jurassic Park* might be shown, but only within a context that defined it as interesting within educational or intellectual terms. Once again, we return to the opposition between the mindless consumer of popular cinema and the intellectual audience and this can also be seen in the Broadway's association with crime and mystery. Here, for example, Wootton has walked a tightrope in his presentation of the audience. He has tried to distinguish the fans of these films from the negative image of the dysfunctional, bloodthirsty popular viewer, while still registering a certain distance from them:

> I find the 'true crime' fans more bizarre because a lot of them are little old ladies who love the prospect of hearing forensic scientists talking about gory details ... You expect them to be people with red eyes slavering at the mouth but they're perfectly respectable individuals who happen to take a ghoulish interest in some of the less savoury aspects of life.[53]

In this passage, the audience to which his comments are addressed is not that of the fans, but one composed of people who appreciate the quality of these genres but have established a distanced rather than a fanatical relationship to them.

Consuming Legitimacy

Despite the arguments of the Broadway's management, issues of social exclusion therefore remain central both to those respondents who were hostile to the Broadway and to those who defended it. For example, the Broadway was not simply a place that people did not visit. In contrast to almost every other cinema, most people had not even heard of the Broadway, and even those that had were often unable to place it within their mental maps of the city.[54] Some people suggested that the reason for this was that the Broadway did not advertise alongside the other cinemas in newspapers and other media, or that they did not frequent the area of the city within which it is located. The Broadway is not in the centre of town like the Odeon or the ABC were, nor is it part of a local area in the same way as the Savoy in Lenton. Furthermore, while the Showcase may not be accessible to pedestrians, it occupies a prominent location on the city's ring road and is clearly visible to all those who pass by due to its design and use of lighting. In contrast, the Broadway is tucked away in Hockley. This part of town is just off the main thoroughfares and has long had a reputation as a vaguely alternative area that features none of the major mainstream shopping chains but rather caters to an exclusive middle-class clientele. Indeed, in recent years, it has become the focus of redevelopment as the old lace-market buildings are being converted into loft apartments for high-income professionals, which, for a time, made it the site of the fastest-rising property prices in the country.

However, even among those who did know of its presence and location, many saw the Broadway as excluding them in various ways. For example, people's most common claim was that they did not frequent the Broadway because it was an exclusive club for which membership was required. This claim may be partly a hangover from the days of the old film society, which was membership only. However, this conviction was not just a result of the old film society, and even when people were reassured that membership was not required, they still clung to this belief. Thus, they seemed to want to believe that the cinema actively excluded them so that they would have an excuse to not use it.[55] This also suggests that many people who knew of the cinema, but did not use it, clearly felt an obligation rather than a desire to attend it. They talked of it as a place they 'ought to go' or 'should visit'.[56] Attendance was clearly something about which they felt extreme conflict. On one hand, they recognised the legitimacy that is associated with the Broadway and desired 'to like what's better to like'[57] but, on the other, they feared that if they went to the cinema, they would only expose the fact that they did not really belong. Indeed, fear of not fitting in recurred in people's accounts of the Broadway.[58] However, while some needed to believe that the Broadway required membership to deal with a sense of exclusion from the culture that this cinema represents, others practised the 'rejection of the rejection' that Bourdieu sees as central to popular taste.[59]

Some respondents therefore referred to the place as 'arty farty',[60] while others described it as 'snooty', 'trendy' or 'elitist'.[61] The descriptions of it as 'trendy' were also related to a more general sense that not only were its audience 'select and pretentious', but also that the place was dominated by young people and hence excluded the older members of the local population.[62] These claims suggested that the audience were in their twenties and thirties, not young children, and although the Broadway does put on a number of children's matinees, many respondents felt that the cinema is 'not for kids'.[63] This was related to a more general sense that the place is serious rather than fun, which led one respondent to call it 'sterile'.[64] However, while the Showcase was described as 'clinical' to associate it with the supposed functionality and rationalisation of mass production and mass consumption, the term 'sterile' carried very different connotations in relation to the Broadway. It implied the dour lack of vitality that is often associated with pure taste, which Bourdieu describes as the 'systematic refusal of all that is "human" ... namely, the passions, emotions and feelings which "ordinary" people invest in their "ordinary" lives'.[65]

In other words, for both those who identified and disidentified with the Broadway, the cinema was discussed in terms of an opposition between entertainment and cultural knowledge, in which both groups associate the Broadway with the values of cultural knowledge rather than the values of entertainment. In one interview, for example, two

The Media Centre walks a thin line between artistic integrity and financial health. The Broadway

friends discussed their understandings of, and investment in, cinema, and while one saw it as primarily a form of relaxation, the other saw it as a means of acquiring and developing cultural knowledge.[66] This situation is hardly surprising and, as we have seen, the Broadway, and the film society before it, has had a long association with the values of education rather than entertainment.

As a result, the cinema can be alienating to those who look to cinema for entertainment, whatever their class background. For example, one respondent, who was a postgraduate student at the university, stated that she saw films as an 'alternative to her intellectual life'.[67] Others, however, felt more directly excluded by their lack of knowledge or by what they saw as the Broadway audience's need to display their own knowledge. As a result, there were several complaints about the 'knowing laughter' of the audience, through which this audience signalled a privileged relationship to the film,[68] while others stated their sense of exclusion and incomprehension more overtly. For example, while the Shots in the Dark festival often asserted its opposition to the 'anti-violence lobby', and Wootton had decided that *Reservoir Dogs* was 'right up our street' on the grounds that it was 'ultra-violent',[69] one respondent responded with outrage to the mix of laughter and violence that they associated with the Broadway by demanding: 'What's so funny about violence?'[70] This question expressed incomprehension at the response to violence that was associated with the Broadway audience, but it also recognised that this incomprehension was also being ridiculed by this laughter. As a result, people claimed to find the Broadway, its films and its audience to be 'strange and obscure',[71] and that the cinema was 'for film buffs rather than film fans'.[72] It is for those with an investment in accumulating and displaying their knowledge of the cinema, rather than those whose investment in the cinema is due to its function as entertainment.

Nor was it just those who felt alienated from the Broadway who associated it with the accumulation and display of cultural knowledge. Again and again, those who identified with the Broadway saw it as a place that was 'challenging and intellectual' and not just as a place that showed 'challenging and intellectual' films.[73] For these viewers, films were often praised for being difficult on the assumption that difficulty not only required effort but also that it would not appeal to everyone. They claimed to like films that 'engage the brain',[74] rather than the emotions or body. It therefore draws on the privileging of the head over the body which, as Stallybrass and White have argued, is frequently mapped onto the distinction between high and low culture: the former is supposed to engage the intellect while the latter is supposed to provoke physical reactions.[75] Indeed, as Linda Williams has argued, the least legitimate genres of film are usually those most associated with the excitement of physical response – most notably horror and pornography which she therefore refers to as 'body genres'.[76] As a result, it is hardly surprising that the films associated with the Broadway are so often opposed to the action movie, a genre that is usually associated with the Showcase and with the incitement of physical reactions – the adrenaline rush, increased heartbeat, sweaty palms.[77]

This sense of distinction is also related to the exclusivity that the Broadway bestows upon its patrons. One respondent, for example, said that he was proud to have had the opportunity to see *Little Voice* at the Broadway before it had become a nationwide hit.[78]

Like Wootton's references to Tarantino, this statement expressed the pleasure of being there before everyone else, of having a privileged and exclusive access while something was still rare and before it became common. This sense is also transferred onto the building itself. While its location means that few people know about the cinema, many patrons talked of the fact that it is 'hidden away' and 'exclusive' as a good thing, and claimed that the cinema would lose its appeal if it attracted the masses.[79] Indeed many saw the fact that it is outside the main area of the town centre as positive in other ways. For example, it is seen as safer and more sedate, particularly on weekends, and one of the clear attractions of the building was less the cinema than the café bar, which was considered a good place to meet people. Clearly, it was not simply that people used the café bar because they used the cinema but that people used the cinema because of their attachment to the café bar.[80] Thus, while many felt alienated from the building, which was seen as 'not for the likes of us', others were clearly attracted because they saw it as being associated with 'our sort of people'. In the process, they did not find the staff and audience intimidating, but 'friendly and accessible'.[81] This sense of comfort within the cinema is therefore explicitly used to judge people and one respondent even claimed that, by taking his girlfriend there, he had been able to confirm that they shared interests with one another.[82] Furthermore, he did not mention the film that they went to see, or their reactions to it, but simply their shared identification with the cinema itself.

Notes

1. See Samson,1986; and Manvell 1944.
2. Unidentified newspaper clipping, Nottingham Local Studies Library files.
3. Ibid.
4. Ibid.
5. NEP, 11 August 1966.
6. *Sunday Times*, 2 November 1969.
7. Ibid.
8. Ibid.
9. Jancovich, 2002b.
10. Gomery, 1992 p. 194.
11. GJ, 13 February 1973.
12. Hall and Jaques, 1983.
13. Crisell, 1997, p. 214.
14. NEP, 15 April 1988.
15. NEP, 15 May 1988.
16. See, for example, Zukin, 1995; and Morley and Robins, 1995.
17. NEP, 11 November 1992.
18. Ibid.
19. NEP, 15 May 1988.
20. NEP, 11 November 1992.
21. NEP, 25 May 1990.
22. *Herald and Post*, 16 October 1991.

23. Ibid.

24. NEP, 25 May 1990.

25. *Herald and Post*, 16 October 1991.

26. NEP, 25 May 1990.

27. NEP, 14 April 1988.

28. *Nottingham Recorder*, 31 May 1990.

29. Ibid.

30. NEP, 26 July 1990.

31. *Nottingham Chronicle* North Edition Issue 9, 31 May 1991, p. 7.

32. NEP, 4 December 1999.

33. *The Times*, 17 June 1993.

34. Ibid.

35. Ibid.

36. See Naremore, 1998.

37. Unidentified newspaper clipping, Nottingham Local Studies Library files.

38. *Nottingham Trader*, 28 August 1985.

39. NEP, 9 January 1992.

40. NEP, November 1992.

41. NEP, 26 July 1990.

42. NEP, 26 July 1990.

43. NEP, 5 March 1990.

44. NEP, 20 July 1993.

45. NEP, 20 July 1993.

46. NEP, 6 May 1993.

47. NEP, 20 July 1993.

48. GJ, 6 October 1969.

49. *Sunday Times*, 2 November 1969.

50. *Nottingham Trader*, 28 August 1985.

51. NEP, 11 November 1992.

52. NEP, 20 July 1993.

53. NEP, 11 November 1992.

54. Whitegates Mothers and Toddlers Group (KE13).

55. Bakersfield and Sneinton Co-op Women's Guild (KE20).

56. One claimed that she had 'been meaning to go for ages!' (Mrs Fairclough, 55, teacher, RSQ). Similar statements were also made by the Bakersfield and Sneinton Co-op Women's Guild (KE20).

57. Brunsdon, 1997, p. 149.

58. Jennie, 32, part-time lecturer (KE7); and Brian, 46, probation officer (KE16).

59. Bourdieu, 1984.

60. Phillip, 32, carpenter (RM2).

61. Lynn, age unknown, housewife/mother (RSQ); and anonymous female, 40, careers advisor (KEQ).

62. Alan, 25, unemployed (RM9).

63. Donna, 30, clerical officer (KE3).

64. Tracey, 37, solicitor (KE4).

65. Bourdieu, 1984, p. 4.

66. Tim, 22, administrative assistant, and Joanne, 25, human resources administrator (KE5).

67. Jennie, 32, student (KE7).

68. Tim, 22, administrative assistant (KE5).

69. NEP, 4 December 1999.

70. Brian, 46, probation officer (KE16).

71. Sharan, 33, nurse/tutor (KE35).

72. Celia, 62, retired cleaner (KE6).

73. Melanie, 34, information officer (RM7).

74. Louise, 34, administrator (RM8).

75. Stallybrass and White, 1986.

76. Williams, 1991, pp. 2–13.

77. Marc, 25, student (KE15).

78. Marc, 25, student (KE15).

79. Stefan, 25, unemployed teacher (KE19).

80. Jo, 22, receptionist (KE1); National Council of Women, Nottingham Branch (KE36).

81. Catherine, 25, student (RMQ).

82. Stefan, 25, unemployed teacher (KE19).

15

Media Revolutions:
Futurology, Film Content and the New Media

New Media and Old Predictions

As we have seen, both the emergence of television and video were seen as threats to film consumption in general and the cinema in particular, confining people within domestic space and rendering entertainment outside the home redundant. However, in both cases, these predictions were never fulfilled. Television has actually made more films available for consumption than ever before and the number of films shown in one week on terrestrial television alone is roughly equivalent to the maximum number of screens in operation in inter-war Nottingham. Similarly, video not only failed to kill off the cinema, but may even have encouraged a renaissance in cinemagoing and cinema building.[1]

However, since the advent of video, a whole series of new media has emerged that are again considered a threat to both the cinema and the city cultures on which it is based. The first of these were, of course, cable and satellite which became the object of intense political and economic investment during the late 1980s. Of the two, cable

DVD is allied with a whole series of technologies that are often referred to as 'home cinema'.
DVD display, Hollywood Video

offered the most opportunities due to its potential for other telecommunications-related media such as the internet. However, while satellite systems could be accessed by any-one with a dish and decoder, cable required a whole new infrastructure that made its development slow, at least until cable companies were given the right to offer telecom-munications packages in 1990. These technologies have also been augmented by the introduction of pay-per-view and digital television. Both promise to expand massively the range of programming channels available to the British public and provide audiences with a greater ability to determine when to watch programmes and particularly films.

In addition to these developments, a whole series of new consumer items has been introduced onto the British market that often identify themselves as, or with, 'home cin-ema'. These items are associated with new information technologies. The first is the laserdisc which never became much more than a gadget for the connoisseur. More recently this has been superseded by DVD which has begun to take off in a far more convincing manner. Unlike laserdisc, it is allied with a whole new series of items, such as widescreen televisions with refined image and sound qualities, and this alliance of technologies is often referred to as 'home cinema' on the assumption that it has over-come the poor visual and aural experience of television, and has achieved a sense of visual and aural spectacle that replicates that of the cinema.

Finally, all these developments are supposed to be in a process of convergence. Soon, it is claimed, different technologies will merge into one complex, interconnected infor-mation system through which we can communicate with others, receive our entertainment and regulate our domestic environment. This technology will therefore liberate us in a number of ways. Not only will communications overcome problems of distance, they will also free us from time constraints, or at least allow us to control our own time. In this situation, people will no longer be dictated to by the schedules of broadcasters but they will be able to download programmes via the internet from a virtually endless archive and watch them anywhere in the world.

These fantasies have been widely diffused throughout society over the last few years and thus we found many respondents who believed that DVD would replace video[2] or that pay per view would render the video redundant.[3] Others claimed that we will soon be able to watch films via the internet on our computers, or that DVD would eventually allow greater interactivity so that films would become more like computer games. How-ever, it is interesting that these technologies were seen as a threat to video rather than the cinema. Indeed, the respondent with probably the greatest investment in these new technologies saw no threat to the cinema because, he claimed, it was already an inter-active mode of entertainment. Here, the meaning of interactivity shifted from one that was primarily concerned with the manipulation of on-screen action to one that stressed the pleasure of 'going out' and watching films with an audience.[4]

Another series of claims is that these technologies will create greater diversity, choice, freedom and hence control. These claims were clearly in evidence among our respon-dents who often seemed highly enthusiastic about the potential for choice. However, as we have argued in previous chapters in Part Five, choice is not always viewed as a posi-tive thing. Not only were there concerns that the choice would not be a 'real' one, but also that the choice already available was creating a sense of 'overload' in which some consumers simply felt swamped by the range available.[5] As a result, despite the more positive images of the new media, there is concern that they will lead to an increasingly individualised viewer who watches these media in a state of increasing isolation. The figure of the computer geek is probably one of the most powerful images to be produced by this type of anxiety, but these concerns can also be seen in the NEP's claim that 'all this technology could encourage couch potatoes to take root in their armchairs and never venture outside their front doors'.[6] In addition to concerns with spatial isolation, many respondents also felt that people will have their own individualised schedules so that any sense of simultaneity and imagined community will be lost.

These predictions also relate to a series of claims about the spatial effects of these new technologies in which social relations are seen to be increasingly disconnected from issues of place: 'Where we are no longer determines who we are – or who we are "with" – to the same degree as it used to because electronically mediated communication has the potential to transform situation, interaction and identification.'[7] In the process, it is claimed, identities are not only less dependent on place but also social relations are less dependent on proximity. As people increasingly communicate via the new media, they no longer need to leave their own homes for goods, entertainment and, perhaps least convincing of all, work. As a result, it is argued that public spaces of interaction become increasingly redundant. For some, this is a utopian image that promises the end of nightmarish cityscapes and a return to a high-tech pastoral society in which the population can return to nature to enjoy the benefits of rural living without giving up the advantages of modern industrial society. For others, however, it is a nightmare of social isolation in which city centres decay and people become increasingly atomised and prey to centres of power, a situation that will spell the final death of cinema.[8]

In other words, the new media figure as both agents of centralisation and decentralisation, and produce either a massive concentration of power or its diffusion. For Nicholas Garnham, for example, these new media are implicated in a process that not only threatens the values of public service broadcasting but the possibility of a healthy public sphere. For Garnham, information is not only increasingly organised as a commodity but we are witnessing an increasingly widening gap between the information rich and the information poor.

It is therefore important to remember, in the face of all the hype about these new media, that many people simply cannot afford them, and that access to electronically mediated communication is still determined by economic considerations.[9] However, while our respondents often used cost to explain why they did not subscribe to cable or satellite programming,[10] other processes were also going on here. While one person claimed that she did not have cable or satellite because she resented paying for them on top of her licence fee,[11] in this case, the remark may also have represented another dynamic altogether. Historically, the take-up of cable and satellite has been precisely among the poorer sections of the population who are most dependent on the television for their entertainment and, as a result, it has acquired the image of a lower-class entertainment.[12] As a result, many people's disdain for it had a class basis, and their refusal to subscribe was because their affluence made them less reliant on television as a mode of entertainment.[13]

Content is King: The Centrality of Film in the Age of New Media

Film presentations have so far been central to the development of these new media and the likelihood is that this situation will intensify rather than decline. The proliferation of media, formats and channels creates a central problem of content. Many of the new media are 'carriage'-centred operations that do not make programmes but are simply concerned with the processes of their dissemination. They therefore depend on others to provide the content that will justify their use by customers. However, even those media that are both carriers and producers face a problem given the sheer amount of scheduling time that needs to be filled. This situation has led to a heavy emphasis on the recycling of material in which media archives become extremely valuable. In this context, film has become central, and all of the major global players have heavily invested in this area, buying studios that will not only ensure their access to top films, but also to their huge back catalogues. It was for this reason that Ted Turner bought the MGM film library, although, in more recent years, media conglomerates have obtained whole studios. For example, the satellite broadcaster Sky is owned by Murdoch who also owns 20th Century-Fox, while Sumner Redstone's empire owns Paramount.

Film is also useful to these empires because it offers a form of programming that can be distinguished from the banality of 'television' more generally. As Crisell points out, while in the past 'the business of being entertained or culturally edified has been more or less separate from the banalities of existence', domestic entertainment is increasingly seen as 'banal'. As we have seen, families often sought to make television viewing a special event in its early days, but as it has become 'more closely [assimilated] than ever before to the daily routines of the individual', television viewing has become less and less special.[14] As a result, even the terrestrial channels such as Channel 4 and the BBC have started to become film producers, if only to present particular programmes as events rather than simply regular parts of the schedule.

In other words, the presence of films is used to distinguish cable and satellite from 'normal' television, and as somehow closer to the experience of cinemagoing, while still retaining the appeals of domestic entertainment. Thus while people discussed the pleasures of cable and satellite in similar terms to terrestrial television, they did distinguish them as somehow more special. Many people commented on the lack of adverts, while others liked to make an occasion of watching films on Sky, opening a bottle of wine to mark it as an event or an indulgence.[15] As a result, one respondent claimed that he regarded satellite as existing in some place that is halfway between video and television, in which video is seen as something special and television as something far more banal.[16] Another respondent said that she had access to satellite for the films, rather than for the sport or what she saw as the 1970s' television series that were such an important part of its programming.[17] Yet another claimed that she thought that television was trash and, as a result, that she wanted to get FilmFour.[18]

These issues are also clearly central to the strategies of the cable and satellite companies that not only heavily use the film channels to promote the attractions of their products but also charge a significantly higher rate for them. While the basic packages are largely made up of standard television programming, it is the film and sports channels that are defined as 'premium' channels for which the highest rates can be charged. Many of the other channels are simply presented as fillers that are used to create a sense of diversity and choice.

However, the responses above are also interesting in another way. All three of the respondents referred to above were middle class and had a relatively high level of identification with legitimate culture. It is therefore interesting that it is these respondents who still made special mention of cable and satellite channels as distinct from terrestrial television. As we have seen, the early take-up of these media was initially among the poorer sections of the population and, by the time of our study, these sections of the population did not feel the need to identify these media as distinct from their normal television viewing. However, these three middle-class respondents clearly saw their identification with satellite as distinguishing them from the 'normal' television viewer. As a result, we may be witnessing a change in the image of these media as they seek to become more legitimate in the hope of attracting those sections of the middle classes that had previously shunned them. The mention of FilmFour is therefore particularly significant in this regard: it is a film channel that distinguishes itself from the other film channels on cable and satellite through its association with the independent and the art cinema, rather than the products of the Hollywood majors.

Convergence or Contrast: the Relational Meanings of Media Forms

If it is unlikely that these new media will destroy film consumption, it is equally unlikely, as Garnham has demonstrated, that these technologies and accessories will merge into one integrated media form. There are two main reasons for this. First, the economic logic that leads hardware manufacturers to develop new technologies that can augment the television or computer would actually work against the development of a single, integrated consumer good. These technologies were specifically developed and introduced as the markets in television sets became 'saturated, so that manufacturers in the consumer electronics sector [were] in search of new products and new markets'.[19] The development of one integrated consumer item would work against the current logic of the market which would not only quickly become saturated, but would also hinder the development and introduction of new accessories and peripherals.

Second, if there is an economic pressure to maintain a diverse range of accessories that cluster around the television and/or computer, there is also a pressure from within the processes of consumption. As we have seen before, while there is a 'tendency for one medium to partially supplant another, that is cinema to replace music-hall and TV to replace cinema, newspaper circulation declining in the face of TV',[20] it is important to stress the 'partial' nature of this process. Certainly some media do go into terminal decline but, as we have argued above, it is more often the case that the meaning of an earlier technology is redefined through the introduction of the newer one. Partly this is through a process in which its cultural status changes. As one medium loses its audience to a new medium, the cost of access to it inevitably rises; as the cost of access rises, the old medium finds it increasingly difficult to compete with new media; and as the audience becomes more select and the taste for that medium becomes increasingly rare, it becomes more likely that middle-class audiences will appropriate this older medium. In other words, middle-class audiences can use it to signal their distance from contemporary popular media by presenting the declining medium as the emblem of a dying mode of authenticity that is posed against the barbarism of contemporary popular forms.

As a result, while the introduction of new media may change the meaning of earlier media they are not likely to replace them, but rather to change their status and function within the repertoire of available leisure activities. Just as television associated cinemas with tradition and nostalgia, so the emergence of satellite altered the meanings of television. Suddenly there were campaigns to protect the quality of television from the threat of 'wall-to-wall Dallas',[21] and the NEP ran a feature on the 'screen debate'. British television, it was claimed, had 'long [been] regarded as the best in the world' but was now 'in for a period of upheaval'. It therefore presented two sets of contradictory responses to the impact of satellite programming under the headings: 'quality is under serious threat' and 'exciting "classic" days to come'. The former largely recounted anecdotes about a golden age of television production, while the latter largely concentrated on the movie packages on offer via satellite: 'BSB promises strong programming and – the jewel in their crown – the best movie catalogue of any television company after deals with the top six Hollywood studios netted them films like *Rain Man* and *Twins*.' BSB are also quoted as claiming that they 'hope we'll be able to make movies when we get richer but we already have quite a substantial investment in British films such as *The Rachel Papers*'.[22]

Furthermore, as we have seen, while many people claim to prefer television to the cinema because they can watch films in the comfort of their own homes, this preference is only a general one. Many still have a firm commitment to going out, even if only every now and then. Indeed, as Crisell suggests, it may be possible that the very ubiquitous nature of television as a medium is actually creating a renewed interest in 'going out':

> The increasing subjugation of broadcasting to the individual lifestyles of its audience in one
> sense devalues the culture and entertainment that it offers. We often speak of television not
> so much as a source of entertainment in itself but as a poor alternative to 'real'
> entertainment ('I think I'll just stay in and watch telly tonight') ...[23]

In other words, different media not only have different meanings but they do so because they offer different types of experience. While a new media may become dominant, it does not follow that it will render the experiences offered by other media undesirable.

New media, for example, may offer greater interactivity but, as we have seen before, while some may value interactivity, they do not necessarily value it all the time, and still others may view interactivity as distinctly undesirable. Some people clearly relished the pleasures of being unable to control the film and the thrill of being assaulted by its visual and aural spectacle. Similarly, while some people might like the interactivity that computer games embody, the pleasure of narrative films is often the inability to control their development, the surrender to their shocks, surprises, twists and reversals: the inability to predict what will come next and even the pleasure in seeing the familiar executed with a sense of perfect craftsmanship. Certainly one could choose to tell one's own stories and make one's own films but, for many, the pleasure of narrative is specifically in surrendering that role to someone else.

Some of these processes can be seen, for example, through the impact of 'home cinema' on the meanings of cinema and cinemagoing. These technologies claim to replicate the 'cinema experience', but this defines the 'cinema experience' in very specific ways. Rather than either a social activity or one that is crucially bound up with 'getting out', the cinema experience is defined simply in terms of the supposed superiority of its visual and aural spectacle when compared with that of television. This is made clear in an NEP article on 'home cinema', which begins:

> Finding a parking space ... queuing for tickets ... sitting behind a woman with big hair ...
> these are the annoying little hazards of going to the pictures. It's the film you want to see,
> not snogging teenagers in front of you. And don't arrive too late – or you'll end up in the first
> row, peering straight up Bruce Willis's nose.

The article does however acknowledge that, for some people, 'the magic of cinema includes all of the above – along with rustling sweet packets and people hissing "sssssh-hhh!" every 15 minutes'. However, such a preference is seen as fairly ludicrous in comparison to those who 'want to watch a movie in peace, with no distractions – and maybe a beer and a sandwich – at home, in fact'.[24]

Cinema is no longer associated solely with 'going out' but is now seen as something that can be recreated within the domestic sphere. The Cinema Store, the Cornerhouse

Ironically, this article appeared in exactly the same edition as an article on the closure of the Odeon, an article that presents this event as a major loss to the culture and heritage of the city. While the article on home cinema claims that it is 'the film you want to see', the article on the Odeon stresses that the venue was about much more than the viewing of films. Most of the people who wrote letters to the paper to lament the closure of the Odeon identified themselves with the dating couples who frequent cinemas, rather than those whose view was blocked by the sight of 'snogging teenagers'.

Indeed adverts for 'home cinema' usually depict a solitary individual watching and listening within a enclosed private space that is frequently distinguished from that of a family living room and identified as a bachelor's flat. There are, of course, sound reasons for this given the demographic at which this technology was originally directed: young single men with disposable income who may or may not live at home but have not yet settled down with a family. In other words, 'home cinema' simply promises to reproduce the quality of sound and image, and it is therefore as much defined *against* traditional television technology as through an identification *with* cinema. It is therefore interesting that not only was the NEP article on home cinema in the property section, rather than either the film or entertainment sections, but it was preoccupied with the technology that one consumer had installed in his home and provided consumer advice on what to think about if one was planning to install one's own home-cinema system. Thus, it is claimed that:

When 'home cinema' claims to replicate the 'cinema experience', this 'experience is defined in very specific ways. DVD display, Hollywood Video

Mike contacted Castle Sound and Vision in Maid Marion Way, Nottingham, and they put together a package including DVD, Sky Digital, video and computer with internet access and remote keyboard and mouse (for business presentations). The system can also play music and, oh yes, there's a karaoke machine ... The room also has remote controlled blackout blinds and the screen is nine-foot wide, that's 124 inches diagonally ... 'The best thing about it is that there is one remote control for everything,' says Jeff Allen, of Castle Sound and Vision.[25]

However, while this passage places the stress on gadgetry, the article also stresses the importance of scale and quality. The article is not only called 'Seeing the Bigger Picture', but it claims that 'for some people, size is important'.

It therefore makes special mention of 'the top of the range Seleco home cinema projector' that 'produces stunning picture quality', and 'the front speakers and subwoofers (low bass)', which are supposed to produce equally stunning sound quality. The article also goes on to note that 'Mike is obviously thrilled with his home cinema' and he is quoted as saying, 'The quality of the old video was never good enough to put on the big screen ... But now with DVD, you get excellent quality which looks fantastic on the big screen.'[26] Home cinema is therefore valued not for the social experience it offers but rather for its ability to technologically replicate sound and image quality, and it is often suggested that the experience of viewing and listening is indistinguishable from that of 'being there'. In this way, it is implied that this technology will not only replicate the experience of 'getting out of the house' but therefore render such action unnecessary. As a result, while the adverts for computer games emphasise the pleasures of interactivity with the game, those for home cinema often present the experience of viewing as a literal assault. One image, for example, depicts the viewer being literally 'blown away' by the image and sound, while yet another drops the viewer into the action of the image where he is reduced to a victim that is pursued and shot at. Far from being in a position of control over, or even interactivity with, the world of the film, he is made into an object that is assaulted by it.

However, despite the claim that home cinema can replicate the cinema experience, as we have seen, the respondent who had the greatest identification with the new media specifically stated that, for him, even widescreen television could not reproduce the cinema experience of watching films with an audience.[27] The introduction of 'home cinema' has therefore had less impact on the meaning of cinema, for this respondent, than on the meaning of television. Indeed, with the introduction of home cinema, computer games and the internet, the television has come to be seen by many as neither technological enough (and therefore inferior to the cinema) nor interactive enough (and therefore inferior to computer technologies).

Local Receptions: Identity, Place and the New Media

Despite the frequent claims that new media are disrupting traditional social relations and identities, whether positively or negatively, their meanings and uses are also defined within existing arrangements. As Shaun Moores has pointed out, the meanings of cable and satellite have been shaped by tensions within families in which younger members of the family have identified with the modernity that they represent, while, for others, the meanings of these media are shaped by their identifications or disidentifications with America or Europe.[28] This was also the case in our study. The young had a sense of ownership of both the new media and the future that they represented, and their identification with them provided them with a position from which they could produce a sense of identity and authority that their parents could not challenge.[29] We also found that while some identified with the American programming of Sky, and saw it as a democratic alternative to the conservatism of British culture, others were clearly opposed to it and saw its Americanness as representing a form of cultural imperialism that threatened to replace a distinctive British culture with a homogeneous mass culture.[30]

Consequently, these new technologies have often been associated with the destruction of local identities, even though some present this process positively: 'Where we are no longer determines who were are – or who we are "with" – to the same degree as it used to because electronically mediated communication has the potential to transform situation, interaction and identification.'[31] However, these new technologies have also relied on, or even encouraged, local identities rather than destroying them. For example, while Diamond Cable used its movie channels to promote itself, it also claimed to enhance a sense of locality and community. From the first, Diamond Cable promised 'three channels for community television', one of which would be 'available for use by local authorities and other organisations within the community'.[32] Indeed, this notion of locality was distinguished from 'existing TV companies and the BBC' which, it was claimed, 'did not operate at a lower than regional level' so that there was 'a vacancy for truly local TV'.[33] For example, one form of programming that the managing director said that he wanted 'to see exploited would be university sport, and perhaps even school sport, which is covered by local cable companies in America'.[34] The company also promised to offer programming for minorities within the local community, and made special mention of its plans for 'ethnic programming – including Asian and European channels'.[35] Indeed, it was claimed that there would be 'a channel specifically aimed at Nottingham's Asian population, with programmes in a number of Indian dialects'.[36]

However, these contributions to the local community were not limited to Diamond Cable's programming. The cable system was also promoted through its ability to create greater interactivity within the community. For example, it was claimed that 'Home computers could ... be linked to each other via the telephone as well as to major computers housed in libraries and other information houses.'[37] Furthermore, one of Diamond Cable's key promotional strategies was that it provided free local telephone calls between its customers in the off-peak period, a strategy that was supposed to bring 'family and friends' together.[38] Diamond Cable was also supposed to help the local community in other ways. For example, it was claimed that the network would be 'an economic "trigger"' that would create jobs itself and simulate the whole economy. Press coverage often made mention of the jobs that the company had created or would create, but it also claimed that 'cable's development was akin to that of the laying of the roads and railways'.[39] This comment is particularly important given the context of Nottingham. It repeats a common claim that the development of telecommunications in the late 20th century was a 'revolution' akin to the 'industrial revolution'. Indeed, the roads and the railways were not only infrastructures that were essential to the development of the industrial revolution, but railway construction was the driving force behind a series of industries such as steel and engineering. This reference has specific significance within the context of Nottingham given that, as we saw in Chapter 2, Nottingham's history was distinguished by a lack of heavy industry. As a result, this comment suggests that while Nottingham may have been marginal to the industrial revolution, it would be central to the 'telecommunications revolution'.

Reports therefore continually stressed that Diamond Cable was 'the first operation of its kind in the world and it's here in Nottingham', a situation that supposedly meant: 'communications chiefs world-wide have their eyes firmly fixed on Nottingham as a unique new service is opened up to householders and businesses'.[40] The supposedly unique feature of Diamond Cable was that it was both a cable TV and telephone company. As Diamond Cable's public relations director put it: 'Until recently the US government refused to allow a direct tie-up between phone and TV companies, so we couldn't develop in the same way there.'[41] Consequently, while Diamond Cable was frequently identified as an 'American cable company', it was not seen as an external imposition but quite the reverse. Rather than a American or even global media imposed upon the city that threatened its identity, Diamond Cable was seen from the first as an organic product of the city that demonstrated and enhanced its unique identity. The city was not only seen as attracting American investors due to its unique character but, as has already been suggested, the city's special conditions were seen as essential to the development of a similarly unique and groundbreaking enterprise:

> The American company currently working out of a small office in Nottingham's Advanced Business Centre, is backed by Robert Wall and Alan McDonald, multi-millionaires with 25 years' experience in US cable who decided to apply for the Nottingham licence because of its business climate and 'progressive atmosphere'.[42]

Diamond Cable's marketing director is even quoted as claiming: 'The Americans have chosen Nottingham because they feel that it's the ideal city and in the right position – between the North and South of England.'[43]

As a result, it is implied that although its backers were American, the company would not simply be the satellite of an American operation. On the contrary, Nottingham's unique conditions made it the economic, cultural and geographical centre of a technological revolution. Furthermore, 'the importance the American backers put on the Nottingham operation' was supposedly demonstrated by the fact that 'senior executives [would be] moving here from Kentucky to live for at least four years to oversee the installation'.[44]

Anxieties about the company's effects upon Nottingham did emerge, but not until the mid-1990s, five years after the company arrived in Nottingham. The process of laying cable, it was claimed, tore up streets and pavements around the city and was 'destroying huge numbers of trees on British streets'. Significantly, the evidence for this claim came from the magazine *Country Living*, which represents the values of a British rural tradition, and claimed that 'cable companies are being afforded an "inexcusable" right to dig anywhere without permission'.[45] Trees were symbolically significant through their association with nature and rural life, rather than technology and urbanism.

However, the city's watchdog on the topic commended Diamond Cable for the 'immaculate' work that it had done, and claimed that problems were due to a fall in quality since the introduction of subcontractors. Diamond Cable themselves also pointed out that its workers and subcontractors 'are all warned about the risk to trees',[46] and it heavily promoted their use of 'a cunning gadget, which promises to wave goodbye to hole-in-the-road misery and could prevent trees being damaged'. This new machine was 'a new radar-directed under-ground digger' that was supposed to resemble 'the Mole out of *Thunderbirds*', and it was also stressed that Diamond Cable was 'the first company in the UK to use it'.[47]

So crucial was Diamond Cable's association with Nottingham as a locality that, when it was purchased by NTL in 1998, its new owners stressed that it would 'continue to be run as an autonomous regional company and the Diamond brand will continue'.[48] Although this autonomy was short-lived, and the company changed its name to NTL Midlands by the following June, the decision to smooth the transition from one brand identity to another demonstrates the importance and value of Diamond Cable's association with the local area. It is also the case that many of the company's local features remain, such as the free local calls to other NTL customers in the off-peak period.

If the meaning of cable was therefore defined through its consumption within the locality of Nottingham, the meanings of satellite and cable were also clearly defined through their consumption within existing domestic arrangements. Often these technologies were explicitly 'for the children', either as a present or else simply to provide them with an electronic babysitter.[49] In another situation, however, we found that in one family, where the parents were divorced and the children lived with their mother, it was their father who subscribed to satellite, a situation that pleased the children when they visited him.[50] Here the subscription may have been a way of encouraging the children to visit, or of making their time with him more enjoyable. It may even have been a way of alleviating a sense of guilt or deflecting a sense of betrayal or resentment.

It is therefore significant that, particularly in the early years, satellite and cable were specifically sold through their association with youth. Not only were the film channels sold, in part, as a youth-oriented product, but satellite and cable were also sold through their exclusive access to cult programming associated with youth culture: *The Simpsons*, *Star Trek: The Next Generation*, *Beverley Hills 90210* and cult channels such as Bravo and the Sci-Fi Channel. Indeed, the cult channels have become a particular point of identification and disidentification with satellite and cable.[51] One respondent was even moved to complain about the ways in which 'ropey films become cult classics'.[52]

However, when cable or satellite was not bought specifically for the children it was either seen as 'a family thing',[53] or else seen as the husband's decision, a decision that is primarily influenced by the presence of the sports channels.[54] The only time that a subscription to cable or satellite was presented as the result of a woman's choice was when the woman was single.[55]

As a result, while new media are creating new forms of film consumption, the claim that they will make leisure outside the home redundant needs serious re-evaluation. Not only are the new media consumed within specific social and cultural contexts, but there are other factors involved in the consumption of film which are often ignored through an overemphasis on these new media.

Notes

1. Hubbard, forthcoming.
2. Stefan, 25, unemployed teacher (KE19).
3. Delma, 40, teacher (KEQ).
4. Andrew, 14, student (KE27).
5. Anonymous male, 44, student (RMQ); Jeannie, 32, student (KE7).
6. NEP, 28 June 1989.
7. Moores, 2000, p. 109.
8. See, for example, Toffler, 1980. For a critique of this kind of position, see Frankel, 1987; and Graham, 1997.
9. Garnham, 1981.
10. Whitegate Mothers and Toddlers Group (KE13).
11. Julie, 31, playgroup co-ordinator (KE34).
12. See Brunsdon, 1997; and Moores, 1993; and Moores, 2000.
13. See Garnham, 1990.
14. Crisell, 1997, p. 256.
15. Sharan, 33, nurse/tutor (KE35).
16. Marc, 25, student (KE15).
17. Tracey, 37, solicitor (KE4).
18. Lisa, 29, teacher (KEQ).
19. Garnham, 1990, p. 118.
20. Ibid. p. 123.
21. For a discussion of the debates over 'wall-to-wall Dallas', see Webster, 1988; Morley and Robins. 1995. For an excellent reflection on the quality debates, see Brunsdon, 1997.
22. NEP, 7 November 1989.
23. Crisell, 1997, p. 257.
24. NEP, 27 January 2001.
25. Ibid.
26. Ibid.
27. Andrew, 14, student (KE27).
28. Moores, 1993; and Moores, 2000.
29. Andrew, 14, student (KE27).
30. Stefan, 25, unemployed teacher (KE19).
31. Moores, 2000, p. 109.
32. NEP, 8 November 1990.

33. Gary Davis, Managing Director, Diamond Cable, 'Diamond Cable – Today and Tomorrow', in *Nottingham Society of Engineers Newsline*, 5 February 1995, no. 3, p. 2.

34. NEP, 19 January 1994.

35. NEP, 8 November 1990.

36. NEP, 22 September 1989.

37. NEP, 28 June 1989.

38. Diamond Cable promotional flier, Nottingham City Library Collection.

39. NEP, 6 February 1991.

40. NEP, 2 December 1993.

41. Ibid.

42. NEP, 28 June 1989.

43. NEP, 22 September 1989.

44. *Nottingham Recorder*, 28 September 1989.

45. NEP, 9 June 1994.

46. NEP, 16 October 1995.

47. NEP, 26 October 1995.

48. NEP, 17 June 1998.

49. Moores, 1993.

50. Andrew, 14, student (KE27).

51. James, 15, student (KE23); and Tracey, 37, solicitor (KE4).

52. Paul, 31, administrator (KE26).

53. Margot, 40, residential social worker (KEQ).

54. Celia, 62, retired cleaner (KE6).

55. Tracey, 37, solicitor (KE4).

Conclusion

We have argued here that the meanings of different modes of film consumption are tied to their location within the cultural geography of the city and that, for this reason, the emergence of new modes of film consumption does not necessarily render older modes redundant. Moreover, the emergence of new modes of film consumption may change the meaning of older modes of film consumption, but this is because their meanings are defined in relation to one another: they are not simply seen as identical. As a result, while we have witnessed repeated claims about a privatisation of 'public' life, 'public' life has simply failed to disappear. While more leisure has become home centred, people not only still feel the need to get out every now and again but 'going out' is defined by its alternative: 'staying in'. However, the meanings of these activities and the places within which they occur are also subject to intense political struggle: not everyone has the same experience of 'staying in' or 'going out', or the same access to different sites within the city. Different sites become associated with different social groups and thus the experience of them involves the exclusion of others.

All these processes are exemplified in the most recent development within the landscape of film consumption within Nottingham: the opening of the Cornerhouse. At precisely the time when it was being claimed that new technologies, such as home cinema and the internet, would render cinemagoing redundant, developers embarked on the construction of a major new cinema and entertainment complex within the city centre, in which the cinema was to act as the major draw of customers. Nor was Nottingham unique in this respect.

In the 1990s, developers turned their attention from the multiplex to the 'megaplex'. As William Paul notes, in 1994, *Variety* published a story on 'a new wave in theatre building that confirms the trend in exhibition' in which:

> Every possible thing is contained under one roof, with free-standing theatres independent of malls that can operate as destinations in themselves by being 'coupled with entertainment centres encompassing everything from miniature golf and virtual reality games to "food courts" and toddler compounds.'[1]

In other words, rather than simply a multiplex attached to a larger out-of-town development, in the megaplex the cinema itself is the central, organising feature of an entertainment complex. Furthermore, as this trend took hold in Britain, it was increasingly associated with developments within inner-city rather than out-of-town locations, and these developments became known as urban entertainment centres (UECs). For example, Star City in Birmingham was referred to as 'one of the first US-style UECs in the UK'.[2] Indeed, in addition to the Cornerhouse scheme, there were also plans for a new ABC complex in the north-west corner of the market square and south of the city centre on the location of the Broadmarsh Shopping Centre.

The main reason for the return of cinema to the city centre was quite simply the result of changing government policy. The concerns about the effects on city centres of out-of-town complexes, which we saw in relation to the multiplex, prompted local and national government to actively encourage developers to concentrate on city-centre projects. As *Estates Gazette Interactive* put it:

> The explanation for this shift [to the town centre] is simple: PPG 6. As Steve Weiner, chief executive of Cine UK, comments: 'It's not difficult to get planning permission for out-of-town leisure schemes. It's impossible.'
>
> A stream of rejected planning applications has forced many of the main operators to rethink their acquisition plans. Mark Atkins at Jones Lang Wootton says: 'Cinema operators want space as quickly as possible. They won't abide being seen to struggle to get planning permission. Deliverability is the key and "town centre" is deliverable.'[3]

Planning Permission Guidance Note Number 6 (PPG 6) required authorities 'to determine planning applications in such a manner that the city centre must be considered before an out of town site'.[4]

If new media are supposed to have led to greater privatisation of leisure, other processes have led to a renaissance of city-centre leisure and the construction of new urban entertainment centres such as the Cornerhouse

There were also benefits in choosing the city centre as a development site. By moving back to the city centre, developers felt that they could create favourable relations
with local and national government in which they would 'see planning and the market
working in harmony'.[5] Local and national governments had an incentive to see city centres redeveloped. New city-centre developments increased the rateable value of the areas
in which they were located and so increased revenue for the local authority,[6] but it was
also believed that these new developments would 'revitalise city centres'.[7] For example,
it was argued that 'a multi-screen cinema should have a knock-on effect in the city centre,
with more people visiting the local bars and restaurants after watching a film'.[8] As a
result, council members supported the construction of the Cornerhouse because the
'part of town' within which it was to be located 'has been terribly neglected and any
development to enhance the area should be welcome'.[9] It was also argued that it was 'a
unique opportunity to create a leisure scheme which will complement and enhance the
existing leisure and cultural facilities within the city centre' and would therefore 'ensure
Nottingham's continuing prominence as the principal regional centre.'[10]

The cinema had another more specific use for the council. Special mention was made
of the new cinema's location 'in an established leisure circuit of the city with the Theatre
Royal, Concert Hall and Old Market Square nearby', a factor that was highly significant
for the Council. As Nottingham's city-centre manager claimed: 'So close to the Theatre
Royal and Concert Hall, it will turn that part of Nottingham into the cultural quarter.'[11]
Nottingham may have had a reputation as 'the principal regional centre', but the bar and
club life of the city centre had meant its nightlife had become associated with youth. The
council hoped that the new cinema's location would consolidate the area's appeal to an
alternative section of the population.

Initial reports of the cinema suggested that it would appeal to older, more affluent
consumers. The cinema, it was claimed, would have screens with 'leather reclining seats',
to which 'gourmet food' such as 'champagne and sushi' would be delivered. It was also
suggested that tickets for these screens would be nearly twice the price of the average
cinema ticket in Nottingham at the time, at around £10 per head, but it was argued that
'Nottingham has a very cultured population ... There is definitely a market.' This appeal
to mature and affluent consumers was also evident in their proposed programming policy: 'Two further screens will aim to attract a different crowd by showing foreign, arthouse
and cult films.'[12] Furthermore, while previous multiplexes had largely been associated
with American culture, the new cinema also sought to distinguish itself in other ways,
and it was claimed that its 'pedestrianised front and its proximity to the Theatre Royal
would give the area a continental feel'.[13]

However, despite the apparent union of interests between developers and the council, there were conflicts between their agendas. For the developers, the value of a UEC
was dependent on its ability 'to convince a customer to buy products'. The function of
leisure was therefore simply to deliver customers to retailers, to 'make a discretionary
activity more enjoyable'.[14] As Richard Kiersey, the property director of Greenalls, put it:
'Retailing is theatre.' The UEC has therefore been described as 'a scaled down theme
park with more restaurants and retail', in which the function of a cinema was not as a

generator of income, but rather as an anchor, or 'magnet for traffic, benefiting both retailers and other leisure operators'.[15] As a result, some developers have been highly sceptical about this approach, and have claimed that they 'were not convinced that a leisure element would increase the property's value'. The 'ideal' for such a complex was a full car park 'with a two-hour turnaround', in which every 'car should average a £100 spend'. Cinemas could therefore be seen as liabilities because they 'will fill the space for two hours, but the spend is low'. As has been claimed, the 'sums don't justify having a cinema in a centre': it is only through their ability to 'attract extra customers' that a cinema can 'add to the value'.[16]

Consequently the complexes were designed to discourage and dissuade customers from leaving the complex to visit nearby bars and restaurants after watching a film, and hence to minimise the 'knock-on effect' which the local council had hoped would benefit the city centre more generally. Thus, while the NEP claimed that the complex would 'open up Nottingham's nightlife and give everyone an even wider range of options', it also referred to the complex as 'a one-stop leisure venue' that would 'be a destination and a circuit in its own right'.[17] In other words, rather than simply drawing people into the city centre, the danger with such complexes is that they are in open competition with other operations and are designed to attract and keep consumers within their own space rather than to revitalise the city beyond. As a result, it should be noted that the opening of the Cornerhouse finally closed the two remaining city-centre cinemas (the ABC and Odeon). Rather than rejuvenate the city centre as a whole, there is a very real possibility that the new complex will simply poach consumers from other areas and so send them into decline.[18]

For the UECs, cinemas are not themselves primarily generators of income, but rather anchors or magnets that attract customers for the other retailers and leisure operators also located within the centre. The Warner Village Cinemas, The Cornerhouse

Furthermore, while the council hoped that the Cornerhouse's proximity to the Theatre Royal and the Concert Hall would consolidate the identity of the area as a space for mature and affluent audiences and so create a culture zone, in practice it may be having a very different impact. Plans for the luxury seats, champagne and sushi all seem to have been sidelined along with the programming of art-house and cult movies. Instead, the cinema was promoted through an association with Hollywood cinema. There were three key posters at the time of its opening and each featured a central image: the first identified the cinema with the horror films that were then popular with teenage audiences; the second associated the cinema with notions of Hollywood glamour though an allusion to a famous image of Marilyn Monroe from *The Seven Year Itch*; and the third associated the cinema with the Hollywood blockbuster through its reference to the special-effects spectacular, *Twister*.

As a result, the cinema has addressed itself to a very different audience to that of the Theatre Royal and Concert Hall and rather than encouraging the creation of a culture zone, the cinema might actually discourage consumers from attending these other two venues. For example, the Trinity Square car park has long had a bad reputation as a potentially dangerous place, but anyone parking there for a night at the theatre or a concert now has to pass through the crowds that mill around the Cornerhouse, an experience that many mature consumers find unpleasant and threatening. As we have seen, for example, elderly respondents frequently stated that they would not go into the city centre at night because of the crowds of youth that frequent it.[19] These perceptions of the new complex as an alienating and dangerous space can also be found in the letters written to the paper. For example, one resident asked, 'What do the police think of another nightclub and ten-screen cinema?'[20]

Certainly some of the cafés and bars still try to convey a continental feel, but these are rarely the kinds of establishments associated with the mature and affluent consumer for which the council hoped that the complex would cater. All these establishments are chains, and ones that are directed at the two key consumers of the traditional multiplex: families and youth. For example, a spokesman for Wagamama, a Japanese-style noodle bar attached to the complex, stated that they were attracted to Nottingham by the 'large and lively student population, [and] an increasing inner-city residential sector'.[21] Both of these groups are assumed to be made up of people who are both young and single, but the developers were also keen to target family audiences through a 'McDonald's, an ice cream parlour and other things to cater for the kids'. As a result, while the complex tried to suggest the diversity of its appeal, its choice of references still clearly identified its appeal with families and youth: 'There are going to be films on from Disney right through to Tarantino.'[22]

However, it is not only older residents who felt excluded from, and alienated by, the complex. There is evidence from other cities that the redevelopment of city centres has alienated sections of the lower-middle and working classes, who see these spaces as the playground of trendy middle-class consumers, and therefore reject city centres as a place of leisure.[23] Furthermore, although the Cornerhouse directly appeals to families, developers have also recognised that UECs are not 'family-friendly'. Not only do they make

The bars and restaurants
that make up much of
the complex try to
convey a continental
feel, to attract quite
specific types of
customers. The
Cornerhouse

much of their 'profit from food and beverage aspects' but can prove very expensive for families.[24] Many parents therefore feel under considerable financial pressure within these complexes and, ironically, even the most affluent sections tended to resent these places. While less affluent parents felt economically threatened, many affluent middle-class parents, as we have seen, regard consumption morally and viewed these developments as encouraging inappropriate behaviour in their children.[25]

As a result, it is hardly surprising that different sections of the Nottingham population viewed its construction in very different ways, and that, from the start, it was the elderly who expressed the greatest sense of alienation from the building. At the beginning, however, objections were largely concerned with the loss of the *Evening Post* building, which had to be demolished to make way for the new complex, and it was not until near the time of its opening that dissatisfaction with the complex itself became evident. Early complaints referred to the plans as a move that would 'wipe out a part of the city's history'.[26] Fear of losing the city's history was felt particularly deeply by more elderly residents who not only tended to have a greater investment in memories of the city, but also saw it as representative of an attitude that rendered them irrelevant. As one letter commented, 'we seem determined to be rid of a part of the city's history . . . It's as though we are going through the 1960s syndrome "Out with the old, in with the new."'[27]

The reference to the 1960s also relates this development to the supposed destruction of the city during this period, which we discussed in Part Three, and, as a result, another letter asked, 'When are the City planners going to wake up?'[28] The demolition of the *Evening Post* building not only met with considerable opposition, but it also revealed a deep-seated alienation from the political process. One letter complained that city council planners:

> are omniscient, they are omnipotent . . . Having once been appointed by an elected body
> they are no longer under its control. They make a decision, they then listen to opinions, they
> carefully consider them, and then continue with the plan they intended to impose.[29]

Another letter claimed that 'the opinions of taxpayers don't seem to matter to the planners',[30] while still another claimed: 'As a resident of Nottingham and a pensioner, I've sadly watched my city being sold to the highest bidders, whose only interest seems to be tearing down beautiful buildings and replacing them with modern monstrosities no one wants.'[31] Nor were these isolated objections; by the final time that plans for the complex came before the planning committee, 11,000 signatures had been collected that called for the building – or at least its exterior – to be preserved.[32]

These concerns with the *Evening Post* building are also interesting in other ways. Shortly before the plans for its demolition were announced, English Heritage had carried out a review of listed buildings in Nottingham and had decided not to list the building on the grounds that it 'was not sufficiently architecturally or historically important'.[33] Consequently, another letter took issue with the campaign to protect the building:

> We're a funny lot, aren't we? For the people of Nottingham, pressing through our city centre
> in a thick fog of supermarket preoccupation, and who normally could not give a damn about
> the architectural merits of their surroundings, that ponderous frowning hulk which houses
> the offices of the *Nottingham Evening Post* currently under the threat of the demolition gang
> is suddenly transformed into an architectural gem.[34]

Others also claimed that there was nothing 'outstanding about it', and that it had only been seen as a beautiful and important building since it was threatened with demolition.[35]

As the opening of the cinema drew closer, however, attention shifted away from a defence of the old *Evening Post* building to a condemnation of the new complex. Just as we saw in the case of the Showcase, while some viewed the Cornerhouse's associations with America positively, others presented them negatively. Thus, it was claimed that the new complex was 'set to be the ultimate popcorn palace of pleasure', in which the viewers could 'plump themselves down in one of the supersoft, highbacked chairs and allow the neon glow of Hollywood to wash over them'. However, while this reference to 'neon' evoked a nostalgia for an earlier era of Hollywood, it was also claimed that: 'Many cinema enthusiasts complain that multiplex entertainment venues sandblast the traditional values of the old-style movie houses.' These complaints again present these places as characterless, global non-places, in which all 'the quirks and crannies which once made local cinemas so distinctive are air-brushed out of existence'.[36]

They are also related to issues of choice, and it is often implied that, like other multiplexes, the Cornerhouse would not provide a 'real' choice but would 'favour the big money blockbusters over the more thoughtful independent and foreign language films'.[37] As Gill Henderson, the then head of the Broadway, put it: 'It might mean you can choose to go to the same film at three different cinemas. That's fine if one of them does your favourite flavour of popcorn, and you want to see the latest blockbuster there.'[38] The implication is, of course, that such a choice is trivial and meaningless, and while multiplexes might bring more screens to a city they 'show mainly the same mainstream films'.[39]

However, while many associated the cinema with bland Hollywood production, the Cornerhouse was keen to stress that it would 'be showing a wide selection of non-mainstream movies along with the blockbusters that you would expect', including 'a weekly Bollywood presentation'. Ironically, the screenings of Bollywood films were rarely mentioned by those who attacked the supposed global blandness of the Cornerhouse, while the cinema itself used these films as evidence of its commitment to the local community. It claimed that it was 'committed to offer the best in Asian films', and supported this claim with the announcement that they had 'employed Ravinder Panaser, a Bollywood expert, to commission their range of features'.[40] It is also interesting that while the promised 'selection of classic and art-house screenings' never really materialised, the Bollywood screenings have proved highly successful and the number of screenings has increased significantly.

Furthermore, while these complexes might seem like global non-places to some, the industry itself views the matter very differently. As the *Estates Gazette* puts it:

> The vast majority of films screened are from Hollywood, and many of the shops and restaurants are either American chains or are selling American-style goods and services. But this does not mean that, from a property point of view, all the developments are alike. The problems posed by projects in Spain are different from those in northern Europe, for example.[41]

It should also be noted that while the Cornerhouse might provide space for chains, some but by no means all of which are global brands, the building itself was the product of two local development firms: Forman Hardy Holdings of Nottingham who later sold the site to developers Wilson Bowden of Leicester.

The cinema opened on 2 March 2001, a year after the completion of our audience interviews and one month after the completion of the first draft for this book. Thus, while we were able to examine the debates over its construction with their projections on potential inclusion and exclusion of the complex, we were unable to study the actual consumption of the new cinema and the impact that it has on other places of film consumption within

Nottingham. This not only demonstrates the need for new research in the future, but also that the history of cinemagoing is not at an end, to say nothing of the history of film consumption more generally. Indeed, if there is one thing that we hope that we have demonstrated, it is that there is no teleology to the history of cinemagoing in particular or film consumption in general: that history is not leading to any predetermined end or conclusion.

Notes

1. Paul, 1994, p. 498.
2. *Estates Gazette*, 4 July 1998, p. 88.
3. *Estates Gazette Interactive*, 6 December 1997, http://www.egi.co.uk/egi2/egarchive/.
4. NEP, Nottinghamshire Commercial Property Weekly, 12 April 1998. For more on PPG 6, see Miller, Jackson, Thrift, Holbrook and Rowlands, 1998, pp. 70–79.
5. John Lett, the London Planning Advisory Committee, quoted in *Estates Gazette*, 4 July 1998, p. 113.
6. NEP, Commercial Property Weekly, 16 July 1996.
7. NEP, 24 July 1997.
8. Ibid.
9. NEP, 17 April 1998.
10. NEP, Commercial Property Weekly, 21 April 1998.
11. NEP, 25 August 1998.
12. NEP, 20 November 1998.
13. NEP, Commercial Property Weekly, 24 November 1998.
14. *Estates Gazette*, 4 July 1998, p. 83.
15. *Estates Gazette*, 8 March 1997, p. 131.
16. *Estates Gazette*, 4 July 1998, p. 83.
17. NEP, 21 February 2000.
18. A similar process has been analysed in Manchester where the Castlefield development has attracted consumers away from the Gay Village, which has gone into economic decline as a result. See Skeggs, Moran, Tyrer and Corteen, forthcoming.
19. See Chapter 11: 'Negotiating Nostalgia: Modernity, Memory and the Meanings of Place'.
20. Letter to the NEP, published 8 May 1998.
21. NEP, 18 August 2000.
22. NEP, 24 November 1998.
23. See Larry Ray and David Smith, 'Racial Violence in Greater Manchester', ESRC Research Award Number L133251019.
24. *Estates Gazette*, 4 July 1998, p. 89.
25. For more on middle-class attitudes to consumption, see Miller, Jackson, Thrift Holbrook and Rowlands, 1998.
26. Letter to the NEP, published 4 July 1996.
27. Letter to the NEP, published 28 April 1998.
28. Ibid.

29. Letter to the NEP, published 7 May 1998.

30. Letter to NEP, published 8 May 1998.

31. Ibid.

32. NEP, 13 November 1998.

33. NEP, 4 July 1996.

34. Letter to the NEP, 7 May 1998.

35. Letter to the NEP, 12 May 1998.

36. NEP, 23 February 2001.

37. Ibid.

38. NEP, 15 March 1997.

39. Ibid.

40. NEP, 23 February 2001.

41. *Estates Gazette*, 8 March 1997, p. 132.

Appendix: Questionnaire

Film Consumption and the City

We are conducting a study of filmgoing in Nottingham, and would be most grateful if you could help us by filling in the form below and returning it to us at the following address: Institute of Film Studies, School of American and Canadian Studies, University of Nottingham, Nottingham, NG7 2RD. Many thanks.

Dr Mark Jancovich

1. **Have you always lived in Nottingham?**   **If not, when did you move here?**
   ☐ Yes   ☐ No

2. **Do you watch films regularly, and if so, how often?**
   ☐ Yes _____
   ☐ No

3. **What are your first memories of seeing films?**

4. **In a few words, describe your feelings about the following cinemas:**
   a) Odeon

   b) The ABC

   c) The Showcase

   d) The Savoy

   e) The Broadway

   f) Other

5. **Please indicate which ones you have visited and why?**
   ☐ a) The Odeon
   ☐ b) The ABC
   ☐ c) The Showcase
   ☐ d) The Savoy
   ☐ e) The Broadway
   ☐ f) Other

6. **Who do you usually go with?**

7. **How do you normally get there?**
   ☐ Car   ☐ Taxi   ☐ Other (please state) _____
   ☐ Bus   ☐ Walk

8. **Do you normally buy food and drink at the cinema, and if so, why?**

9. **Do you usually do anything else before or afterwards (e.g. go for a drink, to a club, etc.)?**

10. **In a few words, describe your feelings about the following:**
    a) Watching a film at the cinema

    b) Watching a film on television

    c) Watching a film on video

    d) Watching a film on satellite or cable

11. **Which of the above do you prefer and why?**

12. **Do you have any particularly memorable experiences associated with going to the cinema?**
    If so, please describe them.

13. **What other kinds of entertainment do you enjoy and how do these compare with the cinema?**

14. **How do you think that the cinema has changed over time?**
    Are things better or worse than they used to be?
    In what ways?

15. **Are there any questions that you think we should have asked but didn't?**

Finally, please give the information about yourself requested below.

16. Your name:

17. Sex ☐ Male   ☐ Female

18. Age

19. Occupation

20. How would you describe your race/ethnicity?

21. Is there any other information about yourself that you consider relevant?

22. Are you willing to participate in an interview or a follow-up questionnaire? If so, please give your address and/or telephone number below. Address/Telephone:

Once again, many thanks for taking the time to complete this questionnaire.

Bibliography

Newspapers Consulted

BBLN *Bulwell and Basford Local News*

EPN The *Evening Post and News* was the result of the merger of the *Nottingham Evening Post* and *Nottingham Evening News* in 1963. The 'and News' was subsequently dropped so that the paper became the *Evening Post* once again.

GJ *Guardian Journal* – The proprietors of the *Nottingham Daily Guardian* and *Nottingham Evening Post* acquired the *Nottingham Evening News* and *Nottingham Journal* in 1953. The *Guardian Journal* was the result of the merger of the *Nottingham Daily Guardian* and the *Nottingham Journal*.

NDG *Nottingham Daily Guardian*

NEN *Nottingham Evening News*

NEP *Nottingham Evening Post*

NJ *Nottingham Journal*

Secondary Sources

Abercrombie, Nicholas and Longhurst, Brian, *Audiences: A Sociological Theory of Performance and Imagination* (London: Sage, 1998).

Aglietta, Michel, *A Theory of Capitalist Regulation* (London: New Left Books, 1979).

Allen, Robert C., 'Motion Picture Exhibition in Manhattan, 1906–1912: Beyond the Nickelodeon', *Cinema Journal*, vol. 18, no. 2, Spring 1979, pp. 2–15.

Allen, Robert C., *Vaudeville and Film, 1895–1915* (New York: Arno, 1980).

Allen, Robert C., 'From Exhibition to Reception: Reflections on the Audience in Film History', *Screen*, vol. 31. no. 4, Winter 1990, pp. 347–56.

Allen, Robert C., *Horrible Prettyness: Burlesque and American Culture* (Chapel Hill: University of North Carolina Press, 1991).

Allen, Robert C., 'Manhattan Myopia; or, Oh! Iowa!', *Cinema Journal*, vol. 35, no. 3, Spring 1996, pp. 75–103.

Allen, Robert C. and Gomery, Douglas, *Film History: Theory and Practice* (New York: McGraw-Hill, 1985).

Amin, Ash, *Post-Fordism* (Oxford: Blackwell, 1994).

Anderson, Benedict, *Imagined Communities* (London: Verso, 1983).

Anderson, Charles, *A City and its Cinemas* (Bristol: Recliffe, 1983).

Ang, Ien, *Watching Dallas: Soap Opera and the Melodramatic Imagination* (London: Routledge, 1985).

Ang, Ien, *Desperately Seeking the Audience* (London: Routledge, 1991).

Ang, Ien, *Living Room Wars: Rethinking Media Audiences for a Postmodern World* (London: Routledge, 1996).

Appaduri, Arjun, 'Putting Hierarchy in its Place', *Cultural Anthropology*, vol. 3, no. 1, 1988, pp. 36–49.

Attfield, Judy, 'FORM/female FOLLOWS FUNCTION/male: Feminist Critiques of Design', in J. A. Walker (ed.), *Design History and the History of Design* (London: Pluto, 1989), pp. 199–225.

Attfield, Judy, 'The Empty Cocktail Cabinet: Display in the Mid-Century British Domestic Interior', in Tim Putnam and C. Newton (eds), *Household Choices* (London: Middlesex Polytechnic and Future Publication, 1990).

Attfield, Judy, 'Inside Pram Town: A Case Study of Harlow House Interiors, 1951–61', in Judy Attfield and Pat Kirkham (eds), *A View from the Interior: Women and Design* (London: Women's Press, 1995), pp. 215–38.

Atwell, David, *Cathedrals of the Movies: A History of British Cinemas and their Audiences* (London: The Architectural Press, 1980).

Auge, Mark, *Non-Places* (London: Verso, 1995).

Austin, Bruce, *Immediate Seating: A Look at Movie Audiences* (Belmont, CA: Wadsworth, 1989).

Avery, Valerie, *London Morning* (Exeter: Arnold Wheaton, 1980).

Bailey, Peter, *Leisure and Class in Victorian England: Rational Recreation and the Contest of Control* (London: Routledge and Kegan Paul, 1978).

Bailey, Peter (ed.), *Music Hall: The Business of Pleasure* (Milton Keynes: Open University Press, 1986).

Bain, A. D., 'The Growth of Television Ownership in the United Kingdom', *International Economic Review*, vol. 3, no. 2, May 1962, pp. 145–67.

Bakhtin, Mikhail, *Rabaleis and His World* (Cambridge, MA: MIT Press, 1968).

Balio, Tino, *The American Film Industry* (Madison, WI: University of Wisconsin Press, 1976).

Balio, Tino, *The Grand Design: Hollywood as a Modern Business Enterprise, 1930–1939* (Berkeley, CA: University of California Press, 1996).

Barclay, John, *Viewing Tastes of Adolescents in Cinema and Television* (Glasgow: Scottish Educational Film Association, 1961).

Barker, Martin, *The Video Nasties: Freedom and Censorship in the Media* (London: Pluto, 1984).

Barker, Martin, 'Film Audience Research: Making a Virtue Out of a Necessity', *Iris*, no. 26, 1998, pp. 131–47.

Barker, Martin and Brooks, Kate, *Knowing Audiences: Judge Dredd, its Friends, Fans and Foes* (Luton: University of Luton Press, 1998).

Baudrillard, Jean, *The Mirror of Production* (St Louis: Telos, 1975).

Baudrillard, Jean, *For a Critique of the Political Economy of the Sign* (St Louis: Telos, 1981).

Beauregard, Robert, *Voices of Decline: The Postwar Fate of US Cities* (Oxford: Blackwell, 1993).

Beckett, John (ed.) *A Centenary History of Nottingham* (Manchester: Manchester University Press, 1997).

Beckett, John with Brand, Ken, *Nottingham: An Illustrated History* (Manchester: Manchester University Press, 1997).

Belk, Russell, *Collecting in a Consumer Society* (London: Routledge, 1995).

Belk, Russell W. and Wallendorf, Melanie, 'Of Mice and Men: Gender and Identity in Collecting', in Susan M. Pearce (ed.), *Interpreting Objects and Collections* (London: Routledge, 1994), pp. 240–53.

Benjamin, Walter, *Charles Baudelaire or the Lyric Poet of High Capitalism* (London: New Left Books, 1969).

Benjamin, Walter, *The Arcades Project* (Cambridge, MA: Belknap Press, 1999).

Bennett, Tony, *Formalism and Marxism* (London: Methuen, 1979).

Bennett, Tony, *Outsider Literature* (London: Routledge, 1990).

Bennett, Tony, *The Birth of the Museum: History, Theory, Politics* (London: Routledge, 1995).

Bennett, Tony and Woolacott, Janet, *Bond and Beyond: The Political Career of a Popular Hero* (London: Macmillan, 1987).

Benson, John, *The Rise of Consumer Society in Britain, 1880–1980* (London: Longman, 1994).

Berman, Marshall, *All That is Solid Melts Into Air: The Experience of Modernity* (London: Verso, 1983).

Bird, Jon, Curtis, Barry, Putnam, Tim, Robertson, George and Tickner, Lisa (eds), *Mapping the Futures* (London: Routledge, 1993).

Black, Peter, 'A Time to View and a Time to Switch Off', *Daily Mail Ideal Home Book* (London: Daily Mail Ideal Home Exhibition Dept. of Associated Newspapers, 1954).

Blumin, Stuart M., 'The Hypothesis of Middle-Class Formation in Nineteenth Century America: A Critique and Some Proposals', *American Historical Review*, vol. 90, April 1985, pp. 299–338.

Blumin, Stuart M., *The Emergence of the Middle Class: Social Experience in the American City 1760–1900* (Cambridge: Cambridge University Press, 1989).

Booth, William, *In Darkest England and the Way Out* (London: Salvation Army, 1890).

Bordwell, David, *Narration and the Fiction Film* (London: Routledge, 1985).

Bourdieu, Pierre, *Outline of a Theory of Practice* (Cambridge: Cambridge University Press, 1977).

Bourdieu, Pierre, *Distinction: A Social Critique of the Judgement of Taste* (London: Routledge, 1984).

Bourdieu, Pierre, *Homo Academicus* (Cambridge: Polity, 1989a).

Bourdieu, Pierre, *In Other Words: Essays towards a Reflexive Sociology* (Cambridge: Polity, 1989b).

Bourdieu, Pierre, *Photography: A Middle-Brow Art* (Cambridge: Polity, 1990a).

Bourdieu, Pierre, *The Logic of Practice* (Cambridge: Polity, 1990b).

Bourdieu, Pierre, *The Love of Art: European Museums and their Public* (Cambridge: Polity, 1990c).

Bourdieu, Pierre, *Language and Symbolic Power* (Cambridge: Polity, 1991).

Bourdieu, Pierre, *Sociology in Question* (London: Sage, 1993a).

Bourdieu, Pierre, *The Field of Cultural Production: Essays on Art and Literature* (New York: Columbia University Press, 1993b).

Bourdieu, Pierre, *The Rules of Art* (Cambridge: Polity, 1996).

Bourdieu, Pierre and Passeron, J. C., *Reproduction in Education, Society and Culture* (London: Sage, 1977).

Bowden, G. H., *The Story of the Raleigh Cycle* (London: W. H. Allen, 1975).

Bowden, Sue and Offer, Avner, 'Household Appliances and the Use of Time: The United States and Britain Since the 1920s', *Economic History Review*, vol. 47, no. 4, 1994, pp. 725–48.

Box, Kathleen, *The Cinema and the Public*, Social Survey, NS106, 1946.

Boyer, Christine M., *The City of Collective Memory* (Cambridge, MA: MIT Press, 1994).

Brand, Ken, 'The Park Estate, Nottingham: The Development of a Nineteenth Century Fashionable Suburb', *Transactions of the Thoroton Society of Nottinghamshire*, no. 88, 1984, pp. 54–75.

Branigan, Edward, *Narrative Comprehension and Film* (New York: Routledge, 1992).

Braverman, Harry, *Labor and Monopoly Capital* (New York: Monthly Review Press, 1974).

Brazier, S., Hammond, R. and Waterman, S. R. (eds). A New Geography of Nottingham (Nottingham: Trent Polytechnic in association with Nottinghamshire County Council and Nottingham City Council, 1984).

Breakwell, Ian and Hammond, Paul (eds), *Seeing in the Dark: A Compendium of Cinemagoing* (London: Serpent's Tail, 1990).

Browser, Eileen, *The Transformation of the Cinema, 1907–1915* (Berkeley, CA: University of California Press, 1990).

Brunsdon, Charlotte, *Screen Tastes: Soap Opera to Satellite Dishes* (London: Routledge, 1997).

Brunsdon, Charlotte and Morley, David, *Everyday Television: 'Nationwide'* (London: BFI, 1978).

Buscombe, Edward, 'All Bark and No Bite: The Film Industry's Response to Television', in John Corner (ed.), *Popular Television in Britain* (London: BFI, 1991).

Butler, Ivan, *To Encourage the Art of the Film: The Story of the British Film Institute* (London: Robert Hale, 1971).

Butsch, Richard, *The Making of American Audiences: From Stage to Television, 1750–1990* (Cambridge: Cambridge University Press, 2000).

Cameron, A. C., *The Film in National Life*, (London: Allen and Unwin, 1932).

Carey, John, *The Intellectuals and the Masses: Pride and Prejudice Among the Literary Intelligentsia 1880–1939* (London: Faber, 1992).

Carrol, Noel, *Mystifying Movies: Fads and Fallacies in Contemporary Film Theory* (New York: Columbia University Press, 1988).

Castells, Manuel, *The Urban Question* (London: Arnold, 1977).

Castells, Manuel, *City, Class and Power* (London: Macmillan, 1978).

Castells, Manuel, *The City and the Grassroots* (London: Arnold, 1983).

Castells, Manuel, *The Informational City* (Oxford: Blackwell, 1989).

Certeau, Michel de, *The Practice of Everyday Life* (Berkeley, CA: University of California Press, 1984).

Chambers, J. D., *Modern Nottingham in the Making* (Nottingham: Nottingham Journal, 1956).

Chanan, Michael, *The Dream that Kicks: The Prehistory and Early Years of Cinema in Britain* (London: Routledge, 1980).

Chapman, S. D., 'Economy, Industry and Employment' in John Beckett (ed.), *A Centenary History of Nottingham* (Manchester: Manchester University Press, 1997), pp. 480–512.

Chapman, Stanley, *Jesse Boot of Boots the Chemists* (London: Hodder and Stoughton, 1974).

Charney, Leo, and Schwartz, Vanessa R. (eds), *Cinema and the Invention of Modern Life* (Berkeley, CA: University of California Press, 1995).

Cherry, Gordon E., *Town Planning in Britain Since 1900* (Oxford: Blackwell, 1996).

City of Nottingham Education Committee, *The William Crane Schools 1931–1952* (Nottingham: University of Nottingham Library Collection, 1952).

Clapson, Mark, *A Bit of a Flutter: Popular Gambling and English Society c. 1823–1961* (Manchester: Manchester University Press, 1991).

Clarke, Alison J., 'Tupperware: Suburbia, Sociality and Mass Consumption', in Roger Silverstone (ed.), *Visions of Suburbia* (London: Routledge, 1997), pp. 132–60.

Clarke, Alison J., *Tupperware: The Promise of Plastic in 1950s America* (Washington, DC: Smithsonian Institute, 1999).

Clarke, David B. (ed.), *The Cinematic City* (London: Routledge, 1997).

Clarke, George, *The Cinemas of Lincoln* (Wakefield: Mercia Cinema Society, 1991).

Clarke, John and Critcher, Chas, *The Devil Makes Work: Leisure in Capitalist Britain* (Basingstoke: Macmillan, 1985).

Clarke, John, Critcher, Chas and Johnson, Richard (eds), *Working Class Culture: Studies in History and Theory* (London: Hutchinson, 1979).

Clarke, Peter, *Hope and Glory: Britain 1900–1990* (Harmondsworth: Penguin, 1996).

Coates, Ken and Silburn, Richard, *Poverty: The Forgotten Englishman* (Harmondsworth: Penguin, 1970).

Commission on Educational and Cultural Films, *The Film in National Life* (London: Allen and Unwin, 1932).

Corbett, Kevin J., 'Empty Seats: The Missing History of Movie-Watching', *Journal of Film and Video*, vol. 50, no. 4, Winter 1998–1999, pp. 34–48.

Corbett, Kevin J., 'The Big Picture: Theatrical Moviegoing, Digital Television, and Beyond the Substitution Effect', *Cinema Journal*, vol. 40, no. 2, Winter 2001, pp. 17–34.

Corrigan, Philip, 'Film Entertainment as Ideology and Pleasure: Towards a History of Audiences', in James Curran and Vincent Porter (eds), *British Cinema History* (London: Weidenfeld and Nicolson, 1983), pp. 24–35.

Crafton, Donald, *The Talkies: American Cinema's Transition to Sound 1926–1931* (Berkeley, CA: University of California Press, 1997).

Crammond, Joyce, 'The Introduction of Television and its Effects Upon Children's Daily Lives', in Ray Brown (ed.), *Children and Television* (London: Collier-Macmillan, 1976).

Crang, Mark, *Cultural Geography* (London: Routledge, 1998).

Crisell, Andrew, *An Introductory History of British Broadcasting* (London: Routledge, 1997).

Crump, Jeremy, 'Provincial Music Hall: Promoters and Public in Leicester, 1863–1929', in Peter Bailey (ed.), *Music Hall: The Business of Pleasure* (Milton Keynes: Open University Press, 1986).

Cunningham, Hugh, 'The Metropolitan Fairs: A Case Study in the Social Control of Leisure', in A. P. Donajgrodski (ed.) *Social Control in Nineteenth Century Britain* (London: Croom Helm, 1977), pp. 163–84.

Cunningham, Hugh, *Leisure in the Industrial Revolution* (London: Croom Helm, 1980).

Cunningham, Hugh, 'Urban Fairs and Popular Culture in Nineteenth Century England', in Lex Heerma van Voss and Frits van Holthoon (eds), *Working Class and Popular Culture* (Amsterdam: Stichting, 1988), pp. 99–107.

Curran, James and Seaton, Jean, *Power Without Responsibility: the Press and Broadcasting in Britain* (London: Methuen, 1985).

Davidoff, Leonore and Hall, Catherine, *Family Fortunes: Men and Women of the Middle Class, 1780–1850* (London: Hutchinson, 1987).

Davies, Andrew, *Leisure, Gender and Poverty: Working-Class Culture in Salford and Manchester, 1900–1939* (Buckingham: Open University Press, 1992).

Davies, Andrew, 'Cinema and Broadcasting', in Paul Johnson (ed.), *Twentieth Century Britain: Economic, Social and Cultural Change* (London: Longmans, 1994).

Davis, Mike, *City of Quartz: Excavating the Future in Los Angeles* (London: Verso, 1990).

Davis, Mike, *Ecology of Fear* (London: Picador, 1999).

Davis, Mike, 'Urban Renaissance and the Spirit of Postmodernism', *New Left Review*, no. 151 2002, pp. 106–14.

Dear, Michael J., *The Postmodern Urban Condition* (Oxford: Blackwell, 2000).

Denison, G. M., 'A Brief History of Nottingham Newspapers', unpublished paper in Local History Library, University of Nottingham.

DeVault, Marjorie, *Feeding the Family: The Social Organisation of Caring as Gendered Work* (Chicago, IL: University of Chicago, 1991).

Dibbets, Karel and Convents, Guido, 'Cinema Culture in Brussels and Amsterdam 1900–1930', paper presented at the International Urban History Conference, Berlin, 2000.

Dickinson, Roger, Harindranath, Ramaswami and Linné, Olga (eds), *Approaches to Audiences: A Reader* (London: Arnold, 1998).

Docherty, David, Morrison, David and Tracey, Michael, *The Last Picture Show? Britain's Changing Film Audiences* (London: BFI, 1987).

Doherty, Thomas, 'This is Where We Came In: The Audible Screen and the Voluble Audience of Early Sound Cinema', in Melvyn Stokes and Richard Maltby (eds), *American Movie Audiences* (London: BFI, 1999), pp. 143–63.

Donajgrodski, A. P. (ed.), *Social Control in Nineteenth Century Britain* (London: Croom Helm, 1977).

Donald, James, *Imagining the Modern City* (Minneapolis: University of Minnesota Press, 1999).

Douglas, Mary and Isherwood, Baron, *The World of Goods: Towards an Anthropology of Consumption* (Harmondsworth: Penguin, 1979).

Egan, Kate, *The Video Nasty as Cultural Object: Censorship and the Changing Politics of Taste*, unpublished PhD thesis, University of Nottingham.

Elsaesser, Thomas, 'Tales of Sound and Fury: Observations on the Family Melodrama', *Monogram*, no. 4, 1973, pp. 2–15.

Ewen, Stuart, *Captains of Consciousness: Advertising and the Social Root of Consumer Culture* (New York: McGraw-Hill, 1976).

Ewen, Stuart and Ewen, Elizabeth, *Channels of Desire: Mass Images and the Shaping of American Consciousness* (New York: McGraw-Hill, 1982).

Eyles, Allen, *ABC: The First Name in Entertainment* (London: BFI/Cinema Theatre Association, 1993).

Eyles, Allen, *Gaumont British Cinemas* (London: BFI/Cinema Theatre Association, 1995).

Eyles, Allen, Gray, Frank and Readman, Alan, *Cinema West Sussex: The First Hundred Years* (Chichester: Phillimore, 1996).

Fainstein, Susan and Campbell, Scott (eds), *Reading in Urban Theory* (Oxford: Blackwell, 1996).

Faire, Lucy, *Making Home: Working-Class Perceptions of Space, Time and Material Culture in Family Life 1900–1955*, University of Leicester, unpublished thesis, 1998.

Falk, Pasi, *The Consuming Body* (London: Sage, 1994).

Featherstone, Mike, *Consumer Culture and Postmodernism* (London: Sage, 1991a).

Featherstone, Mike, 'The Body in Consumer Society', in Mike Featherstone, Mike Hepworth and Bryan S. Turner (eds), *The Body: Social Process and Cultural Theory* (London: Sage, 1991b), pp. 170–96.

Feuer, Jane, 'Dynasty', paper presented at International Television Studies Conference, London, 1986.

Field, Audrey, *Picture Palace: A Social History of the Cinema* (London: Gentry, 1974).

Fishman, Robert, *Bourgeois Utopias: The Rise and Fall of Suburbia* (New York: Basic, 1987).

Flickinger, Brigitte, 'Cinema – A Space to Experience the Urban. Comparative Reflections of Russia and Britain up to the Thirties', paper presented to the International Urban History Conference, Berlin, 2000.

Foucault, Michel, 'Of Other Spaces', *Diacritics*, vol. 16, no. 1, Spring 1986, pp. 22–7.

Frankel, Boris, *The Post-Industrial Utopians* (Cambridge: Polity, 1987).

Franklin, Ashley, *A Cinema Near You: 100 Years of Going to the Pictures in Derbyshire* (Derby: Breedon Books, 1996).

Franklin, Bob and Murphy, David, *What's News? The Market, Politics and the Local Press* (London: Routledge, 1992).

Franklin, Bob and Murphy, David (eds), *Making the Local News: Local Journalism in Context* (London: Routledge, 1998).

Friedan, Betty, *The Feminine Mystique* (New York: Dell, 1963).

Friedberg, Anne, *Window Shopping: Cinema and the Postmodern* (Berkeley, CA: University of California Press, 1993).

Fuller, Kathryn H., *At the Picture Show: Small-Town Audiences and the Creation of Movie Fan Culture* (Washington, DC: Smithsonian Institution Press, 1996).

Garnham, Nicholas, 'Towards a Political Economy of Culture', *New Universities Quarterly*, vol. 1, no. 1, Summer 1977, pp. 341–57.

Garnham, Nicholas, 'Information Society as a Class Society', paper presented to the EEC Conference on the Information Society, Dublin, 18–20 November 1981.

Garnham, Nicholas, *Capitalism and Communication: Global Culture and the Economics of Information* (London: Sage, 1990).

Garrison, L. (ed.), *The Black Presence in Nottingham* (Nottingham: published by the author, 1993).

Gauntlett, David and Hill, Annette, *TV Living: Television, Culture and Everyday Life* (London: Routledge, 1999).

Giggs, John, 'Housing, Population and Transport', in John Beckett (ed.), *A Centenary History of Nottingham* (Manchester: Manchester University Press, 1997), pp. 435–62.

Giles, Judy, *Women, Identity and Private Life in Britain, 1900–1950* (London: Macmillan, 1995).

Gillespie, Marie, 'Technology and Tradition: Audio-Visual Culture Among South Asian Families in West London', in *Cultural Studies* vol. 3, no. 2, 1989, pp. 226–39.

Gillespie, Marie, *Television, Ethnicity and Cultural Change* (London: Routledge, 1995).

Gledhill, Christine and Williams, Linda, *Reinventing Film Studies* (London: Arnold, 2000).

Gomery, Douglas, 'Movie Audiences, Urban Geography and the History of American Film', *The Velvet Light Trap*, no. 19, Spring 1982, pp. 23–9.

Gomery, Douglas, *Shared Pleasures: A History of Movie Exhibition in America* (London: BFI, 1992).

Graham, Stephen, 'Imagining the Real-Time City: Telecommunications, Urban Paradigms and the Future of Cities', in Sallie Westwood and John Williams (eds), *Imagining Cities: Scripts, Signs, Memory* (London: Routledge, 1997), pp. 31–49.

Graham, Stephen and Marvin, Simon, *Telecommunications and the City: Electronic Spaces, Urban Places* (London: Routledge, 1996).

Gray, Ann, *Video Playtime: The Gendering of a Leisure Technology* (London: Routledge, 1992).

Gray, Richard, *Cinemas in Britain: One Hundred Years of Cinema Architecture* (London: Lund Humphries, 1996).

Grieveson, Lee, 'Fighting Films: Race, Morality, and the Governing of Cinema, 1912–1915', *Cinema Journal*, vol. 30, no. 1, Autumn 1998, pp. 40–72.

Grieveson, Lee, 'Why Audiences Mattered in Chicago in 1907', in Melvyn Stokes and Richard Maltby (eds), *American Movie Audiences* (London: BFI, 1999), pp. 71–91.

Grieveson, Lee, '"A Kind of Recreative School for the Whole Family": Making Cinema Respectable', *Screen*, vol. 42, no. 1, Spring 2001, pp. 64–76.

Grieveson, Lee, *Policing Cinema: Regulating the Movies in Early Twentieth Century America* (Berkeley, CA: University of California Press, forthcoming).

Griffin, Colin, 'The Identity of a Twentieth-Century City', in John Beckett (ed.), *A Centenary History of Nottingham* (Manchester: Manchester University Press, 1997), pp. 421–34.

Gripsrud, Jostein, 'Film Audiences', in John Hill and Pamela Church Gibson (eds), *The Oxford Guide to Film Studies* (Oxford: Oxford University Press, 1998), pp. 202–12.

Gunning, Tom, 'The Cinema of Attractions: Early Film, its Spectator and the Avant-Garde', in Thomas Elsaesser with Adam Barker (eds), *Early Cinema: Space, Frame, Narrative* (London: BFI, 1990), pp. 56–62.

Gunning, Tom, 'From the Kaleidoscope to the X-Ray: Urban Spectatorship, Poe, Benjamin and *Traffic in Souls* (1913)', vol. 19, no. 4, *Wide Angle*, October 1997, pp. 25–61.

Habermas, Jürgen, *The Structural Transformation of the Public Sphere: An Inquiry into a Category of Bourgeois Society* (Cambridge: Polity, 1989).

Hall, Ben M., *The Best Remaining Seats* (New York: Bramwell House, 1961).

Hall, Peter, *The World Cities* (London: Weidenfeld and Nicholson, 1984).

Hall, Peter, *Cities of Tomorrow: An Intellectual History of Urban Planning and Design in the Twentieth Century, Updated Edition* (London: Blackwell, 1996).

Hall, Stuart and Jaques, Martin, *The Politics of Thatcherism* (London: Lawrence and Wishart, 1983).

Hall, Stuart and Jefferson, Tony (eds), *Resistance through Rituals: Youth Subcultures in Post-War Britain* (London: Hutchinson, 1976).

Hall, Stuart and Whannel, Paddy, *The Popular Arts* (London: Hutchinson, 1964).

Halliwell, Leslie, *Seats in All Parts: Half a Lifetime at the Movies* (London: Grafton, 1985).

Hallsworth, A., *The New Geography of Consumer Spending* (London: John Wiley, 1992).

Halsey, A. H. (ed.), *Trends in British Society Since 1900: A Guide to the Changing Social Structure of Britain* (London: Macmillan, 1972).

Hammond, Michael, 'Anonymity and Recognition in the Local Roll of Honour Films', *Scope: An Online Journal of Film Studies*, December 2000, <www.nottingham.ac.uk/film/journal>

Hampton, Benjamin, *A History of the Movies* (New York: Covici, Friede, 1931).

Handel, Leo, *Hollywood Looks at its Audience* (Urbana: University of Illinois Press, 1950).

Hannigan, John, *Fantasy City: Pleasure and Profit in the Postmodern Metropolis* (London: Routledge, 1998).

Hansen, Miriam, *Babel and Babylon: Spectatorship in American Silent Film* (Cambridge, MA: Harvard University Press, 1991).

Hanson, Stuart, 'Spoilt for Choice? Multiplexes in the 90s', in Robert Murphy (ed.), *British Cinema in the 90s* (London: BFI, 1999), pp. 48–59.

Harding, Colin and Lewis, Brian (eds), *Talking Pictures: The Popular Experience of the Cinema* (Bradford: Yorkshire Arts Circus and National Museum of Photography, Film and Television, 1993).

Harding, Colin and Popple, Simon *In the Kingdom of Shadows: A Companion to Early Cinema* (Cranbury, NJ: Fairleigh Dickinson University Press, 1996).

Hark, Ina Rae (ed.), *Exhibition, The Film Reader* (London: Routledge, 2001).

Harper, Sue and Porter, Vincent, 'Cinema Audience Tastes in 1950s Britain', *Journal of British Popular Film*, no. 2, 1999, pp. 66–82.

Harris, Neil, 'A Subversive Form', in Jay Leyda and Charles Musser (eds), *Before Hollywood: Turn-of-the-Century Film from American Archives* (New York: Federation of Arts, 1986).

Harris, Richard and Larkham, Peter J., 'Suburban Foundation, Form and Function', in Richard Harris and Peter J. Larkham (eds), *Changing Suburbs: Foundation, Form and Function* (London: E. & F. N. Spon, 1999), pp. 1–20.

Harvey, David, *Social Justice and the City* (London: Arnold, 1973).

Harvey, David, *The Limits of Capital* (Oxford: Blackwell, 1982).

Harvey, David, *The Urbanization of Capital* (Oxford: Blackwell, 1985).

Harvey, David, *The Condition of Postmodernity: An Enquiry into the Origins of Cultural Change* (Oxford: Blackwell, 1989a).

Harvey, David, *The Urban Experience* (Oxford: Blackwell, 1989b).

Hawkins, Joan C., *Cutting Edge: Art-Horror and the Horrific Avant-Garde* (Minneapolis: University of Minnesota Press, 2000a).

Hawkins, Joan, C., '"See It From the Beginning": Hitchcock's Reconstruction of Film History', *The Hitchcock Annual*, 2000b, pp. 13–30.

Hay, James, Grossberg, Lawrence and Wartella, Ella (eds), *The Audience and its Landscape* (Boulder: Westview, 1996).

Hayes, Nick, 'Civic Perception, Decision-Making and Non-Traditional Housing in Leicester and Nottingham in the 1920s', paper to Leicester University Urban History Seminar, 24 March 2000.

Heath, Stephen, *Questions of the Cinema* (London: Macmillan, 1981).

Hebdige, Dick, *Subculture: The Meaning of Style* (London: Methuen, 1979).

Hebdige, Dick, *Hiding in the Light: On Images and Things* (London: Comedia, 1988).

Herzog, Charlotte, 'The Movie Palace and the Theatrical Sources of its Architectural Style', *Cinema Journal*, vol. 20, no. 2, Spring 1981, pp. 15–37.

Herzog, Charlotte, 'The Archaeology of Cinema Architecture: The Origins of the Movie Theatre', *Quarterly Review of Film Studies*, no. 9, Winter 1984, pp. 11–32.

Hetherington, Kevin, *The Badlands of Modernity: Heterotopia and Social Ordering* (London: Routledge, 1997).

Higashi, Sumiko, 'Dialogue: Manhattan's Nickelodeons', *Cinema Journal*, vol. 35, no. 3, Spring 1996, pp. 72–4.

Higson, Andrew, *Waving the Flag: Constructing a National Cinema in Britain* (Oxford: Clarendon Press, 1995).

Hiley, Nicholas, '"At the Picture Palace": The British Cinema Audience, 1885–1920', in John Fullerton (ed.), *Celebrating 1895: The Centenary of Cinema* (Sydney: John Libbey, 1998), pp. 96–103.

Hiley, Nicholas, '"Let's Go to the Pictures": The British Cinema Audience in the 1920s and 1930s', *Journal of British Popular Film*, no. 2, 1999, pp. 39–53.

Hill, Jeff, 'Leisure', in John Beckett (ed.), *A Centenary History of Nottingham* (Manchester: Manchester University Press, 1997).

Hill, John, and Church Gibson, Pamela, *The Oxford Guide to Film Studies* (Oxford: Oxford University Press, 1998).

Höher, Dagmar, 'The Composition of Music Hall Audiences, 1850–1900', in Peter Bailey (ed.), *Music Hall: The Business of Pleasure* (Milton Keynes: Open University Press, 1986).

Hollows, Joanne, *Feminism, Femininity and Popular Culture* (Manchester: Manchester University Press, 2000).

Hollows, Joanne, 'The Masculinity of Cult', in Mark Jancovich, Antonio Lazaro, James Lyons, Julian Stringer and Andrew Willis (eds), *Defining Cult Movies: The Cultural Politics of Oppositional Taste* (forthcoming).

Horkheimer, Max and Adorno, Theodor, *Dialectic of Enlightenment* (London: New Left Books, 1979).

Hornsey, Brian, *Ninety Years of Cinemagoing in Nottingham* (Nottingham: published by the author, 1994).

Horowitz, Daniel, 'Frugality or Comfort: Middle-Class Styles of Life in the Early Twentieth Century', *American Quarterly*, no. 37, Summer 1985a, pp. 239–58.

Horowitz, Daniel, *The Morality of Spending: Attitudes toward the Consumer Society in America, 1875–1940* (Baltimore, MD: Johns Hopkins University Press, 1985b).

Howitt, T. Cecil, *Nottingham Housing Schemes 1919–1928*, University of Nottingham Library Collection (n.d.).

Hubbard, Phil, 'Going Out (of Town): The New Geographies of British Cinema', *Scope: An Online Journal of Film Studies* (forthcoming).

Hunt, Leon, *British Low Culture: From Safari Suits to Sexploitation* (London: Routledge, 1998).

Huyssen, Andreas, 'Mass Culture as Woman: Modernism's Other', in Tania Modleski (ed.), *Studies in Entertainment: Critical Approaches to Mass Culture* (Bloomington, IN: Indiana University Press, 1986), pp. 188–207.

Iliffe, Richard and Baguley, Wilfred, *Victorian Nottingham: A Story in Pictures Volume 1–20* (Nottingham: Nottingham Film Unit, 1970, 1971, 1971, 1971, 1971, 1971, 1972, 1972, 1973, 1973, 1974, 1974, 1975, 1975, 1976, 1976, 1977, 1979, 1983).

Iliffe, Richard and Baguley, Wilfred, *Edwardian Nottingham: A Story in Pictures Volume 1–3* (Nottingham: Nottingham Film Unit, 1978, 1980, 1983).

Ingle, Robert, *Thomas Cook of Leicester* (Bangor: Headstart History, 1991).

Jackson, Brian and Marsden, Denis, *Education and the Working Class* (revised edition) (Harmondsworth: Penguin, 1966; originally published London: Routledge and Kegan Paul, 1962).

Jackson, Peter, *Maps of Meaning* (London: Routledge, 1989).

Jacobs, Jane, *The Death and Life of Great American Cities* (London: Jonathan Cape, 1962).

Jacobs, Lewis, *The Rise of American Film* (New York: Harcourt Brace, 1939).

Jameson, Fredric, 'Postmodernism, or the Cultural Logic of Late Capitalism', *New Left Review*, no. 146, 1984, pp. 53–92.

Jameson, Fredric, *Postmodernism or the Cultural Logic of Late Capitalism* (London: Verso, 1991).

Jancovich, Mark, 'David Morley, The *Nationwide* Studies', in Martin Barker and Anne Beezer (eds), *Reading Into Cultural Studies* (London: Routledge, 1992), pp. 134–47.

Jancovich, Mark, 'Foreword: Othering Conformity in Post-War America: Intellectuals, the New Middle Classes and the Problem of Cultural Distinctions', in Nathan Abrams and Julie Hughes (eds), *Containing America: Cultural Production and Consumption in Fifties America* (Birmingham: Birmingham University Press, 2000a), pp. 12–28.

Jancovich, Mark, 'Genre and the Audience: Genre Classifications and Cultural Distinctions in the Mediation of *Silence of the Lambs*', in Melvyn Stokes and Richard Maltby (eds), *Hollywood Spectatorship* (London: BFI, 2000b), pp. 33–44.

Jancovich, Mark, '"The Purest Knight of All": Nation, History and Representation in *El Cid*', *Cinema Journal*, vol. 40, no. 1, Autumn 2000c, pp. 79–103.

Jancovich, Mark, 'Naked Ambitions: Pornography, Taste and the Problem of the Middlebrow', *Scope: An Online Journal of Film Studies*, June 2001, <www.nottingham.ac.uk/film/journal>

Jancovich, Mark, '"Charlton Heston is an Axiom": Spectacle and Performance in the Development of the Blockbuster', in Andrew Willis (ed.), *Stars: Hollywood and Beyond* (Manchester: Manchester University Press, 2002a).

Jancovich, Mark, 'Cult Fictions: Cult Movies, Subcultural Capital and the Production of Cultural Distinctions', *Cultural Studies*, vol. 16, no. 2, April 2002b, pp. 306–22.

Jenkins, Henry, *Textual Poachers: Television Fans and Participatory Culture* (New York: Routledge, 1992).

Jephcott, Pearl, *Time of One's Own: Leisure and Young People* (Edinburgh and London: Oliver and Boyd, 1967).

Jones, Janna, 'Finding a Place at the Downtown Picture Palace: The Tampa Theatre, Florida', in Mark Sheil and Tony Fitzmaurice (eds), *Cinema and the City: Film and Urban Societies in a Global Context* (Oxford: Blackwell, 2001), pp. 122–33.

Jones, Stephen G., *Workers at Play: A Social and Economic History of Leisure* (London: Routledge, 1986).

Keats, John, *The Crack in the Picture Window* (New York: Houghton Mifflin, 1957).

Kirby, Lynne, 'The Urban Spectator and the Crowd in Early American Train Films', in *Iris*, Summer 1990, pp. 49–62.

Kirby, Lynne, *Parallel Tracks: The Railroad and Silent Cinema* (Exeter: University of Exeter Press, 1997).

Kitses, Jim, *Horizons West* (London: Thames and Hudson/BFI, 1969).

Klinger, Barbara, 'Digressions at the Cinema: Reception and Mass Culture', *Cinema Journal*, vol. 28, no. 4, Summer 1989, pp. 3–19.

Klinger, Barbara, *Melodrama and Meaning: History, Culture and the Films of Douglas Sirk* (Bloomington, IN: Indiana University Press, 1994).

Klinger, Barbara, 'Film History: Terminable and Interminable: Recovering the Past in Reception Studies', *Screen*, vol. 38, no. 2, 1995/6, pp. 107–28.

Klinger, Barbara, 'The New Media Aristocrats: Home Theatre and the Domestic Film Experience', in *The Velvet Light Trap*, no. 42, Autumn 1998, pp. 4–19.

Klinger, Barbara, 'The Contemporary Cinephile: Film Collecting in the Post-Video Era', in Melvyn Stokes and Richard Maltby (eds), *Hollywood Spectatorship* (London: BFI, 2000), pp. 132–51.

Klinger, Barbara, *Fortresses of Solitude: Cinema, New Technologies, and the Home* (Berkeley, CA: University of California Press, forthcoming).

Knight, Caroline and Cockburn, Anne, 'Music Halls of Nottingham: Their Origins and Their History', unpublished paper, Nottingham Local Studies Library (n.d.).

Koszarski, Richard, *An Evening's Entertainment: The Age of the Silent Feature Picture, 1915–1928* (Berkeley, CA: University of California Press, 1990).

Krämer, Peter, 'A Powerful Cinema Going Force? Hollywood and Female Audiences since the 1960s', in Melvyn Stokes and Richard Maltby (eds), *Identifying Hollywood's Audiences* (London: BFI, 1999), pp. 93–108.

Kuhn, Annette, *Cinema, Censorship and Sexuality, 1909–1925* (London: Routledge, 1988).

Kuhn, Annette, 'Researching Popular Film Fan Culture in 1930s Britain', in J. Gripsrud and K. Skettering (eds), *History of Moving Images: Reports from a Norwegian Project* (Oslo: Research Council of Norway, 1994).

Kuhn, Annette, 'Cinema Culture and Femininity in the 1930s', in Christine Gledhill and Gillian Swanson (eds), *Nationalising Femininity: Culture, Sexuality and British Cinema in the Second World War* (Manchester: Manchester University Press, 1996).

Kuhn, Annette, 'Cinema-going in Britain in the 1930s: Report of a Questionnaire Survey', *Historical Journal of Film, Radio and Television*, vol. 19, no. 4. 1999a, pp. 531–43.

Kuhn, Annette, 'Memories of Cinemagoing in the 1930s', *Journal of Popular British Cinema*, no. 2, 1999b, pp. 100–20.

Kuhn, Annette, '"That Day *Did* Last Me All My Life": Cinema Memory and Enduring Fandom', in Melvyn Stokes and Richard Maltby (eds), *Identifying Hollywood's Audiences* (London: BFI, 1999c), pp. 135–46.

Kuhn, Annette, 'Smart Girls: Growing Up with Cinema in the 1930s', in Ib Bondebjerg (ed.), *Moving Images, Culture and the Mind* (Luton: University of Luton Press, 2000).

Laing, Stuart, *Representations of Working-Class Life 1957–1964* (London: Macmillan, 1986).

Langhamer, Claire, *Women's Leisure in England, 1920–1960* (Manchester: Manchester University Press, 2000).

Lash, Scott and Urry, John, *The End of Organised Capital* (Oxford: Blackwell, 1987).

Lawrence, D., *Black Migrants, White Natives: A Study of Race Relations in Nottingham* (London and New York: Cambridge University Press, 1974).

Lee, Martyn J., *Consumer Culture Reborn: The Cultural Politics of Consumption* (London: Routledge, 1992).

Lee, Martyn J. (ed.), *The Consumer Society Reader* (Oxford: Blackwell, 2000).

Leeman, F. W., *Co-Operation in Nottingham* (Nottingham: Nottingham Co-Operative Society, 1963).

Lefebvre, Henri, *The Production of Space* (Oxford: Blackwell, 1991).

Lefebvre, Henri, *Writing on Cities* (Oxford: Blackwell, 1995).

LeGates, Richard T. and Stout, Frederic (eds), *The City Reader* (London: Routledge, 1996).

Lewis, Lisa (ed.), *The Adoring Audience: Fan Culture and Popular Media* (London: Routledge, 1992).

Light, Alison, *Forever England: Femininity, Literature and Conservatism Between the Wars* (London: Routledge, 1991).

Livingstone, Sonia, 'The Meanings of Domestic Technologies: A Personal Construct Analysis of Familial Gender Relations', in Roger Silverstone and Eric Hirsch (eds), *Consuming Technologies: Media and Information in Domestic Spaces* (London: Routledge, 1992), pp. 113–30.

Low, Rachel, *The History of British Film 1906–1914* (London: Allen and Unwin, 1948).

Low, Rachel, *The History of British Film 1914–1918* (London: Allen and Unwin, 1950).

Low, Rachel and Manvell, Roger, *The History of British Film 1896–1906* (London: Allen and Unwin, 1948).

Lury, Celia, *Consumer Culture* (Cambridge: Polity, 1996).

Lyons, James, 'Food Consumption and the Cinema', unpublished manuscript.

Malcolmson, Robert, 'Popular Recreations under Attack', in Bernard Waites, Tony Bennett and Graham Martin (eds), *Popular Culture: Past and Present* (London: Croom Helm, 1982), pp. 20–46.

Maltby, Richard, 'Introduction' in Melvyn Stokes and Richard Maltby (eds), *Identifying Hollywood's Audiences* (London: BFI, 1999a).

Maltby, Richard 'Sticks, Hicks and Flaps: Classical Hollywood's Generic Conception of its Audiences', in Melvyn Stokes and Richard Maltby (eds), *Identifying Hollywood's Audiences: Cultural Identity and the Movies* (London: BFI, 1999b), pp. 23–41.

Manning, Ian, *700 Years of Goose Fair* (Nottingham: T. Bailey Forman, 1994).

Manvell, Roger, *Film* (Harmondsworth: Penguin, 1944).

Marshall, R., *A History of Nottingham City Transport, 1897–1959* (Nottingham: published by the author, 1960).

Marwick, Arthur, *British Social History Since 1945* (Harmondsworth: Penguin, 1982, 1996).

Massey, Doreen, *The Spatial Division of Labour* (London: Macmillan, 1984).

Massey, Doreen, *Space, Place and Gender* (Cambridge: Polity, 1994).

Massey, Doreen and Allen, J. (eds), *Uneven Development: Cities and Regions in Transition* (London: Hodder and Stoughton, 1988).

Massey, Doreen, Allen, John and Pile, Steve (eds), *City Worlds* (London: Routledge, 1999).

Matrix, *Making Space: Women and the Man-made Environment* (London: Pluto, 1986).

May, Lary, *Screening Out the Past: The Birth of Mass Culture and the Motion Picture Industry* (New York: Oxford University Press, 1980).

Mayall, David, 'Palaces of Entertainment and Instruction: A Study of the Early Cinema in Birmingham, 1908–18', *Midland History*, no. 10, 1985.

Mayer, Arno J. 'The Lower Middle Class as Historical Problem', *Journal of Modern History*, no. 47, September 1975, pp. 409–36.

Mayer, J. P., *British Cinemas and their Audiences: Sociological Studies* (London: Dobson, 1948).

Mayne, Judith, *Cinema and Spectatorship* (London: Routledge, 1993).

McCarthy, Anna, *Ambient Television: Visual Culture and Public Space* (Durham: Duke University Press, 2001).

McCracken, Grant, *Culture and Consumption: New Approaches to the Symbolic Character of Goods and Activities* (Bloomington, IN: Indiana University Press, 1988).

McGuigan, Jim, 'Cultural Populism Revisited', in M. Ferguson and Peter Golding (eds), *Cultural Studies in Question* (London: Sage, 1998), pp. 138–54.

McKibbin, Ross, *Classes and Cultures, England 1918–1951* (Oxford: Oxford University Press, 1988).

McQuail, Denis, *Audience Analysis* (London: Sage, 1997).

Mellor, Helen, *Leisure and the Changing City, 1870–1914* (London: Routledge and Kegan Paul, 1976).

Meyerowitz, Joanne, *Not June Cleaver: Women and Gender in Postwar America, 1945–1960* (Philadelphia, PA: Temple University Press, 1994).

Meyrowitz, Joshua, *No Sense of Place* (New York: Oxford University Press, 1985).

Miles, Malcolm, Hall, Tim and Borden, Iain (eds), *The City Cultures Reader* (London: Routledge, 2000).

Miller, Daniel, *Material Culture and Mass Consumption* (Oxford: Blackwell, 1987).

Miller, Daniel (ed.), *Acknowledging Consumption: A Review of New Studies* (London: Routledge, 1995).

Miller, Daniel, Jackson, Peter, Thrift, Nigel, Holbrook, Beverley and Rowlands, Michael, *Shopping, Place and Identity* (London: Routledge, 1998).

Moores, Shaun, '"The Box on the Dresser": Memories of Early Radio and Everyday Life', *Media, Culture and Society*, no. 10, 1988, p. 36.

Moores, Shaun, *Interpreting Audiences: The Ethnography of Media Consumption* (London: Sage, 1993).

Moores, Shaun, *Media and Everyday Life in Modern Society* (Edinburgh: Edinburgh University Press, 2000).

Morley, David, 'Texts, Subjects, Readers', in Stuart Hall, Dorothy Hobson, Andrew Lowe and Paul Willis (eds), *Culture, Media, Language* (London: Unwin Hyman, 1980a).

Morley, David, *The* Nationwide *Audience: Structure and Decoding* (London: BFI, 1980b).

Morley, David, *Family Television: Cultural Power and Domestic Leisure* (London: Comedia, 1986).

Morley, David, 'Changing Paradigms in Audience Studies', in Ellen Seiter, Hans Borchers, Gabriele Kreutzner and Eva-Maria Warth (eds), *Remote Control: Television, Audiences and Cultural Power* (London, Routledge, 1990).

Morley, David, *Television, Audiences and Cultural Studies* (London: Routledge, 1992).

Morley, David, *Home Territories: Media, Mobility and Identity* (London: Routledge, 2000).

Morley, David and Brunsdon, Charlotte, *Everyday Television:* Nationwide (London: BFI, 1978).

Morley, David and Robins, Kevin, *Spaces of Identity: Global Media, Electronic Landscapes and Cultural Boundaries* (London, Routledge, 1995).

Moss, Louis and Box, Kathleen, *The Cinema Audience: An Inquiry made by the Wartime Social Survey for the Ministry of Information*, reprinted in J. P. Mayer, *British Cinemas and their Audiences* (London: Dobson, 1948).

Mulvey, Laura, 'Visual Pleasure and Narrative Cinema', in Bill Nichols (ed.), *Movies and Methods Volume II* (Berkeley, CA: University of California Press, 1985).

Mumford, Lewis, *The Culture of the City* (Harmondsworth: Penguin, 1938).

Murphy, Robert, 'Coming of Sound to the Cinema in Britain', *Historical Journal of Film, Radio and Television*, vol. 4, no. 2, 1984.

Murphy, Robert, 'Fantasy Worlds: British Cinemas Between the Wars', *Screen*, vol. 26, no. 1, 1995.

Murphy, Robert (ed.), *The British Cinema Book* (London: BFI, 1997).

Musser, Charles, *The Emergence of Cinema: The American Screen to 1907* (Berkeley, CA: University of California Press, 1990).

Musser, Charles, *Before the Nickelodeon: Edwin S. Porter and the Edison Manufacturing Company* (Berkeley, CA: University of California Press, 1991a).

Musser, Charles, *High-Class Moving Pictures: Lyman H. Howe and the Forgotten Era of Travelling Exhibition, 1880–1920* (Princeton, NJ: Princeton University Press, 1991b).

Naremore, James, *More than Night: Film Noir and its Contexts* (Berkeley, CA: University of California Press, 1998).

Nasaw, David, *Going Out: The Rise and Fall of Public Amusements* (Cambridge, MA: Harvard University Press, 1993).

Nava, Mica, 'Modernity's Disavowal: Women, the City and the Department Store', in Mica Nava and Alan O'Shea (eds), *Modern Times: Reflections on a Century of English Modernity* (London: Routledge, 1996), pp. 38–76.

Naylor, David, *American Picture Palaces* (New York: Prentice-Hall, 1981).

Nead, Lynda, *The Female Nude: Art, Obscenity and Sexuality* (London: Routledge, 1992).

Needleman, L., 'Demand for Domestic Appliances', *National Institute Economic Review*, vol. 12, 1960.

Nightingale, Virginia, *Studying Audiences: The Shock of the Real* (London: Routledge, 1996).

Nottingham Historical Film Unit, *In Retro: Nottingham Goose Fair* (Oldham: Ronam, 1973).

O'Brien, Margaret and Eyles, Allen (eds), *Enter the Dream House: Memories of Cinema in South London from the Twenties to the Sixties* (London: BFI, 1993).

Oliver, Paul, Davis, I. and Bentley, I., *Dunroamin: The Suburban Semi and its Enemies* (London: Pimlico, 1994).

O'Sullivan, Tim, 'Television Memories and the Cultures of Viewing, 1950–65', in John Corner (ed.), *Popular Television in Britain* (London: BFI, 1991).

Packard, Vance, *The Status Seekers: An Exploration of Class Behavior in America* (Harmondsworth: Penguin, 1959).

Parker, Stanley, *The Sociology of Leisure* (London: Allen and Unwin, 1976).

Partington, Angela, 'Melodrama's Gendered Audience', in Sarah Franklin, Celia Lury and Jackie Stacey (eds), *Off-Centre: Feminism and Cultural Studies* (London: HarperCollins, 1991), pp. 49–68.

Paul, William, 'The K-Mart Audience at the Mall Movies', *Film History*, no. 6, 1994, pp. 487–501.

Pearson, Roberta and Uricchio, William, '"The Formative and Impressionable Stage": Discursive Constructions of the Nickelodeon's Child Audience', in Stokes and Maltby (eds), *American Movie Audiences* (London: BFI, 1999), pp. 64–75.

Peiss, Kathy, *Cheap Amusements: Working Women and Leisure in Turn-of-the-Century New York* (Philadelphia, PA: Temple University Press, 1986).

Peto, James and Loveday, Donna (eds), *Modern Britain 1929–1939* (London: Design Museum, 1999).

Petrie, Duncan and Willis, Janet (eds), *Television and the Household* (London: BFI, 1995).

Pile, Steve, 'Preface', in Doreen Massey, John Allen and Steve Pile (eds), *City Worlds* (London: Routledge, 1999).

Pile, Steve, Brook, Christopher and Mooney, Gerry (eds), *Unruly Cities? Order/Disorder* (London: Routledge, 1999).

Priestley, J. B., *English Journey* (London: Mandarin, 1994; originally published 1933).

Quinn, Michael, 'Distribution, the Transient Audience and the Transition to the Feature Film', *Cinema Journal*, vol. 40, no. 2, 2001, pp. 35–56.

Rabinovitz, Lauren, *For the Love of Pleasure: Women, Movies, and Culture in Turn of the Century Chicago* (New Brunswick, NJ: Rutgers University Press, 1998).

Radway, Janice, *Reading the Romance: Women, Patriarchy and Popular Literature* (London: Verso, 1987).

Radway, Janice, *A Taste for Books: The Book-of-the-Month Club, Literary Taste, and Middle-Class Desire* (Chapel Hill, NC: University of North Carolina Press, 1997).

Ramsaye, Terry, *A Million and One Nights: A History of the Motion Picture through 1925* (New York: Simon & Schuster, 1926).

Rapp, Dean, 'The British Salvation Army, the Early Film Industry and Urban Working Class Adolescents, 1897–1918', *Twentieth Century British History*, vol. 7, no. 2, 1996, pp. 157–88.

Ravetz, Alison, *The Place of Home: English Domestic Environments, 1914–2000* (London: E. & F. N. Spon, 1995).

Reisman, David, *The Lonely Crowd: A Study of the Changing American Character* (New Haven, CT: Yale University Press, 1961).

Rhode, Eric, *A History of Cinema from its Origins to 1970* (London: Allen Lane, 1976).

Richards, Jeffrey, *The Age of the Dream Palace: Cinema and Society in Britain 1930–1939* (London: Routledge, 1984).

Richards, Jeffrey, *The Unknown 1930s* (London: I. B. Taurus, 1998).

Richards, Jeffrey and Sheridan, Dorothy (eds), *Mass Observation at the Movies* (London: Routledge, 1987).

Roberts, Elizabeth, *A Woman's Place: An Oral History of Working Class Women 1890–1940* (Oxford: Blackwell, 1984).

Roberts, Elizabeth, *Women and Families: An Oral History, 1940–1970* (Oxford: Blackwell, 1995).

Roddis, David, *The Thrill of It All: The Story of Cinema in Ilkeston and the Erewash Valley* (Derby: Published by the author, 1993).

Ross, Andrew, *No Respect: Intellectuals and Popular Culture* (London: Routledge, 1989).

Ross, Steven, 'The Revolt of the Audience: Reconsidering Audiences and Reception During the Silent Era', in Melvyn Stokes and Richard Maltby (eds), *American Movie Audiences: From the Turn of the Century to the Early Sound Era* (London: BFI, 1999), pp. 92–111.

Russell, Catherine, 'Parallax Historiography: The Flâneuse as Cyberfeminist', in *Scope: An Online Journal of Film Studies*, July 2000, <www.nottingham.ac.uk/film/journal>

Ryan, Mary, *Cradle of the Middle Class: The Family in Oneida County, New York, 1790–1865* (Cambridge: Cambridge University Press, 1981).

Samson, Jen, 'The Film Society, 1925–1939', in Charles Barr (ed.), *All Our Yesterdays: 90 Years of British Cinema* (London: BFI, 1986).

Sassen, Saskia, *The Global City* (Princeton, NJ: Princeton University Press, 1991).

Sassen, Saskia, *Cities in the World Economy* (Thousand Oaks, CA: Pine Forge Press, 1994).

Savage, Mike, Barlow, James, Dickens, Peter and Fielding, Tony, *Property, Bureaucracy and Culture: Middle-class Formation in Contemporary Britain* (London: Routledge, 1992).

Savage, Mike and Warde, Alan, *Urban Sociology, Capitalism and Modernity* (New York: Continuum, 1993).

Saxon, Graham, 'Class and Conservatism in the Adoption of Innovations', *Human Relations*, vol. 9, 1956, p. 94.

Schaefer, Eric, 'Art and Exploitation: Reconfiguring Foreign Films for American Tastes, 1930–1960', paper presented at the New England American Studies Association Conference, Providence, Rhode Island, Brown University, 7 May 1994.

Schaefer, Eric, *'Bold! Daring! Shocking! True!' A History of Exploitation Films, 1919–1959* (Durham: Duke University Press, 1999).

Schlesinger, Philip, Dobash, R. E., Dobash, R. P. and Weaver, C. K., *Women Viewing Violence* (London: BFI, 1992).

Sconce, Jeffrey, 'Trashing the Academy: Taste, Excess and the Emerging Politics of Cinematic Style', *Screen*, vol. 36, no. 4, Winter 1995, pp. 371–93.

Scottish Educational Film Association and Scottish Film Council, *Viewing Tastes of Adolescents in Cinema and Television* (Glasgow: Scottish Educational Film Association and Scottish Film Council, April 1961).

Scrivens, Kevin and Smith, Stephen, *The Travelling Cinematograph Show* (Tweedale: New Era, 1999).

Sedgewick, John, 'Film "Hits" and "Misses" in Mid-1930s Britain', *Historical Journal of Film, Radio and Television*, vol. 18, no. 3, 1998, pp. 333–51.

Seiter, Ellen, 'Making Distinctions in Audience Research', *Cultural Studies*, vol. 4, no. 1, 1990, pp. 61–84.

Seiter, Ellen, *Television and New Media Audiences* (Oxford: Oxford University Press, 1999).

Seiter, Ellen, Borchers, Hans, Kreutzner, Gabriele and Warth, Eva-Maria (eds), *Remote Control: Television, Audiences and Cultural Power* (London: Routledge, 1989).

Seldes, Gilbert, *The Great Audience* (New York: Viking, 1950).

Sennett, Richard, *Classic Essays on the Culture of Cities* (New York: Appleton-Century-Crofts, 1969).

Sennett, Richard, *The Conscience of the Eye* (London: Faber, 1990).

Shand, Morton P., *Modern Theatres and Cinemas* (London: Batsford, 1930).

Sharp, Dennis, *The Picture Palace and Other Buildings for the Movies* (London: Hugh Evelyn, 1969).

Sheldon, A., *Nottingham Cinema: A Short History* (unpublished, 1999).

Shields, Rob, *Places on the Margin* (London: Routledge, 1991).

Shields, Rob, *Lifestyle Shopping: The Subject of Consumption* (London: Routledge, 1992).

Short, John Rennie, *The Urban Order: An Introduction to Cities, Culture and Power* (Oxford: Blackwell, 1996).

Shove, Elizabeth and Southerton, Dale, 'Defrosting the Freezer: from Novelty to Convenience – A Narrative of Normalisation', *Journal of Material Culture*, vol. 5, no. 3, 2000, pp. 301–19.

Silburn, Richard, *People in their Places: One Hundred Years of Nottingham Life* (Nottingham: published by the author, 1981).

Silverstone, Roger, *Television and Everyday Life* (London: Routledge, 1994).

Silverstone, Roger, *Visions of Suburbia* (London: Routledge, 1997).

Silverstone, Roger and Hirsch, Eric (eds), *Consuming Technologies Media and Information in Domestic Spaces* (London: Routledge, 1992).

Silvey, Robert, *Who's Listening: The Story of BBC Audience Research* (London: Allen and Unwin, 1974).

Simmel, Georg, *The Sociology of Georg Simmel* (New York: Free Press, 1950).

Singer, Ben, 'Manhattan Nickelodeons: New Data on Audiences and Exhibitors', *Cinema Journal*, vol. 34, no. 3, Spring 1995, pp. 5–35.

Singer, Ben, 'New York, Just Like I Pictured It ...', *Cinema Journal*, vol. 35, no. 3, Spring 1996, pp. 104–28.

Skeggs, Bev, Moran, Les, Tyrer, Paul and Corteen, Karen, 'The Construction of Fear in Gay Spaces: The Straight Story', in *Capital and Class* (forthcoming).

Slater, Don, *Consumer Culture and Modernity* (Cambridge: Polity, 1997).

Smith, John, *Adventure in Vision* (London: John Lehmann, 1950).

Smith, Michael A., Parker, Stanley and Smith, Cyril, S., *Leisure and Society in Britain* (London: Allen Lane, 1973).

Smith, Murray, *Engaging Characters: Fiction, Emotion and Cinema* (Oxford: Clarendon Press, 1995).

Smith, Neil, *The New Urban Frontier* (London: Routledge, 1996).

Smith, Neil and Williams, Peter (eds), *Gentrification and the City* (Winchester, MA: Allen and Unwin, 1986).

Soja, Edward, *Postmodern Geographies: The Reassertion of Space in Critical Social Theory* (London: Verso, 1989).

Spain, Daphne, *How Women Saved the City* (Minneapolis, MN: University of Minnesota Press, 2000).

Spanos, John, *The Decline of Cinema: An Economist's Report* (London: Allen and Unwin, 1962).

Spicer, Leslie, *The Spicer Life: A Trip Down Memory Lane* (Nottingham: Beeston and District Local History Society, 1997).

Spigel, Lynn, *Make Room for TV: Television and the Family Ideal in Postwar America* (Chicago, IL: Chicago University Press, 1992).

Spigel, Lynn, 'From the Dark Ages to the Golden Age: Women's Memories and Television Reruns', *Screen*, vol. 36, no. 1, Spring 1995, pp. 16–33.

Stacey, Jackie, *Star Gazing: Hollywood Cinema and Female Spectatorship* (London: Routledge, 1994).

Staiger, Janet, 'Class, Ethnicity and Gender: Explaining the Development of Early American Film Narrative', *Iris*, no. 11, Summer 1990, pp. 13–25.

Staiger, Janet, *Interpreting Audiences: Studies in the Historical Reception of American Cinema* (Princeton, NJ: Princeton University Press, 1992).

Staiger, Janet, *Perverse Spectators: The Practices of Film Reception* (New York: New York University Press, 2000).

Stallybrass, Peter and White, Allon, *The Politics and Poetics of Transgression* (London: Methuen, 1986).

Steadman Jones, Gareth, 'Working Class Culture and Working Class Politics in London, 1870–1900: Notes on the Remaking of a Working Class', in Bernard Waites, Tony Bennett and Graham Martin (eds), *Popular Culture: Past and Present* (London: Croom Helm, 1982), pp. 92–121.

Stearnes, P. N., 'The Middle Class: Towards a Precise Definition', *Comparative Studies in Society and History*, no. 21, July 1976, pp. 377–96.

Stokes, Jane, *On Screen Rivals* (London, Macmillan, 1999).

Stones, Barbara, *America Goes to the Movies: 100 Years of Motion Picture Exhibition* (North Hollywood: National Association of Theatre Owners, 1993).

Storey, Joyce, *Joyce's Dream: The Post-War Years* (London: Virago, 1995).

Strachan, Chris, *The Harwich Electric Palace* (published by the author, 1979).

Straw, Will, 'Sizing Up Record Collections: Gender and Connoisseurship in Rock Music Culture', in Sheila Whiteley (ed.), *Sexing the Groove: Popular Music and Gender* (London: Routledge, 1997), pp. 3–16.

Street, Sarah, *British National Cinema* (London: Routledge, 1997).

Stubbings, Sarah, *From Modernity to Memorial: Changing Meanings of the 1930s Cinema in Britain*, unpublished PhD, University of Nottingham.

Taylor, Ian, Evans, Karen and Fraser, Penny, *A Tale of Two Cities: Global Change, Local Feeling and Everyday Life in the North of England. A Study in Manchester and Sheffield* (London: Routledge, 1996).

Thomson, Michael, *Silver Screen in the Silver City: A History of Cinemas in Aberdeen, 1896–1987* (Aberdeen: Aberdeen University Press, 1988).

Thornton, Sarah, *Club Cultures: Music, Media and Subcultural Capital* (Oxford: Blackwell, 1995).

Toffler, Alvin, *Future Shock* (London: Pan, 1971).

Toffler, Alvin, *The Third Wave* (London: Collins, 1980).

Toulmin, Vanessa, 'Telling the Tale: The Story of the Fairground Bioscope Shows and the Showmen who Operated Them', *Film History*, vol. 6, no. 2, 1994, pp. 219–37.

Toulmin, Vanessa, 'Temperance and Pleasure at the Hoppings: A History of the Newcastle Town Moor Fair', *North East Labour History*, no. 29, 1995, pp. 50–63.

Toulmin, Vanessa, 'Travelling Shows and the First Static Cinemas', *Picture House*, no. 21, Summer 1996, pp. 5–12.

Toulmin, Vanessa, *Randal Williams, King of the Showmen: From Ghost Show to Bioscope* (London: Projection Box, 1998).

Toulmin, Vanessa, 'The Cinematograph at the Nottingham Goose Fair, 1896–1911', in Alan Burton and Laraine Porter (eds), *The Showman, the Spectacle and the Two Minute Silence: Performing British Cinema Before 1930* (Trowbridge: Flicks, 2001), pp. 76–86.

Tudor, Andrew, *Monsters and Mad Scientists: A Cultural History of the Horror Movie* (Oxford: Blackwell, 1989).

Tudor, Andrew, 'Why Horror? The Peculiar Pleasures of a Popular Genre', *Cultural Studies*, vol. 11, no. 3, 1997, pp. 443–63.

Tulloch, John, *Watching Television Audiences* (London: Arnold, 2000).

Turkington, Richard, 'British "Corporation Suburbia": The Changing Fortunes of Norris Green, Liverpool', in Richard Harris and Peter J. Larkham (eds), *Changing Suburbs* (London: E. & F. N. Spon, 1999).

Uricchio, William and Pearson, Roberta, *Reframing Culture: The Case of the Vitagraph Quality Films* (Princeton, NJ: Princeton University Press, 1993).

Uricchio, William and Pearson, Roberta E., 'Constructing the Audience: Competing Discourses of Morality and Rationalization During the Nickelodeon Period', *Iris*, no. 17, 1994, pp. 43–54.

Valentine, Maggie, *The Show Starts on the Sidewalk: An Architectural History of the Movie Theatre* (New Haven, CT: Yale University Press, 1994).

van Voss, Lex Heerma and van Holthoon, Frits (eds), *Working Class and Popular Culture* (Amsterdam: Stichting, 1988).

van Zoonen, Liesbet and Wieten, Jan, 'It Wasn't Exactly a Miracle: the Arrival of Television in Dutch Family Life', *Media, Culture and Society*, vol. 16, no. 4, 1994.

Veblen, Thorstein, *The Theory of the Leisure Class: An Economic Study of Institutions* (London: Allen and Unwin, 1925).

Vidich, Arthur J. (ed.), *The New Middle Classes: Life-Styles, Status Claims and Political Orientations* (London: Macmillan, 1995).

Walkerdine, Valerie, 'Video Reply: Families, Films and Fantasy', in Victor Burgin, James Donald and Cora Kaplan (eds), *Formation and Fantasy* (London: Methuen, 1986), pp. 167–99.

Walkowitz, Judith, *City of Dreadful Delight* (London: Virago, 1992).

Waller, Gregory, A., *Main Street Amusements: Movies and Commercial Entertainment in a Southern City, 1896–1930* (Washington, DC: Smithsonian Institution Press, 1995).

Waller, Gregory, 'Hillbilly Music and Will Rogers: Small-Town Picture Shows in the 1930s', in Melvyn Stokes and Richard Maltby (eds), *American Movie Audiences* (London: BFI, 1999), pp. 164–79.

Waller, Gregory A. (ed.), *Moviegoing in America: A Sourcebook in the History of Film Exhibition* (Oxford: Blackwell, 2001).

Walvin, James, *Beside the Seaside: A Social History of the Poplar Seaside Holiday* (London: Allen Lane, 1978).

Ward, Margaret, *One Camp Chair in the Living Room: A Woman's Life in Rotterdean* (Brighton: Queenspark, n.d.).

Warde, Alan, *Consumption, Food and Taste* (London: Sage, 1997).

Warde, Alan, 'Convenience Food: Space and Timing', *British Food Journal*, vol. 101, no. 7, 1999, pp. 518–27.

Webster, Duncan, *Looka Yonda!: The Imaginary American of Populist Culture* (London: Comedia/Routledge, 1988).

Weightman, Gavin, *Bright Lights, Big City: London Entertained 1830–1950* (London: Collins and Brown, 1992).

Weir, Christopher, 'The Growth of an Inner Urban Housing Development: Forest Field, Nottingham, 1883–1914', *Transactions of the Thoroton Society of Nottinghamshire*, no. 89, 1985, pp. 122–31.

Westwood, Sallie and Williams, John (eds), *Imagining Cities: Scripts, Signs, Memory* (London: Routledge, 1997).

Whyte, William, *The Organisation Man* (New York: Simon & Schuster, 1956).

Wilinsky, Barbara, *Sure Seaters: The Emergence of the Art House Cinema* (Minneapolis, MN: University of Minnesota Press, 2000).

Wilkes, Peter, *The Great Nottingham Goose Fair* (Burton on Trent: Trent Valley Publications, 1989).

Williams, David R., *Cinema in Leicester 1896–1931* (Loughborough: Heart of Albion Press, 1993).

Williams, Linda, 'Film Bodies: Gender, Genre and Excess', *Film Quarterly*, vol. 44, no. 4, Summer 1991, pp. 2–13.

Williams, Linda, 'Learning to Scream', *Sight and Sound*, December 1994, pp. 14–17.

Williams, Linda, 'Discipline and Fun: *Psycho* and Postmodern Cinema', in Christine Gledhill and Linda Williams (eds), *Reinventing Film Studies* (London: Arnold, 2000), pp. 351–80.

Williams, Raymond, *Television: Technology and Cultural Form* (London: Fontana, 1974).

Wilson, Elizabeth, *Sphinx in the City* (London: Virago, 1991).

Woolf, Janet, 'The Invisible *Flâneuse*: Women and the Literature of Modernity', *Theory, Culture and Society*, vol. 2, no. 3, 1985, pp. 37–46.

Woolf, Janet, *Feminine Sentences: Essays on Women and Culture* (Cambridge: Polity, 1990).

Worthington, Colin, *The Influence of Cinema on Contemporary Auditoria Design* (London: Pitman, 1952).

Wylie, Philip, 'The Abdicating Male … and How the Gray Flannel Mind Exploits Him Through His Women', *Playboy*, November 1956, pp. 51–2, 77–9.

Wylie, Philip, 'The Womanisation of America: An Embattled Male Takes a Look at What Was Once a Man's World', *Playboy*, September 1958, pp. 23–4, 50, 79.

Wyncoll, Peter, *The Nottingham Labour Movement 1880–1939* (London: Lawrence and Wishart, 1985).

Yeo, Eileen and Yeo, Stephen (eds), *Popular Culture and Class Conflict 1590–1914: Explorations in the History of Labour and Leisure* (Brighton: Harvester, 1981).

Young, Michael and Wilmott, Peter, *Family and Kinship in East London* (London: Routledge and Kegan Paul, 1957).

Zukin, Sharon, *Loft Living: Culture and Capital in Urban Change* (Baltimore, MD: Johns Hopkins University Press, 1982).

Zukin, Sharon, *Landscapes of Power: From Detroit to Disneyworld* (Berkeley, CA: University of California Press, 1991).

Zukin, Sharon, *The Culture of Cities* (Oxford: Blackwell, 1995).

List of Illustrations

From Spectatorship to Film Consumption: The Capitol, Alfreton Road, illustrations from the *Nottingham Journal*, 17 October 1936, courtesy of the Local Studies Collection, Nottingham City Council Leisure and Community Services; The ABC (formerly the Carlton), Chapel Bar, City Centre, courtesy of the Local Studies Collection; **Contexts of Film Consumption:** The Plaza, Front Street, Arnold, illustration from the *Evening News*, 13 May 1932, courtesy of the Local Studies Collection, Nottingham City Council Leisure and Community Services; The Cornerhouse, Forman Street, City Centre, courtesy of Fisher, Hargreaves and Proctor; **Class, Gender and Space in Early Film Consumption:** Goose Fair in the Old Market Square, City Centre, courtesy of the National Fairground Archive, University of Sheffield; (Shields, 1991, p. 89) Goose Fair, overlooked by the Old Exchange Building, where the City Council had its offices, courtesy of the National Fairground Archive; **Novelties, Fairgrounds and the Exoticisation of Place:** Goose Fair, courtesy of the National Fairground Archive, University of Sheffield; **Constructing the Cinematographic Theatre:** Picture House, Long Row, City Centre, courtesy of the Local Studies Collection, Nottingham City Council Leisure and Community Services; The Elite, Parliament Street, City Centre, courtesy of the Local Studies Collection; **Slum Clearance, Cinema Building and Differentiated Experiences:** The Council House, Market Square, City Centre, courtesy of the Local Studies Collection, Nottingham City Council Leisure and Community Services; The interior of the Savoy, Derby Road, Lenton, courtesy of the Local Studies Collection; **Translating the Talkies:** The Bonnington, Arnot Hill Road, courtesy of Local Studies Collection, Nottingham City Council Leisure and Community Services; **The City Centre, the Suburbs and the Cinema-Building Boom:** The official opening of the Council House, 1929, courtesy of the Local Studies Collection, Nottingham City Council Leisure and Community Services; The Metropole, Mansfield Road, Sherwood, courtesy of the Local Studies Collection; **Consuming Cinemas:** The Ritz, Angel Row, City Centre, courtesy of the Local Studies Collection, Nottingham City Council Leisure and Community Services; The interior of the Adelphi, Bulwell, courtesy of the Local Studies Collection; **Contemporary Understandings of Cinema Closure:** The Windsor, Hartley Road, picture by Mark Jancovich; The Cavendish, Wells Road, picture by Mark Jancovich; The Odeon (formerly the Ritz), courtesy of the Local Studies Collection, Nottingham City Council Leisure and Community Services; The Metropole today, picture by Mark Jancovich; **Locality, Affluence and Urban Decay:** The Majestic today, Woodborough Road, Mapperley, picture by Mark Jancovich; The Ritz today, Angel Row, picture by Mark Jancovich; **From Cinemagoing to Television Viewing:** The Ritz today, Angel Row, picture by Mark Jancovich; The Elite today, picture by Mark Jancovich; The Capitol today, picture by Mark Jancovich; **Negotiating Nostalgia:** The Futurist today, Valley Road, picture by Mark Jancovich; The Savoy, Derby Road, picture by Mark Jancovich; **Regulating Reception:** Hollywood Video, Hucknell Road, picture by Mark Jancovich; Blockbuster Video, Mansfield Road, Sherwood, picture by Mark Jancovich; Hollywood Video, picture by Mark Jancovich; **'The Splendid American Venture on the Ring Road':** The Showcase multiplex, picture by Mark Jancovich; Forbidden Planet, Broadmarsh Centre, City Centre, picture by Mark Jancovich; **Cultural Capitals:** The Broadway, Broad Street, City Centre, courtesy of the Broadway Media Centre; **Media Revolutions:** DVD display, Hollywood Video, picture by Mark Jancovich; The Cinema Store, the Cornerhouse, courtesy of Fisher, Hargreaves and Proctor; DVD display, Hollywood Video, picture by Mark Jancovich; **Conclusion:** The Cornerhouse, courtesy of Fisher, Hargreaves and Proctor.

Index

Page numbers in *italics* refer to illustrations. *n* = footnote; *t* = table